Yor Glory

Talitha Kumi
2000 YEARS LATER

An extraordinary experience gained owing to
the encounter with the living Avatar,

Sri Sathya Sai Baba

Original title: *2000 anni dopo Talita Kumi.*

Published in 2008 by Anima Edizioni, Italy.

Special thanks to the publisher for the cover page.

Translated from Italian into English by Daniela Marinkovic <u>marinkovic_daniela@yahoo. it</u> – May 2011.

First printed in India in 2011.

Reprinted in India in August 2013 (1000 copies)

Published by Lulu.com in January 2013

ISBN 978-1-291-28118-7

I humbly offer this book at the Lotus Feet of the Beloved Divine Master, Sri Sathya Sai Baba, on the occasion of His eightieth birthday, with infinite gratitude and eternal appreciation, for making me understand the origin, the meaning and the purpose of life – why I came to Earth, what the task in this lifetime is and where I am going to.

To Him I dedicate my each and every breath
and humbly ask to serve, with this book,
every soul that yearns to know the Oneness,
but has not found the time,
the way or the place to meet Him yet.

I thank God for bestowing the gift on me
of writing about Him and about all those
from whose thoughts I drew upon, with His guidance,
convinced that what I have written belongs
to humanity and no one in particular,
since Truth belongs to everybody and cannot remain untold.

Repetita iuvant.

PREFACE

This work is for all the brothers and sisters searching for Truth: it speaks to their hearts.

"Every obstacle is useful." This wise adage inspired my heart to revise, correct and expand this manuscript I'd believed had been ready for printing back in September 2000.

Evidently, the mind hadn't realized that time, or perhaps my consciousness, hadn't reached the blooming stage yet. The right season finally arrived.

I believe our relationship with God is tighter than the one we have with our family.

This book is about experiencing faith and trust in God simply and intensely, in every moment in life – day and night, twenty four hours a day – to bring out joy in the heart. Otherwise, it is like no longer swimming while still in the high sea, or trying to stay alive by ceasing to breathe.

I deliberately refrained from naming every person involved – people with whom I'd shared numerous experiences – not because I'd forgotten about them, but because that was the explicit wish of my Divine Master who had asked me to write exclusively about Him.

What I have written is the testimony of a soul "called to rouse" by the Holy Spirit, through multiple miracles of Love that diffused light throughout my life. The fulcrum of my spiritual conversion is the achievement of inner wholeness, or (the regained) joy of life .

This is what I am going to testify to with love and for the love of all the readers – tiny sparks of the Oneness we are all part of.

I

Made you were not to live the life of brutes but to pursue virtue and knowledge.

Dante.

I started to search and investigate many years ago – praying, meditating, reading hundreds of books and studying the teachings of my Divine Master – to "get to know" myself. It feels like yesterday. Time and effort do not count when we pursue the path of the Spirit because we overcome the concept of time in terms of past, present and future. Instead of increasing, weariness fades away.

We are imbued with sacred time, the eternal and continuous *now*, where loneliness is no longer a trap but a blessing as we are no longer self-focused, in a static, barren, depressing, suffocating, self-restrictive way, but become One with the earth, nature, the sky, humankind, the Universe or the Cosmos. On this sacred pathway I have discovered that daily life is but an antechamber of eternal life our true spiritual essence never abandons entirely – not even when, clad in rough matter, it descends to earth in human form.

This essence, or divine spark – our eternal part to which we have access through Divine Love – thrives in us, accompanies and guides us lovingly and patiently, each step of the way, respectfully, devotedly and kindly – provided we are fully aware of its presence. Otherwise, it simply watches us as we go through our troubles and pains, refusing to recognize ourselves in it, or see ourselves the way we really are.

Many decades later, when I found myself again, I realized that divine essence was the starting point of a fascinating, lifelong journey in search of my true Self.

The first thing I remember having learnt from my mother was related to the Divine, and that was surely not by chance. She would ask me to show her where God was and I would point my finger towards the sky. I was three years old.

That was more than fifty years ago. Today I would point my finger towards myself, if she were still here, asking the same question, because I feel that Heaven is within, God is part of me and His Kingdom is in my heart.

I would like to make this journey in stages, slowly, step by step, to accompany the growth of that bud which, slowly and inexorably, turned into a luxuriant flower – my Self-awareness as the Spirit of Truth and Love, my true Self.

When I was six, I was already in turmoil, striving to reveal the secrets God was holding in His hands. To become worthy of His Love, I used to write rules of behaviour with a shaky handwriting on beautiful, gold striped wrapping paper from the pastry shop. I would then cut it and stitch it into a small book. I can still recall some of those rules: always tell the truth, bring comfort to others without claiming it back, give to others, keep for yourself only what is necessary, always bring joy to others and never sadden them with your grief.

Those were the first words written with an insecure hand, as I had just learned to write.

Later on I became obsessed with observing 'rules' imposed by no one but me, in the broadest sense of the word. I was torn between the freedom of the heart oblivious to morality, and a sense of duty that was all about responsibilities. The Inner Master, the Great Priest, or the Divine Spirit, began to speak out. I will simply refer to it as 'my consciousness'. In any case, I was convinced I was talking to God and that He was replying through the Inner Master.

I used to spend every summer vacation in the countryside, in a small village on Mt. Etna, in Sicily. During my walks through olive trees, fig trees and prickly pear trees, the encounters with Him were more frequent and intense.

One summer, when I was thirteen, while visiting a cloister in Assisi, I felt the urge to remain there. My parents disagreed. I didn't know at the time that my path was going to be different.

At sixteen, still at secondary school, I dreamt of becoming a missionary sister in faraway lands upon my graduation from the School of Medicine. I had no idea why I was so attracted to that faculty.

When I was eighteen I finally decided to become a psychiatrist. I was too deeply moved by mental suffering to remain indifferent. Meanwhile, I'd broken my relationship with God, or at least I thought so.

I decided to reach out to the mentally ill in whom I saw my own reflection. They were me. And so, at the age of twenty five, I ended up being a doctor in an Asylum – as Mental Hospitals were called back then – where I came into direct contact with mankind's ultimate suffering without appeal and pain without 'reason' *par excellence.*

With time, I felt less and less comfortable in this role, until it became a 'strait-jacket' and my soul was yearning for freedom.

One day my back 'broke down' under the excessive burden I could no longer comprehend, or accept, and the roles changed: the patient was I. I was thirty eight at the time.

While immobilized and isolated from the rest of the world for nearly two years, I discovered the person I'd used to be - my old self I had lost sight of. I started thinking again about God, whom I had removed from my thoughts at eighteen, about His secrets and the mystery of life.

The official scientific theories on mental suffering I had accumulated over the past twenty years were no longer feasible. As a matter of fact, they were completely outdated. I became a different person.

After my father died in a traffic accident – I was holding him in my arms when he passed away – I considered myself to be an atheist.

I was seventeen and my faith simply did not pass the test and so I stopped talking to God: I refused to believe in His infinite goodness and decided to shut the door on Him, or so it seemed.

I was unaware that He and I were and would always be at one.

His place in my heart was occupied by all the people who were suffering. I was so confused. Although I have never been fond of politics, I became a 'leftist', but not a communist. I was a rebel, but not a feminist. Rigid schematics or 'labels' have never been my cup of tea. The archetypes I was attracted to were not the cultural stereotypes but the deeply rooted ones, common to all, albeit secret and invisible, manoeuvring us so powerfully.

No one ever managed to impose limits on me, but I was doing a good job myself.

When my son was born I was thirty. I welcomed him as a gift from Heaven and indeed he has been.

I was waiting for him, incredulous, since the age of thirteen, when a voice inside me announced with disarming simplicity: "You will have a son at the age of thirty". At the time I thought I would be old at that age, but I made no objections. I waited for the event, trustingly and slightly perplexed. I never spoke about it – for the fear it would come true or for the fear of being considered insane.

His arrival was both joyous and painful. My son found me alone – there was no father around. In fact, the "voice" never mentioned any man. I did find myself several times on the verge of getting married but, as I never met my "soul mate", every relationship was bound to end.

It almost seemed as if God, like some intransigent and jealous lover, wanted me just for Him. Looking back, I see decades of solitude – except for a few spells.

Only now I understand that that was in accordance with the design.

Over the years of gold and the years of lead (in alchemic terms) I was striving to turn worthless metal into gold and eventually into everlasting diamonds and celebrate an entire life together – Him and I.

When I was forty I emerged from a metamorphosis into a new life – it was my second chance. My personal data were the sole detail my new and my previous life had in common.

For years without break, day after day, I searched for the key to what I considered to be the mystery of life in Metaphysics, *Karmic* and Evolutionary Astrology, Numerology, Esotericism, Early Christianity, Comparative Religion (Hinduism, Zen Buddhism, Confucianism), Chinese Medicine, Indian Medicine, Macrobiotics, Gnosticism, I Ching, the Tarot and the Jewish Kabala.

God was back in my life, occupying His post of honour. I didn't quite understand who He was or how He moved through the lives of human beings, but He manifested by organizing every favourable circumstance for my spiritual journey back to Him.

I no longer believed by 'having faith' in God, in religious terms. I knew Him well by then, sensed Him and clearly felt His presence.

When you know God, the ideal becomes reality and what used to represent reality becomes an illusion or something quite trivial. What you can't see is real, what you see is unreal. It became natural for me to believe that whatever happened was for the benefit and timely, as I was aware that the mystery of how or why things happened the way they happened would be revealed to me as soon as I reached self-awareness, the divine essence or the expression of the Self, as the Spirit of Truth and Love.

I was awakened to a new consciousness by various illnesses and a surgery. I discovered that, for reasons of higher order, the veil preventing us from seeing beyond time and space, in the dimension of the eternal evolution of being, could sometimes be removed even for a fraction, but that fraction of time was enough to provide evidence of a reality beyond reality everyone was looking for. However, words cannot convey the right meaning when they refer to generally unknown dimensions, i.e. the 4th or the 5th – at the time I knew nothing about the latter one.

I realized there were two parallel, intertwined realities and the one which was invisible and subtle, the one we could only speculate about, held the key to what could not be understood from the point of view of the other, visible, or manifest reality we lived in.

I am convinced that the soul is sacrificed in the prison of pragmatism of everyday life because it necessitates the lymph of imagination, truth, beauty, ingenuity, inspiration and creativity in order to thrive: that lymph penetrated into my blood through the traumatic events that struck me during those two years[1].

All of a sudden I was liberated from whatever made me feel as though I was climbing the walls – like the law of the world instead of the Law of Love, or conventions, or the roles we had to play – and I could finally take up my search for the meaning of life and transcend myself, against all odds, even at the cost of failure, mistake, complete loss or going insane.

Nothing could stop me, I was no longer vulnerable to blackmails for worldly things because I accepted, or rather, was prepared to accept the conditions: at any price, against all odds.

Once and for all, I delved into the new life to come up with the answers to the many questions I'd had since childhood, or since my teens. I was going to discover who I was, what I was doing here on earth, where I would go after death and how to tell the difference between "the true and the false, the real and the unreal" – answers official science had found neither on the Earth nor on the Moon, where man had already walked, nor on the highest mountaintops conquered so far, nor in the deepest seas ever fathomed by man.

Hence, having obtained a degree in Medicine and having specialized in Neurology, and subsequently in Psychiatry, all this seemed rather disappointing and insignificant. I was taught to fight a mental illness but not to prevail by helping a sick person find his/her lost soul again. A fundamental issue is ignored here: it is imperative to trace down the real causes if we wish to discover the true nature of an event, be it in the mineral, vegetative, animal or in the human realm. Moreover, to proceed in the research, the logic of common intelligence is insufficient. There has to be intuitive discrimination – the faculty which manifests only when we become aware of our own Divinity.

Esotericism has taught me that life starts getting interesting when we get hold of our destiny (*karma*), otherwise we senselessly waste life after life, without fulfilling the scope of evolution and without reaching the goal, namely the Divine Light.

The conflict within the human drama is based on the duality of matter and spirit and the separation of two equally indispensable, complementary parts – the bias between individual consciousness and its divine essence, or the true Self, or universal consciousness, or the Spirit of Truth and Love[2].

In a nutshell, if we try to restore the unity with the divine essence through the use of sexuality without sacredness or through the use of drugs (cigarettes, alcohol, narcotics, drugs, etc.) to expand our consciousness, without the necessary awareness to guide us along the right path, we unconsciously trigger a mechanism of suffering incumbent on all human beings on the hosting earth, like a sentence passed from "Above". Due to modern lifestyle, marriage, family, work, study, cultural interests, pastimes and entertainment prevent the soul from expressing itself. There is no room for the Spirit and it is mentioned only in words or religious rites devoid of significance, addressing an increasingly smaller audiences. The Spirit is kept locked inside the churches – monuments of a less and less attended religiousness – to remind men and women of a God who died in the collective imagery thousands of years ago.

Ignoring the fact that the true goal, which is our divine essence, or Atma, resides within, we pursue illusive, ephemeral goals in everything we do, living the everyday life in its physicality, convinced of being immortal, in order to exorcize what governs us: the fear of death. We work, get married, bring children into the world, buy a house, save money and are concerned about our pension, without any guarantee that we will enjoy its fruits after all. Because, that day might actually never come. Our clothes, i.e. our body with a name and surname, will soon be taken off. That which is eternal, immortal in us is the Spirit, or the divine essence – which owns everything since it comprises everything – knowing neither time nor space, as it transcends the time-space dimension and hence transcends death. To understand this, we should invert the order of priorities acquired from birth. We would discover that we came into this world for a much nobler cause: to evolve spiritually and return home, our real home.

By inverting the order, we grow fond of nourishing everything that enriches the soul, such as imagination, creativity, contemplation, or virtues like generosity, loyalty, purity, sincerity, a heart open to give and receive unconditional Love, spontaneity, the feeling of true friendship extending to all realms: human, animal, vegetative and mineral, including the elements they are made of: air, fire, water, earth and ether, together with the worlds that exist in the Universe, the planets, the stars, the Galaxies – everything which represents life in the invisible world. In short, a desire arises to cultivate friendship with Infinity – with the All, with God, as our only true Friend.

Even though words are absolutely insufficient to express what I've seen, experienced and felt in the course of this spiritual adventure of coming to terms with myself, I feel it necessary to write about it and appease a great desire of mine: to come up with a 'roadmap'[3] of the spiritual world I discovered so that whoever might be willing to venture into this kind of journey could find himself or herself and God, the same way I did, and see that the peace and fulfilment we yearn for are neither far away nor in a distant future, but here and now, within us, because self-aware energy neither abandons nor loses sight of us – not even for an instant.

Going back to human limitations stemming from spiritual ignorance, there is something which has been a constant in man throughout the various ages, habits, customs or moral values: it is fear, the eternal enemy contributing to our ignorance.

I didn't know up until then that when we approach the crossroads of the way of the world and the way of the Spirit and we choose the latter one, the major test is that of loneliness and fear, pertaining to this existential condition. One feels really alone, as the heart is not open for the Divine Love yet.

It happened when I was thirty eight, after I'd experienced one of the most radical upheavals in my life subsequent to a series of major changes, like the death of my father. I was seventeen when he passed away, bequeathing me the memory of his kindness, generosity and non-attachment to material assets. When I was twenty five I moved to the North. My mother died when I was twenty eight and my son was born when I was thirty. I moved abroad at the age of thirty three but it didn't work out. A succession of illnesses followed, bringing me close to death, and the last in the series made me experience the worst Christmas of my life. I was convinced it was the very last.

The trial I couldn't bypass required more braveness than any other. I had to face another side of me, under the most bereaving conditions I'd ever known and start from scratch after years of tough mental work on all fronts: work, family and affections. I had just changed home, town, work, without anyone to help me, without a day of rest, let alone peace. Having neglected a backache for months until I started limping, I still went on with my tasks as mother and doctor. The pain suddenly became so acute one day that I remained stuck in bed. Force imposed on me what my common sense hadn't been able to reason me into. I called an ambulance and was hospitalized in the middle of the night. My son had just turned eight and I had to leave him home alone, while still asleep.

The pain didn't cease despite the painkillers so I was urgently operated the following day. It was on a Saturday morning. The slipped disc operation didn't go well and complications followed, so I was bedridden for a month, head downwards, my bed inclined, and there was more.

At first I thought I would lose my mind. During the very first month at the hospital, due to the position I was constrained to be in, all the blood that flew into my head caused unbearable discomfort. No one was telling me anything about my real physical condition or about the developments of the clinical situation.

While I was lying still in that inclined bed, head downwards, face squashed on the pillow, in absolute desperation, something lightened up inside, unexpectedly. I felt I was not alone. A powerful energy was sustaining me and trying to help me find sense in whatever was going on. I could gradually accept the events as the will of God. Without trying to alleviate the actual problem, I was finding the courage to deal with it, with the best disposition of spirit.

I had to change hospital several times during the years of my ordeal. Although I was fully aware of the fact that the illness and the convalescence had to take time, I didn't know that two long, intense years of suffering, self-observation, study and research awaited me, from which I would emerge fully renewed.

In the important events of my life I glimpsed a thread which went back to a weft that was much bigger than what I was able to make out at the time.

My concern for humanity, the enthusiasm about the beauty of nature, the choice to become a mother and the work related to human suffering – they were all elements which made part of a larger plan. I was implementing it, unwittingly, day after day, looking forward to the day when the work was done so I could pass it back to God as a present, for Him to return it into His cosmic *atelier*.

I felt intuitive intelligence sharpen in me, helping me think with a new lucidity and acumen, clarifying many concepts which had been obscured till then, like, for example, the concept of unity in diversity, a single truth that permeated the entire Universe as we knew it, representing also the substratum of the collective unconscious mind, where the plot of human existence was registered.

I started to understand why so many issues regarding mental illnesses and mental health I'd been dealing with for so many years, so academically and so partially, were still open.

I came to the conclusion that, if we wanted to free ourselves of the needs of the mind, we first had to free ourselves of our corporeal needs and the five senses.

My mind was relentlessly absorbed in the work of self-enquiry, analogical associations, self-criticism and the synthesis of all my revelations. I was never tired.

I wanted to record all the brilliant ideas which seemed to flow in from who-knows-where, with a precise task: taking away that veil of ignorance which had dimmed my inner vision for so many years, causing hardship and suffering.

I had a premonition that that experience would end my life as a 'woman', in terms of romance.

The need to burn all the bridges with the surrounding world resurfaced. The change of house and work might have anticipated what followed soon after. That constant factor in my life, going back to as far as I could remember, seemed to emerge from the insight that being slaves to dependence and emotional conditioning distanced us from the true aim, in spiritual terms, as my subsequent studies of esotericism and metaphysics confirmed. Such reflections were made by the most developed part of my being.

On the other hand, I rationalized and interpreted it as a defence mechanism triggered by my great fear of loss and the conviction that ideal life was beyond reach, also because my love life was littered with loneliness.

As I became aware of a new inner Energy, I realized that God was an essential part of every human being and that finally helped me overcome the fear of loneliness. As I had been by myself and without His comfort most of my life, it did not require a great amount of courage to chose awareness and to surrender not to an adverse destiny but to His Will, knowing that His presence would replace solitude. I didn't know, at the time, that I was going to make the winning choice and become the master of my destiny.

The wish to go beyond appearances, towards the light, was so strong that I managed to overcome that atavistic fear torturing not only me with red hot pincers, but nailing us all to the ground: the fear of leaping into the dark.

The terrible time of my life started when I lucidly realized I was going through the major part of the psychopathological states known to me, ranging from hysteria to obsession, from maniacal disorder to depression and eventually paranoia. Meanwhile, I was in bed, immobilized in a hospital room for several months.

I have always been attracted by difficult, impossible, unattainable and unpredictable things. Most probably, that attitude helped me survive the obvious squalor of life as a bedfast patient.

I was actually learning about a new existential dimension manifesting itself as I was separated from the daily routine of engagements, obligations, clichés, impositions, responsibilities, in short everything my life as a busy professional and single mother had consisted of, until that crucial night when I was taken to hospital.

Just a couple of days earlier I'd taken the Head Physician Qualification Exam. I was later told I'd passed it and thus obtained the qualification.

A mere 'instant' was enough to change the direction of my existence: that job no longer mattered to me.

I discovered that happiness could imply the quality of being content with a break between one emotional storm and the next.

I discovered that pleasure could imply being temporarily free of the stressful needs or obsessive desires. I will keep coming back to this topic in the pages to come, hopefully not in a superfluous manner. Life teaches us the mechanism of repetition as a way of learning and comprehending the daily lessons – only out of Love, always out of Love.

I have always loved all expressions of harmony, since early childhood. On the other hand, any form of violence or discord, even if dialectic, would upset me or create an annoying inner state of alarm[4]. After the spine operation, that state of alarm expanded in all directions, to all my thoughts and all over my body.

I felt as if I were made of glass. Afraid of being lightly touched, unintentionally or suddenly, I avoided crowded places and the use of cars and public means of transport.

I moved with great difficulty and could hardly stand on my two feet. This vulnerable state of physical fragility lasted for nearly two years.

The doctors excluded the possibility of a functional recovery and I experienced the burden of being almost entirely dependent on others like a life sentence.

The spectre of permanent invalidity was looming in my fantasies of failure, inability, insufficiency and incapability, chasing one another in my mind.

I had always considered myself strong, independent, self-sufficient, so much so that I could always face the dual role of mother and father with my son, holding my head high. He would sometimes call me mom-dad. I also played the role of psychiatrist – my illusion was so immense.

I refused to listen to my body speaking out on behalf of my soul. Above all, I didn't listen to my heart which had known a single season till then – the grey, cold and salty one, of the many tears I'd shed.

With a clear vision of my past life spent so bitterly, I quickly realized the major truth.

Even if you have everything, without God in your life it is as if you had nothing, because you feel lonely and incapable of loving truly. Only God, as the Spirit of Truth and Love, enables us to find the capacity and the strength to love unconditionally, to give without expecting anything in return, because love implies experimenting with the joyful, 'energetic' dimension of giving – as the fundamental task in life. It is unlimited since it feeds itself continuously. Paradoxically so, the more you give, the more it grows.

The desperation experienced till then became senseless. The input arrived from an archaic knowledge that came into the light during the arduous delving over the years, the delving that eventually resulted, metaphorically and literally, in the fall of my physical and existential scaffolds.

That is how I discovered that, if you had God, you had everything, even if you lacked everything else, because God is Love, Harmony and Peace. It is everything I'd searched for fruitlessly, far away from Him.

Apparently, I lost my precious independence, my untouchable self-sufficiency, or better, the illusion of both. In turn I received the gift of insight and knowledge of God, as Love and Truth.

Only one possibility remained for me to keep feeling alive: giving compassion and advice, something I had always been capable of, and listening more and more openly. My understanding of life amplified, sweeping over the new fields I'd just begun to explore. Astrology and Holy Scriptures of other religions became my daily bread.

While I was lying in bed, loneliness was not an obstacle but a useful condition for this fascinating research, this adventure into the world of the Spirit: the more unattached I was from the surrounding world, the deeper my dialogue with God was.

I would tell Him, confidentially, that I had realized I was constrained to that bed by Him so that I could realize that my task was to follow Him in the first place, as He was my only friend, the only safe refuge, the divine essence within, a spark or Atma.

I realized where that inner drive to sever all connections was coming from. It was the drive I'd felt for the first time when I was four when, on the occasion of my mother's sudden departure, I found myself unexpectedly without her. Caught by a deep pain due to her absence, I decided that I could live even without her. And so it happened, as a matter of fact, in the coming years, until she passed away. I continued to love her but I was no longer hanging on her.

I learned that true independency was not of financial or social nature but it was about overcoming attachments – material and emotional.

There was an entire world within me to explore and conquer: the Promised Land and the Kingdom of Heaven[5].

Even pain, illness, immobility and death had a deeper sense which was yet to be revealed, understood and accepted.

As I was discovering the sense of reality and forgetting about my physical fragility, my fears dissipated. The more I understood the underlying causes, the more my despair waned, to the point that I was no longer afraid of having to leave my little son for good. I was absolutely certain God would take care of him, of all his needs and necessities, as long as He wanted him to stay on earth[6]. My love for Him, which I had neglected since the age of seventeen, when my father passed away, was coming back with interests, boosted with confidence and warmth, precisely twenty years later.

I dared to go through my teenage diaries and saw that my dream at the time had been to set off on a "great journey" to Heaven or Paradise which awaited me. What a prophetic dream! I had asked God to guide me to His Truth, feeling that the Light of the soul was the longed-for finishing line, with high hopes of being reborn as many times as necessary, to eventually incorporate the body of the holiest and shiniest person and unite with the light once and for all.

The power of my unity with the All was such that I could not conceive my life separate from the rest of humankind.

I read about Saint Augustine, Plato, Aristotle, Tolstoy, Dostoyevsky, Schopenhauer, Gandhi, Yogananda, Aurobindo, Buddha, Confucius and Lao Tze when I was sixteen. I considered God as Truth, Compassion and Tolerance. I found it difficult to see Him as a killer hurricane, a destructive earthquake or a devastating fire. He was the Sun sustaining life – it couldn't possibly take life away.

But my father's death broke the spell[7].

Shortly before his death I wrote that I wished to be inhabited by God, adding: "The objective is not in the far future. It is imminent, before our eyes, now, it is life itself, the life we live in its greatness and simplicity, as it unfolds from dawn to dusk and from dusk to dawn, each day". How innocently wise those words were!

After the accident I wrote: "I believe in humanity and in good will. With the latter we can assist the sun to rise every morning and give life to a new day". Humanity overtook the role of God and my new creed was to try and alleviate human suffering. My prayer consisted in contemplating nature.

My imagination was filled with starry skies, stormy seas, incandescent lava, almond and orange trees in bloom and golden broom flower scents.

Having revisited my adolescent years, I established that the research undertaken in the hospital bed reinstated the knowledge I'd deposited within, many years earlier and even before my birth in this lifetime, or in other lives for that matter, the knowledge of myself as a divine essence, or part of the All.

That hidden knowledge included Love with a capital L, all-embracing Divinity, all-pervasive Truth, service as the major task in a person's life, the 'eternal now' as the only time we have, the 'elimination of shortcomings' as the royal road to self-improvement, stars calling for a contact with other worlds, Divine Grace related to a person's good will, the inexistence of 'earthly happiness', reincarnation, the power of humility, the importance of serving others in order to continue to exist, destiny's immutability unless there is divine intervention, suffering as a tool to ascend to Divinity, abundance stemming from unconditional giving, the power of positive thinking[8] to obtain any form of success, the value of obedience and the fear of God, the awareness of the transience of human emotions, self-confidence as self-awareness, the benevolence of death as it liberates us from physical slavery, the value of meditation, non-attachment to the material world and complete trust in God, the pointlessness of crying over the past and being concerned for the future – notions I rediscovered later on, as a mature person.

I was sixteen when I wrote that earthly life represented the exile and that we should not invest in it all our hopes, since salvation awaited beyond that, adding: "At times I feel as if I were falling down, to the bottom of my inner being, sucked in by the whirl of immensity and infinity... I wish I could get off the planet and dive into infinity, consecrated to Love and giving … do not become attached to what is dear to you, do not love 'too much'. Had I been born as a grain of sand, how less complicated it would have been to be picked by God and taken into the Kingdom of Heaven".

I was starving for true freedom and Truth, being forced to live in a world I considered alien and unreal, feeling I didn't belong to it, wishing to die and be reborn as a superior Being, fused with the All, floating in a Light infinitely brighter than the one I knew.

I wrote: "I wish You bestowed Your Grace upon me, my God, so I could be near Your, as close as possible, away from the material world …This dream has always permeated my thoughts. It might come true one day." It was 1963: the dream did come true thirty years later. This book reveals when, how and where.

I was asking the stars to plead with God and accelerate my earthly journey because the less I was giving myself to God, the more sadness and misery I was uncovering. I hadn't figured out the value of the *karmic* law of cause and effect yet but I already had a vague notion of its great influence in the forging of human destinies and that of mankind through the fluxes and refluxes on planet Earth. As if my wishes hadn't been expressed for myself only but for the rest of humanity as well, to quickly find the way back 'home' by recognizing the true values we could live by and prepare the souls for immortality, or 'the great beam', as I named it. Amongst those values, the most important was altruism: helping others allows for the emerging of happiness, which accompanies the soul during the great journey back to Heaven or Paradise. As I noticed many years after I'd reread those pages in 1985, the terminology I'd used at the time was similar to that used over the past twelve thousand years by geographically distant populations which nevertheless intuited that they belonged to the same constellation or shared a common origin from some unknown star – Sirius, Orion or others still, stars we didn't know the name of. I refer to the population of Egypt, the inhabitants of Cambodia, the population of a disappeared continent south of Japan (Mu), the population of the Easter islands and the Maya of Mexico, all aligned around the Tropic of Cancer and corresponding to the constellations of that time.

Going back to my old diaries, I also wrote about being uncatchable, like the sea. I wrote that I was leaving merely a trace of my transit. I continued: "what isn't there any more has actually never existed, yet the Spirit, which really *is*, never ceases to exist!... Oh night, oh sleep, I wish you never ended, I have always loved you more than I loved the wake and daytime, because you show me where I come from and where I'm going to. You give sense to 'where I am', which is repeatedly brought in by the day, without offering any explanation." Meanwhile, I hoped that my wait for the arrival of the new world, in which we would all be equal, would pass more quickly while I sleep. To 'wash away' the guilt[9] of being born, I asked God to give my joy to others and to pass other people's pain on me.

I complained about being incapacitated from seeing beyond, as if by a mist, so I asked: "Why am I not allowed to see?" I unravelled that mystery many years later.

I knew that the lack of self-confidence derived from not knowing ourselves so I asked the stars to illuminate me on that and added: "We cannot stop the time. It is therefore useless to think about the past or about the future". The 'great fear' both the Egyptians and the Maya had tried to exorcise with every possible means was tormenting me as well – the inevitable passing of time produced yet another victim. I wrote: "I, who have found light in suffering, wish to bring light to those who suffer without seeing the light. One day I will look down on earthly things and go to search for the source of the real Light and, when I find it, I will disseminate it…"

I didn't know the real Light was Spiritual Knowledge but I did know that I would have to go and search for it far away, which is what actually happened. I wrote: "To hope is not much, considering what's in my heart. I could die, if necessary, to find a better world made of truth and peace". And also: "Perhaps I don't fully understand my destiny if the success and failure to observe the laws of nature are left to chance."

I already knew there was no such thing as "chance". We've held it accountable for so many things and events. Yet, each time we are thwarted by ignorance and cannot see the real causes. "I feel the impending burden of age" – I was sixteen –" but I nevertheless wish to get old as soon as possible if it will serve to find the answers to my questions. Sin is not mischievousness but an effect of ignorance…My destiny is to say goodbye to all people and things to be able to continue living with them." Somehow I understood the importance of non-attachment, that is, of being in the world without being of the world. I anticipated the guidance of the inner voice by thirty four years: "If only I could annihilate myself in something sacred; a positive and straightforward thought to replace my prayer… I am always on my own, with the best of companies, God, although I am unworthy of this." By that time I had realized that the only true friend was God, as Love and Truth.

"Every thing must have a final scope and I must never get tired of searching for it. I am sixteen, the age of ungratefulness *par excellence,* ungratefulness being the major of all flaws. I will keep going until I've reached my goal. God will give me the strength … Feeling complete, fulfilled, without wishing for anything - this is what true joy is all about!" I was terribly scared of leading a petty life, merely satisfying the needs of daily existence. "The day of liberation will come …" This thought was confirmed years later, in the voice of the Divine Master Sai Baba.

"It is the mind imposing itself on me and not the other way round. Study and research are life itself, together with the courage to continue along the path … living like everyone else, being like no one else" [10].

I had the clear presentiment at the time that my parents would pass away. I wrote in my diary a few days before my father died in an accident: "Something is about to end, but I don't know what it is!"

Actually, that tragic event marked the end of my youth. With this drastic conclusion of my adolescence, I found myself all of a sudden living an adult life, being responsible and taking care of myself in every sense of the word.

Many years later, I learned that a *karmic* residue from a previous life[11] had come to an end then.

A new life started for me when I was eighteen and it represented the first in a series of great changes in the period that followed. I wrote: "I love to investigate and discover new things that prove the presence of God so that I can persuade those who don't believe He exists". I am of the same opinion today. In spite of all the storms in my life, I have remained faithful to myself, coherent with the way I felt and thought about the world. "I dream of travelling to a far away land, very different from mine, to take care of my brothers in God and forget about myself" and further on: "What good is awareness if it is not awareness of Truth – Absolute and Universal. We can obtain peace through the awareness of Truth and by renouncing what is untrue: our attachments …We must be able to find goodness in everything. Mastering our feelings and getting rid of prejudices fuels the power of will. Between respect and despise, the distance resides in the comprehension … God embraces all, loves all, forgives all and despises nothing … Why are our "desires" so strong and our "will" so weak … the Spirit is an ocean, destiny is a wind that moves the waves of human life … it is the journey that counts, not the arrival, since the goal is in fact here and now."

This synthesis of my notes taken in my teens, which came into the light during that interval in my active life – and here I refer to my illness and the long period of convalescence – was a confirmation that my research at the age of thirty eight was but a continuation of a work initiated many years earlier. It testified of the divine influx as the only drive of life: indeed, as a sixteen-year-old I was closer to the aim than in the several years that followed, up until then.

That's life: a game assigned by destiny, according to the laws of *karma*, or cause and effect.

I had to cross the most obscure and impassable gorges of the soul to find the unique and irreplaceable value of the lost light and the strength and courage to definitely return on the route I'd abandoned twenty years earlier.

The despair experienced in the darkest years of the 'fall' provided me with the decisive impetus to make the big leap in the dark. I realized the importance of despair, as the greatest expression of human suffering in the evolution of humankind. Many years later, when I was studying the teachings of the living *Avatar*, Sathya Sai Baba, I realized that His message had always been at the bottom of my heart, as He addressed me and the rest of humanity.

NOTES: CHAPTER I

1. Suffering has been and will be the herald of renewal and rebirth.
2. To simplify, from this point onwards I shall be using only the term "true Self"
3. Further on, I call it "treasure map"
4. Many years later I understood that the discomfort stemmed from the heavy weight of "discordant" vibrations I perceived with my entire being, as something threatening and alien.
5. I was told years later that it was also called the 5th dimension
6. After a few years it was confirmed by Sai Baba personally, in the course of an interview.
7. The etymological meaning of "Spell" conveys something which is untrue.
8. "Positive thought" is here implied as "understanding of opposites" and "overcoming duality".
9. I was convinced by then that the purpose of suffering was to cancel mistakes and ignorance. Unfortunately, I was still viewing it in the light of "guilt".
10. Out of ignorance, I felt essentially different from the others, although we were similar on the outward. The awareness gained over the years tells me that the contrary is true: although we look different, we are all in the state of Oneness, essentially.
11. In my previous life I lived in Japan and worked in a psychiatric hospital. I eventually fully embraced the Taoist philosophy. My father in that life was the same as in this one.

II

We should learn to love even the most bitter of all things and to renounce the sweetest.

Confucius.

I was released from the hospital in a poor physical condition, without any hope of recovering and being self-sufficient ever again. Although I could hardly get out of bed and move, I walked on my own two legs to the appointment with a Psychological Astrology advisor, fixed quite a while before.

I had been studying different branches of Astrology such as Psychological, *Karmic* and Evolutionary Astrology on my own for a number of years but I'd never consulted an astrologer.

She presented an existential framework, much larger and richer than anything I could have imagined. I met a serious, competent, reliable and professional person who gave a description of my life up till then, which confirmed her analytical skills. Her interpretation depicted the suffering characterizing most of my life in a more acceptable light, albeit still equally tough to endure.

She announced a very significant turning point after five years, after a long period of marginalization and self-marginalization at work.

What can't be cured must be endured, so I utilized that period to deepen my knowledge of metaphysics, astrology, spirituality, etc. I practically lived in solitude over the next five years.

In 1990, I was going to meet the man of my life – by the psycho-astrologer's definition. At last, someone who would give me energy instead of drying me out, which had been the case in the past. It would be an important man, world famous and applauded by the masses. We would establish a profitable collaboration and a true friendship. It was not going to be a marriage in the ordinary sense of the term.

I was baffled by her words, especially because they came from a serious, competent, correct person, an expert in her field. They were difficult to accept for the fear that she might be telling the truth.

How would I approach a man who was important and famous? I have always avoided fame, stage floodlights, public places and the clamour of the limelight.

I would have to go insane, or stop being myself and the shy person who generally chooses to be with serious, discrete, reserved and certainly not famous people.

She also said I would write books with a spiritual topic, with much success. *That* really horrified me. I was not going to write any kind of books. Writing was part of my self-research. I used it as a basis for further reflexion and surely not to display the results of my research to others. My remissive attitude betrayed my insecurity, but I wasn't aware of it at the time. So I categorically denied anything like that could ever happen. I returned home more confused than before, yet reassured about something very important in that moment: I would fully regain my forces and would not remain disabled. I wanted to believe in that with all my heart – it was my anchor of salvation.

I continued studying Astrology and resumed my job between one hospital stay and the next. Since I wasn't as efficient as I'd used to be, I was increasingly marginalized by my colleagues, until I found myself even more isolated than before.

I started getting worried: what I'd been told was coming true over the years, precisely the way it had been predicted.

Marginalization was followed by self-marginalization. I was already disheartened when I arrived back to work but the cold and off-putting welcome gave a *coup de grace* to my career in psychiatry and so I definitely lost all my interest in it.

What seemed like – if I may say so – madness became my point of reference for any possible future project, despite being quite distant from the context I was engaged in at the time. I thought I would meet someone to work with on a philanthropic project. Anyway, it was all very vague and foggy.

I progressed with my studies and was more and more absorbed by the classics of Esotericism, Hinduism, Buddhism and Evolutionary Astrology.

How important was my research? Did it guide me to the revelation of God?

I did meet Him later on, in flesh and blood, in India, in the person of Sai Baba, the living incarnation of Truth and Love – I say it without any fear of being blasphemous – in accordance with the extraordinary predictions of that endearing psychological astrologer who expressed herself in such a peculiar manner (by following analogical thoughts).

I traced her down years later to thank her duly and to apologise for not having given her the credit she had deserved there and then.

In those days I clearly understood that God had always been the only true Love of my life. That was why I'd never been ready to marry a man, despite the fact that I'd nearly done it a few times.

Holy matrimony, in the true sense of the word, could have taken place only with the soul mate. It is a divine and sacred union of two halves separated upon their descent down to earth, subsequent to which they become complete again and can eventually return to heaven.

Today I understand that my vision had been partly idealistic and – yes – a little simplistic.

I no longer counted on the possibility of meeting my "soul mate". God was the only Spouse for me. Still, I didn't feel worthy of Him: I was certainly not ready.

In the context of my thoughts, the idea of meeting a famous man sounded like a delusion, sheer fancy and was not to be taken into consideration. But it *was* referred to Sai Baba.

Years later I found out that my considerations on the soul mate and the holy matrimony matched the esoteric notion of the sacrament of marriage, which was considered to be really sacred in the presence of a union of souls, by the Will of God, and not as a union of bodies, by human desire, ratified in a church or a town hall, as a simple formality.

This fact alone should be enough to illustrate the chaos the entire humanity has fallen into, since the bond of marriage today is aimed at meeting the needs of power and pleasure, rather than those of respect for whatever spiritual there may be in the other person, as the only part capable of expressing true love, with a pure heart. But then, perhaps things have always been that way.

A sick tree bears bad fruits. Consequently, family institutions worldwide are generally characterized by violence instead of Love.

The family structured in this way is the first "school" in which we are educated – or rather uneducated – in the cruellest form of egotism, instead of unconditional Love.

Needless to say, this family imprinting expands in all directions in the surrounding environment, in the society, in the country, in the world. It grows exponentially.

It is enough to look around to see the results.

I joined a triennial course in Astrology in that period. Astrology is a powerful instrument to learn about the visible and invisible reality we are immersed in, unknowingly. It is useful for those who would like to know themselves and find the strength and the maturity to face the truth, without fear. Inner peace is the reward.

Towards the end of the second year of my ordeal, in summer, the season when it all started, I changed three hospitals, at one-week intervals. My "hospital stays" stopped miraculously and so my career as a patient finally came to an end.

When I was released from the hospital, after twenty five months, I slowly realized I was out of the *cul-de-sac*, owing to a divine interconnection of events. Something triggered unexpectedly when, two days before I was discharged with an inauspicious prognosis, with my doctor's refusal to brave another surgery to try and repair the damages incurred during the first operation, I was distractedly leafing through my room mate's magazine and spotted an article on the miraculous healings of Padre Pio. I thought that, if I ever got well again, I would go back to work and help other people. That was it. Considering the condition I was in, I could hardly be of any use to anybody, even to myself.

However, from that moment things started changing in my favour. Just before I was discharged, suddenly, as they were closing my case history, the doctors realized I was seriously anaemic and insisted on extending my stay to do some more checkups. I, on the other hand, just wanted to go home, disillusioned, before I was hospitalized again. But the inner voice told me I should be patient and stay a few more days. And so I did. After a week of therapy, I managed to walk on my own and resume an almost normal life.

That was my last stay in a hospital. I soon stopped taking the prescribed medicines against anaemia.

I went back to work after a month, in spite of the limitations.

I couldn't stand for too long so I worked only in the outpatient mental health clinic (within a PHC centre). The astrologer was right about my health. She foresaw that I would get well and so it was, at least on the functional level, because the damages on the organic level made during the operation remained unchanged. I resumed my life divided between home and work.

In the following year I joined a charismatic prayer group, with a discreet interest. I shared with them the need to do my best for an immediate personal change, without waiting for death or Paradise to come.

They talked about black clouds, or darkness (hatred, doubt, fear), and about white clouds, or light (love, harmony, peace), to distinguish those who were in tune with the message of Jesus from those who were not.

Actually, that simple visual image of life – where black clouds represent the bonds of emotional attachment, among the many aspects of human character, and very strong family ties – illustrates today's society suffering from the gravest of instabilities, right within a family, so much so that we often hear about families at risk, sick families or psychopathology within a family. If families are sick, society can by no means be in good health either.

They said we should give back to Caesar what is Caesar's, i.e. that it was enough to have a job and a family in social terms, as long as we gave to God everything that belonged to God, i.e. as long as we maintained a pure heart, unattached from the world. They also said: he who renounces earthly possessions in the name of God will find them in heaven. We should approach the ocean – God – from which we all originate, without waiting for the ocean to come to us, because when we know the ocean, we cannot be disappointed by the drops. When all the drops are united and purified, there will not be any mud any more.

In other words, when the matter of which creation is made, like drops fallen from the sky mixing with the earth, is purified, it will return to its place of origin, that is, to the Creator Himself, as essence.

I was fascinated by this picturesque vision of life. There was something familiar about it and that inspired me one day to ask for an interview with the group's spiritual leader to discuss the choices I was faced with. He said we should not ask God for miracles, as we were supposed to wait for His "call" in the sense that thinking about daily matters was a call from man, while thinking about the Spirit in everyday life was the call from God.

He believed I was making the right choice, like an apostle of Jesus. Those were his words. To carry on with that task I had to remove all the veils which were still preventing me from having a clear vision, the vision of the heart. He clarified that mental illnesses, which I mistakenly thought I was curing for years in my role of psychiatrist from a medical point of view, were in fact illnesses of the soul, not of the body. He concluded saying that to enter into harmony with the Spirit, I first had to purify myself in order to be able to give the kind of help I had always wanted to give.

I knew I'd always helped my patients more with the empathy that characterized the relationship I'd established with them and not with the therapies administered in clinical practice.

Although the conversation was hermetic and essential, I could discern the direction in which my life was going, more clearly. Right after the interview, I broke down and cried liberating tears. Another knot of my soul was undone.

In three years, he was the second person – the first being the psycho astrologer – telling me about my future commitment of large-scale assistance to others. Although deeply touched by his words, I decided to put everything on the back burner, thinking that what I'd been told could have been but a Pindaric flight of a benevolent imagination.

Anyway, I continued following my path that was gradually outlined before my eyes as I went along, with increasing precision. I knew I couldn't ask for anything more now that I'd been given my health back. I was going to spend my life at the service of others, disregarding my own suffering which would occasionally rush back into my heart and overflow it, like a flooded river.

My suffering stemmed from my loneliness. I deliberately rejected the idea of having a partner, someone to love and share my life with. But then, I also knew that loneliness could be transformed into an expectancy filled with prayers to Him, who was arriving. I noted those words down without actually knowing who that He was.

I continued believing that purification was important in order to advance to a better life, without a distinct idea of what it really was.

I wrote: "I must get rid of my fears because He will come and turn barren deserts into fertile soil, yielding new crops".

Clearly, I couldn't discuss my deepest feelings with anyone so I apparently continued living my daily life the usual way, keeping myself hooked to reality through my job and taking care of my son.

As I progressed in my study of Astrology, I discovered a meaningful analogy between my astrological birth sign, the Virgo, and the symbolic figure of the Sphinx. Through a continuing self-investigation of my growingly intense emotions, I reached a stage in which my transformation crisis – expressed symbolically in the Virgo-Sphinx combination – turned the dramatic loneliness of my individual self, common to all human beings who feel lost in the universal chaos, into a loneliness that was heavy with expectancy for the upcoming fruits, or a state of consciousness open towards the union with the true, universal Self – no longer viewed as an alien, hostile force, but as part and parcel of the same "Being" I was part of, just like everyone else. I thus considered myself to be a particle of a harmonious and perfect "All" or "Oneness" – a microcosm within the macrocosm, but also vice versa.

In fact, only those who have lost everything can realize that they are not what they have lost but something much greater. This experience reoccurred a few years later, marking a fundamental phase of a journey which was just about to begin.

At the time I wrote that I wished to live far away and serve no one but Him, even though I was fully aware that "India", implied as the land of major socio-economical contrasts, was metaphorically also where I lived. My place of work was full of distress and misery and so it was unnecessary to go elsewhere to bring ease to others. It would have been enough to love everybody where I already was. I was still entirely unfamiliar with India, or with Sathya Sai Baba.

To this day I have no idea why I wrote "India" instead of "Africa", or any other country or continent. The truth is, a few years later India indeed became my second homeland on earth.

Could I have considered my choice to follow the way of the Spirit as a "call"? I still didn't have the answer.

Initially, the idea of being the "chosen one" sounded like an ostentation. My concerns were about my spiritual pride – the treacherous enemy of the will to grow and transcend the individual self, that is, the ego. Later on, I was told that I had been predestined.

I learned soon after that pride was a hindrance on the spiritual path, starting from the very threshold of self-realization.

Confirmations of my sensation of being "chosen" arrived gradually, until I started perceiving my destiny as an undeniable fact. Nevertheless, life carried on, as usual. It seemed I had to drink up from its bitter goblet, to the very last drop. There seemed to be no end to bitterness, which was another notion I received confirmation of years later.

Again, I make the point of the fact that confirmations kept coming at a regular pace, since I would like to draw the reader's attention to the constant presence and guidance of the Divine Spirit in everyone's life.

I was fortunately unaware that the "bitter pills" would continue being administered for quite a while. Differently, I might not have had the strength to carry on for twelve long years.

I felt menopause coming prematurely and hoped that this interim phase would be an opportunity to free myself from the power of sexual attraction, recognizing a close analogy with puberty, as when I was thirteen.

Choices, decisions, doubts, longings for faith, hopes or plans are marked with an aura of mystery, when related to any of the two periods – menarche or menopause. The reason is ignorance, or lack of knowledge. In effect, those phases represent a bridge, or a self-managed initiation, between the familiar, or outgoing, and the unfamiliar, or incoming worlds we are about to explore.

As when I was thirteen, it was just as difficult at forty to find someone who could understand me. We perceive only aspects of reality that match our capacity to resonate. In all likelihood, my receptors were quite peculiar.

Occasionally I didn't know how to curb the stream of thoughts, feelings and emotions cropping up in a whirlwind, at times intoxicating and at others disarming. I wrote to myself the way I had done in the past, as a teenager: "I have such a need to put down on paper whatever springs up, that when it emerges into consciousness, it disperses like a downfall, continuously perpetuating its roar. If not to you, who shall I open my heart to? You have always been at my side." Unconsciously, I was addressing my true Self, the divine essence. In a sense, I was talking to God with the same faith I had as a child. "More than anybody or anything else in the world, day by day, night after night, here and everywhere, you have experienced the same things, the same pain. Therefore, who could ever understand me better? The urge to write comes from the wish to testify about what is happening to me. It will be a divine experience, determined by the destiny, beyond the body and the mind, perhaps a metaphysical one. I find myself in the presence of evidence, as if to test my capacity and determination to remain coherent with the choices I'd made. Actually, the test was not so difficult compared with the ignorance and the flaws I wanted to get rid of. Still, it was, compared to the power to resist and persevere. I know that even though I have given up everything, I cannot renounce the cross. I will have to carry it on my shoulders as long as God wants me to."

The letter was concluded by declaring that I put everything back in the hands of God.

When I mentioned the cross or the bitter goblet it sounded almost like an overstatement. Years later, however, I had the confirmation in this regard. My experience was really like that – the bitter goblet and the heavy cross were the right metaphors.

The same terms were subsequently used by the inner voice to describe my past experiences when I'd already forgotten about those writings, when the cross of suffering was transformed into light.

The need to write to myself, unknowingly, derived from the need to testify to the true Self and present the evidence I had picked up on the path to a stable awareness.

While describing this phase of my story, I grasp certain aspects which have remained unchanged and others which have gone through a drastic change in terms of significance and depth, in the light of my present knowledge. The past and the present are surprisingly integrated and so are the familiar and the apparently utterly unfamiliar and unrelated.

Reminiscence of chronologically distant events was food for my thoughts, like deep insights into a new, future possibility to perceive with the heart's eye, having the so-called vision of the heart, to be able to differ what was coming from the individual self, or ego, in the form of unhappiness, from what was coming from the universal Self, in the form of contentment and joy. Inner vision allows us to act in harmony with nature, respecting the cycles and the deadlines necessary for other phenomena to mature in due time, interfering less and less with the increasingly calmer flow of existence. One acts more confidently, patiently and compassionately if inspired by the wisdom of the heart, attainable only through the nobility of the soul and an impeccable character, when the thick veil of material attachments and related desires has been removed. Emotional involvements force us to reincarnate life after life, trying in vain to quench our thirst with a water that doesn't quench: the water of the satisfaction of desires.

Indeed, the true water that does quench the thirst, namely the Spiritual Knowledge, made me realize, by awakening me from the spiritual ignorance which had featured my life till then, that happiness was something impersonal, something one could not own, although it was felt within. In other words, it is a manifestation of the relationship with the inner divine source. Destiny is determined by this flow of positive energy and not the other way round.

During the two years of my illness, due to various physical conditions and complications, I was periodically compelled to stay in bed. I would miraculously overcome every one of those situations, with a strength and courage to continue my life in a new way, increasingly aware that life was a gift. The true miracle was the new attitude to life and its inevitable trials.

Since then, despite my physical condition, compromised by all sorts of diagnosed pathologies, I have never stayed in bed due to an illness, although I haven't spared myself physically and have done unimaginable things according to the doctors who have treated me.

It was then that I recognized that diseases, physical or mental, were a consequence of negative thoughts, that we could lead a normal life and reach the realization of the inner Self, making sure to maintain a pure heart, without being tied down by egotistic intentions. I realized that the most important support we could ever offer consisted in communicating the kind of awareness that had freed us from the needs, that giving ourselves with love without expecting anything in return brought peace, that the greatest misery was not material but spiritual, stemming from ignorance. I therefore felt that aspiring for a higher Spiritual Knowledge to put it at the disposal to anyone who was willing to overcome spiritual ignorance was more important than assisting a single individual.

From then onwards, acquiring true awareness became a full-time commitment which absorbed every crumb of my energy. I mused day and night about what my intuition was revealing to me, as the still vague project I had in mind, or better in my heart, was gaining momentum in terms of consistency and form.

I investigated the deeper meaning of some familiar words. I saw them under a new light, perhaps because I began to perceive them with my heart. Here are a few examples: gentleness means surrendering out of love; mercy means giving your heart to the miserable, that is, to those who are unhappy; compassion means suffering with those who suffer.

I was focusing on the hidden meaning of thoughts, feelings, words, acts, coincidences and events of life.

This alienated me further from the environment. I was often in a state of "transitional absence", which hampered me more and more in my psychiatric career. And so I started considering a resignation.

I often dreamt, in those days, about crossing bridges – small or big, more or less wobbly, each one very different from the other. My dreams would always have a happy ending: I would safely get to the other side. The disappointments and frustrations accumulated with time helped me understand that everything in life was a great illusion, that the "real" world was like a dreamworld, or substantially the same. According to this new vision, I made a meticulous selection of what was to be conserved and what was to be eliminated, to depend less on the unnecessary comforts of life.

Non-attachment to material things, that is the ability to tell what is ephemeral and what isn't, is the easiest type of non-attachment to implement. I didn't know it at the time. As I learned later, the price of emotional non-attachment was higher.

I had an extraordinary dream. I visited a large convent and walked through every room and every garden as if I were visiting a museum. I went to a large window and, to my surprise, saw an outwardly landscape: a field of infinitely colourful, bright and shiny flowers extending as far as the eyes could see and an intensely blue sky. The ecstatic vision was interrupted by a friar who approached me gently and explained it was not allowed to look in that direction. I asked: "Is this Paradise perhaps?" There was no reply. While I was contemplating that divinely majestic sight, I was overwhelmed with immense peace.

Considering the "call" as an opportunity offered by the divine plan for me to renew my life and transform something familiar into something entirely new, yet to be uncovered, I was leafing through my past life and realized that I'd been given similar opportunities a number of times, but felt unfit for the challenge. I remember the most striking events: the visit to the cloister in Umbria when I was thirteen, the wedding proposal by a Japanese friend of mine who wanted to take me to live in Tokyo – I was fond of Japan and Zen culture but I was only fifteen and had other plans in mind – a Catholic mission in South America at eighteen, right in the period of my distancing from the Church, the marriage proposal of an English fiancée – after graduation I looked for a job in London but didn't find any psychiatric hospital willing to employ me because I hadn't specialized yet – the stay in Germany working in a NATO base while awaiting for a possible transfer into the United States, which failed immediately due to the lack of motivation on my side.

Up until then, the only call I had accepted was to work as a psychiatrist on an island in Venice, at an asylum. I'd shut the door to my native island, Sicily, once and for all, having left everyone and everything, and found myself in the North – all within a week.

What I was going through could not be measured with my past experiences and was therefore beyond comparison. At the offset of a new life, I was finally feeling with all my senses, not out of any practical need but rather out of my spiritual need to shoot to the top and answer my true Self's call for a different life plan. The thirst to drink from the fountain of the Spirit was so strong.

I could vaguely see the enlivening glimmer of dawn through the remaining darkness. A new day was breaking on the horizon of life and it was clear by then that I had to finish with my institutional work if I wanted to have a full experience.

I understood that true mental health, or the wellness of the heart, derived from our ability to detach ourselves from worldly things and that, most certainly, could not be acquired with psychotherapy or drugs. I couldn't continue practicing conventional treatments I no longer believed in, or agreed with.

That decision disturbed my economical framework but I couldn't help it. The wish to imbue in the spiritual world was intense. I could see I was at the decisive crossroad of take-it-or-leave-it. It was like: you are either with God or with the world. I couldn't remain lukewarm with respect to the Divine and that was patently clear.

I began to understand what seemed to be incredible, impossible or even madness, not long before. My firm determination to pursue that goal triggered a new outlook on life.

The Kingdom of God was among us, right within, and it was sufficient to love truly with a pure heart to instantly gain that awareness. The words of Jesus palpitated with life.

By "loving" I don't mean giving charity, which is generally meant in the Christian world, or serving others while still enslaved by the ego, seeking personal gratification. I mean giving yourself, your affections, your time, your life, all the priceless things that can't be sold or traded.

Was I going insane?

As a psychiatrist, I tried to make a self-diagnosis. I sometimes thought I was switching from depression to delirium and back again. At the same time, it was quite obvious that, given the circumstances, it was hardly probable that I could maintain the lucidity and the critical mind and reach the conclusion that I was delirious. It was a contradiction in terms.

Another miracle was actually taking place. My physical healing was followed by the healing of my heart. My love for other fellow human beings, not as a whole but as parts of the Unique Whole, and the concept of death as a birth into the true life of the Spirit gave birth to an inner, rare and unfamiliar flower. It was optimism.

My vision of life had always been sombre, quite foggy and elusive. It didn't bring me much joy. A smile was finally peeping in my eyes and on my face. I often went to church, after a twenty years' break, especially between the services, to meditate and talk to God. In the silence, occasionally interrupted by the screeching entrance door, I contemplated the shaky flames of the lit candles, whose liveliness emulated His presence. I talked to Him although He never replied. Still, I was convinced He was listening.

I was growingly persuaded by the value of the Christian concepts I'd rejected in the past. They became indispensable for my spiritual approach to life.

One of the concepts particularly difficult to "digest" was the claim that Divine Grace could be attained only through the cross, or that Grace was proportionate to one's effort to purify the heart and the mind.

My study of Esotericism, Gnostics, the Apocryphal Gospels, St John's[12] Aquarian Gospel and the like progressed and opened my eyes to "the other face of Jesus". I was finally putting together my knowledge, i.e. water, with the love and the spirit. My strength outgrew the obstacles before me.

This knowledge, filtered through my faith and trust in God, made me see that people were neither good nor bad but more or less perfect, that serenity and inner peace were the prerogatives of health, that disharmony and discord were the bases of all ills and that harmony was the origin of happiness intended as peace, joyfulness and fulfilment.

To be able to love unconditionally, it is necessary to comprehend and accept all the facets of the people around us. Only then we can see the others the way they really are and accept them, without idealizing.

Harmony comes from God and disharmony comes from man. Hence, evil comes from man as an expression of spiritual ignorance and a consequence of the erroneous use of free choice.

I realized that being incarnated on this earth represented a greater disturbance for a soul, since incarnation embraced the slavery deriving from the laws of matter, whereas in death the soul broke free from it.

Consequently, the cross *is* slavery deriving from the laws of matter we automatically obey, from birth. When it becomes too heavy and painful, we refuse to accept it. Hence, the more we detach from matter and its limitations, the less we suffer. This is the only way to escape its overhanging influence and the heavy dominion of its laws.

The concept of the cross, austere and hard, became almost soothing, like a gentle advice by a loving Father or a loving Mother. I could catch a glimpse of the transformation of its essence of pain into the essence of light.

The Glory of the Lord, that is, inner peace, is attained only after the ego has been tempered, the play of the desires toned down and the chains of emotional and material attachment undone – in a word, after we have carried the cross, experienced slavery and liberated ourselves from it, to re-conquer the light and the dignity of freedom and immortality.

With this vision of heightened awareness, the renouncement or non-attachment to worldly "illusions" loses its bitter taste the individual self or ego covered them up with. Instead, they acquire the unique taste of freedom – sublime, intangible, celestial. The goblet turns from bitter to sweet.

But what becomes bitter and hard are the bonds of "sweet" slavery which stick to us like addictions until we are able to recognize ourselves in our true essence and be no longer at the mercy of all the poisonous fruits of illusion, like fear, anxiety, insecurity, doubt and isolation of the true Self. Clearly, what we really miss is our own Self, although we think we need all those things to survive. Dimmed by the numerous addictions, we cannot even notice the major peril before us and the fact that we have lost our soul by not having acknowledged our true Self.

Neurosis, one of the modern illnesses, is typical of someone who trusts his individual self or ego, instead of trusting God, and so ends up in desperate isolation, impermeable even to Divine Grace.

Speaking of disharmony as the origin of all evils, I refer to all its multiple expressions like egotism as the counterpoint of unconditional love, pride as the counterpoint of humility, attachment as the counterpoint of generosity, anger as the counterpoint of patience and grudge as the counterpoint of forgiveness.

In a nutshell, the mentioned manifestations of negative energy, characteristic of those still subject to fear and a sense of guilt – rooted in childhood experiences with our parenting figures, when we discovered their imperfections and flaws, which conditioned our lives as adults – stem from our failure to abide by the laws of nature (*karma*) regulating the course of existence. A reassessment of those features in the light of Truth and Love, leaving aside our pride and illusions, will bring out courage and impartiality, and we will be able to see things in a new perspective and overcome them.

A lifetime dedicated to matter and its needs merely perpetuates disharmony, creating dissatisfaction, depression and a feeble body: factors that predispose to illness. A lifetime dedicated to the Spirit and its yearnings, on the other hand, frees us from all evil and brings peace and harmony.

Now I know that the only force that can set us free is the power of the Spirit: a man is free when he has learned, wisely, to love Truth as God. Those who love Him freely accept the will of Universal Intelligence, that is, the will to do only good.

I reconsidered my habits and cut down consumption in the light of the approaching retirement.

I had travelled a lot until then. My destinations had been places where I could freely experience and contemplate nature, to love and admire it in its magnificent grandeur and variety of beauties. To immerse in it and its seas, forests or mountains has always been an outstanding and enlivening relief. I had to contain this aspect of my life drastically as well. The last pilgrimage to a natural sanctuary, a desert, took place in 1990 when I went to Africa with my son.

It was the first time in my life to encounter such inimitable beauty shaped exclusively by God's hand. I heard it speak the most eloquent of all languages, the language of God – silence. I listened to that silent voice telling me about the Spirit: it was a pilgrimage to a place where the finite met the infinite. It was love at first sight[13].

When one is able to listen to that Voice and understand it, a spark in the heart lights up – the spark that has always been there without us knowing about it – never to be put out again. This is what happened to me when we met.

A Tuareg proverb says that God created the world to give the man a home and a desert for him to find his soul.

That short-lived, almost furtive encounter, a few hours stolen from a timetable packed with forced stops in various places I no longer remember the name of, remained impressed in my heart, with two important lessons on what it takes for an undertaking to be successful. We should have a strong character, that is, the will and determination to remain coherent and in harmony with the Universe and the courage to nurture a tender heart, comprehend everything and everyone with compassion and generosity, recognize our own shortcomings in other people's limitations and flaws and accept everything and everyone with Love. Not surprisingly, the hardness of the heart and the weakness of character increase attachments and make us incapable of loving.

Back home, the need to find the dimension of inner silence pushed me to attend a course in Zen meditation. In that context as well, spiritual ignorance was defined as a source of suffering and disharmony. A phrase from Buddhist readings kept coming back into my mind: "If you don't find it within, where are you going to search for it?"

To me, that question was a fundamental cue on which to delve. It invited me not to give in to the tide of my desires, needs, broodings over the past and daydreaming about the future. The mind is a good servant but a bad master. I had always known that, having assisted in its relentless hustle and bustle, in both roles – as a doctor and a patient – at the expense of my life.

I knew I had to be present within, in the here and now, striving to merge with the All, that is, with the surrounding energy which is at the same time pure vacuity and unfathomable essence.

I silenced my desires and needs. The only real fortune we can ever possess is our Love for God, in our thoughts, words and acts. To surrender myself to God in that way, I first had to know myself but even prior to that, I had to find myself.

Mine was the highest objective one could aim at. Only by reaching it I would be able to discover my true Self. That was the fortune I was after.

You are rich only if you can give of yourself and share generously. It is the act of Love *par excellence* which makes us find and perceive Divinity within.

As I was trying to adjust the individual self to the true Self and realize who I really was, I continued to meditate. A part of me, no doubt the wiser one, knew that meditation was the shortcut to the Self as the expression of the inner Divine.

My long lasting love for Japan, dating back from my early teens, was based on my empathy for the Zen culture and its intuitive compassion[14], simplicity, straightforwardness, essentiality, reservedness, self-awareness, objective images devoid of personal emotions, great love and respect for nature, disregard for death and acceptance of adversities. It is a culture that invites to experiment with reality without the deceptive intervention of the intellect that tends to categorize and analyze. Apart from Astrology, it taught me the transition from logical to analogical thinking which considered comprehension possible only when we ignored the intellect and carefully followed intuition, thus contributing to the development of antirational thought, an anti-mind, which was not difficult for me, since I had always thrived on intuition rather than rationality.

This inborn attitude helped me understand aspects of eastern philosophy (Confucianism, Taoism, Buddhism and Zen) which might at first disorient a rational mind, like any other paradox. The following statement is just an example: "to see implicates senses but in the final analysis it must transcend them".

I found this "religion of quietism and calmness" indeed very congenial and the meditation group analogous, but I nevertheless decided to interrupt that experience after a few months. I couldn't share the group members' veneration for their master whom I considered human. I therefore simply withdrew, out of coherence. I thought that the man was fine, competent and respectable, but nothing more than that. I hadn't met anyone worthy of veneration yet.

I was looking for a Master with a capital M, I'd been looking for Him my entire life, but I hadn't met him yet.

And so, I was by myself again, contemplating and praying, of course in my own way. My prayers were conversations with God, mostly soliloquies, or at least that is what I thought before I realized that God had been, was and would be part of myself.

Nine years passed before I resumed meditating regularly and experiencing meditation as a simple but unutterable jewel of union with my divine Self.

I continued studying esoteric and sacred scriptures of varied religions, namely the Upanishads, Ramayana, the Bhagavad-Gita, Tao Te Ching, Dhammapada, the Bible, and so on. I was growingly convinced that man could be saved from his involution only by giving priority to his spiritual education over his academic learning.

Just as the ground must be tilled before sawing, we must first eliminate our flaws to replace them with virtues by educating our character according to the human values, depending on the life stage (childhood, adolescence or adulthood). Then we should consider what kind of seeds to plant in schools, universities or colleges. All that without losing sight of the fertilizer of coherence which should always be there, at every stage, without any exception and without any contraindication.

If it is true that only a fertile soil can yield good crops, how can we expect to have a "good crop" from a humanity "infested" with flaws and oblivious to the meaning of virtue?

Why be amazed at the youth without values, at the fading of the family as an institution or at the violent society?

Spirituality is life, or better, the essence of life[15]. It cannot be given away in specialized settings, studied by "authorized people", theologians or priests or in religious circles, or be a cult object in rites devoid of their original, vivifying meanings.

"Churches are empty all the time" cries the Catholic Church.

"It's useless to close the stable door after the horse has bolted".

How much damage has been inflicted on the entire humanity, albeit unintentionally, by the people of the church! They have deprived ordinary people and families which constitute our society of the Spiritual Knowledge for two thousand years.

These ordinary people and families have been cut off from every possibility to establish a direct relationship with God so that everything could be mediated by the church and its official representatives.

Nobody will ever admit what was supposed to be safeguarded and why. However, it becomes self-explanatory if one takes a closer look at the ecclesiastic policy over the last millennium and compares it with the life of Jesus. The two have nothing in common.

It took me decades of study and reflection to reveal the meaning of the words written in the Gospel of Jesus. The only kind of help I received from the church in this matter was that it made me give up and stop trying to understand – at least that was my experience.

I did not give up, nevertheless. My thirst for God was unquenched. The frustration due to the failure to find Him was stronger than the fatigue.

Without submitting to the pain and the hardships, I kept on struggling until I found myself on the right pathway to Him, the path of Spiritual Knowledge leading to the awareness of being "Divine", made in God's own image and likeness.

I was fascinated by Spiritual Knowledge, as the only true knowledge, and felt enlivened by its grandeur without limits of time and space in the generous embrace of infinite galaxies, with its flavour of timeless eternity, the limpid and pure sound of its silence and the explosive effusions of its brightness.

As my work of self-observation continued, I noticed more and more manifestations of significant coincidences, real phenomena of synchronicity[16] which became a constant in my daily life spent mostly in the name of the Spirit.

It was in that period that I stopped feeling ridiculous for my "magic thought". By then I'd realized that magic equalled to sacred, in a language well forgotten by the civilized man.

Actually, magic thought, intuition, coincidences, the language of symbols, the language of numbers, the language of nature and the language of the stars were all access keys to Spiritual Knowledge from which I'd been cut off, together with the vast majority of humankind over the past two thousand years. The twentieth century – industrialized, robotized and technicalized – saw science reach its maximum, at the detriment of true knowledge.

I've always thought I would not be able to end this life without giving sense to my personal story. It would be a futile sacrifice, a waste. That was the scope of my relentless reading of Astrology, Anthropology, Psychology, Numerology, Gnosticism, Esotericism, Taoism, Buddhism, Hinduism, Mysticism and Early Christianity.

I still didn't know that the source (Father), the river (Mother) and the water (the Son and the Holy Spirit), the microcosm and the macrocosm, were within. The universe of the heart would make me feel united with the rest of humanity, like one heart and one soul.

I didn't know yet that the recently made decisive choice had come from a well defined source: the Grace of the Holy Spirit. I received Grace, the miracle *par excellence*, which I called the miracle of all miracles and which intoxicated me until I felt mad and ridiculous. It happened also to the apostles of Jesus – people thought they were drunk when they were inundated by the gifts of the Holy Spirit.

The Spirit had come to bring light to my eyes and warmth to my heart. The light was the knowledge of the deep sense of things and events in life, as revealed Truth. The warmth was the love and the imperturbable joy which embraced everything, as the fullness of existence.

The gift of intuitive intelligence or knowledge, or the light that illuminates the mind and the heart, was given to me, to become familiar with the Godly matters and plans and free my mind from the veil of ignorance. I was reborn in the water and in the spirit, in Knowledge and Love.

I was about to have an extraordinary experience which changed the course of my life once again, so I could be in Paradise on Earth. I was going to meet God and His Glory that become visible when we are illuminated by the Holy Spirit.

I still didn't know that predicting future events, understanding mysteries, perceiving hidden things, realizing desires and the likeness and closeness to God were the gifts of the Holy Spirit, as the source of all goodness which, once settled in His position in the heart – and acknowledged by us – enlivened, renewed, transformed, purified, illuminated and made us Divine, filling us with Love and Knowledge.

NOTES: CHAPTER II

12. All the quotations have been taken from St. John's Aquarian Gospel.

13. Later on I found out that Sai Baba defined life as a pilgrimage to God.

14. Japanese letters are ideograms and are related to the right, non-verbal brain hemisphere, the one linked to intuition, creativity, poetry, painting, etc.

15. According to the Catholic Church, only the baptised and the ministers of the cult are "inhabited by the Spirit". But can the Spirit be limited? Jesus said: *"The Spirit where he willeth doth blow"*

16. Synchronicity: temporal coincidence of two or more events, unrelated in terms of cause and effect but with the same or analogous content in terms of significance.

III

Comprehension does not take place due to a shock but due to identification.

Jaspers.

In September 1990 a friend of mine lent me a book about a great mystic, an enlightened man called Sathya Sai Baba. He lived in India and was depicted as the man who had come from heaven. I also read in the book that phenomena such as telepathy, clairvoyance and palmistry were once "normal" powers of the human mind, that man had forgotten about the power to communicate with his own Self when he had lost Paradise, although it was unclear how – perhaps man had stopped feeding himself adequately both psychologically and physically, taking in substances that gradually dulled his extrasensory skills or maybe life conditions on earth changed.

One evidence of the lost or forgotten abilities might be the fact that even a slightly altered state of consciousness, like hypnosis, can bring out temporary precognition, retro-cognition, or cause regressions into previous lives.

In the part dealing with mysticism as a science whose scope is to awaken the awareness of the Self in a person, it said that, in order to reach that state of awareness, one had to cross the territory of the unconscious mind where the divine spark, or the Self, or *Atma*[17], resided and pulsated at the feet of the Divine. That particular topic stirred up great interest in me.

I had been interested in the unconscious mind from a viewpoint of psychodynamics for decades, without being able to quench my thirst of the Knowledge of the Spirit, with a capital "K".

Phenomena I had personally verified or seen in other people, e.g. that the unconscious mind could cause and cure illnesses, were clearly described.

I started to make out a rather clear indication leading to this "inner place".

Being able to connect with the unconscious mind implies having overcome all the obstacles between individual consciousness and the universal Self and, accordingly, having got in touch with the inner All.

It is the realization of the Self, or the state of expanded consciousness, in which we perceive the universe and us as one single thing.

To acquire this, the path can go either upwards or downwards. What matters is to arrive to the Ocean and merge with it, like tiny drops into Him – the Absolute.

Saint Ignatius wrote in his Spiritual Exercises: *"It is not the amount of knowledge that satisfies and pleases the soul but the inner feeling and tasting."*

And that was actually happening to me in the course of that reading.

Within, I was savouring each word on this great Indian living Master, Sai Baba. It was an entirely new feeling: enlivening and tasting of something unique and rare.

When I closed my eyes and thought about Him, I was gently immersed in His ineffable mystery. Here are some phrases taken from His teachings, which astonished me for their vastness and universality of judgment.

"I teach you to live with righteousness and to die with benefit."

"Start loving your parents, friends and enemies."

"Where Love is, there is Peace; where Peace is, there is Truth; where Truth is, there is Bliss; where Bliss is, there is God."

"Start the day with Love, fill the day with Love, finish the day with Love – this is the way to God."

"Love is God. God is All-pervasive. We are all incarnations of Love. Live with Love, serve with Love, rejoice with Love and merge with Love – this is the fundamental task of serving the others. It is in the service for the others that the Love of God manifests. Give Love and you will receive Love. In Love you will find God."

Love is neither born nor does it die. It is unchangeable and it always shines in the hearts, beyond joy and pain, praise and contempt."

I finally found the supreme reality I had been looking for all my life.

Sai Baba says that man will be free only when he detaches himself from the ties and desires binding him to the world.

Spiritual Knowledge can be revealed by the Spirit only if the mind and the heart are pure and filled with good thoughts and feelings.

Desire is born out of selfishness, as the root of all evils, flaws and deficiencies.

'Life + desires' makes you feel human. *'Life – desires'* makes you feel at one with God.

The inscription on the temple at Delphi says: "*Know thyself and you will know the Cosmos*". I found what I had searched for all along and I was absolutely sure about it.

Perhaps Sai Baba was a starting point, or a destination, or both. What I know is that He was the first and the only One who opened my heart to the enlightenment of the knowledge of the Self – of me in terms of Self.

The key of the golden gate of the unknowable resides within. It is called the experience of the Divine within and it is our best teacher. He confirms it.

All the books and all science are nothing compared to the direct personal experience of God, resulting in the knowledge of the heart.

With His arrival on earth, Sai Baba made the greatest gift, a messianic one, by returning God to humankind. He points out that God has no intermediaries between Him, the Self and man, regardless of race or religion.

The Messiah is back with us, as promised two thousand years ago, to inaugurate an age of full human and cosmic renewal, when man's divinity will be acknowledged as irrefutable reality.

I was given the possibility to experience this long awaited advent in person and it seemed quite incredible. It was true, though! I *was* the chosen one!

Representatives of all churches should review their role as intermediaries between the Divine and the rest of mankind and take heed of the new age advent of the Spiritual Knowledge, of the Light within.

When the heart and the mind are purified, there is no need for any intermediaries. One becomes the priest and the healer of oneself.

At the beginning of each age, the Messiah comes to illuminate the way and heal the broken hearts: Sai Baba arrived duly to redeem and bring solace to the tired and heavy-laden humanity approaching the third millennium, longing for a new life, a new knowledge and a new spirituality.

Since human law considers acts and Divine Law considers intention, Sai Baba says that today's thoughts and actions build our future, just as yesterday's thoughts and actions built our present life, according to our intentions embedded in them.

Sai Baba has come to recommend us to put His message of Love into practice because, as Jesus also used to say, those who listen to the words of God without putting them into practice deceive themselves and God and build castles in the sand.

He came to warn us not to persevere in our errors. Over the last two thousand years, few people have really put into practice the message of Jesus – also a message of Love – and our society is a clear evidence.

Each one of us is hence the creator of his/her own destiny. I was beginning to acknowledge it myself and realize that the moment had come for me to put myself trustingly in the hands of His spiritual discipline.

Sai Baba spoke about familiar things I had always been aware of and acknowledged as being true, although I had not understood that they were the essence of life. I had searched for them elsewhere.

Experience showed me that being 'in the right time' and having a pure heart wasn't enough if we wanted to find what we were looking for. We had to be 'in the right place' as well.

First of all, we must know what we are looking for or what we are aiming at. If it is Love with a capital L, we can be sure that we have found it when we meet the One who can open our heart to Love with a glance, letting us know that He is Love, that we are Love, and that we are at one. That is a true Master.

This is actually what happened to me when His Grace overwhelmed my life, teaching me that the path leading to freedom and subsequently to self-realization consisted in accepting the surrounding world of duality, patiently, with balance, inner peace and harmony.

I have always loved harmony. He made me realize that God was Harmony and that we should stop considering joy and happiness as our friend and pain and suffering as our enemy. They are two sides of the same coin, just like fear is the other face of attachment and doubt the other face of mistrust in God.

We should embrace everything with Love to convert everything in goodness. Jesus said: *"Love thy enemy"*. For the very same reason, Sai Baba says: *"Your enemies are your best teachers"*. Suffering and pain serve the purpose of our spiritual health, because they poke indolence and presumption. They are the tools that have aided the greatest mystics to see beyond. It is not a coincidence that the first Christians used to say *"per crucem ad lucem"* (To the light through the cross.) and the old pagans: *"per aspera ad astra"* (To the stars through difficulties.).

Non-attachment prevails over fear and surrendering to God prevails over doubt.

Time was no longer a hindrance but a means to realize God's plan, as much as possible, and so it had to be spent in the best way. Sai Baba says: *"Time is God."*

I started thinking of Him more and more and this often filled my days, even if I was busy doing other things.

I read all the books about Him and all His speeches I could get hold of.

I wished to see Him, meet Him, and get to know Him. In my heart I felt I had always known Him.

I talked to Him – in silence – in my heart.

I asked Him – in my thoughts – to make my big dream come true: being in India, in His presence, at my son's fourteenth birthday. At the age of fourteen, Sai Baba proclaimed to be the *Avatar*[18] of the new age and started His mission as Sathya Sai Baba. He left His family and set up His *ashram*[19].

I understood I had found the One who would give me fulfilment, the One who would give me energy instead of taking it away, the One who was acclaimed by the masses and world famous. The prediction made by the psycho astrologer precisely five years earlier came true.

I was witnessing something I had considered impossible, unimaginable and incredible. That man existed, very far away from my place of birth, the One I was born for was waiting for me, the One I was living for, the One I would die my earthly death for, to be reborn in the life of the Spirit.

Like the Samaritan in the Gospel of Jesus, I was going to drink the water that quenched the thirst once and for all, the water of the fountain which was Jesus[20]. I was going to be at one with Him, in the Christ Consciousness. I was going to become a fountain of life by opening myself to Freedom and Divine Knowledge, by adoring God in Spirit and in Truth.

Jesus said: *"I shall ask the Father and He will send another Paraclete, the Holy Ghost of Truth!"*

The Spirit of Truth was back among us and I recognized It in my heart and was about to receive the Grace and be recognized by Him.

Winter and spring passed and I was still waiting for an encounter with the Divine.

In early summer the moment finally arrived to step on the holy land of India and leave for the long awaited appointment – my dream was coming true. I was travelling with my son and sister. That was the first in a series of numerous dreams, realized owing to the Divine Omnipotence.

When we find ourselves eight/nine thousand meters above the ground, on the plane, the sensation that everything is in the hands of the Cosmic Intelligence I call God is stronger and I believe that no one gets on board without fear, confiding in mere chance or in the flight captain, that is, in another human being. You know your life is tied with a thread and the only thing that really counts is not trusting yourself but something much greater and more powerful. It is the moment to surrender to God.

This should always be the way we feel, even when our feet are on the ground, because life *is* hanging on a thread, in any case, also when we are unaware of it.

I had never been so far and yet so close to home.

As soon as I was out of the airport building, I was struck by a wave of air so hot and humid that I could hardly breathe any more. It was a shock but I was prepared for anything.

That world was totally different with respect to the one I had just left but, paradoxically so, it was somehow familiar and I loved it already – and love is blind, as we all know. I liked everything about it, didn't mind the delays or any other hassle. To think how relieved I had been when I had left Sicily about twenty years earlier, considering it too hot. In India I endured everything, even the 40°/45°/50° centigrade I sometimes experienced there. I found everything so fascinating. Yes, there was much misery and poverty around. In this sense, Mumbai is a megalopolis full of contrasts. Wealth and poverty cohabit and nearly get along well. I was struck by the colourful vitality[21] in the smiles and the eyes of the people, kids in particular – something you cannot see in the west any more. Provided it has ever existed, implied as the joy of living, we might have lost it with the sought-after economical wellbeing of our society.

It was the monsoon season and it was raining all the time. It was a different kind of rain; in fact, it was a deluge.

I took another plane to Bangalore, a town at 1000 m of altitude, considered to be the garden of India. I arrived at Puttaparthi by taxi in a few hours. It is a remote place on the Deccan Plateau – a mountain chain dividing central India in two. It was not the tropical India with the luxuriant vegetation I was expecting to see. The surrounding land was desert-like: fairly arid and bare. Sai Baba's *ashram* was a celestial sight, an oasis in the desert. Inside it, everything was special, albeit austere and essential. My home had never been so close – I was back to my origins.

I was positively surprised noticing that my son was sharing the same sensation. My sister was respectful but displayed less enthusiasm. We were staying inside the *ashram* and started getting ready for the solemn encounter, with trepidation.

While we were waiting for Sai Baba to arrive inside the temple called *Mandir*, perfect silence resounded the Glory of God.

These waits, which can last for hours, twice a day, when He comes out to join His devotees for the *darshan*[22], became the sweetest waits of my life.

So many hands to transform the world and so few eyes to contemplate Him! This phrase stated by who-knows-whom was really appropriate for that moment. There were at least three to four thousand people expecting Him.

But what was that compared to the rest of humankind, outside, in a world that knew nothing about Him and kept living and ignoring that Grace, so within reach?

Sai Baba – by His own words – hasn't come for the few privileged but for the entire mankind and the day will arrive soon when He will be acknowledged by everyone.

When I saw Him for the first time, I recognized Him as the One I had been looking for and I felt I knew Him in my heart. It was a silent communication with mutual glances of understanding, just like old friends understanding each other, without needing to say anything.

My mind was completely empty and I was left without thoughts and desires, without anything to say or ask. I recognized myself in Him and that was it. It was up to Him to do the rest.

He acted promptly and woke me up from that surreal, dreamlike atmosphere which lasted only a week, into a nightmare: I had to go back immediately.

I had just laid my foot into Paradise and yet I had to leave already. I cried warm and bitter tears and finally gave up before the evidence. My sister had joined us but her motivation was different from mine. Rightfully, she wanted to see other parts of India, not just the ashram of Sai Baba.

I realized then why He hadn't approached me, spoken to me or made external signs of attention. He allowed me to get used to feeling Him in my heart and speaking to Him with my heart. In this way I would never be disappointed in my expectations of feeling Him close to me, as I would always carry Him in my heart wherever I went[23].

I would have suffered so much more had I been forced to leave Him after I had gathered His splendid smile or after I had heard His sweet and melodic voice, after I had lightly touched His delicate feet, soft like silk. The pain was great anyway, as if a part of me had been torn away, and I remained impaired, with an open wound in my heart.

Surely this was not the right way to love Him but I didn't know it at the time. It took some time to learn to get rid of the many attachments, one of which was sublime – the attachment to His physical form, the living manifestation of God.

It might sound blasphemous but Sai Baba invites us to detach ourselves from His physical form and learn to see Him everywhere in the realm of Creation, in the world, in nature, above all in our fellow men and women, in the heart of each one of us[24].

I experienced the joy of seeing my family at His feet, although this does not sound appropriate, because when I think of my family I think of mankind and not about three or four or ten people united by a blood tie. I am definitely in favour of universal brotherhood.

What else could I wish for? I had asked Him in my heart months earlier to bring me there but not to stay with Him as well, so I couldn't complain.

During the last *darshan* which seemed like the very last for the disconsolate tears that blurred my sight, I found myself in the front line. He passed close to me and looked at me with eyes so sweet, deep like night, bright like day, and looked into my eyes which were like a river in flood and walked on. I had to contain my pain of that excruciating separation, not to distress those who were close to me. I resigned myself and we continued the journey.

The Divine Master's card was written with my tears, expressing acceptance and not attachment, not constriction but Love.

God wants our faith to be founded on an act of freedom, i.e. on an act of Love for our neighbour who is just as at one with God – we must always bear that in mind, or otherwise we might lose our direct contact with Him.

With my heart still at Puttaparthi, we continued our journey southward. I hadn't learned yet that we should always be present within, with all our heart, wherever we might be in a given time.

As I was leaving Sai Baba's native place, where He still lives, I asked Him for a sign, to let me know if my job resignation was in accordance with His Will.

Over the past years an idea was gradually taking shape. I felt an imminent decision coming through but I needed His approval. I was not going to take any decisions unless approved by Him.

The sign arrived in time, in a unique but "painful" manner. I was staying in Pondicherry, a world famous place hosting a spiritual centre, Auroville, inspired by the teachings of a great, enlightened master of the past century, Sri Aurobindo.

I decided to stay in the hotel due to the high temperatures (45/50° centigrade), while my son and my sister were playing the game of the daring tourists and defying the burning sun. Through the closed window of my hotel room, I was silently contemplating the beach and the dark blue sea of the Gulf of Bengal, thinking about Sai Baba and the week I had spent with Him, in His *ashram*, while the fishermen were drawing the nets in the distance.

I was brooding over the possibility that the experience I had had could have been the last for me in this life and that made me feel even sadder. My mood was not good in those days – and I regret it so much now, when I look back – but this happens in life, when we are unaware of our divine essence.

In a few words: after I'd spent two days as a recluse in my room, I went out, fell down the hotel stairs and ended up with a plastered leg. We returned to Italy earlier and I was soon back home.

The journey ended with a clear indication of what had to be done: it is so true that bad luck often brings good luck. Actually, bad luck always brings good luck....our Spirit. I still remember the proverb my sister taught me "Each impediment is an advantage".

The "accidental" fall took place right below a large picture of an Indian divinity unknown to me at the time. When I asked for its name, I was told the image represented Lord Krishna and afterwards I learned that Sai Baba was one of His reincarnations.

A perfect plan was accomplished before my eyes. Others saw it merely as an accident.

A month upon my return, my irrevocable letter of resignation was signed. I also had my name struck off from the medical register before the departure, as the proof of my blind faith, feeling His presence and His divine essence within me. I have never practiced the medical profession again, of my own free will, and to this day I could well be the only person who has ever done that.

I was a different person with a new life and the old, official role did not belong to me any more – I couldn't help it.

Evidently, no one understood that gesture. It was of course interpreted as sheer eccentricity and extravaganza.

I closed the chapter "Psychiatry" and with it the life that accompanied it. I crossed the point of "no return" and took a leap into thin air.

Once I had taken the decision, a new energy surged within. This helped me realize that only those who were really determined could be saved, provided they knew the Truth, while the others remained in their state of slavery. When Truth doesn't warm up, it burns[25]. In other words, it can harm.

As the years went by, all those who had disapproved of my decision changed their mind and admitted it had been the right thing to do.

According to Indian ayurvedic medicine, when it comes to spontaneous healing, there is a constant common to all spontaneously healed patients. Healing is immediately preceded by an inner personal transformation, in people with a strong faith, courage and a positive attitude to life, who get rid of prejudices and, unprompted, put themselves in the hands of their silent intelligence – which unmistakably knows what is good for them. This intelligence of the heart accepts both joy and pain with gratitude and appreciation; it supports the eternal contradiction between the understanding of the mind and the feeling of the heart, knowing that God resides in both and everything is but an expression of Him. There is, therefore, a sense of reconciliation with life which produces the awareness that we are all a human family and not just separate individuals.

This is what happened to me years earlier, when I found myself miraculously healed and "on my feet" again, above all with a new state of consciousness, no longer feeling like an "orphan, abandoned in the Universe".

Many years had to pass before I recognized that "mental health" was a possibility to realize the real Self within, through the spiritual (or mystical) experiences which helped us transcend – and not to go against – the individual self, or ego, and the surrounding environment, accepting everything and everyone.

The reinstated condition of inner wellbeing allowed me to accept Sai Baba as the Master with a capital "M" I'd always hoped to find.

My strength, tenacity and courage to pursue the way I'd chosen to follow stemmed from the awareness that our body was immersed in the Cosmic Body of God, just like the human mind was immersed in the Cosmic Mind, or our heart in the heart of the Universe, just as the microcosm was immersed in the macrocosm, one reflecting the other. I was aware that we were not spectators but co-creators, being able to change our destiny with God's aid in the supreme Cosmic Game, even though, paradoxically, the spectator's part was even more significant and performed by the true Self within, witnessing all events and thoughts all along, guiding our destiny industriously and reliably. The more I understood, the more responsible I felt and the more determined I was to get to the bottom of the game of life.

I discovered that, in India, when one reached the age of retirement, at the age of sixty, having enjoyed the benefits of material life such as family, work, and the like, one generally decided to dedicate the rest of one's life to the inner world and the unity with God. The mind, having experienced the habitual dulling of the fascinating albeit tricky state of wake, seeks to stop thinking, through meditation, to return to its source, the silence of pure divine energy, because in effect it acquires importance only because our senses get involved in the surrounding world, giving shape to scents, colours, etc., also made of pure energy.

When we succeed in perceiving the world as a living universe, with a pulsating heart expanding beyond its normal limits to contain us lovingly, as a mother's womb contains a child, we can feel the comfort of fulfilment and the blissfulness we yearn for all our lives, as incredulous adults.

I am not sure if such experiences can be defined as "peak experiences" but I am certain, from my own experience, that they are moments of pure happiness, when all doubts, fears, inhibitions, tensions and weaknesses dissolve. In those instances, there is a healing, regenerative power that transcends the duration of time and so minutes, hours or days do not count.

Feeling united with the entire world, being its integral part, is indeed an exceptionally livening experience – it is the fusion, or better, the annihilation of the individual self in the true Self, i.e. Cosmic Love.

I started dreaming of India and Sai Baba and His *darshan* at Puttaparthi. He was inviting me to stop thinking about death and return to Him soon, since death was the overwhelming thought at the time.

The Bible often mentions the presence of God in people's dreams as 'special moments of direct communication with the Divine'. But man stopped conceiving God as the privileged interlocutor and so God stopped "disturbing" him in his dreams, which eventually became an object of psychoanalysis in the century I was born.

Psychoanalysis has played an important role in restoring the dignity of the reality of dreams, as a small step towards the deserved acknowledgment of this essential aspect of human life and its additional re-evaluation, thus improving our Spiritual Knowledge and that of the world we live in.

The said anticipation of a future trip to India, announced in my dream by Sai Baba, literally imbued my heart with joy and brought me into a state of bliss that lasted several days. I felt free and light, like a butterfly.

I enjoyed pondering upon the beauty of nature, sharing life with the elements – earth, fire, water and air. I realized I felt joy for everyone or rather for the fusion with everything, within and without. I wish to point out that my dreams of Sai Baba described in this book have, to me at least, the same value as everyday reality. I am firmly convinced that they are made of the "same substance". I had the opportunity to verify this on numberless occasions. If we are sometimes unable to comprehend the subtle meaning of oneiric experiences, it is due to ignorance, lack of awareness and our inability to see beyond. Unfortunately, our rationality cannot help us extricate ourselves from the world it doesn't belong to (the 4th dimension?).

I speak specifically about the dreams in which Sai Baba appears. As for the rest of my dreams, there are ways to clarify them, all based on the topic of this book, but I cannot take them into account.

Since I decided to leave my job and submit my resignation, a strange period followed. It seemed that a good part of my friends and acquaintances had agreed to leave together for a better place and departed at the same time. I thus attended ten funerals of people dear to me, some of which I'd looked after, day after day, until their terrain experience came to an end.

A whole year passed in the sign of this special commitment: being close to people living on the borderline, between life and death, and share that experience.

Paradoxically, Sai Baba told me in my dream not to think about death. He was actually communicating that I should start considering it differently from the way most people did. To them, death represented the end.

I had to start viewing it simply as a new beginning and there could hardly be a better opportunity to take note of it than to live constantly in its wake, day after day, for a year.

One of those people was an extraordinary woman who had introduced me into Sai Baba's knowledge. She had been miraculously saved by Him ten years earlier and dedicated the remaining years of her life to Him.

I was by her side over the last six months of her earthly life. During that time, despite her precarious physical condition and suffering, she succeeded in passing something special on me: the joy of living. It was one of her features, which distinguished her from all those around her.

She used to say that both of us were strong, courageous and determined in life and in our faith in Sai Baba, but, unlike me, she always managed to do the right thing, while some sort of profound joy always transpired from her gestures, words or actions.

She was loved and appreciated for this gift. It remains fixed in my heart's memory as a great lesson.

Less than a year from the first encounter with Sai Baba, I found myself in India again, just as He had announced months earlier.

And that was an adventure in every sense of the term, spiritually and physically.

I could never have imagined what awaited me or that I would have succeeded in overcoming the difficulties and trials I was about to face.

I soon realised that every trip to India, to Sai Baba, represented a unique and unrepeatable experience, never allowing me to use known references to simplify things. Each test was different.

That particular adventure-trip developed according to the Divine Game, wished by Him, for me to be purified quickly – to burn my *karmic* debts, as they say in India. I realized that eventually, back home, once the adventure was concluded.

On my second journey I went to Whitefield, to His *ashram* a few kilometres off the city of Bangalore.

I departed with a group of fifteen people for my first collective experience.

During a *darshan*, Sai Baba spoke to me for the first time, asking me where I came from. I was so excited that I replied neither in Italian, my native tongue, nor in English, the language I only managed to speak, but in French, the language I had studied at school but never used. I have never comprehended the reason for that curious reaction. He gave me the possibility to make some photos of Him while He was walking through the crowd, which I have kept with care, also because coming to a *darshan* with a camera was soon banned and so that experience remained unrepeatable.

I found accommodation inside the *ashram*, staying in a room my travel mate and I shared with an Iranian girl.

She was meditating and praying all the time. Still, I could feel that she was very sad. Worried about her health, I asked her if she would like to tell me her story. Allegedly, in the course of an interview, Sai Baba had invited her to stay at the *ashram* for a few months. She unfortunately ran out of money, didn't know how to keep her promise and stay and was therefore thinking of packing her suitcase and going back to Iran. I tried to convince her to accept some money but she refused at first.

Upon my insistence, she agreed to write a letter to Sai Baba and ask for advice, as one way for the devotees to express questions, prayers, thankfulness and the like to Him was by writing letters.

The morning after the *darshan*, Sai Baba took that letter and so she accepted to receive the money which enabled her to stay until the fixed date. We agreed not to exchange our

·names – she did not know who I was and I did not know who she was. I was just a channel of Sai Baba's generosity towards her.

A week later, with great surprise, I learned that Sai Baba was moving, for a while, to a place in the mountains in southern India. I decided to move with the rest of the group to that place at two thousand meters of altitude. I had no idea I was going to face one of the worst moments of my life.

During the exhausting travel – sixteen hours without a break in a shaky bus, of the kind we have not seen in Europe for decades – I was feeling strange.

I was looking through the window at the sky all the time, praying and crying, deeply moved, feeling a very strong presence of my parents, both deceased years earlier, asking me to forgive them. It was cathartic.

With extreme lucidity, I realised something which had never been so clear to me: to be able to forgive the others, to be really able to do it, we must be able to forgive ourselves, first of all. That was my father and my mother's message. But why there, so far from home, in the midst of the Tamil Nadu (the Indian state I was passing through) mountains, and why then and not before? In the many years after their death I never felt them so alive, within me. I was agitated but at times also bewildered for what I was going through.

Meanwhile, a person who had already given signs of anxiety at the departure started being more and more bizarre in his behaviour, until he eventually reached the state of total confusion, at the end of the journey.

I was deeply worried when I established that his condition was getting worse with every passing day.

I had a *darshan* twice a day, begging Sai Baba with all my heart to do something about that person in whom I could see terrible deterioration. He lost his luggage, money, and documents – luckily they were found soon after – and stopped taking care of himself.

The situation kept worsening noticeably and I realized there was no other way out but to put him in a mental hospital.

My *karmic* debt to mental health was not paid off yet. Those days were a nightmare because the closest mental hospital was 600 kilometres away. To accompany him, I had to return to Bangalore, where our journey had started from. But what was most terrible about it was the fact that I was suddenly compelled to leave Sai Baba, once more.

Departure was again experienced as a cruel, unavoidable game of destiny. I couldn't deny my help to this man who was refusing any type of cure, oblivious to his illness.

Reaching the hospital was quite an odyssey. It is too painful to remember, but I know that I learned many a "life lesson", all in a package, through the suffering, desperation and humiliation due to my powerlessness. It was an intensive course and Sai Baba partly cured my ignorance and flaws, without even answering my articulated prayers.

I realised I couldn't ask God to do something I had to do myself. I asked Him to provide me with the strength to do it and He gave me a lot of strength. Secondly, I realized one should never rely on others. We should rely exclusively on the One Friend we have, God, implied as the true Self, within, because He is the only unselfish One, who never abandons us, being our integral part.

I actually repeated the lesson from the previous journey, but this time for a different reason: I was repeatedly forced by the circumstances to leave the Divine Master in advance and spend ten days in a wonderful city I cared nothing about, visiting that guy who was finally put in a mental hospital, twice a day. From riches to rags, and worse. That was my "*darshan*", twice a day, over the remaining ten days in India. It cost me a lot to grasp that. It is difficult to see God in a mentally disturbed person, especially if aggressive, violent and desecrating. The test was tough but very useful for that matter. God really is inside every one of us.

Acceptance, not attachment, together with humility and forgiveness, were the lessons I had to learn fast. As I said, an intensive course.

The unforeseen expenses I had to cover for myself and for that person, the hospital etc., were well over the liquidity in my possession. Besides, I was so physically exhausted that I could not afford to dissipate my energy further and so I relied on Him, on Sai Baba. He would somehow let me know what to do. He always helped and I had been a direct witness of how He had helped through me, as in the case of that Iranian girl. He was certainly going to help me, too.

A couple of days prior to my departure, despite the little change left and all the unsettled bills for the taxi, the hotel and the hospital, I felt I had to visit an orphanage in a sanctuary in Mysore, a town near Bangalore, dedicated to Sai Baba, and pay homage to Him, since I could not see Him in person due to my imminent trip back home.

Coming out of that place, I found a roll of Swiss francs, brand new, unused, the kind they usually issued in banks. Without hesitation, I found the guard and offered the money to him. Curiously enough, he refused the money. Instead, he took the few rupees (Indian currency) I had with me.

An idea flashed through my mind: it was Sai Baba who somehow made me find it.

Back in Bangalore, I went to a bank. I was so confused that I forgot the value of the currency, although I knew it in effect. The supreme surprise arrived when I was told that the amount of the money I had just found, expressed in Italian liras, was equivalent to the amount I had given, upon arrival, to the Iranian girl.

I started crying tears of excitement and delight. It is true, Sai Baba, the expression of the Divine, had followed me through all my ups and downs, even in the darkest moments when I was afraid that He was not listening to me. After I passed the trial, He awarded me – not with the money I had found but with the new certainty in my heart that I would never be alone again in my life. Only God can be so great and merciful to grant us the perception that the Universe is not only within but on the outside too.

I paid all my bills with that money and I was left with 300 Swiss francs. I kept them with me for many years, as a relic, as they no longer had the value of money but of the gift of God. I would show it to people to whom I happened to retell the adventure of that trip so arduous, yet brimming with Divine Grace. Amazingly, I needed it many years later, for the very same purpose it had served me the first time. Incredible, but true.

The gift made to me by Sai Baba on that occasion, literally without looking at me, was immense: He gave me the certainty of His presence within me, in my heart.

Back home, it took me two months to recover. I used that period of forced inactivity to ponder on what I had been through. I was almost certain I had let myself be involved more than I should have and that was an important lesson to bear in mind.

I learned that we should not take other people's destiny upon our shoulders, adding more weight on our own. It is not always a good thing to assist those who must make it on their own, in that particular moment and situation. We must be able to carefully discern when it is good to do something for others from when it is better to refrain ourselves, because, paradoxically, we might be more helpful in the latter case. Most importantly, we should not or, rather, must not take anyone's place, ever.

Illness arrives when we are unable to take the decisions necessary for our development. It is nature's reaction against hesitation, when we can't choose between the sublime and the ephemeral, between spirit and matter. Unless we find the willpower to choose, we either fall ill or succumb.

We all have a role to play in the game of life and it is enough for us to do our best, at least to understand what our limits are.

I've learned, at the expense of my life, that we are always fundamentally alone, even when we think to be in a company. The kind of solitude we choose determines the quality of life, as we become either slaves or masters of our destiny, experiencing solitude either on our own or with God.

As far as I was concerned, I had to go through that bitter experience of being abandoned by the group I was in. That was the only way for me to realize the Power and Grace of God, as the only Friend, Comforter and Saviour.

I understood that we felt alone whenever we failed to acknowledge our real value, our real essence, the divine essence within (the Self).

Those two travels to Sai Baba were the beginning of a long series of "missions" which brought me, through continuing perseverance, courage and willpower, from unconsciousness to consciousness, from consciousness to awareness, from awareness to the divine within.

In those months I was dreaming of seeing the Divine Master again, of being recognised by Him as His devotee of all times, just like I'd recognised Him as Master and God, in my heart, even before meeting Him in India.

During my first visits, I didn't talk with Him. There was just an exchange of words regarding the place of my origin and my limited mind thought about the earthly place. But Sai Baba intended to stir up the memory of my true, divine roots, common to all human beings.

Sai Baba says that He calls to Himself those who have recognised Him already, in their previous lives, alluding to the times when other Avatars were present on earth, like Jesus, Krishna and the others.

The certainty that He was the divine incarnation on earth stemmed from my strong perception of His presence in my own heart which I retained to be the same as anybody else's, and consequently I recognized that His power could reside and be perceived in the heart of every human being.

My trust in Him was absolute but I had a human desire to receive a confirmation of His Love. When a child seeks his mother's embrace, it knows well that she loves it, but it nevertheless wishes to feel the "warmth" of her love.

Just as a loving mother and father respond to the child's desire for Love, so He responded and in a couple of months I was getting ready for a new trip: I strongly felt He was expecting me.

The third travel to India was memorable in the history of personal encounters with the Divine Master.

A few weeks before the departure I dreamt of receiving a phone call from abroad telling me that Sai Baba was sending me an absolutely cryptic message: "I am not Epiphany".

The dream became true when I departed on 6th January of the same year (Epiphany day).

Epiphany means "apparition". That was the meaning of the message and Sai Baba was informing me that He was not an apparition but sheer reality.

He demonstrated it when I arrived in India, in His presence, responding to my wish for a physical experience with the Divine. The wish confirmed that the original wound, the source of all human suffering, even if we are unaware of it, comes from our separation from Him as the Spirit of Truth and Love, in a remote time, and the fact that we have become excessively attached to the surrounding world.

I travelled with a friend of mine who had lent me the first book on Sai Baba. I knew He was waiting for her as well. In fact, I felt as if I were accompanying her through that experience. She had never been to India before.

After He spent fifteen days at Puttaparthi, Sai Baba left for Madras. The time flew away and we found ourselves like "orphans", without His reassuring presence. We went to Bangalore while waiting for Him to go to the *ashram* of Brindavan, at Whitefield. Several days passed devoid of interest and all attention was focused on the news about His return.

On a Saturday morning, the long awaited moment arrived. Sai Baba was going to give a *darshan*, He was back with us.

I felt a strong emotional tension which brought me an unequivocal foreboding of a special event.

At the *darshan*, I was in the front line, waiting with trepidation for Him to arrive. I was hoping He would come to me and give His blessing, with all my heart. Everything occurs by His Will and so I was in that special place owing to Him.

I caught a glimpse of Him for afar, gliding slowly, lightly and elegantly, carved in the Absolute, in eternity, out of time and space. He returned my glance. There was a single cry in my heart, oblivious of any other request, except for *"Come to me, I've been waiting for You all the time."*

Moments out of time passed and the distance He was approaching me from was endless, but He arrived at last. He responded to my call, just as I had responded to His.

He stopped right in front of me. Confused, excited, my heart beating hard, overwhelmed by His Love, I stooped to His feet, gently touching them with my hands and, out of respect, I only kissed the marble on which they were laid. Then I brought my joined hands to my face, crying with joy. I thanked Him for the immense gift He had granted me.

I subsequently learned that touching the feet of an *Avatar* was the greatest homage He could ever grant to us. He gave me even more. Several months after I had returned to Italy, a friend of mine presented me with a film in which she had recognised me in the act of touching the feet of the Master. The 'film director' was a friend of hers, but didn't know me and so the magical moment was shot by the Will of the real director, the greatest one, Sai Baba.

On that fantastic day, when He manifested in the heart, I felt as if I had been born for the second time.

But there were more gifts lined up for me. Another important and unforgettable event was going to take place.

In the afternoon of the same day, I had an appointment with an expert in palm[26] leaf reading to whom I'd given my birth data.

I was in a state of Grace. I felt weightless – so great was my inner lightness.

I had to concentrate hard to listen to him. I immediately noticed he was going to tell me very interesting things and so I tried to be present and register what he said about my previous lives, my present life up till then and about my future.

After the experience made eight years earlier and since all the predictions made by the astrologer were coming true, I learned to carefully discern all important messages, even those arriving under odd conditions or from strange personalities, but still messages of truth, from other, perhaps purely informative messages. It was as if I had had an antenna in my heart which received the truth of things or people and their importance.

I discovered that I'd lived most probably in India, which I took for granted, due to the familiarity the country and its people inspired from the moment I had laid my foot on its soil. I had spent other lives in China, Israel, South Africa and the last one in Japan.

I was deeply moved by hearing him say very naturally that I would end my earthly life right there, in India. It meant that I had been "accepted" by Sai Baba, to be by His side for the remaining years of my life, just as I had asked with my heart that very morning. I had found the ultimate landing place.

It would have been so agreeable to leave my body on that day, having found *the* source and being immersed in it, also because I was concerned that continuing to live could compromise the aim I felt I had finally reached. Life was not supposed to end there and then, however. There were still many debts to be paid, in the hope that I would not keep creating them any further, notwithstanding the normal life I was leading. Nevertheless, nothing was normal in that particular moment of my life. Everything was special and I felt all-powerful and invulnerable – I felt like His protégée.

I was conscious of the fact that all the important appointments in life had been pre-arranged and my study of Astrology had but anticipated it. The picture was clearer now: the reason for having chosen to be a psychiatrist, but not to work as one was that I had done the same in my previous lives, helping others with herbs or other techniques or with words.

I avoided getting married three times because fundamentally I was not supposed to get married.

Sai Baba was the Master who had been waiting for me all along. I could not recognize any other master in my life and each time I met someone important from the cultural sphere, I would think: "Sure, this is an extraordinary person but it is not Him."

I was going to do what I always have: assist others to be at peace with themselves.

Unfortunately, as we know, enthusiasm has a short[27] lifespan and it can mutate into disappointment at any moment. When I left, I was content and thrilled about the place, but on my way back to Whitefield I was immediately faced with another harsh surprise: Sai Baba had just left for Puttaparthi – His "workplace", as He defines it. Whitefield is His residence.

A few moments of bewilderment followed, but I was not discouraged. As I said, I felt invulnerable and omnipotent and, although I had to fly back to Italy in three days, I still decided to take a taxi to Puttaparthi.

It was dark already when I departed. Sunsets are brief in India and daylight turns into the darkness of the night from one moment to the other. I was on my own as my friend did not come along, having decided to join me the day after, with some other travelling companions.

I spent all my travelling time in silence and my eyes were captured by an immense, starry sky, basking in a dimension I could only define as "bliss".

I felt I was in the right place, in the right time, doing the right thing. There was plenty of inner fulfilment and I could barely contain it.

I was reconsidering my prayer to Sai Baba expressed in my heart that morning. Apart from what I wrote earlier, this is what I also asked from Him: "Come to me. I have been waiting for You all this time. If You allow me to touch your feet, it will be a confirmation that I may leave my body in the same place where You will leave Yours!"

I could envisage the cremation and the ashes scattered in the river flowing through Puttaparthi, the Chitravati – in which Sai Baba had announced He would leave His physical body in 2021, at the age of 95 – shrouded in deep, infinite peace.

Immersed in the starry sky and in my thoughts on Sai Baba and my future with Him, I found myself blocked on the verge of the road to Puttaparthi. We met the taxi driver I had previously requested to be driven by – considering him to be my guardian angel on the uneven journey I had made a year earlier in the mountains of Tamil Nadu, returning to Bangalore – and Sai Baba was ready to meet my smallest wishes. I ended my travel driven by him and arrived "home" at midnight. It looked like Christmas, at least for me, considering the hour of the dark Indian night, illuminated only by stars and a few lights in the village, which made it appear like a living Christmas crib. Jesus was born in my heart, turning on a light which anticipated the arrival of Christ Consciousness – the awareness of being Divine.

That light has never been turned off since then. It has illuminated each error, each trial, each fall, so I could avoid or overcome them afterwards, without infringing on the desire to proceed on my illuminated path. I have stuck to it, without ever abandoning it, transforming every challenge into victory.

Exhausted but happy and at peace with myself and the world, I fell asleep thinking about the remaining two days I was going to spend near Him.

During the second-last *darshan*, I told Sai Baba in a trembling voice, while He was passing by, that I was soon to leave and asked if I could have an interview with Him. He kind of stopped and asked how many we were and where we came from and allegedly added a "yes". In my mind I knew He said: "I will see", which implied He might summon us in a few years, as we learned. We were a group of seven.

I burst into tears as He was leaving, questioning myself absurdly: "What have I done wrong? Where have I failed?", and the like.

Much later, I learned that when the moment arrives to encounter Him personally, if it is beneficial for us, He calls us wherever we may be, even thousands of kilometres away. This happened to me personally and to some other people I met: He called them in a dream and received them as soon as they arrived in India and simply continued the conversation initiated in the dream.

While I was looking at the sky in bewilderment, the silence was broken only by the sound of palm trees, caressed by the wind. I was in India for three weeks and in that moment it felt both like eternity and a split second.

I had that profoundly intense encounter with Him only three days earlier. How could I leave the next day without talking to Him once more, at least briefly.

In my heart I felt an impulsive crescendo of emotions which fed an inner river in flood. I could not embank it with mere leaves of grass – so tender were my rational motivations with regard to what was transpiring.

That river in flood was my love for Him and its urge to manifest itself was at the same time indescribable and uncontainable.

Endless minutes passed by. Sai Baba finished His *darshan* and headed for the porch of the *Mandir* where He used to invite people to whom He conceded an interview in a small room, where they retreated.

I was suffocating with pain caused by His disappearance when, to my immense surprise, I noticed, notwithstanding the distance, that He turned towards the female[28] section, pointed His finger in my direction – and I felt its effect on me – and made a sign to me to stand up. He was calling us.

I didn't notice the distance I had to walk to the porch. I just know I found myself next to Him, my heart beating with joy, still incredulous about what was befalling on me and my companions.

He made a sign to me, like an old friend, and we comprehended each other.

I had understood earlier, with my heart, that His was an assertion but then I let myself be deceived and mislead by my mind and by appearances.

Inside that room I experienced a new dimension . In there, rationality has the value of a torch without batteries – zero! Anything can happen and afterwards one doesn't remember a thing. One understands unknown languages and does not understand one's own; one can hear without being able to see what others can feel and see; what is quite common to everybody is a peculiar state of confusion mixed with euphoria, at times prolonged well after one has left the room. One can testify of most extraordinary materializations or miraculous episodes, like disabled people standing up and walking and so on. All this is experienced as something normal.

One discovers in there that Sai Baba knows even the innermost thoughts of each one of us, He knows all about our lives, and more. He knows what's behind us and what awaits us, what our exigencies and those of the people around us are, what our most hidden desires are, our longings, aspirations, everything.

When my turn arrived to talk to Him, I offered my life to His feet and asked Him to make me work with Him. At the time I still believed my life belonged to me and it was still unclear to me that we all belonged to God because He is All and Oneness is All.

Three days earlier in Whitefield, approaching me, Sai Baba showed that He knew me. A little while before, in the *Mandir*, He confirmed it by calling me with a gesture of His hand. It was me He was calling, the same me who had lost all my omnipotence, in that precise moment. I felt like a dismayed girl, as if I'd lost the person I'd been holding by the hand, or like someone who had just awoken from a dream that lasted two thousand years.

In this regard I realize that, even though I continue to age chronologically, I feel younger in my heart with every passing year. When Sai Baba speaks to me in my dreams and in person, He calls me "girl". I am a "grey haired" girl because the true Self is ageless and sexless and this is why He considers us all as "Embodiments of Divine Love".

While entering the interview room, I kissed the floor on which Sai Baba had just walked as a sign of respectful thankfulness, feeling an intense scent of jasmine emanating from His Holy Feet[29]; I was literally intoxicated by that scent.

Sai Baba talked to me at length, saying I had always worried too much about my son. But life was a simple game and we'd better play it more lightly; He would take care of my son who had been His even before he became mine. On the other hand, life was the challenge I had to face and He would always be within me; He said I would come and work close to Him and there was no need to ask for permission because that was my home; I first had to finalize a task in Italy and then He would give me the special visa to come and stay with Him. He concluded saying *"I love you, I love you, I bless you, I bless you, God is with you, I am Shiva!"* I was dismayed, speechless, amazed. A little earlier He materialized some white ashes *(vibuthi)* and poured some into our hands and on our heads; He then fetched some orange robes, identical to those He usually wore and presented them to us, together with many sachets of *vibuthi,* and filled our hands with them. There are no words in any dictionary to describe how I felt. His words were much more important than the materializations He made in the course of the interview, such as gold watches, gold necklaces, etc., as tangible manifestations of His immense love for His devotees and for the entire humanity.

My friend also came to understand, finally, that Sai Baba had been waiting for her. He spoke to her for quite a while and anticipated, among other things, certain personal events which took place in the following years, precisely as He predicted.

At the end of the interview, on the way out, I dared to touch His shoulders lightly and, something I never again had the impudence of doing, His hair. I was shocked by the soft inconsistence, it was like caressing a cloud.

As I let Him leave, I kissed His hands and uttered in my heart: "I love You too, my God, my Love, my All, my imagination and my reality."

He was the only reality, the supreme reality, or *Shiva*[30] (the destroyer of the ego).

He confirmed what He had announced in the dream: He was not an apparition, He was the Supreme Reality.

This experience strengthened the perception of the surrounding emptiness, which continued to grow in the following years.

An inner voice I heard more and more often – from this point referred to as 'inner voice'– reassured me with the words: *"Understand and accept your limitations and your imperfections. You will become perfect one day, without limitations, you'll pass from nothing to everything, but there can be no knowledge of the Self without the knowledge of one's limitations. The gates open up to those who overcome ignorance. Knowing one's limitations should be a means to overcome them – not to remain imprisoned in them. Don't be afraid, the search does not necessarily imply loneliness. You will find a multitude of friends along the way to share your tender love with!"* It was like saying that only a pure heart can see God.

Not being able to consider loneliness all the time as a divine blessing was a considerable limitation. I was alone as a girl, as an adolescent and eventually as an adult and, from time immemorial, I had a strange presentiment that I would not live through my old age.

I asked God to give me the strength to accept the destiny with serenity and without bitterness. I knew that we came into this world primarily to purify ourselves, not to enjoy it and that it is not physical death we should be afraid of. On the contrary, we should prepare ourselves for the next life because, as the *Bhagavad Ghita*[31] says, "Death is certain for anyone born, and birth is certain for the dead."

When I returned from that trip, the resolution to surrender completely to Him became definite.

I kept repeating: "May my body exist only to serve You and to honour You, as long as I am capable of serving and honouring You. I commit myself to You, I trust You, I accept everything that comes from You."

I was offered the major opportunity to know the purpose of my life and to evolve through whatever I experienced along the path to God. The journey consisted of three stages: listening to God, turning my mind to God and putting into practice what I had learned. I would like to add another item to this list: passing my knowledge on to others. There was nothing else for me to do except to live, day and night, and orient my life in that direction, in coherence and truth, according to Sai Baba's message which is essentially identical to the message of Jesus.

NOTES: CHAPTER III

17. *Atma*: divine spark in Sanskrit.

18. *Avatar:* Divine Incarnation according to Hinduism.

19. *Ashram:* Place consecrated (monastery or retreat) to spirituality, where a Master lives with his disciples and devotees.

20. Intended as Christ Consciousness.

21. According to a research by the London School of Economics, the happiest country in the world is Bangladesh. India occupies the 4th and the U.S.A the 46th place.

22. *Darshan:* Vision of the Divine in Sanskrit.

23. He personally confirmed it to me years later.

24. Those who still speak of monotheism, polytheism and pantheism have not come in touch with the divine essence yet, which resides within each one of us and reminds us, with every breath, that: All is Oneness.

25. From the point of view of Esotericism, there are two types of fire. One purifies and the other destroys.

26. *Shuka Nadi:* reference to a planetary "birth register", called "*Akashic* Archives" by the initiated and generally in India. This library of life contains the universal memory (and the collective unconscious mind) and it can be consulted for the past and for the future. The 4th dimension (to which the said archives belong) is the eternal now. This dimension is partly parallel to and it partly overlaps the 3rd dimension (the earthly one) in which we are immersed.

27. As Sai Baba says, "Pleasure is a moment between two sufferings."

28. Women and men are rigorously separated both in the temple and in all public places in the *ashram*, such as shops, the canteen etc.

29. In India, the holiness of the Master's Feet comes from them being part of God's body, which is in direct contact with our planet Earth.

30. *Shiva*: the third person in the Trinity of Hinduism: Brahma, Vishnu and Shiva.

31. Hindu Holy Scripture.

IV

Our life is determined by our thoughts.

Marcus Aurelius.

Just like my childhood and youth, my adult life was characterized by the concern of committing the sin of pride whenever I realized that I was not understood, that it was impossible to establish a dialogue with the other person or that I was risking to be considered different – which was usually the case – to say the least. I thus preferred to confront myself directly with God, through all the channels He allowed me to recognize as preferential. Obviously, feeling different and being considered as such added an additional burden on my existential loneliness.

Over the years, my awareness was raised and I discovered that loneliness was actually a divine gift, as it nurtured and strengthened my ongoing search for God, or better the search for the Divine within, the real Self.

In that period, I learned something very important for the continuation of my search and self-inquiry which concerned the capacity to experience the present. It might sound trivial unless we realize that nobody can really succeed in doing that and that most of our fears and difficulties derive right from this inability.

Our bodies – physical and mental – are synchronized with the present moment, whereas the emotional or astral body eludes this synchronicity and this is what we must work on very hard if we wish to evolve and get to know unconditional, true Love.

This means that, when we fail to experience the present reality, moment by moment, be it for the fear of the future, be it for the longing for the past, be it for desiring what we don't have or don't experience, we do not make the most of the energies granted to us by nature – which is divine. And so we get depressed, dissatisfied, anxious and suffer from a vast range of physical illnesses.

Accepting to experience the "here and now", with our full participation, becomes a spiritual message, or rather a survival message because, by not experiencing the present and not being able to draw our energies from the Cosmic tank, we are forced to suck energies from other people, to their and to our own detriment.

As for me, the borderline experience I had – fantastic and magical – transformed my uninteresting life into a wonderful dream. I had had an interview with the Divine Master, placed before Him, so nothing else really mattered. Therefore, the return to the triviality of the daily routine scared me to the point that I wished to avoid it.

I was not fully aware yet of all the contradictions in my lifestyle. The road stretching in front of me was so long – and to think that for a few brief moments I thought I had reached the final destination[32]!

Having made an assessment of my daily routine, I reassured myself that what really counted in life was being myself, not what I or the others though I was. I knew that other people's opinion didn't matter and that it only conditioned my choices.

I discovered that emotions associated with physicality generated euphoria and exuberance. The joy of living we see in children testifies to this. On the other hand, diseases and fatigue result from the conflict between mind and physicality. Substantially, the mind harasses the physical-emotional body with excesses and humiliations, that is, by inducing models of behaviour which are contrary to our wellbeing. It is the mind which creates the heaviness, with its load of pessimism, prejudices, with the negative thoughts that distance us more and more from the only source of energy, which is the "now", as we experience it – whether in its fullness or in its vacuity, it doesn't matter, as long as it is experienced.

To relive the past with nostalgia or to inquisitively fantasize about the future is just a waste of energy and vital force.

For me, there was another major limit to overcome – the aptitude I had nourished all my life to project myself into the future, perhaps because in the past I had always been discontented with life. Those projections showed traces of pessimism and the lack of self-esteem for not having understood myself fully or what I wanted from life.

Things were changed now, although a certain degree of doubt concerning my ability to succeed remained, until one night I dreamt of being alone, on my knees, before Sai Baba, very penitent and repeating that I felt undeserving of His Love.

He came close to me and told me, very softly, as if He were caressing me, that I should never accuse or condemn myself again since in my heart there was a huge treasure I had to cherish: devotion.

I was pardoned. After that night I never had a single occasion for self-pity. Sai Baba awakened my heart to devotion, to the love for the Divine and to Him who, like Jesus, heals the body and the mind by purifying the soul and the heart.

I finally realized the danger and futility of such aptitudes which can only obstruct the cosmic, divine energy flowing within, establishing health, wellbeing and peace.

Miraculous healings are spiritual healings. I can testify to that, as I wrote earlier, and that is what brought me back to God.

Unconditional, Divine Love is the most superior and powerful energy in life. Not being able to experience and accept the present, not being able to love, or feeling unloved, can be the primary causes of all diseases, as a consequence of the blocked energy flow in one or more bodies – the physical, emotional and the mental bodies constituting the human being.

Sai Baba says: *"When your faith meets My Love, the cure arrives".*

Jesus used to say: *"You were healed by your faith".*

This is what happened to me, first in the reality of wake and then in the reality of dreams, during my encounters with the Divine Master.

Something changed within, permanently. The Spirit took the guidance of my being and the Self supplied everything necessary for my growth, to meet the needs I was not fully aware of.

From the point of view of spirituality, I could really reiterate the words from the Gospel: *"I do not lack anything".* When we rely on God, we are not short of anything any more. Even loneliness becomes sweet because we are always in His company.

However, we must not mix up the spiritual needs and those related to ordinary, material life – it is the first group I'm referring to.

Clearly, spiritual growth could not exclude suffering, which should be seen as spiritual food, or better, a spiritual medicine, necessary to transcend the individual self (or ego), or as an indispensable premise to reach the Self. It comes with the lessening of the individual self – each time the ego is frustrated by its expectations, we suffer – which is an impediment to be what we really are: divine creatures.

Indeed, being self-centred keeps the person away from appreciating and being thankful to God for all the things that happen because everything manifests by the Divine Will, everything is divine and man is immersed in the divine just like fish in the water. Our very breath is God. But egotism is an impediment to perceiving this reality.

In this sense, suffering should be first accepted and then comprehended, for us to be able to transcend it as an expression of ignorance.

Going back to the question of the need to live in the present to tap the energy granted by Cosmic Intelligence, we can readily comprehend, for example, that we can love or be loved only in the present time – not tomorrow, or yesterday.

The dimensions of past and future are illusory to begin with, but we nevertheless continue to devastate our energetic body with their ghosts, so much so that we do not live well in the present, although it is the only time dimension we can really experience and use for our growth.

What is life if it is not lived to rid ourselves of pain, fear and ignorance?

I am going to address the question of the meaning of suffering right away, to clear the field of the recurrent misunderstandings related to the attitude that "if He loves us", he should make sure that we don't suffer and rescue us from diseases and misfortunes. This is impossible because it does not reflect reality.

Suffering does not exist outside man. It is the product of self-centredness and thus it will continue to exist, as long as there are traces of ego within us.

My prayers had been answered in the past, when I'd asked Sai Baba, in my heart, for a possibility to go to India with my son and, once there, for a sign, so I could know if I should end my professional life. Furthermore, in my more recent journey, He answered my prayers when He showed that He knew me and when He allowed me to touch His feet.

He presented me with His robe – symbolically the most important material gift – as a sign that I could take the assignment offered to me shortly before my departure and become the President of the Sai Centre in the city where I lived.

Never in my life had I accepted leading positions before, because I was not cut for such roles. However, I could not decline the offer, since this was His wish.

I found myself running a Centre within the Sathya Sai Organization which included thousands of centres for the dissemination of His message, devotional activities and service.

I was still harbouring a few perplexities in my heart due to my innate reluctance towards head positions.

Strange phenomena, coincidences, messages, encounters, dreams and predictions by the inner voice I call now "the voice of the Spirit within" started manifesting in that period. They were all incredible, one way or another, but, after the initial moment of dismay I started accepting them with serene humility, as a part of the Divine Game which is life.

I was certain I would sooner or later understand the sense of life in its entirety. I'd always felt confident about coming to understand it, eventually, and that nothing and no one could stand in my way.

I knew that my intense desire and the tension due to my aspirations for the still unreached goal – the knowledge of the real inner Self – would touch the heart of God so much that I would be conceded the Grace of seeing with the heart's eye and becoming aware of the events which I had been, was and would be the witness of, not only for my own sake but to share the constant and timely testimony of His presence within us and with us in the course of our lives.

I wished not only for me but for all humanity to stop feeling separated from the Absolute, from God, and see the ocean inside a drop, as a metaphor of a human being, because we are all made of the same essence – the Spirit.

If we purified our hearts and minds to view life through the heart's eye, in this age everybody could discover to possess prophetic skills, see the Truth with clarity and try to convey it to those who do not see it.

The suffering I had experienced up till then had to have a purpose. I found it useful because I managed to overcome it. But, apart from that, it was supposed to be a user-friendly roadmap, for other fellow men to find a way out.

I discovered a glimmer of light in the suffering. Hopefully, I would be able to contribute with the light of intuition and insight in the suffering of those who hadn't been able to see that glimmer yet, having ignored the presence of the Spirit within and deeming it distant, although the divine essence was actually the liveliest part in us.

Those who believe in reincarnation know that the Spirit in terms of the Self – the only part which lives eternally and outlives all incarnations – unites with the mental body (our thoughts) and the emotional or astral body (our emotions) from life to life, in an aggregate which subsequently takes its form in a physical body, functioning like a clothing.

The Spirit is only free to choose whether to connect itself to one or another of the past lives and pay the pending "bills" or "debts", according to the immutable laws regulating the realm of matter. It is good to know that we get back to earth with a very precise mission: to purify or improve ourselves.

By entering the material world – the 3rd dimension – we lose power and freedom, since we have to obey much stricter rules than those regulating other dimensions permeating the world we live in.

Therefore, we don't reincarnate for sheer pleasure, which is quite obvious even to those who turn a deaf ear or a blind eye to Truth.

Our spiritual guides accompanying us along this journey called life can advise us on the most appropriate choices to make, but they cannot compel us to make any specific choice.

It means that we create our destiny, with our free will.

After a "contract" is forged for a given life, the Spirit – the true Self – reviews all the previously lived lives, including the one it is going to live in the physicalness, but it cannot establish the total duration or the final destination. It can however choose the places and the length of the various phases it will have to go through in the upcoming lifetime.

Thereupon, the aggregate forgets the "plan" and starts its journey as a soul "in exile", or in punishment, primarily due to this "forgetfulness".

I felt like a tormented soul for so many years and so many people like me have gone through the same harsh and disquieting experience without making sense of it. Why? Because we overlook the task we are here for, on the beloved albeit harassed "Earth".

So, this is the root of the cruel dilemma around which life folds and unfolds, the dilemma destined to remain unresolved until we acknowledge the Divine within and without, as the key to the understanding of life in its totality, and expand the consciousness of our existence in the world, from individual to collective and eventually to Christ or Cosmic Consciousness.

Who am I? Where do I come from? What am I doing here? Haven't we all raised the same questions at least once in a lifetime?

Just as everyone has to face death, sooner or later, we all face the great questions. They are the undeniable proof of our universal, unacknowledged brotherhood.

The lives we have come to live can be distinguished by most diversified qualities, ranging from a life of complete rest – if we had worked hard in our previous lives – to terrible, hard lives, chosen actually to quickly settle the many debts created by the "mistakes" made in the earlier lives, or lives full of love and devotion, spent to bring relief to mankind, to mention only a few. What can possibly mean a medium duration of a human life, compared to eternity? The final scope for everyone is to stop being subject to the laws of matter, to return to the Light, or God, or the dimension of the Spirit (the 5th Dimension)[33].

I learned from Esotericism that enduring suffering with courage strengthens the emotional or astral body and facilitates a reincarnation in a healthy physical body, with high moral values. Living life with Love predestines a long and healthy life.

In a nutshell, we carry along our distant past written inside and on us. Holistic Medicine utilizes this concept appropriately.

Our past contains our suffering as well, registered as an expression of ignorance and forgetfulness of the task we were born to do. We mask this condition with our desires for what we don't have and our bitterness for not being able to obtain it – I am referring here to our attachment to the world of objects.

This is why the past is the best prophet of the future.

Aspirations from one lifetime become skills in the next, the will to realize oneself is transformed into the power to act and vice versa; missed opportunities are transformed into incapability or impossibility to act.

All this unfolds not on the principle of award and punishment – as many people would erroneously presume – but consequent to the natural law of evolution from which no one is exempt, taking a heavy toll on us, as inner emptiness tormenting the vast majority of people in modern societies aggravates to a degree which is directly proportionate to the level of "civilization", or better, degree of affluence.

In accordance with the law designed to resume balance, every disease is at the same time an effect of former excesses and a means of purification, to keep us away from passions and desires compelling us to repeat the same mistakes.

The repetition of errors is an aggravating circumstance that weighs upon our destiny enormously in terms of suffering. Among other things, it prevents us from benefiting from Divine Grace, exposing us to the risk of having to expiate our debt fully, which extends our "exile"[34] further.

My insight into reincarnation corresponded to my knowledge of Evolutionary and *Karmic* Astrology and allowed me to deepen the spiritual aspect of the "chronometer of destiny" - the personal astrological theme – in order to fathom the depth of the unconscious mind, understood as condensed experiences gained in previous lives and in other dimensions.

This kind of interpretation of life was more congenial to me than the scientific one – offered by psychiatry or psychoanalysis – when it comes to the "knots in the heart" that must be undone to allow the healing of the illnesses of the soul – such as neurosis, various complexes, etc. – which are not the illnesses of the mind. That had been the subject of my work and study for so many years, but it had given me very little satisfaction.

Relevant to this, a highly eloquent proverb says: "Your destiny is not decided by fate but by the wisdom and the kindliness you operate with."

Reincarnation does not disavow the stance that destiny is in our hands. It actually supports it. It is the mental indolence of the less evolved (laziness prevents the knowledge of God!) which causes a distorted, fatalistic interpretation. Facts teach us that life is a projection forward and not a return backwards. Stars do not dispose – they propose.

With this perception, I could savour more intensely and with a deeper awareness the message of Jesus and the deep and serious wisdom of His words:

"Do unto others as you would have them do unto you." "You reap what you sow." "Judge not lest it will come back to you in the same measure." "Live by the sword, die by the sword."

His message was familiar to me from earliest childhood, even before I went to school or studied Catechism.

Science and religion, or rather spirituality, come in tandem by the Divine Law of cause and effect – the law of nature encompassing both the ethics and the everyday reality of the physical world.

The Greek philosopher Plato said that learning was remembering our lives or unearthing knowledge which was ours already, to experience it more appropriately and grow spiritually, regardless of our beliefs. The Self or the spark which testifies of the Divine is in all of us, without exception.

I found the explanation of so many things in this simple law. It became a new, albeit ancient key to an understanding of facts, events, situations, feelings, conflicts, etc.

With this interpretation of life I could finally unravel numerous subjective and objective, seemingly impenetrable phenomena I had encountered, like the sensation of having already experienced certain situations, the "fatal attractions" to people I did not know, the attraction to certain unknown places perceived as familiar, the unaccountable repugnance for certain people, places or things, the so-called coincidences – which in effect do not exist – seemingly unexpected vocations, the ingeniousness in a child or adult, artistic talents, sanctity or perversion.

The direct contact with the Divine Master inaugurated the first stage and the most important part of my spiritual path in search of the real Self within, the path of devotion which Sai Baba defined – in my dream but also in reality – as the greatest fortune a man possessed in the heart, unknowingly.

Without devotion[35] one cannot attain the awareness of the Divine. In other words, without a loyal and trusting submission to God we are not capable of "seeing" the Oneness in All. Devotion, or the Love for the Divine, is self-sustainable, whereas love in terms of human attachment needs others.

Devotion – an intimate relationship between the devotee and God, or the Self, or *Atma,* or the divine spark – is an ageless and indestructible relationship of eternal unity, inspiring man with the true knowledge of reality, the Spiritual Knowledge, infusing him with wisdom, which is the second stage on the spiritual path. It is exclusively owing to the attained wisdom that man is able to reach the third stage, the stage of non-attachment and renouncing egoism and its illusions or delusions, in the form of desires. It guides him to the

71

liberation from slavery to matter, once he has transcended the individual self, which is the fourth stage on the spiritual path. The fifth and the last stage on this evolutional track is the realization of the Self (*Atma*) and the end of suffering.

I recall the most poignant parts of the code of conduct Sai Baba invites us to observe in everyday life:

"Take care of your parents with love, respect and gratitude."

"Tell the truth and act virtuously."

"Whenever you have time, repeat the name of the Lord."

"Never speak badly about or seek others' faults."

"Do not cause suffering to others in any way."

He synthesized the points in the above essential phrases that contain the wisdom of the entire holy Hindu literature of the *Vedas*.

"Love all, serve all. Help ever, hurt never."

"Hands that help are holier then lips that pray."

An "egoless" service, practiced not to gratify ourselves (the individual self or ego) but done with devotion, that is, with the "Love for the Divine", in terms of humaneness, with the awareness that we are at one with the All, seeing God in everyone and everything, is the preferential way to liberation.

I recognized the words of Jesus in the message of Sai Baba, when he said: *"Love your neighbour as you love yourself."* I understood that Jesus was alluding to the Divine Self – certainly not to the individual self.

We should love and serve the others the way we love and serve the Divine in ourselves because we all share the same essence and are part of a single, immense Spirit[36].

I learned that whatever came from the heart, unless contaminated by personal interests or desires, was "pure idea or thought" which, when put into practice, became selfless action (righteous action or *Dharma* in Sanskrit). *Dharma* makes everyone happy, without hurting anyone.

The purity of thought, word and action as a whole distinguishes coherent behaviour as an indispensable instrument to master the individual self or ego and access Knowledge through the discernment between what is real and what is illusory. Coherence – the unity of thoughts, words and actions – as an instrument of Truth or wisdom of the heart or intuitive knowledge enables us to distinguish between the true and the false.

The Divine Spirit manifests in man as Love and Truth, since Love and Truth are the divine essence in us.

The Divine Law considers the human heart and gives importance to the intentions behind the actions, unlike human law which judges from actions.

Sai Baba, like Jesus, does not view actions but what lies behind them. He points out that 'being' matters – not 'having', or 'appearing'.

For example, if we do charity out of our need for self-gratification, we'd better forget at once about our illusion of having been generous and hence deserving rewards from Heaven, because we have actually only done service to our individual self or ego – strengthening it further - and not to the cause of the Spirit. Jesus would call us *whitened sepulchres*, which means 'candid only in appearance'.

I recognized myself more and more in the teachings of Sai Baba. They helped me reveal the hidden meaning of the teachings of Jesus I had never understood so clearly.

When people listened to me, they understood I was speaking from my heart, although I kept saying "Sai Baba says", "Sai Baba said" each time I mentioned Him – I felt I owed it to Him – until I realized that I and He were at one, in the heart.

And so I stopped referring to His name each time I mentioned His teachings, but I never stopped repeating His Holy Name in my heart, day and night. Every moment was useful to remember Him[37]. It was a way to express my Love for Him.

If devotion, or the Love for the Divine, is the medicine against egotism and attachment to the body, the disease which strikes all human beings, then discipline is the necessary diet to overcome it or at least to keep it under control. It consists in observing the teachings of the Divine Master or putting His Message into practice.

In the first stage of His advent, Sai Baba said: *"My life is My Message!"* He was nearly seventy when He announced the beginning of a new stage: "Your life is My Message!" Sai Baba's message was simple to understand, if we listened with the heart. It was identical in form and substance to that of Jesus.

It seemed impossible that a disease – egotism – could cause all the evils in the world, from physical to social or natural, with their respective upheavals. In this regard Sai Baba says that the lack of water on earth is related to the lack of good sentiments in mankind and that until humanity does not change for the better, this sore is destined to deteriorate. Therefore, problems linked to cataclysms, wars, disharmony and chaos are rooted in egotism and spiritual ignorance. Why did we fail to notice it in the past and why have we denied it to this day? Perhaps because egotism possesses a self-preservation mechanism. On the other hand, a righteous action protects the one who performs it – it is the law of nature. By blinding our awareness, egotism prevents us from seeing and knowing the truth about ourselves, human life, nature and the entire Universe, but above all it prevents us from "Loving" in a divine way, that is, by giving and forgiving – everything and everyone, unconditionally.

Sai Baba came to earth with a precise mission: restoring Truth in the world and initiating the age of Truth or *Sathyayuga* (the age of Love, Harmony and Gold in terms of knowledge of the Spirit), as Baba's very name *Sathya* (Truth) says. This age will replace the current age of ignorance or *Kaliyuga* (of darkness, disharmony, lack of Love and Unity).

He is the fully empowered Avatar who descended to earth as the Messenger of Love, Peace, Righteousness, Truth and Non-violence – His five principles.

In Him shine the figures of all the Divine Masters who previously descended to earth – Rama, Krishna, Buddha, Jesus and all the others with their respective messages of Love, Righteousness, Compassion and Redemption.

Humanity must restore all those values to make the most of this opportunity of being born as human beings in this messianic age, which is doubly a fortune, not to be wasted. Being born as human beings is already a major gift of the Spirit to help us evolve towards more spiritual and subtle dimensions, but being born in an age, which sees the presence of the Messiah among us, offers an extra opportunity to be "pardoned" by Him.

In this respect Sai Baba says: *"You ask me many things but not what I came to offer to you, which is the liberation from the enslavement of repeated births."*

He reminds us that the Divine Grace is proportional to the effort to respect, with a due discipline, those human values He called everlasting and irreplaceable, because they are the manifestation of the divine essence within, as evidence of divinity in mankind.

Disavowing those values equals to disavowing God because those who do not love Truth do not love God, who is Truth. All this entails the payment of a very high price we all know the name of. It is called "suffering", implied as disease, death and destruction.

God implied as righteousness is the "preserver", but He can become the "destroyer" of egotism, discordance and disharmony – always out of kindness – when man refuses to acknowledge Him as the "preserver".

Sai Baba arrived as the creator (*Brahma*), the preserver or the comforter (*Vishnu*), the destroyer or the redeemer (*Shiva*) to bring the message of the extreme make-over of Mankind, due to take place with the support of the Holy Spirit – the divine energy of Love and Truth – within us and around us.

It is enough to fill your heart with unconditional Divine Love to ensure all the goodness in the world. Why do we not do it with every breath? How come it is not our primary objective?

My existence was swarming with questions when I said "yes" to Sai Baba and His message, a "yes" contemplating that anything might appear on the horizon.

I was torn by my perplexities and most disparate queries on the role I had accepted to carry on, when an absolutely extraordinary encounter took place in the premises which later became the Sai Centre. An American healer had arrived from the U.S.A., anticipating his business trip to Italy for a day so that he could be there on a Thursday evening. He was accompanied to the Centre.

Nobody understood the reason of his presence as he said nothing about the purpose of his visit. The devotees who accompanied him knew nothing about his "mission". After the devotional chants (*bhajans*), we all said goodbye to each other, in a friendly manner. While everybody was on the way out, at my greatest surprise, I found out that the man had come, or better, had been invited to meet not me but my soul!

Actually, although we were both normal people in our physical form, his soul was talking to mine thanks to his capacity to be a channel for a message coming from another dimension, the fourth dimension.

I met him briefly a year earlier during a seminar on self-healing and never saw him again.

He was meditating all the time and did not take part in the devotional chants. When the moment arrived to get up and leave, he came towards me, determined and impersonal at the same time – we really didn't know each other – as if driven by a force unknown to me and gave me a warm and welcoming hug which lasted during the entire communication. It seemed endless to me.

That day was the anniversary of my father's death and I was already particularly moved. I prayed for him all the time. The man's strong embrace stunned me, but I was even more stunned by his words pronounced so gently and sweetly that I felt a lump in my throat. For a few moments I caught a glimpse of his shining eyes and then nothing, as my face was leaning against his chest, in that encircling embrace. After he had kissed first one and then my other hand, he whispered in my ears words of appreciation and continued: "What a joy, how happy I am to be with you. You work a lot for all of us. You must do something for yourself, too. You have the right to be happy the same way you give joy to others. Love, Love, thank you for the joy you give us." Then he kissed my hands again.

I could not understand why he was speaking in plural so I spontaneously said: "Thank you for coming". And he replied: "Thank you, you are wonderful." That man was transmitting Love. I was confused and embarrassed when I realized, after I had removed my face from his chest, that people stopped to look at us with curiosity, not knowing what was going on. He continued: "You are useful here." I interrupted him saying: "Here in Italy? I don't think I'm doing enough in this period." He replied: "No, here on earth, Italy or India, it makes no difference. Now, in this particular moment you are useful here. Therefore, bring your heart back to where you are now. Do not break it in two. Here is where you should give love wholeheartedly. This is where it is beneficial now." Actually I knew that my heart had remained in India, with Sai Baba. "You are free after all. You can go wherever you wish. Baba will take care of your son." Sai Baba had already told me that during the interview which took place exactly a month earlier.

The encounter ended just as it started – unexpectedly. He moved away from me and recovered his composure. He said goodbye to everyone, aloof, and left with those who had accompanied him without looking back, as if we weren't there any more.

I immediately realized that there was something unusual about that encounter. In any case, it was somehow linked to Sai Baba. It took me days to regain my balance after that extraordinary experience.

At the end of the day, that man touched two issues only Sai Baba could know about: the perplexity concerning my capacity to be in charge as the President of the Centre and the firmness of my devotion.

Clearly, he was sent in a support mission in the moment when I started performing a duty which was so out of the ordinary for me. Indeed, He, the Divine Master, never left me alone.

I entered the life stage of "divine accomplishment" and perceived it with a lucidity which was sometimes baffling.

Intuition, the knowledge of the heart, or the voice of Truth, made me understand that I was moving according to a previously developed Divine Plan. My soul was probably in accordance with the Divine, Universal Intelligence.

That encounter was one of the first confirmations I received. Throughout the years, I have received many more and I will try to put them down, one by one, as evidence that human life can be divine if we open ourselves to God – to the Spirit within.

Having drawn strength from this inner divine support, I wasn't afraid of any task and no obstacle could stop me any more.

The strength and the enthusiasm grew as I felt Sai Baba, or God[38], sustain my efforts. I dreamt about Him more and more often, which confirmed that His guidance was guaranteed not only while I was awake but even during sleep.

The path of devotion suited me perfectly. It was an intense call perceived from my earliest childhood, although neglected for a while.

Sai Baba says: *"I have come to give you what you request from me, hoping that you start longing for what I'm actually here for."*

The Divine Master has come to help us awaken the Inner Master, the Self that resides in each one of us, in every devotee's heart, as Christ Consciousness, or the consciousness of the Christ within, when we transcend the individual self by turning our attention inwards instead of pursuing worldly things.

However, our daily surrender to the Divine Will through the practice of His message enables us to dominate the ego, instead of being dominated by it, and awakens a new consciousness within.

Spiritual practice helps us forge and strengthen the character. Sai Baba says: *"A man without character is not a man."*

Character implies will, determination, perseverance, courage, discernment, decisiveness, honesty and loyalty. The force of our character will allow us to perform an important spiritual task in the Cosmic Game we take part in. This is so because the Divine Knowledge of the Spirit cannot be taught. It can only be realized with the help of God and by His Grace.

Forging a good character requires effort, through prayer, study, self-inquiry, research, service and above all by being oriented inwards and not outwards because the purifying, illuminating and ever-quenching source is within us. It is therefore useful to meditate. Meditation – getting in touch with the Self – represents for the soul what air represents for our body: the very breath.

If we remain calm, unattached, equanimous and fair, the Spirit can lead us. But when we are immersed in the whirl of the world, that part of us dies out and we can no longer feel it within.

In that period I had a vision and saw a connection with the true Self, or the Spirit in me.

I saw a stormy ocean. A dry cave was placed on my belly – I was lying on the bare ground – and a child took shelter inside. While it gradually transformed itself into light, it filled the cave, until it dissolved and the child emerged. All of a sudden the tempest came to a halt and the ocean became calm, smooth and shiny, like a mirror. That imaginative scene seemed to convey that, when the Self (the child) is self-illuminated, the body (the cave of the ego) becomes weightless and breaks free from the physical world (the tempest) and so Spiritual Peace finally emerges.

Speaking of the spiritual path, Sai Baba suggests to *"dig a single hole but a deep one, instead of digging many shallow holes"*. In other words, He invites us to follow only one Master with perseverance and full time, not part time as we westerners usually do. Many of us haven't forgotten the Christian rituality of "observing the holy days", in the sense of going to church on Sundays but dedicating the rest of the week to worldly things, to the individual self and not to God who is the true Self within. This is an example of a part time faith.

These two characteristics of devotion – perseverance and full time coherence – pave the way for God's blessings and, occasionally, cancel our past debts. When it comes to the present, by doing everything in the name of God, without thinking about the fruits of our actions, leaving the failures and the accomplishments to Him, we can stop accumulating new debts. It is important to know all those features of the "Geography of the Spirit", of our inner world, and the many opportunities He offers to help us on the path of salvation.

We are left with the choice to either take them or to miss them and keep groping in the darkness of confusion and ignorance.

I spent the three following years immersed in my service at the Sai Centre which became my life. I worked there full time and was grateful to Sai Baba for giving me the opportunity to evolve together with my travel companions.

Sai Baba kept visiting me in my dreams. Once, in a dream, during a conversation He said: "What else can I do? I carry most of the world's misfortunes on My shoulders. There is nothing more I can do."

In that period several friends died, leaving behind their inconsolable friends and family. He might have referred to them.

In another dream, I was accompanying Him to the South of India where He was going to inaugurate a school. I told Him I would like to live and work by His side all the time. While getting on the bus on the way back, He intertwined two *japamalas* (Indian rosaries consisting of 108 beads), one made of wood and the other made of crystal, and said: *"Forces of good and forces of evil, unite!"* Then we sat down, next to each other. He allowed me to rest my head on His shoulder and told me: *"We must love each other."* Moved by so much grace, I confessed my love for Him.

Those dreams helped me create an increasingly familiar rapport with the Divine. As I said, I was experiencing the dimension of dreams in the same way I was experiencing daily reality. He was the friend I could turn to, to ask for assistance or advice, at all times and everywhere.

Sai Baba invites us to be good, to love each other, see goodness, listen to goodness, utter goodness and think good thoughts to avoid the weight of the natural law of cause and effect (*karma*) because we can benefit from the Divine Grace by behaving well. He came to bestow Divine Grace upon us profusely, but we must open our hearts to Him – or to God or whatever we called it, it doesn't matter.

He maintains that Love is the natural condition for man and mankind and ignorance prevents us from realizing that. Developing divine qualities, such as unconditional Love, tolerance, patience, compassion, charity, kindness and forgiveness, is the only cure against our ignorance about our real nature as "divine creatures".

Ignorance about our true nature cannot be eradicated as long as the mind is at the service of the individual self, or ego, which on the other hand fears God as its destroyer and consists of prejudices, preconceptions, likes and dislikes, differences and mistrusts, etc... It can be overcome though with the divine qualities deriving from the wisdom of the heart. This is intuitive intelligence.

I kept asking my friend Sai to help me understand, to illuminate me, as I didn't known that light was within me yet. The child made of light in the vision described above pointed precisely at that.

I often went on a pilgrimage in my dreams, including certain Catholic holy sites. I was once visiting the Sanctuary of Our Lady of Divine Love. I saw Our Lady as the feminine aspect of God, or the Divine Mother. I kissed the rock on which her statue was erected in the same manner I had kissed the marble floor on which Sai Baba had walked, during the encounter in His temple at Whitefield (Brindavan).

In a dream I had during the night of 11th February (anniversary of Our Lady of Lourdes), I was on my way to a Marian underground Sanctuary, climbing down a very steep stairway. There was a multitude of pilgrims coming and going. I finally arrived at an immense white church. The vault was extremely high. In an apse, covered by a white veil, there was a statue of Our Lady, all white. I prayed, went out and found myself in a beautiful park, thinking about the fact that people, instead of travelling around so much, should get familiar with the magic of those holy places and taste true happiness.

I also dreamt of being in an *ashram*, in India. The Master was passing among His disciples and when He arrived near me, He said: "You are the one who will go to work as a volunteer to Puttaparthi, at the *ashram* of Sai Baba, but you sleep too much." As if he was telling me:

you would like to work at the place where God decided to incarnate, yet you are not preparing yourself adequately for your future task.

Perhaps, through that dream, the Self was reproaching me for having stopped getting up at four o'clock in the morning to meditate.

On that occasion I understood I was not only guided, which was fully ascertained, but I was also held under "strict surveillance" and this made me feel uncomfortable. Being an "around-the-clock disciple" of the Divine School was a great responsibility.

The difficulty consisted in the fact that I felt constantly observed and heard by the Self. I was the witness and the protagonist but I had not evolved enough to be completely unattached from my actions.

That was the basis of my perplexity. Was I supposed to judge or just to observe myself? Had I let my mind decide, it would not have acted freely. I would have been under the control of the ego and therefore unable to abandon my habitual patterns, entangling myself further. I eventually gave up, waiting for my intuition to come to my aid, in its wisdom, and help me resolve the dilemma.

As a matter of fact, awareness was awakening after a long torpor, but it was not always easy to recognize it.

I could see that the Divine Master was taking care of me and I thought I did not deserve so much attention and kindness. At times, paradoxically, I seemed to wish to be on my own, being influenced by the ego – which I understood only later on. Those moments were very brief since, unconsciously, I wasn't leaving much space to my ego. I would turn to my best Friend and ask for His complicity, forgiveness and understanding whenever I made a mistake or failed unintentionally, one way or the other.

I realized subsequently that mine was merely a human vision of God. He does not have to forgive anything. He has always loved His children because He is Love.

Mystics of all religions speak the same language, like the one spoken by Sai Baba: *God is Love, Unity, and Truth. Turn your back to the world and you will find God.*

Jesus said: *"You cannot serve two masters, so it is either God or the world"* and : *"Whoever embraces the cross finds liberation and salvation, that is, enters the Kingdom of Heaven".* Sai Baba says: *"Only renunciation and sacrifice bring liberation".* Those were also the words of Jesus.

A Christian mystic, the Blessed Angela of Foligno wrote: *"Good and bad are divine. So great is the Father's joy upon the return of the sinners that He bestows His supernatural grace upon them for them to attain salvation."*

Sai Baba came to earth to bring that Grace. In my dream in which I travelled with Him to the south of India, He intertwined two rosaries and said: *"Good and evil, unite!",* to convey that evil is defeated by goodness, with Love, just like Jesus said: *"Do not oppose evil. Love your enemies!"*

The Arab mystic Rumi wrote: *"You are a drop, you are the sea, you are grace, you are anger and you are poison: therefore, stop tormenting me!"* and: *"It is God's habit to create from nothing. Consequently, unless man becomes 'nothing', God can do nothing about him." "God can be heard only through the mouth of prophets or men of God".*

The Russian novelist Tolstoy wrote: *"Know yourself and acknowledge God.", "God is someone we can't live without. Knowing God and living is the same thing, since God is life, happiness, service and truth." "If you spend your life searching for God, He will manifest in all aspects of your life. Everything around you will brighten up and that light will never abandon you", "True discipline must follow you like a shadow. It must never move away from you, otherwise it is false discipline. Peace is the consequence of faith and obedience to God, whereas pain comes from man's innate aspiring to God and his failure to adjust himself to his commandments."* Sai Baba has been telling us the same thing for 80 years!

All those who have realized the inner Divine speak the same language to express the wisdom of the heart.

Whenever I ran into words similar to His own, my heart filled with joy. Men and women of all ages, religions, races and cultures found God in the same way and were illuminated by the same Light – the light of Love and Truth – because the bright path of spirituality is essentially the same, notwithstanding the different itineraries it may follow.

I really started to believe that my experience of suffering, mixed with joy, amazement, surprise and confusion could provide a better understanding or help for those who were on the same path, for them to feel less lonely. Anyway, it was important to discover that those were but the "necessary stops" on the way and being able to testify personally was useful for the others, to encourage them in this effulgent and magic adventure.

Inner maturation requires a lengthy "setting in" period characterized by confusion, whereas spiritual growth takes place through numerous rebirths, as obligatory stages of arrival and departure. It takes much patience and trust in our inner sensations. Our deepest desire reveals the task we have been called to perform in this lifetime – to get to know ourselves and be authentic.

Comprehension was not enough to know Truth, or the Spirit, and my desire was to be the living witness of the Spirit within me, to serve as a mirror to those who were still mistrustful about their own feelings and therefore risked missing the opportunity to reveal the presence of God within – God who was peace, joy and serenity – and no one could do it in their stead. This research has to be done personally and it requires refining our perception until it becomes crystal clear, so we can fully rely on it.

Only from there can we start noticing a tangible progress, because we begin to interpret and trust the signs, symbols, coincidences, dreams and out-of-body experiences through which the Divine manifests or the Spirit speaks. What others might consider as pure fantasy – people who care little about the search for the Spirit – is reality to those who pursue Truth. This reality is ready to fill up a vacant space in the right moment and bring clarity in the interpretation of the human experience on earth.

I realized that the world of ideas moulded the manifest reality. Just like numerous enlightened people, like Pythagoras and Plato, claimed in the past: thought becomes matter. It is our ideas which tie or set us free, depending on how much we rely on the illusions fed by the world of duality (matter vs. Spirit) by means of the individual self or ego. When we realize that life is also a "dream dreamt with open eyes" and that we populate it with scenes, situations, events and more or less pleasant or more or less terrible facts, we will be able to apply ourselves to prevent the dream from turning into a nightmare. Through this effort, we will eliminate so much suffering.

We – and no one but we – can help ourselves, because the law of cause and effect (*karma*) manifests by presenting a statement of the account we opened, which can be settled only by us. How many times have we done everything to try and "save" someone – to no avail. Sooner or later, in those desperate attempts there was always a moment when we had to surrender and, as we say, let things go their own way.

With time I realized that the terrible feeling of impotence we are seized by in those instances is, in fact, an expression of the hurt ego and a sign that we do not trust the Divine Work, although it is merciful without exception, even when our limited and quite imperceptive mind desists, deducting that Divine Mercy does not exist.

And here lies the importance of learning to maintain equidistance from the good and the bad, from joy and pain, success and failure, because our emotional involvement is the primary cause of our slavery, the kind of slavery that determines the return of the physical body down to earth, with all the consequences we know so well. It is the fourth dimension we should transcend, to move beyond.

I dreamt in those days about being in a child welcome centre, taking care of some children together with my friends. One of them unexpectedly started pointing at my right hand: a gold ring with three diamonds suddenly materialized on my ring finger. Sai Baba made me a present from afar. I was amazed, just like the rest of the group. Seven years later, I forgot about the ring when, in the course of an interview, He materialized an identical ring in the presence of the same friend who had appeared in the same dream, along with some other people, from the same group. He put it on the ring finger of my right hand Himself.

NOTES: CHAPTER IV

32. What I didn't know at the time was that the spiritual path was unfinished as long as there was life in the physical body (the 3rd dimension). A spiritual path consists of continuous arrivals and departures for the next stage, until we are ready to pass into the 4th dimension.

33. It is the "coarsest" among the subtle, spiritual dimensions (6th-7th dimension etc.)

34. It is what not only the Catholic religion but also Esotericism calls 'sin against the Holy Spirit'. It cannot be simply forgiven - in the sense that it must be "paid for".

35. Devotion: love for the Divine which entails a feeling of love for all things, or experiencing Oneness with everything (intimacy, friendship with God).

36. When it comes to the origin of man, we read in the *Vedas*: *"I have separated Myself from Myself in order to love Myself"*.

37 Repeating God's Name – any of the respective names attributed by the various religions or beliefs (*Namasmarana* in Sanskrit) in this dark age (*Kaliyuga*) – is the simplest way to obtain God's Grace.

38. Sai Baba or God: I would like to specify that those two names for me express the same Oneness: Sai Baba is for me the living incarnation of God, as the Spirit of Truth and Love. I refer to both at the same time, with a familiarity I do not deny.

V

Lord, I have not received anything of what I have asked from you, but you have given me everything I needed."

Rumi.

Jesus claimed what Sai Baba is saying today: *"There is nothing outside man which could contaminate him if fed into him. However, he can be contaminated by what he produces."* As a matter of fact, thoughts are the only thing which can purify or poison the food we eat, but also life itself.

Studying a text on "The Secret Sayings of Jesus", I found some phrases which were clarified further in the messages of Sai Baba. At the end of the day, the Spirit that nourished or has nourished both of them is Unique – and Truth is Unique. The Divine Master (or *Guru,* meaning 'the light that dispels darkness') kept enlightening me.

Jesus said: *"When you turn two into one and when you make the inner like the outer and the outer like the inner, and the upper like the lower, and when you join the male and the female into one whole, then you will enter the Father's Kingdom."*

The female is Creation, the manifest universe or matter (what has been created is considered female; only the Creator is male, Non-manifest and Absolute – Father God, or Spirit) and it must become male, in other words it must be transformed into the Spirit to be able to enter the Kingdom of Heaven and realize the Divine (that is, to see God).

Sai Baba says: "Only when you realize the Androgynous within will you be able to find harmony as the only precondition to see the Divine."

With the gift of Christ Consciousness bestowed on those of us who have purified the heart (from worldly cravings), the Holy Spirit makes us attain the Androgynous within and realize that we were created to "His own image and resemblance".

After years of contemplation and research, I understood the subtle meaning of the words of Jesus and Baba: the Androgynous is the divine man, the angel in us, the real man who loves with the heart, "poised" in his spiritual heart, feels compassion for everybody, having reached equanimity, and loves all humanity unconditionally (being at one with the good and the bad) because he has overcome the duality of good and evil and male and female.

The spiritual heart corresponds (according to esoteric knowledge) to the eighth chakra that is developed together with the ninth chakra (spleen) in the mankind of the future that will experience the Golden Age (of Spiritual Knowledge).

Sai Baba says that a woman's *Dharma* (righteous path) is generally the path of sacrifice because she covers the distance to attain the Spirit more quickly than a man. He says that while a woman carries a hundred men to God, a man does not carry a single woman and that patience and perseverance – typical virtues in a woman – are hard to find in a man (being more subject to anger, passion, pride and jealousy).

How can an ordinary person overcome the duality of male and female, being male or female by nature?

Jesus said: *"What are you waiting for to sublimate the two tendencies, the male and the female, in one point of your body which is the spiritual heart?"* It is an invitation to sublimate sexuality as the stronghold of duality in human life.

A harmonious encounter of the female and the male principle on the physical plane gives life to a new birth, that is, the union of the male semen and the ovule (again, energy transformed into matter) generates a new life (that of the baptism of water),. Likewise, on the spiritual plane, the union of the soul and the Spirit, as the gift of the Holy Spirit, generates a second birth (that of the baptism of fire).

By sublimating the energies associated with the primordial instincts of survival and procreation and transcending the psychic energies of the rational logic of the mind, man can see and feel with the heart (have the inner vision and knowledge of the heart) and thus follow the safe guidelines of wisdom coming from the true Self.

To purify the heart we must transcend the senses and the mind because these two instruments are subordinate to the ego. Only then we will be able to grasp the Self within, or the Spirit manifesting in the body, and stop feeling like a body in search for the Spirit.

When Jesus was asked: *"Give us the knowledge of the one thing which will draw upon us the Love of God."* He replied: *"Hate the world and God will love you."* Sai Baba says: *"Turn you back to the world and you will find God."* The two statements are essentially identical. *"The only indication is to keep watching and be prepared, as no one knows the day and the time." This is not the time to be tepid. You must chose between hot and cold or otherwise you will miss the very last train".*

One day I heard an "inner command": *"I beseech you, announce the Word."* What magniloquent words! Especially considering my humble being. Was I going insane? Well, now, what comes to my mind, I wondered, am I perhaps emulating the exploits of Jeanne D'Arc?

I knew I had no foolish aspiration to be the centre of attention and I don't think Jeanne D'Arc had any of it either. We have one thing in common: attraction to the Spirit.

But who was I and what was I supposed to announce that hasn't been announced already? I couldn't reply to myself and, just like so many times before, I put everything on the back burner.

In the same period I found (by some strange coincidence) a book on the secret language of the dates of birth.

The day I was born was marked by the number of the "spiritual warrior"

It was enough to make me think of a "benign conspiracy" orchestrated by the Spirit, possibly to remind me of my primary task.

It said: *"A Spiritual Warrior is he who does not consider inactivity as an option. He is one of those hard workers, one of those soulsmiths who will not desist from a waste land. What is the use of words if the promise is broken? What if the deeds betray them? Words must be accompanied by action. If we intend to use divine energy to attain Divine Love, we must put into practice the teachings of the Divine Master. To know them is not enough.*

The Warrior's ideal is to progress without ever looking back. He enriches himself by proceeding gropingly, is able to move mountains and becomes a living symbol of determination in overcoming adversities, dedicating an immense amount of energy to serve a noble cause."

It was all part of the plan. There was no escape for me; I had to stop hesitating and do something. I had to go back to writing, as I couldn't see anything else for me to do to give body to the instructions contained in that message, apart from what I was already doing.

I was actually aware of the fact that mankind was running out of time and the moment had arrived to follow the Spirit, or Truth and Love, in every instant of my life. But, considering my situation, it was also true that I was quite privileged for being able to retire and dedicate myself exclusively to the inner research through service, study, self-search, "missions" in India (travels) and the like.

How many people have been given the opportunity to discover what I managed to synthesize over the many years, under the guidance of the Spirit (the true Self within), from the material I collated, having gone through hundreds of books? Had it been only for my own sake, it would not have been the right thing to do, seven days a week; it would have been sheer, meaningless selfishness. I could see it clearly after I had met Sai Baba and gained my self-confidence. However, the notes I kept to gain a better understanding of life and myself were inadequate for a book.

I thought that the inner commands might have been referred to the need to transform the material collated over the years in a cogent synthesis, for it to be considered as a roadmap of the world of the Spirit, or a guide for travellers eager to explore this new territory within reach yet so inaccessible – so much so that some people questioned its very existence.

To start with, I could have written: "I have tried this for you", like an advertising slogan of an adventure-travel agency.

Going back to my shiny spiritual path, I have already written something about suffering and confusion but now I would like to say something about the import of being authentic.

Being faithful to ourselves first of all implies making sure we know who we are, without denying our imperfections (transforming ourselves, remember, is divine). We should then forgive ourselves while calling things by their proper names and recognizing our flaws, such as envy, jealousy, pride, laziness, anger, falsehood, ingratitude, distrust, greed, inflexibility, touchiness, impatience and the like, as the major obstacles on the path to the realization of the divine essence in us.

On a daily basis, we all tend to conceal from ourselves and from the others the above sampling of facets that distort our personality and weaken the character, in the unsuccessful attempt to "simplify our lives" and "adjust ourselves to the standard model" imposed by society.

The fact of the matter is that, in this way, we become less and less spontaneous and more and more artificial, less and less authentic and more and more seductive, increasingly less free and increasingly more slaves to the world of appearances, distancing ourselves dangerously from the divine essence as the only source of life in us.

We are so absorbed in our physicality that we worry about losing a limb or an eye or any other body part. Yet, when the contact with the divine essence is broken, we don't even realize that our soul – our noblest part – risks withering.

This painful aspect of the human nature was the reason why I decided, over the years, to withdraw. Living in a group or in a society was not my cup of tea.

Coherence, compassion, patience and acceptance were still unripe fruits in the garden of humanity.

I had to work on my flaws for a long time before it sank in that I could only change myself and not the world. The world was supposed to be loved as it is.

I understood though that we could overcome our imperfections only if we recognised them and if we were true to ourselves. On the other hand, it was of no use being intolerant of other people's faults.

Sai Baba states that, being the divine incarnation, He personifies both the masculine and the feminine principle of cosmic energy, called *Shiva-Shakti* in Hinduism. In addition, He points out that *Shiva and Shakti,* or this marriage of divine energies, are present in each one of us as the inexhaustible fountain of life (the true Self, or *Atma,* or divine spark).

Shakti, the feminine principle, the water of renewal which characterizes the age of Aquarius, or the Golden Age (of Spiritual Knowledge) we are in already, representing compassion, trust, humility, flexibility, receptiveness and intuition of the human being, was the fountain I wished to drink from.

Man is the thirst (as the individual self or the ego with its annexes) but he is also the fountain (as the universal Self in him, the Spirit of Life). He contains the water that quenches the thirst once and for all – the water of the Spirit Jesus referred to when He said: *"He who fails to become a fountain himself will never quench his thirst".* Otherwise, he remains unfulfilled and cannot satisfy his incompleteness (inner void) with whatever form of evasion.

No desire – except for the yearning for the Absolute – will ever be satisfied because man will always remain thirsty.

The water that gushes out from every human being is the energy that waters the heart. In this way, the heart will not dry and wither and the skill to listen to life will flourish again, overcoming mental resistance and drawing directly upon the Self (Spirit of Truth and Love).

I was still the prisoner of the mind and its confusion. I still believed that the strength to go on was something external and not an integral part of me, still projecting myself in the future instead of being present within to seize the fleeing moment in its eternal existence.

I was still wearing my "character shield" made of pride, rigidity and the fear of revealing my weaknesses. Yet, only by undressing completely could I find myself again, or the true Self. I understood that much later.

About a year passed from the last trip to India and, although I was convinced that a higher purpose (I was not aware of) justified that lengthy absence from my second homeland, I was still longing to see Sai Baba again and find myself in front of Him.

When I left India a year earlier, I knew in my heart that I would not be back soon to see Him in His physical form. He gave me so much that I could not ask for more.

Confusion, dissatisfaction and insufficiency do not touch those who have found the fulfilment of existence and stopped desiring, since they no longer feel separated from anything, they don't miss anything. I entered that state of bliss every while and then.

I would experience that fulfilment intensely, although briefly. We feel safe when we are in direct contact with the cosmic energy and the cosmic force, as its integral part. It is the only energy that can give us the strength and the courage to affirm that we are at one with the All through this sensation of gratifying and overwhelming fullness, like a tide of beneficial bliss. In those moments I realized that I lived in Paradise. I was already in the Kingdom of Heaven, or better, the Kingdom of Heaven was within me.

The people around me were not aware of this the way I was. What they considered as normal, everyday routine for me was Paradise, owing to my inner perception.

This realization fostered in me the wish to share what I had discovered, step by step, not without strain: that the Kingdom of Heaven was within reach. I was still unable to stabilize that state of unity (i.e. the realization that the Self was me), but at least I wanted to make the attempt. I couldn't back out from it.

I wondered what the major obstacle might be for someone willing to hear about my experiences. Was it the fear of change or incredulity, self-consciousness or alienation, the fear of having to renounce the "false" certainties or having to choose between the familiar and the unfamiliar? I couldn't reply and so I stayed still, hoping to come up with an answer.

I kept probing the profusion of the inner realm, in the hope that I would become a useful tool for the Divine one day, to testify about the wonders of His manifestations and present concrete, irrefutable facts.

With Sai Baba, everyday life became sacred and magic at the same time. Dream and reality merged into one. I was the testimony that that dream was not utopia; it was true and anybody could verify it.

Sai Baba says: *"Make sure that your life speaks the religion you practice, make sure it is a life of friendliness and simplicity, humility and love, service and sacrifice."*

I was trying to act in this direction, motivated by the desire for insight, for my sake and of all those who were unable to demand something they were rightfully entitled but oblivious to.

A tragic aspect of human life is determined by the fact that, very often, man is unable to find peace. He does not know what he wants or what to look for because he neglects his real needs or does not even know what he lacks, no longer remembering what it is that he has lost. And if it is difficult to find what we have lost, it is even harder, if not impossible, to find something we possess unknowingly. This sterile search for search's sake continues until we become clearly aware of our true nature....which is divine!

The limelight of life illuminates the places that attract us like smoke and mirrors, with the cajolery or illusion of happiness at a bargain price and so we keep running left and right, attracted by noise, confusion, ostentation, advertisements or whatever might seem to offer more satisfaction.

Until we get to know ourselves or our true inner essence, none of the desires we try to fulfil can appease our needs because they are phoney, unreal, just as we are unreal when we feel unaccomplished and empty, disregarding our most noble aspect that is the basis of human dignity.

It is another kind of illumination and another space – internal rather than external – in which we retrieve what we have lost. It is important at least to know that it is within reach and accessible to whoever might have the good will to pursue it.

Jesus said: *"Peace on earth to men of good will!"*

Peace is God or the manifestation of God in man and in the world.

Peace is not the absence of war but a state of the soul. It is a virtue or a disposition to benevolence, justice, trust and Love.

Good will is the Divine Will acting by the Will of God.

I understood what Jesus meant: God ascends in the form of peace when people act according to His Will or when they implement His message.

God is manifest within – only if we really want it, or else He keeps watching us, His children, like a witness.

Sai Baba claims that God protects those who stand for truth and behave righteously, but nowadays man tends to kill the truth and imprison righteousness. Sadly, we can all see the consequences.

What blocks the will while we make our decisions, or choices, or act according to the divine teachings? Nothing but the individual self (or ego), in its multiple forms, all related to the fear of being nullified.

Doubts about the actual existence of God within and the fear of being alone in the world, threatened by everything around, stem from the sense of loss, abandonment and insecurity deriving from a remote nostalgia of a union which once became fragmented, as I wrote earlier, a nostalgia of a contact which was interrupted when we descended to earth. Those feelings have always been common to all mankind, without any distinction of race, sex, creed, culture or age.

Jesus said that the fear of death would end with the cessation of rebirths, or when women stopped giving birth. Why? Because the state of ignorance about our origin is the price we have to pay for being born in the physical form (the 3rd dimension) on earth, where we learn new lessons at the school of experience, one life after another, in order to evolve and settle the debts created in our previous lives, because we were unaware of our true, divine nature.

Consequently, not only ignorance, but also fear and doubt will also persist in man until the curtain is parted between the real and the unreal, the ephemeral and the sublime, the limited and the unlimited, duality and unity and the manifest and the hidden. The curtain is an allusion to our failure to recognize our divine nature. The Spirit is not separated from matter, since it is the very substance matter is made of and, in man, it is his very breath.

Sai Baba says that, as we breath, each day we repeat 21600 times: I am God, I am That, *So ham* (in Sanskrit), i.e. I (the individual self) am I (the universal Self), without even being aware of it.

Man, in the physical body, has to be subordinate to the categories of time and space, while the Spirit within him has neither limits of time and space nor fears or doubts or, most importantly, selfishness. Therefore, the Spirit can be our best friend – but only if we wish so, because it does not impose itself on anyone.

I have personally seen concrete evidence of His capacity to "wait " for us, until the time is right.

I started meditating many years ago. Then I made a break, resumed a few years later and stopped practicing again. That was such a tremendous loss for my inner wellbeing. The Self was waiting (respectful of my unwise choices) for many long years, until I reinstated that wonderful practice one day, to have "close encounters" with the Spirit, but this time with a different awareness that enabled me to experience them daily, and I am sure this will continue for the rest of my earthly life. Those "encounters with the Spirit" have become as important and essential for me as my very breath.

When my mind is silent, it is much easier to get in touch with the Cosmic Intelligence permeating the entire Universe. It manifests in man as balanced awareness or wisdom of the heart, as intuition or intuitive intelligence which is Truth, Universal Love, Compassion and Bliss. It is the source gushing from one's spiritual heart, the essence of Spiritual Knowledge. When life is enlightened by this Knowledge, it ceases to be a mystery and becomes pure life.

Speaking of it, there is a constant in human life: attraction to mystery. I would like to say a word about it to clear the misunderstanding it is surrounded by and try to explain its roots.

Attraction to mystery, to darkness instead of light or clarity, can partly be explained by the logic (of the individual self[39]) according to which pleasure leaves us dissatisfied – or never fully satisfied. In this regard, consider all the addictions linked to the search for "negative" pleasure, namely alcohol, smoking, drugs in their infinite variety, sex, etc.. It is a mechanism by which the mind, subject to the ego, tends to justify deficiencies, faults, attachments, fears and senses of guilt, inducing us, with excessive self-indulgence, to become unconscious victims of all kinds of conditionings.

From the point of view of the ego, there is only pleasure related to passion, which is destructive, negative pleasure. There is, though, another kind of pleasure which is positive, creative and related to the intellect. When life is characterized by the former type of pleasure (desired by the ego), it is good to know that there can be no room for the latter one. They do not coexist.

Having said this, we should take a moment of reflexive pause and evaluate what we are doing in this very moment in life with regard to the two outlooks of experiencing pleasure and question ourselves which of the two we opt for.

We can also remain silent and avoid answering, but it is important to know that we can't be well or improve our quality of life unless we have acknowledged our self-destructive impulses. We should then accept them, forgive ourselves and transcend them.

Only in this way can we stop deceiving ourselves and bring our existential displeasure to a stop. We will finally be able to surrender in a healthy way, trustingly, and open to the world that will no longer appear like a hostile place.

First of all, this mishmash of emotions, or human nature, is about the power of the ego to execute our continuous condemnation and perpetuate the condition of slavery, insinuating doubt, scepticism, mistrust, touchiness, desire for revenge, vengeance and so on.

Those negative feelings keep us from knowing true Love and opening ourselves to real life, paralysing our will with fear. All negative emotions are heavy energies acting like a ballast, anchoring us in matter. We should always bear this in mind.

When we are enslaved by the ego, deprived of our own will, we have no chance of improving our lives. The ego will keep us in its power as long as doubt, guilt and fear remain on stage.

Until we become our own masters and in charge of our own will, we continue to be the victims of circumstances and other people.

Negative feelings and the lack of will feed incoherence, contradictions and compromises in our behaviour, putting an additional burden on our already restricted condition.

All the conditionings that subjugate and confine us under the power of the ego, draw us towards "forbidden", distorted, negative and destructive pleasures, in order to stupefy us and cover up the underworld of negative emotions we don't want to see or know about. That world made of hatred, envy, jealousy, anger, guilt, regret, resentment, insecurity, mistrust, sadness, hard-heartedness and more, is the fertilizer which stimulates man's attraction to mystery. Ignorance is cloaked into "mystery". Captured by the seductive power of everything that's "obscure" or "mysterious", we give up of the discovery of the origin of our dissatisfaction and lack of fulfilment, fearing clarity, coherence and truth. Consider how many satanic sects are flourishing, along with sadomasochistic behaviour and similar phenomena. K. Gibran said: *"Man is two men, one is awake in the darkness and the other is sleeping in the light."*

Sai Baba says: *"In this age of ignorance and darkness, man, instead of loving God and fearing sin, fears God and loves sin."* And this is really true, man has turned the natural order of things completely upside down.

Mystery is nothing but a pretty miserable baggage and it would be just fine if we could get rid of it quickly, but to do this we need the light of true knowledge, the courage to look within with objective open-mindedness and the will to call things by their proper name.

Following this serious self-investigation, we must accept our limits and forgive ourselves for the present and for the past, for our wrongs or mistakes, inflicted or suffered, which generated guilt, insecurity, resentment and fear.

The way of forgiveness is simple and varied at the same time. With one stroke, it frees man from all inner outstanding matters, senses of guilt, desperations and depressions in order to restore the taste for True Love, truth, peace and the *joie de vivre*.

Once the choice is made, there is no more room left for suspiciousness about life or God and we are filled with faith in Him. This new feeling takes us back to being open to the world, to the light and the dissolution of darkness in us.

Spontaneity, simplicity and authenticity are possible only when our thoughts and feelings are positive, constructive, creative and vivifying.

When we renounce the perverse game of the ego and destructive pleasure, we can put an end to fears, doubts, insecurity and self-deceit, that is, to suffering and dissatisfaction.

Finally, we can let ourselves go to the creative, positive and constructive joys of live and savour peace, grace, love and realization – in a nutshell, the divine presence within.

This is the climax of the spiritual path of a human being. Inner divinity activates itself through peace and joy and not through anxiety and pain. Peace, joy, creative delight and fulfilment are the primary purpose of the spiritual search and, at the same time, its final aim.

People living with their inner conflicts cannot fully understand the truthfulness of the above statement. Those who do not live in the truth cannot grasp its meaning and so the conflict arises each time the divine, natural law of Love and Truth is infringed on any level. Consequently, they are unable to see clearly, or recognize the fruits of self-deceit.

We cannot trick the life that flows within, or deceive ourselves, pretend to feel fine and avoid the suffering caused by inner conflicts. Considering all the wonderful things we have been called to do or share, we cannot avoid paying the price of frustration and inner emptiness if we live a lukewarm life – half-way, sparing ourselves and dodging "going for it".

As a matter of fact, we are not short of anything, there is nothing to look for and if we keep on suffering, it is because we have not allowed ourselves to live fully. We have not allowed our noblest part, the Spirit in us, (our essence) to speak out. We have not given voice to the Love and Truth within.

We are distracted from the inner, true Self by countless fake certainties and false pleasures.

Ramana Maharsi, the enlightened Indian from the previous century said: *"See the false as false and what remains is true!"*

How simple, easy and beautiful is the life that flows in Truth.

Sai Baba says: *"I am always happy. Be happy al the time"*. If we live in Truth, which is God, we shall always be happy, fulfilled and blissful.

I was completely absorbed in my study of Holy Scriptures and the service at the Sai Centre over the long year that went by. Then, out of nothing, something happened which put me in the condition to decide to leave for India quickly. Actually, He decided it in my stead. The confirmation of that arrived while I was in India, during certain events that took place there later on. It was He who inspired each one of my travels and this has been evident to me ever since. I moved only when I felt His call within my heart or else I would stay home, where He would certainly give me the tasks to perform.

A group of devotees from the Sai Centre were planning a trip to India for quite a while, in the next January (precisely a year after my previous journey). I did not feel I should join them.

A few months earlier I drove a friend of mine to the airport. He decided to spend the last days of his life next to Sai Baba (he had AIDS and little time left to live).

I promised him that, if he died in India, I would bring his ashes back to Italy (he wished to be cremated according to the Hindu custom) so that his mother could have a tomb to go to and pray.

I asked Sai Baba if I might do that if necessity arose, as I had promised to my unlucky friend.

Towards the end of the year, the distressing news arrived. And so I decided to leave with the group for that extraordinary journey.

On New Year's Eve (prior to departure), I dreamt of being in India, at Sai Baba's home. I was going to talk to Him under the porch of the *Mandir*. There was a constant coming and going of elderly men dressed in white inside the *ashram,* as usual,. They were all Indian. As we talked, I passed Him a child of about a year of age, from my arms to His. He looked at the child. At first His mood was pensive, but then He started joking with it, making it laugh. He suddenly passed the child back to me, left and stopped by the elderly devotees.

The encounter left me ecstatic and it took me a few moments to "get hold of myself", in the dream, from that state of bliss. Still carrying the child in my arms, I followed Him, cleaning the best I could, with my hands, the lane He would walk on, for the fear that His constantly bare feet could touch something unclear.

One of those elderly men approached me and said we should have empathy for our neighbours because when we understand the others, we get closer to Sai Baba. I agreed and added that I, too, felt Sai Baba close to me owing to the same inner intention I nurtured with regard to the others.

The dream confirmed what I already felt within: our empathy and unconditional love for the others is the manifestation of His constant presence in us. Indian Holy Scriptures say that all the grace in the world is born from wishing joy to others and all the pain in the world from wishing joy to ourselves.

The dream that conveys a clear spiritual message is certainly the expression of the living presence of the inner true Self, guiding and illuminating us on the path of true knowledge because it is beyond time and space and it interprets the visible and the invisible, the conscious and the unconscious mind, our thoughts and feelings, even when we don't see or feel them.

The true Self depicted my own experience of myself. I was that child, because I felt alive from the moment of my rebirth, when I met Sai Baba, during the previous trip.

The Divine Master says: *"Celebrating one's birthday is not important. What is important, though, is to celebrate the day when we felt that God was born in our heart"* ...that is, when we recognized Him in our divine essence and became at one with Him.

For the upcoming journey, I was setting about to celebrate my first birthday into a new life (the dates coincided perfectly) with Him. We are all children in the arms of God, after all.

The elation from experiencing the sweet, infinite fulfilment a year earlier was still alive in me. I can never forget the moment when a passage for the light was finally opened in my heart.

Sai Baba says: *"Why rebuke the Sun for not entering the heart if you keep the door locked?"*.

The door to my heart was opened at last and I realized that worldly life should never be disconnected from the life of the Spirit. Otherwise we lose the opportunity to see unity everywhere. Love and empathy allow the understanding that God is within.

The true Self was sending me more comprehensible messages and lessons. Perhaps intuition made me more receptive, so that I became increasingly aware of the Spirit within.

Concepts such as devotion, wisdom, renunciation, liberation and the realization of the Self were the subjects of my daily contemplation. Like beads of a single Japa Mala (rosary), I used to carry them along at all times, striving to discover the access key to every one of them. I eventually realized that I had to be patient and wait for the right moment, to reach my goal.

The fourth, long awaited but still unexpected journey had other revelations and gifts in store.

Precisely a year after the last encounter, Sai Baba gave our group an interview. Sitting by His side, at the feet of His armchair, I felt as if I had never left the small room. In the course of the interview, the answers to my heart's questions came through the replies Sai Baba gave to others. This happened also in the future, in other interviews. Sai Baba talks to us in a myriad of ways and it is up to us to hear what He says, that is, listen carefully.

During my entire stay at Puttaparthi, I basked in the feeling of the live, incisive presence of the Divine Master in my heart.

I realized he provided us with whatever we needed, at the right time. In the economy of the divine, cosmic energy, the accounts are always closed positively. The good and the bad have, as the last resort, a single function: bringing us back into the light, that being our sole and eternal common goal.

Compassion and discrimination gradually grow as we detach from the fruits of our actions and recognise His presence within, as the *"primum movens"* of all things, including ourselves as simple spectators. We should also detach ourselves from the senses, to purify the heart, which at this stage happens quite naturally. It contributes to stabilizing the will, for us to control the mind instead of vice versa.

Once more, when the moment arrived to depart from Sai Baba, the experience was traumatic. I subsequently learned it was an interim phase I had to go through but also get out of if I wanted to raise "the child" I saw in my dream, held in Sai Baba's and in my arms.

I filed a request at the Italian Consulate in Mumbai and managed to bring my friend's cinerary urn home. I never parted from it during the entire journey.

Upon my return I handed it to his family and so his wish was granted – he was buried close to home, in accordance with his wish.

As soon as I was back I felt ready to leave again because the more I drew upon the Divine Master, the more I wished to draw from His fountain.

Life in the West no longer met my inner needs - my only remaining needs as a matter of fact.

I received two messages from the Spirit through a friend of mine. I was cheered up in a sense, but in another I was worried. One message said: *"Heard you have already the call of My heart, beautiful girl*[40] *to whom I dedicate my song, beautiful in the heart and in your appearance. Do not fear the future. You know it has no consistence. You are here today, somewhere else tomorrow, yet your abode will always be within My Being. Do not worry about what you leave behind, it is up to Me to put those things right.*

No one will miss you because everybody will have a place in their respective lives. You will play a beneficial role in other people's lives since you will be telling about Me things which are still difficult for obscure souls to comprehend. You have been chosen as the daughter of the Spirit and I empower you with the teaching skill.

Coarse souls will approach you and you will certainly know how to explain My Presence and the reason of My coming. This incarnated Spirit wants to make the world understand what you have already assimilated in the course of your many lives. You were present when "another One" was crucified for humankind.

Have faith and persevere, as total happiness is not far, although the moment of your return into the Cosmos – to reassemble your existence in a new way, adding the experiences gained in this lifetime to those gained previously – is still distant.

And I tell you, my darling: sing, sing, and sing the praises of Love and Hope.

Peace to you."

Between one message and the other, I dreamt of Sai Baba presenting me and a friend of mine (also a devotee of Sai Baba) with two saris. Mine was orange (in India this colour symbolizes renunciation; Sai Baba usually wears orange robes) and hers was white. She got married two years after, just as I had intuited. Here is the integral transcript of the part of the message concerning me: *"Beautiful soul, your grief is unfounded. Do not be disheartened by what is petty and insignificant. You will by all means encounter greater and smaller obstacles in the course of your mission, but you will be able to address them wisely, at times even cheerfully, because not all problems are grave. Do not think that you are not up to this challenge – you would not have been chosen if this were so.*

If you are at this stage of development, rest assured that the One in charge knew and knows that you can compensate and face trials beyond your imagination.

In physical life, peace and tranquillity are not always there for you. Moreover, you must conquer peace and then tranquillity will reach your soul, untroubled by things which can be resolved. You know, the meaning of meditation and prayer is not unfamiliar to your soul. Therefore, my dear girl, do not be bothered by human issues.

You are there to assist those who are still unable to comprehend this.

Love your brothers and try to understand them, as you would do with small children. Do not allow yourself to be disheartened by their contradictions and lack of understanding[41].

You are like a mother to all of them and you would certainly attach no importance to the words uttered by your sons who feel lost before the small things.

Again, my darling, try to understand that those who enter truth should know that the storms of life will continue to shatter it.

Love and empathy – this is our mission.

Do not fear. It is utterly human for human beings to be afraid, isn't it? Peace, Love, Empathy and Solidarity.

Cast away all the prejudices and misunderstandings. Cast away all the fears and insecurities.

Out of faith, you will undertake things which are unimaginable in your present state of mind. With time, you will understand my words, my dear, my beloved daughter.

Peace to you."

I did have a vague feeling that I'd been chosen for a task. However, by whom and why was still a mystery. I couldn't see it yet.

Could it be possible that the King of the Universe troubled to talk to a common creature like me?

If so, it must have been really God, that is, Sai Baba. Only He can love everybody with so much care, even the most ordinary beings.

I doubted that the messages originated from God because I felt so "small" with respect to the grandeur of the Spirit, or the Absolute.

I hadn't realized up till then that we were small if we thought "small", that is, in terms of material (worldly) things. We are big if we think "big" – in terms of the Spirit (heavenly)[42].

Ancient Chinese wisdom teaches us that you can tell if one has a noble soul or a mean personality by what he is fed by: he is noble if fed by sublime and mean if fed by ephemeral things. But one is also given the possibility to sublimate what one is nourished with – be it food or thoughts. We are what we think because thoughts become matter and hence we are co-creators (together with the Absolute) of our destiny.

Only in the recent years scientists have started agreeing on this aspect of daily reality: within and without. In antiquity, Pythagoras, Plato and other scholars were familiar with it.

Since man makes himself "small" by thinking primarily about material things, he risks losing the major opportunity of taking control of his own destiny at any time and making a positive shift in his life.

I can personally testify that when we meet God or the Spirit in us, our destiny can change radically, by His Grace.

Sai Baba recommends choosing a good, or better, a holy environment, although this might be more difficult in a sense. It is easier to have God as a friend, all the time.

Most importantly, when it comes to human relationships, the elder or the more mature have the duty to understand the younger or the less mature. Therefore, if we are not sufficiently mature or mentally and emotionally stable, we are more likely to get involved – in stead of evolving – in dubious companies, generally offered by the world.

Another message arrived informing me, among other things, about a gift I would receive by Sai Baba: the "materialization of a diamond ring". I paid little attention to that part of the message. Instead, I was more interested in the part highlighting my previous incarnations in ancient Egypt, explaining to me certain *karmic* involvements in my present life. One part of my distant past was gradually emerging, the part linked to the unravelling of the major "knots" of my present incarnation.

Three years after I had received those messages, I was certain they were not coming from the angels or some elevated spirits, but directly from God, or Sai Baba, because, in the course of an interview, He confirmed I had to write a book and said that He would bless it. A year later, in another interview, He stated I had to write only about "Swami" (The respectful and affectionate epithet by which the devotees address Sai Baba. It means 'Master'.).

I already longed to go back to India although I had just returned to Italy.

I felt the need to discuss with Him all the questions raised in my heart since those messages started arriving. Yes, I was still coping with a "desire", albeit a noble one.

I would like to pause at this personality trait surrounded by an aura of confusion and ignorance, to try and clarify certain aspects of it.

When it comes to desire, and it is indeed a widely discussed topic nowadays, we are often unaware of the fact that it is the fruit of the mind, although it uses the world of emotions to manifest itself, in its various facets.

It is useful to know that, when we speak about "feeling" we imply the feeling of Love which creates unity. On the other hand, "identifying" implies the kind of thought that creates separateness. Feeling is born in the heart and it tends to unify, while identification is born in the mind and it divides.

Desire is a surrogate of love – sustained, fed and manipulated by the mind or by thoughts – and as such is the source of separateness, division and discord, it is masked by attachment and it is falsely and inappropriately retained to be a sign of affection when it comes to human relations, or a sign of dedication when it comes to work and so on when it comes to any form of attachment – to money, home, "our things", etc..

While experiencing emotional or material attachment, most of us fail to notice that they are dealing with negative energy (negative in the sense that it drains our vital force and that of the people around us).

Let's consider for a moment the meaning of "identifying". The need to identify with or to be attached to another individual originates from the supposition that the two are apart. Being divided from other people or being on our own in the world feeds insecurity, anxiety, distrust, diffidence and the like.

Being attached to another person should fill the gap between them. But who created the distance in the first place? The mind, that is, the thoughts create the distance, the divisiveness and by consequence also the "remedy" – the attachment. In this case it is totally appropriate to say that the cure is more dangerous than the illness. This is why it is wrong to desire even the most sublime things, such as enlightenment, liberation, sanctity, etc. That too is an expression of attachment.

We should stop wishing and start Loving, with a capital 'L', since wishing belongs to the mind and loving belongs to the heart. At times we happen to "feel" that someone is very "close to us". The mind cannot explain why and it can even stay apart, annoyed by its own impotence to control the deep empathy it is registering.

The heart, on the other hand, needs no explanation because it generates nothing but Love and there is no division, distrust, closure or coldness in Love. There is only unity, understanding, warmth, trust, openness and fulfilment.

Thus, instead of wishing, we'd better Love and all the pieces will come together. Jesus said: "*Love God and you will be given everything*".

We should not "desire" God but Love Him, since Love brings us closer to Him.

We can love without "desiring". This truth does not sound convincing to most people but it is still the Truth, as true Love is not fed by desire but by acceptance, understanding, deep sharing, respect, trust, loyalty and Truth.

I learned very quickly not to long so much for returning to India to see the Divine Master and to Love Him the way He deserved to be loved, wholeheartedly, because I could perceive Him more and more in my heart, as the Spirit within.

Do not be frightened by this statement which might sound like an expression of fanaticism. As a matter of fact, only by giving ourselves to God (who allows us to experience ourselves as being at one with the All), can we obtain the necessary awareness, give ourselves to the others and serve God and humankind or simply maintain healthy, constructive relationships. He says so.

NOTES: CHAPTER V

39. From here onwards I use the term 'ego' when I refer to the individual self.

40. Time is definitely irrelevant for the Spirit. My hair was already grey at the time.

41. My discouragement stemmed from my emotional involvement at the Sai Centre and my often excessively intransigent attitude with respect to other people's incoherence.

42. Sai Baba says: *"If your thoughts make you feel apart from God, then you are apart. Clear your mind, or thoughts, and you will discover that God is within you. Enjoy this reality by diving into yourself".*

VI

You can do what appears to be sinful, as long as it helps other creatures.

Milarepa.

The way to accomplishing my greatest yearning and achieving the union with all things – the fusion of the individual self with the universal Self as the inner expression of the Absolute – was both simple and complex: by learning to love everyone and detach from everything. That was the highest point we could reach in the heart.

Pursuing that divine target implied not only the purification of the heart and the mind, but also the unification of the soul and the Spirit. The goal was truly enormous, almost out of reach, but my hopes were fairly high as well.

I accepted the invitation to accompany two friends to a place in the mountain where Sai Baba usually resided in that particular time of the year (our spring corresponds to summer in India), which was around March and April.

I was rather familiar with that part of the country which had been the theatre of my adventure two years before. At the time, the very thought of it could well send shivers down my spine.

That place, defined by Sai Baba as His holiday residence, attracted me like a magnet. I felt that the invitation was coming from Him. In fact, that journey (the fifth in the series), ended up being the umpteenth gift by the Divine Master, bearing in mind that divine gifts implied as Grace can entail either joy or pain, in the sense that they can manifest either as something being given or taken away from us.

The enlightened Indian Aurobindo used to say: *" Grace is that tide that can either save your life or take it away from you".*

In this sense, both giving and taking are certainly beneficial for our development.

God (the Divine Master or Sai Baba) is only interested in the Spirit and not in our daily, materialistic affairs, which tend to absorb us completely, and are of no avail. In the messages received a little earlier, the inner voice defined them as "trivial, inconsistent matters".

In spite of their inconsistence, trivialities often turn into "harmful and dangerous matters", as they are good at distracting us from the only true goodness which is always and only God, as the Self within.

In our daily routine, we sometimes feel disappointed and so, may it not sound blasphemous, we 'run out' of God. Yes, Him, right. It is a bitter statement that ordinary people are characterized by spiritual ignorance and scarce discernment.

We are disappointed by God when we are displeased by Him or when He doesn't fulfil the thousand requests we place before Him in the rare moments when we remember Him at all, trying to win Him over to grant our wishes "as soon as possible".

This is the kind of rapport humankind has established with God in this dark age.

Unaware of that, and judging from our lifestyles, we are doomed to perpetuate the vicious cycle of dissatisfaction, as there is no end to the fulfilment of desires. As soon as we satisfy one, two more crop up, and so on, until we die.

Sai Baba invites us to put a "ceiling" to desires. He knows our suffering and where it stems from, He knows why we suffer, for how long we will have to suffer, when our suffering is going to end and so on. Actually, He has always known us.

Kodaikanal, where I was headed, is a tourist site in Tamil Nadu, a state in southern India.

Forests with eucalyptus trees stand out against the sky, often crossed by an infinite variety of clouds, like tall witnesses of the magnificence of God. The air is intoxicating at 2000m of altitude. At times it is sizzling and light, but at times it can be penetratingly humid. Consequently, I felt heady, albeit happy, all the time .

It was clear from the beginning that my friends were accompanying me and not vice versa, as I had initially thought. They took care of me in an extraordinary and awesome manner throughout the stay which turned out to be a time of outstanding purification.

Life is indeed fascinating, with its successive "revelations" unfolding like Chinese boxes. When you think you have come to the last box, there is still another one, and again another one... There is no end to discovering something new and interesting, which gives sense to what seemed absurd just a while before, until we reach the stage in which chaos – or at least what appeared to be so due to our ignorance – becomes perfection.

I was never ill during my stays in India, unlike everybody else, sooner or later, during such travels. The health condition should by no means be linked to the country itself or the climatic, environmental or hygienic-sanitary conditions, as one might be induced to think if one is not familiar with all the circumstances. The less gullible know that, in such occasions, health disturbances can be related to the process of purification which should be respected, without putting additional stress on the body by taking medicines, of course only after a judicious medical check-up has excluded the presence of serious pathologies. I here refer primarily to phenomena like flu, or a sore throat, cough, fever, dysentery and the like, which aren't justifiable by sanitary conditions or food. Whoever has ever visited Said Baba's *ashrams* knows about the high hygienic standards there and that the cleanliness of kitchens and public facilities is entrusted to volunteers operating with maximum good will. In my case, external causes were not accountable for my "attacks of fever". I stopped eating and I had exclusively liquids. I felt weaker and weaker. Nevertheless, I never missed a single *darshan.*

Despite my physical weakness, I would stand in line, waiting to get in, just like everybody else. Recklessly, several times I lightly touched Sai Baba's feet with my hands, being so lucky as to find myself in the front line. One of the two friends, a sensitive clairvoyant, strongly advised me against doing that, claiming that my physical condition was already too feeble and that I should not expose myself directly to His energies since they were too powerful for my debilitated state.

She was almost certainly right because I remember that, as I was touching the feet of the *Avatar*, I felt enraptured in a rarefied atmosphere. While he passed and stopped in front of me, in those few infinite instances it seemed absurd not to take advantage of the opportunity to touch Him and to think about my physical condition instead. To tell you the truth, I couldn't have cared less even if I'd died, there and then.

I went back to my room with a new attack of fever every time. This went on for several days. Meanwhile, my friend saw "black clouds" (using her own words and unaware of any better terms myself) coming out of my body and thought that was the outcome of my work at the psychiatric hospital, where I had absorbed (according to her) plenty of negative energy[43]. I could understand the meaning of her words much better years later and see how truthful they had been.

The other friend took care of my health. She used to wash me and even fed me and stayed up, like a tender mother during my nightly sleep. I will never forget that tender, loving care, especially because I always tried to be self-sufficient and never allowed anyone to "serve" me except for the period of immobility, during my illness, when I depended on everyone and everything. That was certainly a major lesson to my pride which came out quite harassed from that period of invalidity and, subsequently, semi-invalidity.

Under the circumstances, I would never have imagined doing incredible and unrepeatable things. I had promised to the devotees of the Sai Centre who had never visited that *ashram* that I would be back with a video-documentary so they could admire its beauty. I therefore asked my son to lend me a video camera I'd never used – actually, I'd never touched it before. I would like to point out that, after that incident, I never touched that strange object again. In fact, one of my many drawbacks is technophobia – being unable to handle or utilize any object possessing an electronic mechanism. When it comes to the video camera in question, I knew no more than two of its functions, namely how to use the *on* and the *off* power button.

In a nutshell, I managed to bring the task to its end and filmed not only the natural beauties but also, and this was miraculous to me, Sai Baba in person during the *darshan*, while he was walking towards me and while I was handing down some letters to Him with the other hand, free from the camera. In addition to that, he conceded me another long shot, made from a few meters' distance, during the session of devotional chants (*bhajans*), on Rama Day that coincided with our stay.

There was really nothing more to ask from Him. It was a dreamlike[44] experience. He made sure I would be taken care of with so much love in that place connected with the disturbing experience I'd had, almost as if to reciprocate the care I'd given to that sick person who had been hospitalized, two years earlier. During my stay in Kodaikanal, I dreamt of Sai Baba offering me some food blessed by Him (it is called *prasad* in India) and presenting me with one of His yellow robes He wore on special occasions such as Krishna Day.

He talked about gold, saying that it symbolized light, with a clear reference to the process of alchemic transmutation through which a non-precious metal is transformed into gold. His intention was to explain the analogy: through the spiritual search of the true Self, a human being is transformed into a divine creature. He was evidently hinting at my search and urging me to pursue it.

After a few days, I dreamt of Him again, directing a light beam, similar to a laser beam, towards me, straight onto my heart chakra. I felt a strong pain in my chest but was not worried at all. That energy was coming from Him and I was perfectly at peace because of His positivity. God wishes nothing except our wellbeing, in every circumstance. And so, the trip was indeed characterized by purification.

The clairvoyant friend of mine claimed I had absorbed, like a sponge, all the pain and suffering of others and advised me to learn to differentiate, in the future, before allowing anyone to approach me and above all to keep a certain degree of distance and avoid being hugged by everyone without distinction, until I was sufficiently "screened".

I hadn't acquired a permanent inner balance yet, to safeguard me against external influences. I don't have the gift of clairvoyance, but I know I have always been capable of feeling other people's pain and suffering. Not knowing much about invisible realms and their respective energies, I had no idea what it meant to be charged with other people's tensions, fears or anxieties.

I can't deny I was in a way alarmed by this revelation, having suffered for a week, emanating "dark clouds"[45] day and night (my friend watched me during my sleep as well).

In the years that followed, other clairvoyant people reasserted that I had that predisposition (to absorb other people's emotions) and advised me to avoid possible emotional involvements.

I gradually realized that the only screen against negative energies consisted in having a pure heart, untainted by any type of shadow and so I kept orienting myself in that direction, with the constant and caring support of the Divine Master who was always with me (and with anyone who was ready to feel Him in the heart).

Comprehension is the first and putting into practice the second step. Through His teachings, I realized that having a pure heart was the most important quality in a human being, indispensable for reuniting with the true Self or the divine spark within – itself being the source of power and strength. Hence, there was nothing else left for me to do other than putting His message into practice.

Sai Baba says: *"Do not give in, do not be mean, do not sell out your self-respect; strength is your nature, you are the children of immortality."*

A wise man governs his own stars; only a fool remains in their slavery, since the stars predispose destiny without determining it, as I said earlier.

Let us boldly claim back the right to belong to the light. We are all children of the light. Some of us dismiss this notion and get lost in the darkness for entire cycles of lives on earth and end up considering themselves to be the children of darkness, out of ignorance. They say that the children of light conceal, within their DNA[46], the code of true Knowledge (I cannot prove this statement though) and that they can be distinguished from the children of darkness (despite being brothers and children of the same Father and Mother, i.e. God) by their involvement in the world and their humanness, as they have come to help the others, while the children of darkness are on earth to satisfy their own needs, in their illusory, desperate and vain search for happiness. The children of light are aware that the only happiness awaits them in the realm of the Spirit, once they take off the clothes, that is, when they leave their physical body to go to live in the Kingdom of God.

Don't you know the story about the ugly duckling that felt so and was considered as such only because it dismissed the fact that it was a swan? It grew up and the day arrived for it to reclaim its lost dignity.

That journey experienced on the brink of reality, due to the naturalistic landscapes immersed in the mist or for the unexpected showers which seemed to swell everything or for my constant physical malaise and confusion (altitude contributed to my state of chronic anaemia), generally improved my communion with the Spirit and strengthened my internal, increasingly close and intimate dialogue with the Divine Master.

Back home, strangely enough, sensations I considered long forgotten returned after about a decade, dating back from my spine surgery. As if I had suddenly become much older, not by several years but by several centuries – the kind of aging that enveloped the history of humanity, from its origins. It was of course a most unpleasant sensation.

I believed that the true Self had me experience that to help me distract from the physicality. Only when we get rid of the attachment to the body can we perceive the Spirit within. My determination to progress on the enlightened path was getting firmer every day and I could envision it more and more clearly.

I kind of retired from the world for a few weeks and dreamt about Sai Baba coming to visit me.

Whenever I dreamt about Him, I would wake up in the middle of the night and it felt like daytime, regardless of the hour. I woke up at two o'clock that night to write down what I had just experienced in the dream.

I was in India, at the *ashram*, in the company of a girl. She was about thirteen, dressed in white and a student of one of the schools founded by the Divine Master. Thanks to her I could approach Sai Baba in that instance, outside the *ashram*. He was talking to an Indian elderly devotee.

After the conversation, he made a sign to us to come closer. I kissed His hands and He looked at me with infinite love and asked who the girl's mother was. I replied with a question: *"Am I doing enough?"*

He replied:*" Instead of being the President,[47] you will have to do something similar to what I am doing, considering your disposition to humility; you must get involved in the discovery of the new world."*

In my dream I could perfectly understand what He was referring to but when I woke up, in the middle of the night, I found myself amazed and confused for that divine revelation. It took me years to comprehend who the girl's mother was. He is the Divine Mother to all of us. He *is* Love. I recognized myself[48] in that girl who represented the ideal of purity.

I will try to describe the itinerary which conduced me to the discovery of the new world, as announced by Him.

The symbolic value of the reality in a dream is even more poignant than that of the wake because truths emerge that are otherwise shrouded and covered up by the mind during wake, because rational consciousness censors everything that is potentially jeopardizing for its integrity.

To remove the veil of ignorance which hides reality from us, we must work constantly and tenaciously so that we don't miss all the messages the unconscious mind (an instrument of the Self) sends in the form of symbols, dreams, etc., to assist us in our discernment.

It is written in the Apocalypse that Truth must be taught in a hierarchical order because what enlivens the strong, could kill the weak.

Every revelation has its evil side – one man's meat is another man's poison. It is like saying that the fire of Truth burns when it does not illuminate.

Sai Baba addresses each person in a language he/she can understand and He specifies with infinite compassion[49] that whenever telling the truth might hurt someone, we'd better remain silent.

We must proceed gradually, as when we learned to read and write. We first learned the letters of the alphabet by heart. Likewise, if we want to learn to feel with the heart, we must also know and be able to explain the meaning of the events from the surrounding reality written in the book of life – our life experience, expressed in symbols, numbers, ideas, thoughts, messages from the world of nature and the realm of the Spirit.

As I said before, we are what we think, since thinking is equivalent to creating. We are also what we feel "with the heart", as feeling is equivalent to experiencing the knowledge of the heart and not that of the mind – which is not true knowledge. This can be of aid in "creating" a better world because intuitive intelligence helps us discover what we really are, as opposed to what we think we are, according to our rational mind. This realization modifies our very thoughts, offering us the possibility to think and create anything – from a new personality to a new world – by means of our will to do good.

All thinkers live in the world created by them, but which world did Sai Baba mention in the dream? I didn't know it yet.

It took me years of hard research within and without to unravel that question. His loving guidance enabled the realization of specific facts which illuminated the path I am still treading.

John the Apostle claimed: *"In the beginning was the Verb, the Verb was with God, the Verb was God."*

The Verb is the Word of God; the Word is God. God symbolizes an idea; we all symbolize an idea, the idea of "man".

Therefore, if we can discern the idea behind the symbol, we can trace the Universal Soul that permeates it.

To feel at one with the blueprint of all things – and consequently that multiplicity is just an illusory game – will give us Power, Wisdom, Love, or the divine attributes we need to speak and not only feel with the heart. In other words, we will know the language of Truth.

Power is righteous behaviour associated with force because greatness and righteous behaviour are inseparable, as there can be no greatness without righteousness. With willpower and righteous behaviour, man acquires the "power" to sublimate everything he is fed by, the power to "divinize" himself and become a "divine creature", or a solar angel.

It is therefore evident that there can be no real power in evil. Power resides only in goodness, in light and in righteous behaviour (*Dharma*), as we can see from the evidence provided by the world and the society we live in. Despite the omnipresence of evil, the Ruler of the World remains to be God, representing the power of light into which everything converges, sooner or later.

The power of evil, with all its derivations, is manifest only in the absence of goodness; it is but a chimera, a fruit of seduction and a powerful instrument of the ego whose great destructiveness is still underrated by man. In fact, it cannot manifest in the presence of the divine essence, or the pure life energy in man.

And that is why we are attracted by the world of matter and driven away from the world of the Spirit, because to "see God" we must turn our back to worldliness as one cannot serve two masters – God and the world – at the same time.

The laws regulating the world of matter say that opposites, the positive and the negative, attract each other, whereas similar objects (plus and plus or minus and minus) repulse each other. This entails the perpetuation of separation, opposition, division and disharmony and an implicitly unsuccessful attempt to overcome them, as long as we are anchored in the world of matter and duality.

Life in a physical body, never disjoined from suffering, derives from the union of opposites, or attraction for dissimilar objects. So, transcending physicality or the individual self is the pathway to freedom from pain. Once we have transcended the physical dimension of duality, the laws regulating the Spiritual dimension follow the similarity-attraction principle, to guarantee perfect harmony and unity.

Love, divine essence and true peace belong to the dimension of Oneness, or the Spirit (the 5th dimension) and not to the material dimension of duality (the 3rd dimension). Hence, Love is Unity and it knows no counterparts such as hatred, fear, discord and the like.

When man acquires inner power stemming from a righteous life, lived according to the will of God, he is given access to the knowledge of the Spirit (of Love and Truth). This wisdom is never separate from humility, enabling us to maintain the fear of God, obedience to His Will and the respect and understanding for our fellow men. The two divine attributes, namely power and wisdom, open the heart to Love. At that stage we become Love. The Verb, the word of Truth and the Christ as Christ Consciousness, are the very same thing: the language of Love, of the heart, dictated by the Spirit within. This is the language shared by all humankind, the tongue understood by everyone because what springs from the heart unifies (the will of good), whilst what comes from the mind divides (desire).

Once again, just as fear is a universally proved negative emotion, we can state the same thing regarding free, unconditional Love: it is a sentiment or rather a condition universally acknowledged as positive. That also confirms the fact that we are all in a state of Unity, that is, Oneness, which is Love.

Be pure and you will find the Self within your heart. Be Love and you will find the unity of creation. Everything will be light, freedom, happiness and peace when you start seeing God in everything and in every creature.

This means bringing Heaven down to earth, that is, Paradise into our lives and around us. The Kingdom of Heaven is within.

That was the new world (the 5th dimension) Sai Baba mentioned in the dream. That revelation had an explosive effect and gave me the energy I needed to carry on with my fascinating life project.

Step by step, learning to see things from a broader viewpoint, equidistant and increasingly unattached from the ties of the physical world, we unveil a new world around us: a wonderful world populated by angelic creatures, both corporeal and incorporeal, spending their "lives" only to bring us support and aid. Many of us have already experienced them and many more will do so as well in the future. They are the earthly angels. The 4th dimension of emotions, or the astral dimension, manifests within the 3rd dimension, the earthly dimension we live in. Likewise, the 5th dimension, the spiritual one, manifests in our search for salvation from duality through unconditional Love.

As I was engaged in a full time self-inquiry, it became increasingly evident that I would be able to read from the book of life in general and from my own in particular, provided I purified myself and got rid of all the limitations and flaws of the ego.

There was no other way for "impersonal", Holy Love to free me from the imprisonment of the ego and make me enjoy my own divine beauty, so that I could finally find, within, the ideal I had always pursued outside. This void had caused all my suffering up till then, manifesting in the form of angst, lack of satisfaction and restlessness – emotions experienced from my earliest age.

In other words, the complementary, divine inner part, the real Self, the spiritual essence, the divine spark (the greatest fortune a man possesses), was hidden behind the ego, waiting to be discovered so that I could regain my long searched completeness.

I believed I was holding in my hand the solution to the enigma of my unhappiness and that of mankind, but in my hands there was only the illusion of a victory conceived again by my mind.

This interval of "inner embroidery" lasted for many years before I could see or, better, feel that it was "completed" during an encounter with my true Self.

In those years I never gave up or doubted that I would make it and achieve inner fulfilment thanks to the inner divine essence.

Some time elapsed after my last dream of Sai Baba, when I found myself in India again, during an astral journey (out-of-body experience) – I subsequently learned the term for that kind of experience. I first thought they were simply dreams. Well, He invited me to a work meeting at Puttaparthi and so I found myself in India in a flash, in flesh and blood (so I thought).

When the meeting was over I crossed the sidereal space studded with diamonds – that was my perception of the stars that seemed to surround my nonmaterial thought-form. I felt as if I were studded with stars, that is, I knew I was myself but the body was not there any longer, just as on my way there – at the speed of thought, wrapped in a vortex of air which I felt as the Divine presence. So I found myself back home.

The thing I was mostly impressed by – although I experienced it as something very natural, as if I had been well accustomed to travelling with my thoughts and cover such distances in a split second – was the strange, entirely new sensation of being on my own in the universe, at the same time being its integral part, inseparable from the All. I wasn't afraid of the darkness of the sidereal space, or the brightness of the stars. I was at one with God, but even to say this is not really appropriate, because it limits what is unlimited by its own nature. I felt it as such. Words cannot express what I really felt, apart from this statement: I felt fused with "Infinity", or with "Nothingness".

I felt I had no limits or boundaries and realized that melting with the Absolute cancelled the dualities. I was all and nothing. There was neither fear nor solitude – only fulfilment and peace.

Since then I have always been certain that life continues in the integrity of thought beyond this material world. Thought extends its existence beyond the physical body, in the form of the mental body.

It is thought that creates matter and not vice versa, under the direct guidance of the Spirit as the divine spark. The physical body ceases to live when the divine essence (the vital blow of the Spirit) abandons it. Subsequently, other bodies gradually move away from it, namely the ethereal, astral, and mental body, fading one after another, in brief intervals, leaving the inert matter of which the physical body was composed, to disintegrate into dust.

In the so called nothingness, in that nonmaterial dimension in which I happened to be, intellectual capacities are perfectly efficient. I was aware of my existence and I continued "being" myself, although I was no longer in the physicality – the only reality I had known till then.

Therefore, thought (or energy in the form of thought) makes use of the human brain to express itself in the physical dimension of human life but it does not need it in the higher dimensions.

For analogy's sake, this can be proved with individual awareness. When we are in the state of wake, individual awareness is indispensable for us to live and relate to the world appropriately, but it disappears in the state of deep sleep and dream, without impeding a parallel life which is at times even richer in terms of content and creative sprouts with respect to daily life. We sometimes meet people leading a flat and empty life during the day, with an intense and satisfying oneiric life at night.

I went on with my everyday routine trying to establish a connection, whenever possible, with the Absolute, to receive a confirmation that the contact established with the Divine was still alive.

I often made questions to the Spirit, or asked for confirmations. I once spotted a scarab that seemed to have materialized out of nothing in the room where I used to write or read. Or, a robin appeared on my window or outside, in the garden. For me, their appearances were expressions of the Spirit in my surrounding.

I took my research very seriously and continued to study and contemplate, without a break. I sometimes forgot that life was also about the joy and lightness of being. However, the Spirit did not forget and, whenever I became oblivious to that, it promptly drove me to look for books, open the pages and read about whatever was necessary for me to bear in mind, whatever I was neglecting in that given moment, such as that God is Joy, God is Life, God is Love, Life is Love and therefore we should make the most of it.

When the above mentioned episode occurred, I was rather tired and fatigued. As I read those words, I recalled that Sai Baba had told me the same words during the first interview and so for me it was a double confirmation of His care in my regard. This awakened my drowsed energy and put me back on the track.

I was thinking a lot all the time, worried about the fact that I didn't see in my environment much interest for the issues which absorbed my life, like the question of death, for example, as the only thing which empowered man's awareness. Death has always been a taboo and people usually chose not to discuss it. When it came to destiny, it seemed that no one was interested in being unhooked from their personal *karma*.

The enlightened sage Aurobindo, like Sai Baba, said: *"Man is in love with his chains."* and I was beginning to see the truth of that.

Why did I feel so different, why did I engage in matters which did not interest others, and yet I considered them of vital importance?

I was delving in similar topics when I received another gift from Heaven.

I dreamt about meeting an eighty-year-old Indian sage, very tall and thin, of noble bearing. He was wearing a robe, candid like his long hair and beard. It was a celestial vision. He came to greet me and handed me something. Standing in front of him, I noticed how short I was compared to him (he was nearly two meters tall). I saw he was holding a case in his hand. He said: *" The secret of your initiation is inside this case."* I simply replied that I knew I would be initiated by a master introduced to me by Sai Baba because He was not going to initiate me personally. In my dream everything was crystal clear. But when I woke up I was quite confused and could not understand the meaning of the case, or of my initiation either. The detail about Sai Baba sending another master to me seemed totally inappropriate.

After years of contemplation and experience, the entire content of the dream came true in real life which, ironically enough, seemed like a dream.

The events that took place later on were truly on the borderline of reality. Three years later I actually met that old Indian sage and after six years I was initiated into meditation by another master.

As I went on, progressing on my spiritual journey, the Spirit was making sure that I had everything I needed for my growth. I, on the other hand, was only trying to do my very best, without expecting anything in return.

There were moments when I felt all-powerful and was preoccupied with that. I was concerned that the discoveries I was gradually making would make me proud. The inner voice said: *"Behave well, with a pure heart, and I will give you anything you ask for."* My requests concerned the knowledge of the Spirit because I was sure that those were the fruits I wished to collect and give to the others. I have always believed that learning (true knowledge) belonged to everybody and that it was not in anybody's ownership. It was supposed to be shared among all those who were interested in it.

The deeper I went in my research and the more unattached I was from my own environment, also because I couldn't find anybody to fully share my experiences with. This gave me the sensation that people were even more unreal than what I had initially believed.

However, it didn't prevent me from enjoying a childish behaviour of ludicrous gaiety, like chasing the wind or dancing under the rain, so intensely that I was sometimes overwhelmed by the feeling of inner fulfilment. It was as if I had inhaled a laughing gas, as if I was intoxicated, experiencing an inexplicable light-heartedness.

Transforming ourselves is a divine task. For me, it was wonderful to imagine being a direct channel of the Spirit one day. I had to progress and evolve, until the individual self flew into the universal Self, to become the divine mirror in which His light was fully reflected. Happiness resides within us, like an inexhaustible fountain of Love, waiting to be discovered, so that everyone could quench their thirst. Those fully perceived moments allowed me to feel increasingly confident about the presence of the divine essence within.

I ardently hoped for the day to arrive when I would be permanently imbued in that awareness.

I felt I had nothing more to do with the rules and laws of the world. The only thing that counted for me was the voice of God, which transcended common morals to take us across the threshold of the golden gate of knowledge.

When we hear and recognise that "Voice", we remain enchanted and captured forever. Since Love has the power to transform everything it touches, as soon as I started loving my destiny, it became something special and unique to me.

I asked Sai Baba, every day, to fill every vacant space in my heart with Love. He heeded my prayer and filled it with Him.

So I found myself ready to leave for India for the third time that year. Sai Baba was realizing my dream to be there at least once in my lifetime on the sacred and magic festivity – at Christmas.

I spent forty days with Him, including Christmas, which is observed Puttaparthi due to the numerous Christians among the devotees of Sai Baba, coming from all over the world.

As always, that stay was also totally different from the rest of my stays at the *ashram*. I imposed a very strict discipline upon myself from the beginning, in terms of timing and daily tasks, isolated in my inner world. I used to spend eight to nine hours a day at the temple. They were hours of waiting, spent in morning and afternoon prayer. I did not know why I was behaving like that, but I felt it was the right thing to do. My ego often complained against the many restrictions. I would ask Sai Baba why He kept telling everybody: *"Be happy"* in every circumstance. Weren't we supposed to continue suffering on the spiritual path, although it was supposedly the calmest, safest and truest pathway in this fake world? The question was really naive but I was unaware of that at the time. My ego formulated the questions and caused the very suffering I asked explanations for from God, instead of looking for the answers inside. This is how I actually realized that the individual self or the ego resisted "merging" with the universal Self and did not allow me to surrender to the Divine and become His "possession", to experience unconditional, impersonal Love.

It was clear that, in the heart, there was place for only one Love – the Love for the All, or Oneness (God). It enables us to love unconditionally and to reconcile ourselves with the entire Universe, that being the only condition to eradicate suffering. Nevertheless, my awareness wasn't high enough to enable me to exit the perverse game of the ego.

During the long waits, twice a day, at the *Mandir* (temple), expecting to see Sai Baba, I would abandon myself to the blue sky, following the swallows' low and sinuous flights (it was a dance of heavenly harmony), admiring the progressive modelling of the clouds cut into the blue colour of infinity. It was always a wait full of magic sacredness. I was glad to gaze at the shining, bright gold of the temple domes where Sai Baba lived, carved into the blue sky. I could almost fuse with the colour of the Spirit (gold), until I heard the divine spark palpitating within (the inner dweller, the true Self).

I understood the subtle meaning of the expression I'd often heard since childhood: "to have a golden heart". Those who are constantly aware that they live for the others and not for themselves, seeing their own reflection in others or, better, the reflection of God (the divine within), they have a golden, or a pure heart. Is all humankind and the entire creation a reflection of God?

I dreamt of Sai Baba one of those days, in a magnificent cathedral, bigger than St. Paul's cathedral in Rome. He was passing through the crowd in the packed church. As He was approaching me, I breathed my yearning to fuse with the Absolute.

I would like to make a point here.

I was convinced at the time (a conviction created during my illness, about ten years earlier) that I would have to leave my worldly life on a certain date, precisely a year from then.

I thus believed that that Christmas was going to be the last Christmas of my life, in this world. My mute and sorrowful cry was accompanied by a prayer: I was asking Him to give me the strength to transform my spiritual search into a creative work (creativity is linked to the Spirit) that would "sing" His presence and His might to mankind, or at least to those who were ready to listen, or hear the "song"[50].

In one of the messages I received, He turned to me and invited me to sing the Glory of God. "Sing, sing, sing", He repeated three times.

I thought I was running out of time and thus I felt the need for my request to be granted the soonest. This would allow me to finalize what I felt like a task useful for the others too and, in this way, my worldly life would end with a flourish.

The prayer was answered in a couple of days. As if guided by His hand, I went to the central area of the *ashram* and stopped in front of a blackboard displaying one of His quotations daily.

That day, I could read the following words: *"One must be firm, powerful, unyielding, like the eternal snow on the highest tops of the Himalayas, unaffected in their purity by the tumult and noise of the bazaar of the mind. If you put your passions and emotions under the control of your supreme nature, the Lord will take the responsibility of your progress in His direction: the Universe will be your friend.*

This does not mean that you are without shelter or guardian. He is always by your side, manifest as consciousness, as a companion or guide".

Through that message Sai Baba was affirming that the situation was under control. He was taking care of me. Still, "divine discontentedness" was tormenting me without relent.

For those who, albeit unconsciously, yearn for the Absolute, there is no life of ease in the world of relativity. I knew that but could not be at peace all the same, although I felt I was on the right track. I didn't know there were many more years in front of me and, above all, that Divine Intelligence always sized the ordeals according to our strength.

Those three travels in that year were such a grace – bathing three times in the Absolute (using faith instead of soap and practice instead of water) was very useful for my purification from thoughts and negative energy. Obviously, the seekers of the Absolute are fed by purity and by being close to divinity, as Sai Baba stated: *"As long as I can share every day with you, from the beginning to the end, nothing can destroy you in between."* He is nourishment and He is purity.

I was trying to permanently integrate rationality and intuition with the awareness of the Spirit, which was beginning to blossom in me, timidly.

This slow, gradual inner evolution helped me understand that Divine Love or the Love for the Light was the longing for the Absolute which, paradoxically, was the longing for renouncement (of what is relative) – and not for conquering or dominating, which are intrinsic of human love. I also realized that pleasure was undifferentiated ecstasy, without object, and not the attraction of opposites. Anything can be transformed into joy if an individual, after feeling separated from the All, finally discovers to be an integral part of the Cosmos – a Cosmic Creature.

I learned that nothing was impossible because impossibility was the starting point of all possibilities, the total sum of the major possibilities which are yet to be realized.

Dreams remain dreams until we realize them, when they become the so-called "reality".

God was no longer in my thoughts. It became "*the* thought".

That stay was longer than my previous stays in India and it allowed a more profound connection with the Divine Master.

I happened to be in the front line almost every day and so I could see Him from close up when He was passing by during the *darshan*.

I kissed His hands a few times and touched His feet as well. But what really warmed my heart was His intense look. We exchanged glances several times and He lit a fire within me which increasingly nourished my will (His Will, in fact) to proceed on my spiritual path.

All those days spent in His close and permanent physical Presence left an indelible trace in my heart. True Love knows no barriers and it goes "into the heart of things". The more we Love, the more we are at one with the object of Love, with God. The climax of Divine Love is a total fusion between the lover and the Beloved, the soul and the Spirit. It is the mystic matrimony of the Self and the soul, which is self-realization.

I hadn't achieved peace of mind yet, and so my knowledge remained in the mental sphere – although I knew that the union with God was the right conclusion of the spiritual journey.

Divine Wisdom has its way to unblock situations which have become an obstacle in the process of development. We recover our wits through a shock: a collision with tailor made circumstances force us to think, see and act differently and our progress is prompted. That extended absence from Italy, from home and from my son, was in many aspects a shock and it marked an important stage on my journey to God.

Being away from everything and everybody for such a long time served to reconsider many things from a different angle, see people and situations from a more distanced perspective and be more objective. Once again I noticed the emptiness and the transience of all the things that had been my daily life until then.

I could clearly and sharply see that our task was to become masters of our destiny and realize unhoped-for dreams, like replacing hatred with Love, mistakes based on ignorance with knowledge, the pleasure-pain dichotomy with happiness, the birth-death dichotomy with spiritual power, diversity with unity, war and discord with peace and harmony....in a word, to realize God within.

I also noticed that undesired behaviour repeated itself not so much for the lack of awareness as for the lack of putting what we know into practice. We sometimes deceive ourselves by pretending not to know about something, for the fear of losing what we are attached to, and thus some of the greatest impediments to our development often derive from not being sincere with ourselves.

Apparently, everybody knows that God is their best friend, judging from what they say. However, when it comes down to facts or everyday practice, this truth is neglected or put aside. People continue to flounder in the ocean of life, forgetting that they can swim. I could see it each time I tried to help someone who had asked me for advice. My function – no longer as a psychiatrist but as a spiritual aide, of which I received confirmation years later – was to assist those in search for the Self, even if the person didn't have a clear understanding of what he, or she, was looking for.

Initially, it is a blind search and we don't even know that we are searching for the Divine within, or the true Self, because our starting point is the darkness of materiality that envelops the Self being nonetheless part of us.

I felt on the same boat with the person asking for help, the difference being that I had an intuition (Intuition is a spiritual faculty beyond the intellect; it is the eye of wisdom made of Love in terms of devotion, compassion, peace and truth.) about where the boat was heading to and what was to be done to reach the destination.

I used to say that I loved bringing the Light (i.e. the Divine Knowledge) I had found in the suffering to those who hadn't found it in their suffering yet. That was my adage.

The Universe is the expression of the joy of God; it is a child's game. To grasp this vision of reality, you have to be able to see the light, or to see, with your heart, the light as a divine presence in us and everywhere around us. This is extremely important. At the beginning, when this light starts to manifest, we feel as we are going blind until we gradually begin to really "see". However, those who are satisfied with the small, ephemeral things of the world, cheap gratifications or mediocrity, have never been fascinated by the light I am talking about.

God's response to the search is obscured until the heart is completely pure. God and Nature are not unlike a boy and a girl, playful and in love, hiding from each other and fleeing as soon as they get a glimpse of each other, only to seek, chase and catch each other again. I used to stop now and then to dwell on God's image and address Him, in a monologue: *"You are the God of everything and nothing, you are the Absolute and the relative, good and evil, joy and pain, light and darkness, beauty and ugliness, power and weakness and courage and cowardice. My heart is Yours. Take it, so it can merge with You, so there may never be an "I" that sees, thinks or lives in duality, but is forever at one with You".*

Once, as I was dwelling upon this, Sai Baba appeared under the porch of the *Mandir* and looked in my direction. Without a second thought, I expressed my love for Him with an affectionate, yet typically western gesture: I sent Him a kiss by slightly touching my lips with my hand. Just as a mirror reflects our image in real time, He contemporaneously brought His hand to His lips and sent the kiss back.

Surprised and amused, the mixed crowd of Indian and western women applauded with delight.

I was the only one who knew, in my heart, the secret of that gesture which reunited me with Him, in a profound intimacy.

I learned that egotism was the only sin, that meanness was the only vice, hatred the only crime and that all the rest could be easily transformed into a goodness of highest virtues: Courage and Love, emanating a unique warmth that can transform doubt into trust. Sai Baba infused courage and filled my heart with Love.

I've learned that when you love, you love every thing and this creates fulfilment – the fulfilment which annuls every void, concern, fear or doubt.

I've learned that there are two types of soul: those whose intelligence controls the emotions and those whose emotions control the mind. Those who are dominated by emotions are unfortunately bound to be slaves of their destiny and can never master themselves. Divine Grace is bestowed only upon the former category.

As for the latter group, God is merely present in their consciousness as a witness, without guiding their steps dictated by free will and emotions, as they are still subjugated to the illusions of the world of duality (matter-Spirit) littered with desires, passions, attachments and addictions.

These souls have a long way to go until they are purified and able to transform passion into affection and affection into unconditional Love and definitely overcome the dominating fear.

The fear manifesting in this case, including the fear of Divine Love, apparently paradoxical, is in fact linked with the idea of losing our familiar identity, the idea of an abyss we might fall into upon losing our ego. In the absence of our faith in God, this fear reveals the lack of Love or the inability to Love.

Due to these shortages, such souls are content with a sexuality which is not on the same wavelength with the other levels, namely the emotional, mental and spiritual level, and they call it Love. Yet, Love is not sexuality in terms of mere physical attraction or mere physical pleasure which is the fruit of the ego. There can be no Love in the presence of the ego.

Jesus used to say: *"No union is more sacred than matrimony".*

But which matrimony was he speaking about?

"The chain connecting two souls in love is forged in Heaven and no man can ever undo it. The two souls are united by Divine Love." (We continue to speak about souls and not about physical bodies.)

"Physical passion between a man and a woman can create a union of two beings, just like oil and water. Then, a priest, or a civil servant if it is a civil proceeding, can forge a chain and unite the two individuals. This, however, is not a real matrimony. It is a legalized counterfeit and in this case the imitation is displayed before the eyes of God and is guilty of adultery. The priest, or the civil servant, is involved in a perpetuated crime."

In the Sacrament of matrimony, the water of purity (of the heart) becomes the wine of the Spirit. The transformation of water into wine takes place: and this is the explanation of the parable of Jesus. In a "holy" matrimony, two "pure hearts" are at one, in Spirit and Truth. In the future, in the Golden Age, "alchemic weddings" will take place between souls who are on the same evolutionary level. By exchanging pure Love, they will be able to neutralize the possible surrounding negative energies in the "fusion of hearts" and not in the "fusion of sexual intercourse", where the attempt to dominate and use the other is predominant, in a power game similar to what we see in the world of animals, because instinctual nature is characterized by the same instincts of survival, conservation of the species and procreation.

Man has a consciousness and a thinking mind thanks to which his life may assume a predominantly animalistic imprint if it is not used appropriately.

Therefore, no priest, or civil servant, has been empowered by God to unite two souls in a conjugal Love. That power comes only from Love itself.

Jesus stated: *"What is therefore the unity of matrimony? Is it contained in a priest's words? Is it a roll of parchment on which priests write the authorisation for the two spouses to live within the bond of the matrimony? Is it the promise made by the two spouses to love themselves until death separates them? Is love passion, subject to human will? Can love be bought or sold, like a sheep? Love is the power of God which connects two souls into a union. There is no power on earth which can dissolve the bond. The bodies can be separated by force, by man or by death, for a short time, but they will meet again. This Divine bond is the union of matrimony. All other unions are a straw in the wind and those who live in them commit adultery. God knows the pure in the heart. Lustful men and women are nothing but creatures of the greedy self (ego). They cannot be united with another person or be at one with God. Carnal eyes will never see God. Men are not considered pure simply if they are unmarried. A lecherous person is adulterous whether married or unmarried. On this level of life, men get married simply to recompense their egotistic self (or to perpetuate the human race) but in the world to come and in the day of resurrection, men will not take upon themselves the vow of marriage. Like the angels and other children of God, they will not unite for the pleasure of the flesh or to perpetuate the human race[51]".*

Just as apostle Philip said two thousand years ago, I could repeat today: "Lord, those who have been united in the bond of the holy matrimony by You are few".

It is not difficult to verify how truthful this statement is. If we look around, we can see discordance, violence, disharmony and absence of Love characterizing the institution of the "family" today, worldwide.

The souls whose intelligence dominates their emotions (and consequently the senses), bask in the Divine Grace and draw the necessary strength from it to face the trials of life, overcome the weaknesses and find the "beacon" or the contact with the Divine Knowledge, that is, with the Christ or Cosmic Consciousness which brings peace, joy, balance and harmony, the indispensable ingredients for attaining God, as Truth and Love.

Once we have identified the "beacon", our confidence in achieving the goal infuses plenty of strength into our veins, so that we can fight, challenge and resist the hardships of life.

How sweetly safe I felt while imagining myself immersed, one fine day, in the source of existence, merged with the Absolute.

I realized that loving God was the most complete form of Love. Experiencing the Love for the Divine leads to loving no one but Him. But then, He resides in all the people we love and in the rest of humankind, in all the natural realms and in the Universe.

My intuition was becoming sharper every day, which was a clear sign that I was on the right path.

Intuition allowed me to "see" (with the heart's eyes) God in the person of Sai Baba, both as nonmaterial, creative energy and as a divine incarnation, vesting the Spirit with His characteristic form/non-form and fluctuating in His solemn, elegant gait, both humble and sublime. The Self was guiding my pace, still shy and insecure, and I was in safe hands. I understood that being myself meant being spontaneous, simple, disinterested, sincere, open and natural, as opposed to being unnatural, artificial, insincere, closed, self-interested and complicated, like the victims of spiritual ignorance, hypocrisy and incoherence of the ego.

Hypocrisy is therefore severely condemned by Sai Baba – and by Jesus – because it leads to the mortification of the Spirit, precluding the soul any possible possibility to evolve and return home.

Under the guidance of the Divine Master (within), I flowed like water, without making resistance, being certain that true freedom resided in the acceptance of our divinity. Perhaps this was the "Way of the Tao", i.e. the way of the flowing water.

In a certain way, I transcended the moral patterns of behaviour which never suited me. Therefore, whenever I happen to "stumble" on them again, my reaction is calmer than it used to be in the past. I am also less intransigent about hypocrisy and other people's lack of coherence. In the past it took much less to upset me.

I realized that it was not the good and the bad but the wise and the foolish and the true and the false who determined the quality of everyday life. An authentic person is wise, whereas a hypocrite is merely foolish because he/she keeps ignoring the true essence, which leads to depression and perpetual lack of satisfaction.

The union with God manifesting as Cosmic Consciousness within was my far-fetched aim. The Divine Psychiatrist, Sai Baba, made me understand that I had to keep tempering my ego. I was not an "empty vessel" yet. I was not ready to be "filled up" with Him and help others by setting an example for having achieved my aim.

I could see the "pinnacle" in the distance, dominating the valleys and the plains of the world, and dreamt of climbing it one day. In reaching this dream, I always hoped to find a way for the rope to pull up other people too – all those who shared with me the desire for a mystical ascension and truth, or those I knew nothing about, who felt attracted by the same yearning – out of solidarity or simply out of Love.

From the very start of my spiritual journey, I have always connected Oneness with multiplicity, the Divine with the human, the Wings of God (Love and Courage) with man's progress.

I felt God closer and closer to me, or better, I felt Him within me and I was no longer a woman or a man. I *was* and that was enough. Jesus used to say that we should become eunuchs to enter the Kingdom of Heaven, in the sense that we should not fall a prey to lust. Sai Baba claims we should become androgynous to be able to see God. Was the Holy Spirit about to set me free from the slavery of physicality, preparing me to enter the Kingdom? I could not tell. I was still unable to "merge" with everything around and make my heart equally fond of beauty and ugliness, the great and the small, the old and the young, the healthy and the sick. I had not freed myself yet from the illusion of worldly things and was still perceiving the dualities, except for certain moments in my everyday life, when I became suddenly overwhelmed by a feeling of Oneness with the All and could no longer tell beauty from ugliness, when everything was magical and useful for seizing that holy essence which unified everything, as sublime as it is simple. In those instances, the mind was unsuitable for distinguishing determinate concepts and unable to grasp, from its own meanders, the categories of the twofold reality (beautiful, ugly, good, bad, etc.) ... and reason remained astonished.

I would then wonder how come I was not making the difference between the various faces. They all looked beautiful to me. It took me a while to realize that in such moments, out of the blue, I was no longer viewing the surrounding world with my physical eyes, i.e. with my mind, but with the eyes of the heart, or the vision of the heart.

Life would be wonderful if we could experience this condition permanently. Those light "flashes" were actually evidence of the presence of a much vaster light source residing in each of us, however incredible it may sound.

This unidentified and unutilised fortune lies hidden in the mine of our spiritual heart. This is our treasure.

NOTES: CHAPTER VI

43. To put it simply, the condition of wellbeing is the manifestation of positive energy and vice versa, the condition of illness is a manifestation of scarce energy or negative energy.

44. I could hardly believe my eyes when I saw, back home when we projected the film, that it was really well done.

45. That expression reminded me of a Catholic Renewal group I had attended many years before, where someone mentioned "dark clouds" and "white clouds" to define negative and positive energies.

46. Apart from the esoteric interpretation of this statement (which I am not going to elaborate), I must specify that science (Molecular Biology) is moving in this direction, coming up with the hypothesis of a "divine" gene within the human genome (see *Time* magazine, of 29th November 2004).

47. The mandate of the President of the Sai Centre was coming to an end.

48. I refer to the girl resurrected to the Light of the Spirit by Jesus, as He pronounced the words: "*Talitha Kumi!*"(A parable of Jairus' daughter), Gospel according to Mark 5:41.

49. By compassion I mean balance between strength (fear of God) and mature Love (indulgence), made possible through the experience of suffering, which in the case of the Divine is the metaphoric suffering of the entire human race.

50. *Bhagavad-Gita,* the Hindu Holy Scripture, actually means "the divine song".

51. Extract taken from the Aquarian Gospel.

VII

I slept and dreamt that life was joy. I woke up and discovered that life was service. I started serving and found that service was joy.

Tagore.

God gives us everything we need when we surrender to Him, but what we need is not necessarily what we desire.

So, a whole year passed before I returned to India. In return, Sai Baba often paid me visits in marvellous dreams, as if to make up for my longing to see Him.

Shortly after my return, one night I woke up at four o'clock. I meditated and suddenly dropped off to sleep again.

I dreamt about being at Puttaparthi. Sai Baba had just returned from one of His many customary visits to schools, hospitals, etc. Arm in arm, He presented me to some Indian devotees who were working at the *ashram* as volunteers because I was soon going to start a new job. Deeply moved and thrilled, I asked Him (in English) if the moment had arrived for me to work near Him, that is, in India.

He specified: *"Yes, but you must first balance your backbone. It will not take long, however".* He might have been referring to the seven chakras situated along the spine. He then left us and walked towards the *Mandir,* where he was welcomed by a large crowd. Only then I realized that they had prepared a big feast. Sai Baba looked as if He were about 30 years old (He was actually 70), dancing through huge bunches of flowers, moving His arms gently around in the air, as if drawing invisible circles. Garlands materialized from His hands and fluctuated in the air, dancing with Him. He was looking at me and smiling. I was overwhelmed by a sensation of blissful amazement and could hardly contain my enthusiasm, also because I had never seen Him dance before. According to a Hindu belief, the Universe was materialized from the holy dance of Shiva and Sai Baba is His incarnation. He told me that personally, during the first interview. All of a sudden, I noticed that, in the thousand varieties of colourful flowers, there were also many peacocks, big and small (the spreading of the peacock's tail represents the Cosmic deployment of the Hindu Spirit). Dumbfounded for so much beauty, I asked some Indians, who were also watching the event in admiration and enthusiasm, about the significance of such feasts. They answered it was Peacock Day. I woke up and my heart was beating hard. It was five o'clock in the morning.

Still deeply moved by so much greatness, I got up and wanted to write down my dream.

In Hinduism, the peacock symbolizes immortality, eternal bliss and purity of the heart in terms of giving up of worldly assets. The peacock belongs to the symbolism of the Sun and it represents the power to transform the poison of passion (the killer snake) into the potion of immortality (bliss). It also symbolizes a soul's direct vision of God. When I realized how much grace was bestowed upon me, I started crying warm tears of gratitude to the Divine Master. It was an immense gift He decided to present me with on the anniversary of the first two interviews. It was a confirmation that nothing was closer to us than God, not even a mother or a friend. God is our very breath, the vital energy that pervades and moulds us continually, sustains and makes us feel alive. God is cosmic energy. He is the yin and the yang of Taoism, according to which "*Relationships with the yin and the yang are closer than those with one's own family*" (according to Chinese wisdom, they are the male and the female energetic flows permeating the entire Universe).

Sai Baba is a Master who is difficult to follow because He directs us towards the longer pathway to reach the aim, that of transforming the heart and not something external. In this way, we are faced with our greatest limits. Once we manage to overcome those limits, He assures us there is no going back and we are reassured by His constant presence.

To continue searching for my inner peace and the harmony needed to realize the divine essence within, or spark, or *Atma*, the pathway of devotion was most congenial to me, in addition to discipline, determination, discernment and non-attachment.

I would silently repeat, day and night, the five words beginning with the letter D, Devotion, Detachment, Discipline, Determination and Discernment because their meaning, put into practice, stimulated my spiritual growth.

Every spiritual seeker's primary task is to manifest Love in his actions, thoughts and words and by Love I mean sacrificing the self for the beloved ones, or in other words giving up of the small self, or ego, to realize the true Self, or the divine essence within.

This raises our awareness and we open up to the revelation of Truth, the word of God and the plan He has in store for us.

We have all been created out of kindness but we often utilize our gifts – like the ability to chose, or our free will – inappropriately.

The man's grandeur, or otherwise his pettiness, is determined by the direction he chooses his life to take.

Sai Baba says that the only way to freedom leads through acts of Love, doing good deeds and living a righteous life, because "*Love in terms of thought is Truth, Love in terms of action is Righteous Behaviour, Love in terms of feeling is Peace and Love in terms of understanding is Non Violence. Therefore, Love is Truth, Righteous Behaviour, Peace and Non Violence*".

It is the principle that unites the other four, like wheels of a single cart, the cart of human life in the physical body.

The five Ds embrace the integral message of Sai Baba, and their implementation provides guarantees for a positive life.

After many inner struggles and a lengthy, disquieting silence of the soul, I was finally convinced that everything was pre-established. Actions have already been recorded in the "book of life" and what remains in our power, as free choice, are the intentions behind our actions. If positive, those intentions will settle or cancel the cost or debt we must pay in this lifetime to reach harmony. We have somehow determined our particular type of destiny and enabled the natural law of cause and effect to manifest, having accepted it by returning into the world of matter because this law governs the entire physical universe. If our intentions are negative, they additionally weigh on the load consisting of past debts, for the present and for the future, that is, for the coming incarnations, creating complications, problems and illnesses which serve to purify, correct and revise our behaviour because God, who is Light, never gives up but leads us back to Him, sooner or later.

This truth is the same in all the Creeds in the world, from East to West. All human suffering, of any nature – physical or mental – exists to help us distinguish what is real from what is unreal and it persists until the given human potential is fully developed. In this regard, Sai Baba says that an action is less relevant than the intention behind it. And this is why doing service to assist others is true service only if we are able to see "ourselves" in the others, as a divine expression, or, better, as God. Jesus said: *"Love thy neighbour as thyself".*

When we realize that by doing service to others we are, in fact, serving ourselves, we shall be able to manifest gratitude to those who accept our assistance and that is the greatest gift we can receive. There will be no need then for any external gratification – which is nothing but food for the ego.

The confirmation as to whether we have made the right choice between the positive and the negative intentions comes from our own sensations. In the first case, and only in the first case, we find peace because we are being righteous (*Dharma*), being on the right path. In the second case we encounter suffering because we are pursuing a mistake (*Adharma*) and we are on the wrong path.

It is enough to look inside to understand, without anyone's help, which path we are on and ask ourselves, simply and sincerely, if we are at peace or in conflict with ourselves. The answer should be clear, without ambiguity or falsehood.

The "divine folly" I was living in for years, with time seemed to become increasingly acute instead of chronic.

The road leading to the Divine – unlike the one leading to the world which may initially appear easier and more alluring, only to end up in a prison – is difficult from the start. It is rough at first, compelling and hard, but it later becomes smooth and easy (anybody of good will can check this) as we gain serenity, impassiveness, amiability, brightness and confidence, stemming from our faith in God.

The initial strain of spiritual life is linked to the overcoming of the major obstacles, namely our flaws and attachments, but this occurs to allow pain to destroy what gives origin to suffering. This revelation was revolutionary for me, although the mystics and the sages of all times have spoken about it. There is no evolution without suffering because the renouncement and the distancing, that frighten those who are still firmly connected to the world, represent the royal road to cancelling all the suffering. The pain born from the ego dies with it, that is, it ends when the ego ceases to dominate the individual self and merges with the universal Self.

True suffering is in fact ignorance to which we are condemned as long as we are subdued to the ego and the natural law of cause and effect (*karma*), regulating the physical world.

My faith in God was stronger every day and I was convinced I could reach the goal in my heart only through Him, granting me the access to the Kingdom of Heaven within.

I was moved and upset by the gradual awakening into this new life. The continuous effort to evolve and differentiate between what was relative and what was Absolute, enabled me to catch a glimpse, once in a while, of the described state, in which all restlessness or bitterness would be conquered. I knew I could never give enough to the others before I found light myself.

What could we possibly give to others, if not what we already possess inside?

I did not get tired of knocking on the door of the Absolute, certain that it would open, sooner or later. Perseverance and determination were my inseparable companions, through thick and thin.

I learned by reading Sai Baba's discourses, collated over the Divine Master's sixty years of relentless activity, that the destiny of earth was modified and, likewise, the destiny of every human being could be modified, by Divine Grace.

Sai Baba claims that the dreaded global destruction of the planet will not take place. There will be an evolution in mankind's consciousness that will allow everyone who is ready for that moment, not specified further, to recognise His descent on earth as the *Avatar*, or Divine Incarnation, and participate in His Grace He will bestow on the awakened humanity in the form of Love and Knowledge (Power and Wisdom), as Jesus Christ did with the Holy Spirit. Here is the description of that moment in a text revealed to an enlightened sage with regard to the Gospel of Jesus: *"The Eternal is a musician playing higher and higher notes, whose tone was born from His blow and ascends for one grade every two thousand years. At the end of the sixth of those tones, worlds cross into a new vibration stage. I tell you that I am the Main Artificer of the sixth tone* (it is Jesus Christ speaking), *or the fervour which must make the door of the hearts vibrate in a different manner, at the end of the two thousand years to come. "*

We have reached the end of those two thousand years. Sai Baba is with us. He is here to urge us to open our hearts and manifest the divine spark we all share in the collective awakening into Unity, (through the transition from individual to collective and finally to Cosmic Consciousness), through the etherification of matter. Ether is the forever active divine substance, the Creator and the Creature (Creation), the immense eternal matrix, the fifth element, or quintessence.

A human being is the ethereal vibration of two flows: the positive masculine and the negative feminine, the inseminator and the inseminated, giving birth to the two magnetic laws of polarization and equilibrium that sustain eternity.

This process can take place through the purification of the heart and the elevation of the state of consciousness of each one of us, through Love, spiritual – not technological – Progress and the Insight into what is ephemeral vs. what is eternal. From the fusion of blue (the colour of spirituality) and yellow (the colour of knowledge), emerald green will result, that is, the beam of the "healing heart". Those are the colours of the New Age.

Planet Earth and all mankind have been summoned to take part in the Kingdom of Heaven, in the coming decades. Are we going to accept this divine invitation to enter the 5th dimension with exultation?

The Spirit blows where and when it pleases and it is not going to get out of its way more than it has, because it has been warning us for sixty years already.

We are at the threshold of the deadline for a possible passage from the 3rd to the 5th dimension, which is the spiritual, ethereal dimension (and why not even to the 6th dimension, that of the solar angels, the so-called Paradise), the one closer to ours.

To conceive our divine nature and hence our task on earth is the reason of our very existence, bearing in mind that each of us can modify only his/her own heart and thought.

We live in an age of major changes. To ignore Truth – i.e. the mother of all relative truths, the Truth we can unveil[52] with the faculties we possess as human beings – is a mistake born from religious teachings, wanted by people and not by God. Dependence on an ecclesiastic body to communicate with the Divine encourages the false belief that safety is something external to us – with the church, family, state or job. Throughout the thousands of years of prejudice and preconceptions, dependence on everything external to man has been one of the worst forms of violence, exerted and perpetuated against mankind.

What followed this distortion of reality patently revealed that the "remedy" was more detrimental than the ill cause.

Since Christian (and non-Christian) antiquity, the belief has been that an ordinary person, in the sense of inferiority, could not handle the so-called mystery of faith by himself. Truth is, to this day – and we are in the third millennium – we have been kept in the dark concerning some facts with regard to faith in God which could only bring light into our lives and our consciousness.

For centuries, churches of varied confessions, through their representatives, have arrogated themselves the right to mediate between man and God.

As a living divinity, Sai Baba teaches and shows undeniably that there is no intermediary between man and God and woe betide those who profess themselves as such.

God is there for everyone, belongs to everyone, He is within the range of each atom and *is* every one of its elements. He is in each grain of sand, drop of water, breeze, sun beam and every cell of the human body. We all make part of His plan in the manifest and in the hidden world, no one excluded.

30 years have passed since my father passed away and I have realized that I've been completely transformed. A new life is throbbing inside me and I view the world differently. My taste, my points of reference and my interests have changed. My attention was gradually withdrawn from the outside world and redirected inward.

I thank God every day for the opportunity I was given, to live a second life in the same body. The new life consisted mostly of solitude, silence, meditation, reading, silent conversations with the Divine Master whom I used to call *Swami* (Master), in a familiar manner. At times I committed the sin of (spiritual) pride, believing I was ready for the call and up to any trial coming from Him.

It was definitely an excess of zeal which was put into the right perspective in the years that followed, to the advantage of humility which helped me accept my smallness, which was not meanness but immaturity and scarce awareness.

So many incredible and surprising experiences awaited me, to fill my life, lived for the Spirit, with plenty of magic.

My immature soul did not stop me from imposing challenges on myself, ignoring the risk of not being understood, or misunderstood in my often clumsy attempt to set an example of faith in God.

On the mental plane, the resolve appeared bold and unattainable, but viewed from the heart it was simply inevitable.

In the stillness of my heart I often repeated words of Love for the Divine Master: *"I love you more than anything, take me with you, I am yours, I no longer belong to myself, or to the world"*.

I even lost interest in travelling and stopped marvelling at the beauties of nature. I was only interested in my inner journey, fuelled by those visits to India, to the home of the Father. That was the sense I gave to my visits to Sai Baba. India, fascinating and disturbing at the same time, was just a landscape where my only object of interest, the Divine Master, stood out, giving me the possibility to see Him, listen to Him and be close to His golden aura. Being tied to the material world makes us see diversity in the unity instead of seeing unity in the diversity. This tie gives value to form at the detriment of essence, from which everything is born and which imbues everything.

Still convinced about my imminent death, one day I decided to send a letter to Sai Baba, asking Him to help me break free from the prison of ignorance and the life in the physical body, without awareness – in other words, to end my worldly life. If He took the letter directly from the hands of the person who carried it to India for me, it would signal a positive reply. The reply arrived promptly – Sai Baba did not take the letter. Clearly, the answer was negative.

I put my anxiety aside, I patiently rolled up my sleeves and went on with my struggle, now that the end was not as near and imminent as I had thought for about ten years.

Then one day, while I was walking in the mountain, at high altitude, in the ice and the snow, thinking about the Divine Master, I spotted an ermine in front of me. In its immaculate candour, the little, rarely found animal symbolizes incorruptible moral purity. It chooses extreme sacrifice – or even death – to escape contamination. It lives in immaculate places: in the snow, at high altitudes, or in the Arctic. That encounter was the call for the great commitment: to search for the purity of the heart, the treasure to conquer immortality, to reach the highest pinnacles of the Spirit. In order to be free, paradoxically, we must get rid of ourselves, or better, of the small individual self. Only then, the heart, our precious gem, will be perfectly pure and will be able to actuate the Divine Will and express balance, coherence and harmony.

Not before the individual self (the ego) flows into the universal Self, can we prevail over the eternal enemies of inner peace and the unfathomable calmness of the Spirit, namely fear, doubt, insecurity and lack of satisfaction – manifestations of the fracture between the external and the internal, the relative and the Absolute, the unreal and the real.

When the will of man is connected to the Divine Will, it finds its utmost expression in the power of Harmony.

Sai Baba says that harmony is coherence of thoughts, words and actions and coherence is balance – an indispensable element for attaining true peace.

When there is inner Harmony and perfect balance, there is peace of mind. That premise is necessary to "see" God, the Divine within and without, with the eyes of the heart. I often repeated those words, talking to myself.

I wanted to see Him and meet Him, not only when in India, in His presence, but always, in every moment of my life. I wanted to seize in His look (a beam of gold, emanating an ocean of compassion for all creatures and worlds) and His Love[53], so it could be part of me, forever, to transform me into pure love, in that holy fire burning discretely deep in the heart. He brought that fire to life and I had to keep it alive, like a vestal at the temple of my heart. For this, I still needed His help, although I could see more and more, over the years, that God was actually guiding every little step on my way, patiently, skilfully and kindly. And so *Swami* (Sai Baba) came to my aid with another dream. His Love manifested in one gift after another, through the use of symbols that have not changed over the centuries albeit they are never the same, becoming the state of dream and becoming the state of wake, as the universal non-verbal language, and enriched my consciousness with awareness, or Spiritual Knowledge.

Night time, spent dreaming and in deep sleep, is as important as daytime, when we are awake.

People who knew me smiled at this affirmation, considering it over-simplistic.

I would frequently "turn the hands" of my inner clock and fall asleep at any moment, convinced that I would clarify, in my sleep or in my dream, whatever I couldn't unravel with my mind or with my intuition, which cannot be activated deliberately.

Sai Baba says that, whenever we are faced with a problem we can't resolve, it is enough to repeat the name of God and remain quiet, or go to sleep. The problem will find its way to a solution because if we stay in tune with His message, we don't have to ask for anything. Grace is automatically bestowed upon us. Grace was bestowed upon me also through my dreams.

I dreamt of being in the *Mandir* (at Puttaparthi), together with a large crowd of people during the *darshan*. Sai Baba was passing through the crowd, materializing *vibuthi* for some women. Unexpectedly, he interrupted His elegant, solemn walk and, as if by magic, a passage opened through the crowd separating me from Him. I found myself opposite Him. He was smiling, wearing His pristine white[54] robe, arms stretched out, holding a large white Lingam of light in His hands. He came towards me and handed it to me, like an offering.

Dazed by so much magnificence, I woke up in the middle of the night. I was happy and peaceful. The night seemed to be over and I felt restored. As I said earlier, it always happened that way, whenever I dreamt of Him.

For me, that dream was a divine confirmation of the progress I had made in my inner search. The *Lingam* (the cosmic egg) represents, in Hinduism, the primordial form of creation from which the entire universe originated. It is connected to the microcosm, the centre, the heart, or the pointer of the mind-body scale (the 4th *chakra* is between the three lower and the three upper *chakras*), on whose pans we oscillate from the cradle to the grave.

When I saw the white *Lingam* of bright light, I thought Swami was offering me what I wished to achieve: a large and pure heart containing Love for everyone and everything. In other words, unconditional Love.

He promptly reacted to my desire to see Him and merge into His Love.

Sai Baba defines the *Lingam* as the principle that guides and protects us along the spiritual way. It is the centre of a man's heart and the only provider of Joy, Power, Peace, Love and Wisdom.

"Bring your attention to your inner life so that the Lingam can grant you the first three gifts[55] and then your mind will be comforted by Love and Wisdom".

I read the above lines in one of Sai Baba's talks, a few days after the dream[56]. It was such an extraordinary coincidence. The oneiric experience echoed in me.

In other words, intelligence and will in the service of Love unleash the Power in us, revealing that we are "divine" creatures. It is the power of harmony. Intelligence and will are expressions of our higher nature, while our lower nature is linked to emotions and desires. If we use our higher nature altruistically, or at the service of others, with unconditional Love, we can master the lower nature, that is, the world of emotions, causing our repeated returns to earth, in a human body, according to the natural law of cause and effect, or the law of *karma* (according to Hinduism).

Love comprehends everything: wisdom and ignorance, abundance and poverty, the world of ideas and the soul. Love dissolves everything because it is forgiveness, understanding, sweetness, kindness, and compassion. It even dissolves the *karma*, or the necklace God put around our neck when we were born – the only ornament we are always distinguished by, from one life to another, through the impressed memory of the ancestral, yet so topical principle of "give and take". The part which was temporarily removed from the impenetrable puzzle of Cosmic Consciousness will be quickly put back, considering that a lifetime, brief even from our perspective, is but a fleeting flash in a timeless dimension. And so the best way to annihilate evil is by making progress in goodness and neutralizing it with Love, instead of fighting against it with force.

Sai Baba says: *"Grace is proportional to effort"*.

Divine Grace intervenes when there is devotion, discipline and determination. Many people believe that devotion in the heart is an attribute granted to us by fate, as if to say that it cannot be acquired if it is not there already.

Let us try and think about what happens at birth.

When a child is born, will it not become fond of and progressively nourish a deep affection, which will then turn into deep love towards a mother, or a father, or a substitute playing the role of a parent, strong enough to result into something like the blind trust in the parental figures who raised him, unparalleled to any other future relation to be established in the course of its life?

Experience teaches us that we grow fond of those who take care of us and not of those who brought us into this world.

Affection and trust should be constantly cultivated and nourished, day by day. Trust in those who raised us is not inborn – it is cultivated by the reassuring warmth emanated from the behaviour of those who are close to us, be it a natural parent or otherwise. Trust is fundamental to faith. Without trust, faith withers and it can die.

I experienced something similar many years before, after my father's death, when I thought I had lost trust in God. For no less than twenty years I stood on my own and never spoke to Him, because I felt abandoned.

How can we doubt the possibility of nourishing trust in God, who is the Father and Mother to all of us? Such doubts are based on the spiritual ignorance we were raised in and in which we live. Nobody lets us know that we are divine, but we are taught, inculcated, explained and handed on from previous generations that there is a God outside us and that we can reach Him only under certain conditions.

This is possibly the most tragic aberration that determined the degeneration of human values and their gradual depletion to the point of thwarting the greatness inherent in human nature – the divinity within, as the very best part in every human being.

Nothing is closer to us than God, not even our mother, family or close friend. God is our dearest friend and we are conscious of it, so much so that we complain to Him about our existential solitude.

We can place our total trust in no one but Him, until we surrender completely. There is no greater or more sacred opportunity for a man. When we realize this, loving God is inevitable.

God is the Love that accepts and forgives everybody, it is the only key that opens the door of every heart to truth.

I've read somewhere that:" *The hope of those who are on the side of truth is quick and it flies on the wings of swallows; it transforms kings into divinities and the most humble creatures into kings.*"There is so much truth in those words.

For the "goblet" to be filled, it must be empty. If we wish to fill it with the water of eternal life, we must first empty it from the water of desires and attachments to worldly life. We, or our lives, are that goblet. How much space is there left in us for the Spirit, in our lives dominated by pleasure, greed, thrift, or simply egotism? What are we waiting for, why do we not fill the chalice with the water of eternal life? May this hope full of Love illuminate all those who still doubt their own divinity, so that they can recognize the silent, inner guide which never leaves us. May the divine seed sowed by God in every human being bloom and thrive under the warmth of Love in the New Age we are about to inaugurate.

Sai Baba says that there are three types of people: those who have accumulated Love, those who are intimate with Him and those who are the personification of Love. While I tasted the sweetness of the intimacy with Him, I was aspiring with my heart to attain the third condition, as He defined it – the personification of Love.

I've realized over the years that if we are in harmony with our level of development, we never get ill (I will discuss this further on). In this regard Sai Baba says: *"The duration of a lifetime is under the control of the One who originally granted it – the Creator.*

It does not depend on the calories in the food we eat or the quality of the medicines that are prescribed. The main causes of bad health and death are fear and the absence of faith.

If we concentrate on the Atma (divine essence within) *which is beyond decay, senility and destruction, we can defeat death.*

Hence, the most efficient prescription for all kinds of illnesses consists in administering the "Knowledge of the Self".

Many years of my life had been marked by a series of illnesses, debilitating my health, but I realized that, since my life had taken a new turn, I was never ill and I even forgot to take care of my chronic diseases I was still suffering from, like anaemia.

Talking to myself, I used to say that the Divine would take care of my health if it wanted me to do something useful for the others, in His name. Purity is the medicine No. 1 in a spiritual therapy. My task was to do my best to pursue the purity of my heart and the rest was up to Him. Experience has demonstrated that by doing our best to assist others, unconditionally, we are at the same time working on our inner balance, that is, our wellbeing.

Sai Baba says:" *It is not I who want your death, it is you who determine it with your actions and intentions",* and *"Unless you destroy your desires, they will destroy you."*

The meaning of these affirmations was becoming clearer because, if it is true that the course of our life is determined by our more or less right or more or less wrong choices, we inevitably deduce that our physical death is determined in the same way.

How can we not be aware of the effect of anxiety, fear, mistrust, dissatisfaction, frustration or the lack of Love, at the onset of a disease?

Sai Baba says that all diseases originate from the mind. In the last century of the past millennium, official medicine took into serious consideration the psychosomatic origin of many illnesses.

I dreamt of Sai Baba again, dressed in white, sitting under the porch of the temple (*Mandir*) at Puttaparthi. The sun was setting and the sky, kindled by the hot light of the sun, painted His candid garment pink. The sight was indescribably beautiful.

I was not far from Him, with a friend of mine. He suddenly called my name and I approached Him with reverence. He introduced me to an elderly Indian lady standing by His side, in charge of the female voluntary service, and asked her to invite us to lunch[57] when we come to India next time.

While taking leave, he advised me to be less intransigent with myself and others. He was so patient with me. I was in fact rigid at the time towards whoever was turning a deaf ear to His call, quite embittered when I clearly saw that certain people were giving lip service when they claimed they were convinced of His divinity as the *Avatar,* i.e. the divine incarnation on earth (in the Kaliyuga or dark age of spiritual ignorance) to save humanity from illusion and egotism just as Jesus did two thousand years ago, when He came to restore Truth and Love but in practice they went on living their everyday lives without a change, as if that truth was something to be offered on the altar, at which they could, once in a while, make a plea, a prayer or, above all, a request for help.

I failed to understand that they behaved like that because the voice of God could be heard only by a pure heart. Listening is a talent. Its power lies in the resonance, from one heart to another. That is the only way to listen to God and other people. We cannot listen and hear God with the mind. In the same way, if we listen to others with our mind, we don't allow them to feel truly understood or empathized with. Empathy belongs to the heart, while judgement belongs to the mind.

The key which opens all the hearts to empathy is the ability to listen with a pure heart, full of Love. So, those people did not understand that they should lay the Truth of Sathya Sai Baba (*Sathya* means Truth) on the altar of the heart. Analogically, the sacred heart of Jesus – adored in the churches today – is our own heart consecrated to God, i.e. to unconditional Love. We are the Church and the heart is the tabernacle where God resides. The day is not far when the light of Christ or Cosmic Consciousness will enlighten our consciousness, when everyone will realize the gift of Grace that the Holy Spirit will bestow upon mankind, as the Divine Master promised.

I took the advice received in my dream by Sai Baba and tried to modify certain features of my personality, to be more compliant with the others and with myself. Sai Baba came to open the heart to Love, with Love and out of Love and to offer a world of light and immortality. But we are more familiar with the world of matter, illusion, darkness and death, which almost scares us less We are still rather unfamiliar with the world of light, in spite of its brightness. I dare say it takes courage to turn His message into a life project – with power, ingeniousness and creativity.

Admittedly, the possibility to reach bliss, peace and fulfilment only through the right behaviour seems quite utopian for those who are fully committed, day and night, in their search for pleasure and the means and tools to obtain more pleasure, having mistaken it for the very scope of life, in terms of conquest of worldly happiness.

Hence, it was pretty difficult for me to listen with the heart to those who were not searching for the truth. I remembered the words of Sai Baba: *"Those who speak reasoning with their mind should be spoken back from the same mental plane*. I cared very little about that and so I became even more selective about my acquaintances.

Apart from the few friends, my isolation increased and I gave priority to my dialogue with God. I could communicate directly at least with Him: from one heart to another. I felt privileged sometimes, but other times I felt really isolated from the surrounding world. The feeling initially weighed upon me but it diminished over the years, as the reality of the inner world was gaining clarity and strength.

Someone drew my attention to the fact that my strength in a dialogue was the ability to be concise, which I used to resolve dilemmas and smooth out differences. My trust in God helped me develop it. Starting from what was essential for the analysis of the given issue and putting together all the most salient aspects, I would quickly come up with a synthesis and find a possible solution or interpret the issue appropriately.

As a matter of fact, God is the essence of all things. My thoughts were constantly focused on Him, always coming back to Him. I believe that He, as the Divine Spirit within, illuminates every question, to help me interpret situations or come up with solutions. Is He not thought Himself, or better, is He not intuition Himself?

Some people complained of not being able to understand what was asked of them in order to embark on the journey of the Spirit and that the Spirit did not speak out. In those situations, I asked how much time, in 24 hours, they dedicated to the Spirit. Generally, there was no answer or the answer was a facial expression of thoughtfulness, perplexity or even irritation.

Apparently, my words sounded like heresy to those who, in good faith but strangers to the life of the Spirit and unaware of its value, were convinced of being in the right because they spent most of their time working and what remained of it with the family, or having a well deserved rest.

The most common phrase was: "We must work for a living," and I would add: "...and die to discover that you actually never really lived."

For most of them, it was not easy to understand that, for a living, we had to "be" rather than "do" (a Taoist saying reads: *"the path of doing is being"*).

We blame life, the world and even God for the perverse mechanisms we fall victims of, while in reality it is we who trigger and pursue those mechanisms to the extreme, with our ego and its fictitious needs. We eventually end up ruining ourselves, unaware that we did everything ourselves, with our own hands.

Worry and discontent, inappropriately residing in every human heart, turn us into soldiers, in a hidden war involving the entire mankind. It is the worst and most devastating war, timeless and limitless, as old as human life on earth. Its lethal arm is invisible to many of us and it is almost invincible: I'm talking about the ego.

Can we avoid taking part in and perpetuating this war? Apparently yes, since more and more people are, one way or another, involved in the knowledge of the arrival of the New Age – the Golden Age or the age of Truth, Spirit and Love.

Symbolically, gold is the most precious metal. It can be seen, touched and owned and man still needs to see, touch and own. Nevertheless, gold, being incorruptible, also symbolizes the Spirit, Love and Truth, which come in a package. In order to see, touch and own the Spirit, we must first open the door of the heart to awareness: therein lies purity, or the gold.

Awareness enables us to read between the lines and beyond the lines of the book written by us, in every moment, with every breath we take, with every heartbeat, with our emotions, thoughts and actions. It is the book of life which registers the permanent flow or the rushing stream running towards the ocean of the awareness of the Spirit. This is the target of every human being, with or without faith in God.

What can be our task if not that to reach this calm ocean, unfathomable and imperturbable, waiting for us from time immemorial, to "dive" into the stream of His Love and become at one with the All.

Whatever the path to get there, be it the roughest or the easiest, the most sinful or the most saintly, once we are at the source, or in the ocean, there will be neither time nor space, or difference between body and Spirit. There will only be Absolute Bliss.

Sai Baba is not here to impose anything, but to show us the way to the light and to goodness. It is up to us to decide whether we want to follow His message or not.

I tried to refine my perception, to be in tune with the presence of the Spirit in every moment of the day. I stopped talking about Him (of my own initiative at least). I talked about Him only when asked by others, that is, upon request. However, whenever I thought about Him I had to contain that river in flood which seemed to burst every dam put up by rationality.

I was finally learning not to worry about whoever was still deaf for His call, or was not yearning for Truth more than anything else in the world, like me. I was sure that the Spirit would sooner or later take care of them.

I used to be concerned about being insensitive, while I tried to avoid getting involved in the normal events of life. But I realized it was about having more faith in the Work of God, in the sense that I believed it was up to God – the Spirit – to see that everything turned out the way it should. I, on the other hand, could only engage in my personal growth and that was all.

Sai Baba invites everybody to be loving, kind, smiling, silent and radiant. When the heart is filled with devotion, we see everything as a divine manifestation and there is no need to choose between dedicating ourselves to God or to the world. We can attain Godliness by seeing Him in every person and thing. The path of Love for the Divine resolves all limitations, or conflicts.

Owing to this particular possibility, everyone will reach God, sooner or later, while still living in the world.

I dreamt of being "snatched" by a vortex of light, whirling in a spiraliform movement, lifting me up, off the ground and higher and higher. It was a fantastic sensation, a sublime lightness of being.

That oneiric experience was, for me, the nth confirmation of the progress I was making on my spiritual path.

But I was not protected from disappointments and the backlashes of destiny, always lurking, waiting in ambush, within the worldly context.

I gullibly believed I had found the solution for every problem, only because I understood the equation: *man – ego = God*.

It was not that simple to get rid of the ego once and for all and life provided new evidence of that, day after day. Apart from that, I started liking and accepting myself for the first time in my life, with all my strengths and weaknesses which still make part of my personality.

True, serenity resulting from forgiving and accepting ourselves is an indispensable premise to pursue spirituality.

I learned not to struggle against certain limitations but to offer them to God instead, invoking His intervention in the alchemic transmutation of "coarse matter" (flaws) into gold (the purity of the heart). He would strengthen my will to pursue only goodness and intuition, to avoid making mistakes.

Intuition, this supreme faculty, the gift of the Holy Spirit, helps us read the destiny between the lines of the book of life, where reason has no access; it helps us achieve the very scope of life when we share our love with tenacity, perseverance, dedication and ego-abnegation – qualities which allow it to evolve and manifest in its original richness.

Personal experience has taught me that the more authentic we are, the more our intuitive capacity grows; we become receptive to the inner voice of the Spirit. Only through this "voice" can we amplify the knowledge of ourselves as the divine essence and of the surrounding life as the manifestation of the divine.

This knowledge reveals that the more authentic we are and the more clarity and coherence we develop. Those are the prerequisites for the development of trust, joy, serenity and Love and the eventual unification with the All.

Having faith in the destiny as the divine plan, or feeling to be a part of a great, unique plan, helps us develop the skill to synthesize, mentioned above.

Sai Baba says that God has neither face nor name. He is beyond anything and envelopes everything as the Truth. It would be over-simplistic to recognize Him in a name.

Truth is crystal clear and it does not envisage separation or a need to defend itself. It thrives in a pure heart, freeing us from the bonds and addictions, to foster real human nature which is Love. He invites us to follow the way of the Truth, just as Jesus did two thousand years ago, pointing at the Kingdom of Heaven within as "Truth".

We have reached the end of an era which has contemplated divisions of different creeds and religions. Jesus and Sai Baba's have urged us to know ourselves, our divine essence, and to search for the Kingdom of Heaven within, as the only Truth. It is more topical than ever, despite the thousands of years of history, at the outset of the New Age, the age of Truth (*Sathya Yuga*), when the unity of all human beings in the Oneness, like multiple sparks in a single Light, that of the Spirit, has been acknowledged.

Today, more than ever, the Light, our divine essence, is pushing and driving us to God. Nevertheless, our longing for Him must prevail if we wish to attain Him.

Years ago I realized that my roles as a doctor and later on as a mother were transitional, so I stopped identifying with the roles.

I did my best to identify myself with the true Self and started hearing a soundless voice of the Spirit, lovingly confirming His presence in me.

Renewal and death are two sides of the same coin – we chose one or the other.

Some people do not know that deviant expressions such as violence, anger and rage are the other side of desperation, depression and apathy in human life and that all of them lead to disease and death. This burdensome human luggage is related to our identification with the ego and our distancing from the soul, to the point of losing contact with it and ignoring the existence of the Spirit within (as the divine essence).

Involution, i.e. our common search for negative pleasure, generates losses of energy, without the possibility to restore it, weakening our willpower, our higher abilities, our state of consciousness and our physical body.

Under those terms, the common opinion seems to be the following: a guaranteed dish of soup in jail is better than risking to starve outside, where one must work hard to provide food.

This opinion dictated by the generally accepted common sense prevents most of us from tasting the nectar God is ready to give, to nourish us with Him, when we chose the path of renewal.

Once we are able to savour that nectar, that is, when we find the courage to get out of that "prison" of selfishness in order to provide the food for the soul (unconditional Love), without any fear or doubt about remaining hungry, or suffering for having renounced our attachments, acting upon His Will, which is the will of goodness, God will make us feel in harmony with the Universe and this is when we will get to know peace and fulfilment.

I kept on taking down every impression, coincidence, dream, synchronicity and each sign I perceived as originating from the realm of the Spirit. This aptitude helped me maintain my mind firmly focused on my life project, allowed me to evaluate progress and the forced pauses, but, most of all, to reassess the events and the considerations in the light of a renewed perspective and greater awareness.

It was encouraging to realize that my understanding of Sai Baba's message and that of Jesus was getting better and it was a tangible evidence of my heart's openness for the Divine Knowledge.

In that period of great inner turmoil, I dreamt of being at Puttaparthi during the *darshan* hour. Sai Baba was passing through the crowd. He stopped in front of me and I gave Him some letters and kissed His hand while he was telling me: *"Grace! Grace! You are always ready to make requests but not ready enough to give things up"*. Was He admonishing me?

What are we supposed to renounce to obtain grace and inner peace? I learned from experience that reason could not coexist with passion (passion is "blind"). Therefore, not before we overcome the lower joys of passion can reason be enriched with the ability to discriminate.

Continuing to experience the lower pleasures of life, those of the senses, we cannot avoid restlessness and suffering. In this case the only alternative is either experiencing blind suffering, i.e. without knowing anything about its meaning, its origins and causes (hence not being able to defeat it) or learning about its causes to be able to prevail.

Becoming aware of the causes of suffering and acting upon them (by elevating awareness beyond our emotions and acquiring the ability to differentiate between what is good for us and what is not), we can gradually overcome and annul the suffering.

Peace is also experienced along this way. Actually, our emotional attachment to physicality deters us from our true nature – and not the physical body *per se*. The body is just the means, or the packaging of the higher faculties. It is used by the elevated level of awareness to advance from individual to collective consciousness and eventually to Cosmic Consciousness.

I new that it was necessary to restore the lost ordination of true human values to understand and overcome the state of imprisonment in the evils of life, to be equipped with the faith in God, as we get off the path paved by habits (perpetuated over the centuries) that keep us subservient to the ego.

We ought to cut off the logic of common sense, made unusable by the load of the so-called advantages of pervasive materialism, and leave more free space for spontaneity, imagination, intuition, creativity and the faith in the divine potential still dormant in us.

By acknowledging our divine nature, we can defeat the fear of living and dying. Faith in the inner divine is the antidote against any type of fearfulness.

Our trust in the abundance of divine essence within can quench the thirst of material and emotional possession, as the basis of any fear in man, which would provide the opportunity to live not for what we manage to "have" but for what we manage to "be".

The fear of loss pesters our existence from the cradle to the grave. Its *raison d'être* vanishes when we realize that what we really need is within us, belongs to us and can never be taken away.

The constant presence of the Spirit kept guiding me. It was an invisible presence, yet intensely perceptible, coming to my aid each time I stepped out of the pathway traced by the habit of living according to the slavery conditioned by the ego. I could then release new inner energies I never imagined I had. The revolutionary force unblocked by this new way of life was surprising. It was the confirmation that, until a precept becomes fully efficient through its constant application, the wealth it is supposed to produce cannot be revealed in full. The precept was Sai Baba's message which was essentially identical to that of Jesus, given two thousand years earlier. To me, efficiency consisted in the daily commitment to put it into practice, to carefully observe all the consequences in terms of thoughts, emotions, occurrences, dreams, encounters, messages of the inner voice etc..

What I found most important in my constant scrutiny of the evolving of life was the possibility of a change which manifested every time I managed to modify my way of thinking about a situation, fact or relationship, from negative to positive.

Reality seemed to be modelled or shaped only and unavoidably according to this new approach. Reality could become a magic dream. Paradise was not behind the corner (as it was in a dream I had one night) but right inside me.

That magic required purity, integrity, clarity, audacity, sincerity, simplicity, faith, self-control, discipline, surrender to God, or, to put it briefly, the capacity to live wisely, unattached from our ego.

Why is it important to detach ourselves from the ego, from the little individual self? Because it is the only way to stop identifying with the limitations dictated by the senses, desires and fears and start identifying with the divine essence, the Self within. I started harvesting the crops of the choice I'd made many years earlier, well-aware of what I was doing. I found the courage to live in accordance with the needs of my heart, risking to lose the (false) security provided by the mediocre life I had been leading up until then, to realize greater aspirations, i.e. to find the true Self or the divine essence within.

As I was gradually approaching this goal, I felt safer and I also felt it was the right kind of security – not the fictitious one granted by a safe job or a family I belonged to. I came out of the "prison" to look for new nourishment, risking starvation, but it was worth the effort.

I was no longer alone and I was never going to be alone again. Whatever I did, the most challenging or the most trivial thing – looking for a notebook or an important object, choosing a book or magazine, meeting people, planning trips or making decisions – everything was sieved by this silent intelligence which accompanied me always and everywhere, day and night. I may even say that we became one single thing.

Coincidences or phenomena of synchronicity became the norm. An Irish dictum says that synchronicity is a miracle in which God wants to remain hidden. Dreams, messages and objects I found again were constant revelations of the presence of the Spirit. The experience of the inner voice was beyond a shred of a doubt His most extraordinary manifestation in me, from that moment onwards. I was quite upset by it initially, due to its unfamiliar origin and the cryptic content of the messages I received.

My rationality was not helping me at all to get a better understanding of things. On the contrary, it suggested that I was going insane, but I discarded it readily. My intuition came to my rescue, as it didn't fear judgments, or logical or moralistic objections. It simply made me realize that what I was hearing unexpectedly within, in different moments of the day or night, was the voice of God (or the Holy Spirit, or Sai Baba). In this regard, it was a great comfort to read in the Holy Scriptures that this phenomenon occurred in the past centuries, more often than we imagined.

I was at times ironical with myself to downsize the experience but I was unable to reduce its magnitude and holiness that I even found embarrassing at times.

Considering the compelling content of those messages, I could not have doubts about the sender as being God as the Holy Spirit, that is, Sai Baba, being certain that no other spiritual entity, however elevated, could speak in His stead, in that manner.

I can't find the right words to express the sense of fulfilment mixed with amazement which pervaded me each time I experienced it.

How could a normal person like me become the object of so much attention from the Holy Spirit? I didn't know. The only thing I could do was to continue following my path. I learned that loving implied knowing and serving implied loving and so the key words for being in tune with the Divine were: "knowing, loving, and serving".

The inner voice was the Truth, revealed by God to teach me the Knowledge of the laws of nature regulating human life. The teachings served to open the narrow angle of the ego to a broader vision of things – I had only been able to imagine their real essence and logical consistency up till then – amplifying my awareness and ability to give advice in an entirely impartial manner, without being mentally and emotionally involved, which had characterized my previous, informal activity of spiritual aide, or as a psychiatrist prior to that.

I was sometimes tormented by an issue, without being able to draw a plausible explanation, e.g. the issue of the life-long suffering of a person who turned to me for support and advice. I would turn to God with utter humility to gain a clearer picture of that particular destiny.

After a while, the inner voice would come up with an irrevocable and final answer, expressed in a few words, albeit hard as stone in their essentiality. The veil of ignorance was suddenly removed and I could see the situation with amazing clarity, perfectly reflecting the Divine Law. I cannot say more about this matter without involving the people concerned.

As I replay my past experiences, step by step, I will report only the revelations related to my own life and pathway.

I wished other people could share the same enthusiasm for this type of rapport with the Divine and experience the Grace that results from it. We all have the possibility to hear this voice. It is enough to desire it intensely, instead of drowning in the mental laziness which can block us until we are unable to believe that we can change our nature, and consequently the surrounding world.

But to change our nature and the world, our words and ideas must be illuminated by the light of Truth. *"Carpe diem"* was a Latin proverb, meaning "seize the moment", *"hic et nunc",* or "here and now" – if you wish to turn your life into magic. I would never wish to discover, in the moment of death, that I haven't really lived fully due to indolence, cowardice, blindness or ignorance.

On my way from minus to plus, my destiny was guided by the Above, exerting a pressure which was relentlessly, albeit slowly, removing every obstacle along the way, not without pain.

Making use of the tools of wisdom, such as discernment, intuition and emotional non-attachment, I managed to identify the time for courage and the time for caution.

The Spirit was constantly by my side. I wasn't afraid any more because I felt safe, and I wasn't tired because I felt sustained.

The suffering experienced while overcoming the obstacles, like the attachments to inferior goals, was a form of training in objective insight and an impact test for my faith.

Spiritual life is not a "walk" but a "climb" and we should not see it as a friendly attitude of devotion to noble ideals but as an inner adoption of a new existential attitude, in order to address the crises which keep arising in more or less regular intervals. It is therefore crucial not to surrender or cede or retreat. We must never lay our perseverance and tenacity aside during this journey, since they are the lymph of our spiritual growth.

When we live in the Truth, with a pure heart, we discover something we would never expect to find: freedom and necessity coincide. Indeed, what we must follow (our *dharma*[58]) – not what we would prefer to follow – sets us free.

True, there is no other freedom except doing what makes sense for the ultimate scope – the self-realization of the inner Self – and making a leap from nothing to everything, from matter to Spirit.

Our faith and trust in God makes us great because it elevates the ethereal vibrations of the living matter we are made of, which is again ethereal matter, until we attain the divine vibrations of the dimensions which look forward to hosting us in the coming decades, the dimensions of the Spirit, when the seeds of Knowledge and Truth will spring in the pure hearts, open to Love.

Those who remain deaf to the call of Silence (the voice of God) and Truth (His Word) will remain slaves of errors and darkness.

As I contemplated my life again, I noticed that whatever turned out to be useless for my development did not withstand the test of time and was thus changed, while what was still valid for the same purpose remained unchanged.

The courage to be honest and true, beyond the rules, the laws or the current morals, has always been my favourite feature and lifestyle. With time I realized how important it was to follow the heart, but only the pure heart, guided by intuition and not by reason.

And so following the (pure) heart and being authentic, at any cost, also became my motto.

Sai Baba says that the Truth must be defended at the risk of one's reputation and social tranquillity and that the debts accrued in the previous lives are quickly settled if one wishes to climb the ladder of divinity because the results of the spiritual practice are visible after the debts are extinguished, and not sooner.

This was patently clear from the first direct contact with Him. On that occasion, I was foretold (in the interpretation of the *Shuka Nadi*) that, from the age of forty nine (that date was close) till the end of my earthly life, I would be engaged in the realization of the Self and nothing would ever stand in my way to God.

I was entering the most important period of my life and I was finally going to realize the true Self, the divine essence within.

Jesus said: *" The Spirit is strong, the flesh is weak".* Man is unable to renounce the pleasures of the senses and so he misses the opportunity to realize God.

When our thoughts and emotions are fully engaged in the satisfaction of material needs, it is impossible to gain the awareness.

If we could go back in time and be like children, without a structured defence mechanism, limitations, mental censorship, prejudices and pressing carnal desires, and be spontaneous, trusting and sincere, we could re-learn how to live.

Jesus spoke two thousand years ago (for example, He said, *"You must become small to enter the Kingdom of Heaven within"),* but who listened to Him?

As I progressed on my spiritual journey, I occasionally felt as if I was one step away from the aim and everything seemed easy. But putting out evil (the ego) is everything but simple, since it is elusive and concealed most of the time.

A voice in my heart started telling me to be careful and avoid making any wrong moves. Since then, I was alerted each time I ran the risk of making a mistake, but, alas, I made so many of them, without realizing it immediately. I shed many tears in my attempt to understand the flimsiness of the surrounding world.

The moment of my retreat from worldly engagements was approaching. Almost three years passed from the opening of the Sai Centre in my hometown and that presidency was going to be my last engagement before I became fully focused inwards. The retreat lasted nearly ten years, although I didn't think it would.

I continued devouring dozens of books as if I had to prepare for some kind of final exam, or perform some kind of task. I was in a hurry to learn whatever I deemed necessary to feel ready for something, but I had no idea for what.

Studying Sai Baba's teachings, I was more and more convinced that *Swami*, the Divine Master, was the Christ heralded by Jesus two thousand years before, and that we lived in the age of His return to earth and to our hearts.

In that period I met a friend who revealed me a secret, including me in his personal story. The encounter took place a couple of days after I'd made a dream, unique and extraordinary primarily for the location in which it took place. I dreamt of being in Palestine, as a woman in her thirties, dressed typically for that period, waiting, together with other people, for Jesus to come down the dry and barren country road. I suddenly saw Him in the distance. He was coming surrounded by a large crowd, singing "Hosanna" and crying out His name.

I was standing aside, albeit anxious to look closely at His face. He walked slowly, stopped near a large mass of stone and sat down. I came so close that I could touch Him. He turned to me and patted me on my right knee a few times. I was so deeply touched that I woke up and went on thinking about this wonderful, incredible encounter all night.

So, a couple of days later, this friend reveals that he was a member of the Essenian Community in the time of Jesus, adding that I was also part of it, just like many other people who nowadays acknowledge Sai Baba as the Avatar who has come to inaugurate the *Sathya Yuga*, or the age of Truth.

In the same period Sai Baba sent me a message through a friend who was residing in India, saying: *"A major change is on the horizon for you"*, letting me know that a change could be so deep that our consciousness cannot grasp it.

"Don't put off till tomorrow what you can do today" warned Jesus two millennia ago. Sai Baba repeats it today, as if addressing the same individuals from that distant period. Just as then, most of the people seem to pay no attention.

Most often, we grasp the truth of such affirmations only under extreme conditions, when it is too late to make up.

Why is it so hard to recognise and accept the Truth, even when we are confronted with it or told directly and openly?

I did recognize it, but it was still not in my power to do much about the others and make them "see".

"Seeing" is an ability that can be developed subjectively (because it requires working on ourselves) if we purify the heart from attachments, desires and negative thoughts that generally fill our "goblet" (or the channel through which we receive the divine energy, or Grace, provided it is empty), as I said already. In this way, our heart becomes usable.

Nobody can do it in our stead. We – and no one else – can "cure" ourselves and then the Truth will become visible. It will illuminate us, radiant with His light, allowing us to see that marvellous landscape which is life with God, both within and without. Sai Baba says we should expand, or broaden our heart and open it to all mankind if we wanted to reveal the Divine within, instead of remaining enclosed in our limited individuality. The heart's cure is its expansion.

NOTES: CHAPTER VII

52. We cannot realize Absolute Truth in the mundane, physical life. It would be unthinkable, with our dual nature (mind and body), to recognize the Absolute. In the realm of the Spirit, beyond matter, only similar others recognise each other.

53. As it is the case with all those who visited and recognized Him, after every trip to India my eyes shone with a different light, thanks to Him. The Self within Him and the Self within me got in touch, triggering a spark, but mundane matters would gradually cover it up.

54. Sai Baba wears a white robe on rare occasions (e.g. on His birthday).

55. The three gifts are: joy, power and peace.

56. Sai Baba claims that the dreams related to the Divine are real.

57. Eight years later, that invitation turned into reality for me and the friend who appeared in my dream.

58. *Dharma* refers to the respective, individual task every person must accomplish.

VIII

There is a concealed unresolved issue behind every misfortune: Truth is the cure.

Quinby.

It was a sultry afternoon in August when some friends gave me five small keys: each seemed to belong to a small case. I immediately remembered the dream I had the previous year about the case, but I couldn't put the two events together.

I asked for an explanation and one of them replied hermetically that I had already opened three doors and was supposed to open the remaining two by the end of the year. This coincided with the date that would allegedly bring a major change in my life – my forty ninth birthday.

On top of all the material I had to elaborate, there was this additional, complex riddle which stimulated my already alert spiritual curiosity.

One of the first things I started considering was the combination of words I often used in my attempt to put into practice what I'd learned from the Divine Master: the "3Ps and the 2 Ds", namely: Patience, Purity, Perseverance, Discernment and Detachment.

I associated the "three open doors" with the 3 Ps, and deduced that the remaining two doors were about the 2 Ds. In other words, I was supposed to put into practice discernment and non-attachment within a year. What an enormous task!

I didn't know and it would have been hard to believe at the time that I'd be delivered two more keys the following year. It was true however and there was more.

Reality exceeded imagination by and large over the past years, or precisely from the outset of my spiritual journey.

Symbolically speaking, "having the keys" implies having been initiated, or having access to (and entering) a spiritual state or realm, or degree of initiation. The key has the power to open and close and therefore symbolizes initiation and insight. Keys allow us to tie and untie (the alchemic definition deals with the power to coagulate and melt, or in Latin *"solve et coagula"*).

Apart from the symbolism of the keys, I could not help contemplating the number five which corresponded to the third identity in the Hindu trinity, or Shiva (manifest in Sai Baba), bearing in mind the importance of numerical language (rooted in the Hebrew and Pythagorean schools of thought) in deciphering and decoding the various aspects of reality I happened to live in and those I was yet to reveal or "eliminate".

I thought about the five aspects of psychological perfection (sincerity, faith, devotion, aspiration, surrender) in the light of my research. Thousands of other hypotheses emerged, and so I finally stopped investigating what happened and continued with the self-inquiry.

I knew that the silent, guiding Intelligence would help me discern whatever was useful for me to discern, when appropriate, just as it had already helped me see the great, approaching change (as foretold by Sai Baba): the transition from the horizontal plane of everyday life to the vertical one, i.e. the search for the Spirit.

The choice had been preannounced years earlier in India in the reading of the *Shuka Nadi* and the timing was perfect. My task consisted in searching, selecting and prearranging the various pieces of the puzzle, to put them together and compose the picture of the ever-changing circumstances, carefully checking whether it coincided with what the Divine Master expected of me. And He promptly signalled His approvals or disapprovals, depending on my achievements.

I cannot think of a greater tragedy than that of a wasted life, lived (so to say) without realizing why we were incarnated, what our special task here on earth is, why we depart from it and where we go after the "death" of the physical body.

Those questions, still harboured in the human soul, can be answered only with the Knowledge of the Spirit. Thankfully, we were incarnated in an age when this Knowledge is within reach. So, why not take this unique and rare opportunity?

As I delved deeper into this Knowledge, I did my best to examine every clue offered by my intuition, to complete the puzzle of my inner world – the microcosm in the macrocosm.

Along the way, the only difficulty consisted in the daily effort to make progress. The "indications" were hidden by the ego and so I had to resort to my intuition and my faith in God all the time – a sixth sense supported by the blind faith in Him – to maintain my perception of whether I was heading in the right direction alive. I could not afford making any mistakes, as they would immediately dull the confidence of being guided by a Silent Higher Intelligence.

I discovered that having a pure heart implied having control over our five bodies (physical, ethereal, astral, mental and causal). Five are also the steps to the Self: devotion, non-attachment, discernment, liberation and realization.

I associated those steps to the five keys I'd received that could hopefully help me identify the steps I had to climb and check that I was on the right way.

On the outside, I gave the impression of wishing to evade the world and my commitments, but the reason for rejecting that rather responsible role within the Sai organization was my confidence that work had to proceed within me from that moment onwards, until further instructions from above.

I think every spiritual seeker must face this difficult moment – when we are likely to be least understood by those who were, until recently, our peers.

The priority of what is invisible from the outside, i.e. the inner development, can be difficult to affirm if we are immersed in the worldly dimension of life, where spirituality is considered as a luxury of the few elected, without understanding that anybody can be a self-pronounced seeker of the Spirit, without exception. This search does not require academic titles or noble origins, as thousands of years of history have shown.

Undeterred, not paying attention to other people's criticism, I proceeded along my way, resolutely, certain that my pure heart would provide me with the key to the Kingdom of Heaven, the most important 'key' for the realization of the Self within, or the Constant Integrated Awareness[59].

Few of us come to understand that the mood, determined by the thoughts, that is, by the mind, conditions the events in our everyday life, which is why it is so useful to think positively.

Our daily life improves as our thoughts and mood become positive, attracting nothing but goodness, like a magnet. In this sense, a coherent behaviour, i.e. when our thoughts, words and actions are in tune (saying what we think and 'walking the talk') is a precondition for a real change. A message arrived in those days to clarify certain aspects of that imminent change I started feeling in the air, in a vague and disturbing manner,

It said: *"Smile to life as it is, you know well what it is. Let us play together, without any problems, without any objections. Everything comes and goes, Love, friendship, friends and foes. What remains is the creative, everlasting, Cosmic, spiralling essence.*

Sea tides carry all of you together to the beach of earthly life. You are drops of the ocean, separated for a few instances, only to become ocean again. Accept everything you have been given as a great gift, whether you understand it or not, without wondering why. Simply accept it with Love, because everything is given to you with Love.

Accept what I send you, with less apprehension, without paying much attention to other people's words that fuel your confusion.

Stay calm and wait for the events to take place, those for which you have been prepared. You will not have to wait for long. Your assignment at the (Sai) Centre is about to end. You will come to India afterwards and receive an assignment, by My side. I am working on that. You will be happy, finally.

Do not wonder what it is, it is beyond your imagination. I love you".

The message was a good lesson, as I was trying to predict the future in order to make plans.

Sai Baba hinted that the way I was progressing was not acceptable for the Spirit. I had to surrender to Him, who had always been so generous with me, confirming His safe guidance, and all the rest would come by in due time.

Everything tallied perfectly. He was preparing me for a task and I had to continue with my inner work, to be ready and impeccable, because the call could arrive any moment.

That explained what I'd felt from the moment I came to terms with God, many years before. Reconciliation (in the form of forgiveness) allowed me to receive His grace and helped me make the right choices and perhaps transcend destiny (*karma*).

It was as if destiny had been modified. Instead of being marked by physical death, that year was marked by an initiatory death of my life prior to then and a new birth into a life dedicated exclusively to the Spirit.

In my personal view – supported by the predictions made by other people from different areas of study, who had examined my birth chart, all of them reaching the same conclusion – it was as if divine intervention had extended my life to allow me to settle the *karmic* debts in the best possible way, for me to attain liberation during my earthly stay, before I leave the physical body.

Was I raving? Even if it were so, it was useful to know that Sai Baba claimed that the world would be a much better place if more people were afflicted by this type of (divine) folly. As a matter of fact, (again, according to Sai Baba), true folly is forgetting God and depending on other human beings to survive.

The words of Jesus echoed in me: *"Don't put off till tomorrow what you can do today"*. Those words were reinforced by the recollection of the parable of the virgins waiting for the Spouse. The wise virgins, those who had brought the oil to light up the lanterns, were admitted to His presence, while the foolish ones, who had not provided themselves with oil, were left behind the door.

I see the wise virgins (those with the pure heart) as those who light their heart (the lanterns) in time with the light of the Spirit (oil), or insight, and enter the Kingdom of Heaven (temple), to be next to the Spouse (God as the Divine Self), whereas the foolish ones (tied to this world), that is, those who do not prepare themselves for the encounter, are hence excluded from that joyous matrimony (mystical wedding of the soul with the true Self or the Spirit).

I was constantly repeating the name of God, just as my heart dictated, at times saying SO HAM SHIVO HAM, other times saying OM SAI RAM, or OM NAMAH SHIVAYA, or OM SAI BABA NAMAH (all names of God in Sanskrit).

Sai Baba claims (let me remind you again) that repeating the name of God (Namasmarana), whatever holy name we may use to invoke Him at the turn of the ages (the end of Kaliyuga), could help us realize the Divine: *"You will be as you feel. Feel divine. Feel that nothing is impossible for you and it will be so in the reality you live in"*.

We can all have direct access to the Truth revealed by God as the Holy Spirit. What is required is humility and the purity of heart.

Jesus used to say the same thing two millennia ago: *"Unless you become small like children, you will not enter the Kingdom of Heaven."*

I learned that knowing others implied wisdom, but knowing ourselves brought Enlightenment and revealed our inner divinity. I did my utmost to know and understand others, but now I was getting ready to climb to the top of the Knowledge of the true Self, or the divine essence, or Atma, within.

It is quite strange to consider this to be the most challenging task for a man. When you think about it, the true Self is the closest thing we may ever have. It has always been with us, or better still, it had been with us even before we became what we are today and will continue being so and representing us, even when we cease to be what we are today, that is, after our physical death.

Many think this belief is the millionth eccentricity of the human mind, born out of our need to give sense to life.

When Jesus said:*" The Kingdom of Heaven is within you"*, was he not referring to the divine essence within that gives dignity to human life and that is the source of Love, Beauty, Purity, Truth and Wisdom?

So, life becomes authentic only when we get in touch with the inner divine essence, the true Self. Without this connection, we find ourselves vegetating instead of living, on the narrow and miserable tracks of the daily routine, quite mechanically, driven by habits, and this keeps our individual consciousness in the state of continuous sleep through a myriad of more or less fictitious and artificial engagements. Accordingly, life becomes a fantastic dream, or a nightmare, not different from what we experience in the oneiric states of mind.

When Jesus asked: *"Give us our daily bread"* (bread and wine as the flesh and blood of Christ are Knowledge and Love, Truth and Spirit), which bread was he referring to, if not the bread of Wisdom, understood as the Knowledge of the Self and the Will of goodness, the only food which renders life worth living – the 'heavenly' bread of the soul. He was certainly not speaking about the bread that sustains the physical body.

Just like many times in the past before a great change, I felt the urge (and destiny was my ally) to retire from the world to meditate and contemplate.

I have been a maverick most of my life, swimming upstream to the source. I felt I was approaching the destination.

Ten years earlier, I had been foretold that I would step into a period of social and self-marginalization. It was supposed to be a favourable period for starting an inner work, useful for my future life choices. That is precisely what happened from the moment I met Sai Baba, five years later. I sensed that something similar was just about to take place, but on a much deeper level. I'd always taken care of other people's suffering, trying to help those who could not manage to detach themselves from their own emotional inner jungle. But now I wished to focus on my own psychological mechanisms, my thoughts and emotions, to be able to orient myself clearly and lucidly, in my own "jungle" within and get out of it once and for all. I wanted to be clear-headedly objective and go beyond the ego.

Sai Baba might have referred to this search when He mentioned a new world (the 5th dimension?) in my dream.

Self-scrutiny and self-inquiry are the only way to get to know ourselves and to change accordingly. Above all, this search brings awareness and opens the door to the Knowledge of the Universe we become part of as we attain Cosmic Consciousness.

In reality, we live in different dimensions contemporaneously. The worlds we can easily investigate, as ordinary people, are the surrounding world (the 3rd dimension) and the psychic world (the 4th dimension).

Our behaviour, which is as far as we can go to manifest ourselves externally, is an expression of our personality which is in its turn shaped by the character. Within us, there are three worlds connected with their respective dimensions which, to simplify things, we consider as levels, namely the physical (the 3rd dimension), emotional and lower mental (the 4th dimension), higher mental (the 5th dimension) and causal (the 6th dimension).

Those levels are the bearing structure of one's character.

Sai Baba says that *"we are humans only if we have character, otherwise man is similar to animal."*

Character[60] represents man's richness or poverty, depending on what prevails – either the virtues, such as goodness, sincerity, loyalty, faithfulness, honesty, generosity, humility and the like, or the flaws, such as envy, jealousy, pride, falsity, greed, anger, craving and so on.

It means that (however paradoxical it may seem when observed superficially) it will be given to those who have and it will be taken away from those who lack, as Jesus claimed in the parable of the prodigal son and the talents. In other words, those who have a character attract goodness and those without character attract evil, while on earth.

We have all seen that it is easier to obtain something if we don't desire it, i.e. if we don't miss it or if we can do without it, because we are already full as a matter of fact, we are rich within. When a man possesses the wealth of virtue, fire cannot burn him, water cannot drown him, the cold and the heat cannot affect him, nothing can harm him. To earn this fortune we must put into practice the spiritual teachings because knowing them is not enough.

We must put our devotion into practice, our Love for God, and this will release the kind of energy that can transform us, making us sensitive to the grace God wishes to bestow upon us.

Sai Baba says: *"May your words be as sweet as nectar, you character as soft as butter and your mind as cold as the Moon.*

Therefore, leave behind your anger, hatred, desires and attachments".

I realized I became more sensitive and noticed easily when someone's sincerity lacked guarantees.

It is a very basic spiritual "semeiotics"[61], verifiable by everyone.

Whenever vanity, pride, narcissism, seduction or hypocrisy emerge in someone's behaviour, there is automatically no coherence between words and actions and consequently there is no authenticity, spontaneity or ingenuousness.

In order to practice Sai Baba's message (which is also the message of Jesus), the heart has to be pure and tolerance, compassion and truth exercised in our daily activities. This is the method of transforming the plumb of egotism into the pure gold of unconditional Love.

When Jesus said we cannot follow two masters (God or Mammon), he intended that there are two ways of living which cannot be reconciled: the dimension of the ego and the dimension of the Spirit. In other words, we can live according to the seed of egotism or according to the seed of unconditional Love.

The roots of (dark) evil, when we live egotistically, reside in our intentions that precede our actions.

Intentions are not visible and so it becomes so difficult to transform evil into goodness, because it tends to hide and camouflage itself. Even ostentatious goodness is an expression of selfishness and not of Love.

Intentions are concealed from others but also from ourselves. One does not necessarily have to act badly to hurt the next person. It is enough to think badly and this hurts others. Thoughts are substance, including a conceived action. For example, thinking of stealing qualifies as actual stealing according to the Divine Law.

God watches and observes the intentions harboured in a man's heart, those that determine his destiny.

Sai Baba says: "*It is not the actions that matter, but the intentions behind them. He tells every woman: see every man as a father, if older than you, as a brother if you are of the same age, and as a son if he is younger than you. Speaking to men he advises: see every woman as a mother, if older than you, as a sister if she is of your age, and as a daughter if she is younger than you*".

He suggests such behaviour to avoid nurturing bad intentions, since it is bad not only to think badly of someone or something but also to think contrary to the Spirit, or against the Divine Law.

I went on with my inner search, working hard, at times obsessively.

With regard to this, Sai Baba says: "*No human being in the world is without love. This love however can be expressed in many ways. In a mental hospital, you can meet mentally ill people who went through all kinds of disappointments. In a way, the entire world can be considered as a mental hospital. In the world there are people who are crazy about money, others are obsessed with their fear of diseases, others still are crazy about power and social status. Every individual is obsessed with this or that desire. There are also people obsessed with the idea of God: this is the only advisable obsession*".

I felt acquitted by Him (maybe not by others, though) and this was sufficient to continue my journey with unshakeable resoluteness.

At times I went against certain aspects of my character and my behaviour, to the point of invalidating the confidence of being on the right path.

Promptly, the "invisible aides" became "visible" (as in the past, when pursuing my inner path became extremely difficult), under the masterly orchestration of the Divine Intelligence (for me it is synonymous of the Divine Master, or Sai Baba), coordinating and sustaining everything.

I was foretold a few weeks in advance that I would attend a meeting of great importance for my inner search, foreseen to take place right when it actually did take place.

I went to dinner with friends, to a place in the countryside. I disliked going out at night and so it was not customary for me.

We were sitting at a table, among friends, and the seat next to me was empty. I asked who was missing and a young man came along immediately and explicitly stated he had come to give me a hand. I found this thing extraordinary at the least, all the more because I had never seen him before. How could he know who I was or that I needed help? After all, I was there only due to a strange coincidence. At least, this was what I thought.

The encounter seemed fortuitous but in reality it was prearranged in its smallest details and timely.

I never saw that person again, if not after several years, only at a glance. I wasn't given the opportunity to re-experience the intimate fraternity of those moments presented to me by Divine Intelligence (I was though, when I think of it, nine years later, but with regard to another message), which sometimes manifests as "strong arms ready to give us a warm hug" in the right moment, showing its continuous and unrelenting care for a single human being and for the entire humanity.

It was another gift from afterlife (for the moment I cannot come up with a better definition of this dimension which has been so generous with me) which filled me with peace, joy and Love.

We were standing next to the table, while the others were having dinner (quite curious about our familiar and affectionate attitude they couldn't explain), when he embraced me and told me he had been sent by someone who loved me a lot to help me transform myself. My chronic suffering (added to that accumulated in my past lives) blocked the heart chakra and prevented energy from flowing freely within. I was full of Love but I did not allow it to flow freely.

He went on saying that, if I wanted to improve my capacity to listen in order to assist others, being helpful did not suffice. I had to open that chakra for the energy of Love to flow and completely dissolve the pain and suffering accumulated inside since who knows when, or in who knows how many lives.

He said that, from then on, others should not respect me for my suffering but for my capacity to give Love and warmth. I ought to stop thinking of my duties (referring to my activity at the Sai Centre which came to its end), responsibilities, rules, let go of all the rituals and start loving with my heart. The Divine Master was asking me to do that in the face of the imminent change.

He said I had so much to give and do, there was no more time to waste. He added that the 6th chakra was opened to make me feel well inside, to facilitate my intuition.

He mentioned the "Master" and spoke about a "transformation", and so could I not help thinking of Jesus or Sai Baba and the message He had sent me only a little earlier.

Until then I believed I had nearly reached the final stop of my worldly life, but the fact of the matter was that my old modality of addressing life was going to die out. I was going to be born again, with a new approach to life.

That evening I fell asleep in the embrace of Cosmic Love and woke up in the morning in the same mood, full of joy, with peace in the heart.

The following day, I went to the airport to welcome a group of devotees returning from Puttaparthi. When we met, they said I was full of light, as if I'd just been with them in India.

Tightly locked in my heart I kept the secret about the encounter with the Light of the evening before.

It is not easy to describe what you feel during such encounters because they are so different from anything else. It is like waking up in the morning and discovering that you had been sleeping on a treasure all the time, or on a gold mine (divine experience), without ever noticing it, or as if you found the genie from Aladdin's lamp, or revealed a password like "Open, Sesame", or the recipe for happiness, which is actually the divine essence within.

My features changed from that moment, according to those who had known me for years. I noticed it afterwards, looking at my old photos. I was really different prior to that magic moment. Time seemed to run backwards instead of forward and I felt rejuvenated. Divine Intelligence was keeping me on a silver tray and I could feel it all the time.

Almost a year passed from the last trip to India. Meanwhile, I learned that, apart from being present within, it was necessary to maintain the light, the love and the peace in the heart without putting them at risk if I wanted to be well and useful to others.

Once we get hold of this Light, we need to nourish it carefully to keep it alive, make sure it does not extinguish itself. In this way the Light will help us find the roots of optimism, the strength to shape our destiny, the determination to leave behind the pursuit of personal pleasures and finally the joy of a new birth, becoming (if we stick to this path) ourselves the "Light" for other people.

I discovered there was only one way to pay off the past *karma* and that was by earning Divine Grace, i.e. by loving and giving unconditionally.

Jesus said that, unless we offered it to others, our life was lost. Also, an Indian proverb says: *"man has only what he has given away".*

That is the secret of the continuing progress, without any backfalls (the greatest asset is indeed renunciation).

In this sense, I was kissed by fortune: I'd never been nostalgic for the native land I had left a long time before, or for the affection of my dearest or what I'd left behind, such as friends, job, or the like.

I never looked back and my eyes were always fixed ahead, on infinity (an Indian friend of mine used to say that what she loved about my look was this very trait. Till then, I was unaware anyone could notice it.), knowing that my corporeal form was a grain tied to the temporariness of the mundane illusions by a thread, in spite of the fact that it contained the divine essence as well – the seed of the Light of the Absolute.

It also served not to lose myself in the silence I lived in – not in terms of emptiness, but in terms of enjoyable fullness.

Silence is the voice of God. I loved to listen to Him and to hear Him, interrupted only by the swish of the wind, the singing of the birds, the pelting down of the pouring rain or the sounds of nature in general. I even stopped hearing sacred music, so filled I was by that dimension from the moment I started channelling the divine energy that flowed within, in the right way.

We often complain of being tired. In fact, we get drained by directing our energy incorrectly, thus blocking the channels which would otherwise allow us to draw from cosmic energy and flow with it to infinity.

We can't expect to become spiritually rich if we keep "channelling erroneously", without even trying to redirect our energy.

This is the state of things for most people: things do not work out, one is not satisfied, but the pattern of behaviour remains the same, until the last crumb of energy is consumed, that is to say until the soul runs out, until death.

If you trust a friend, you will never nurture any doubts about him, even when appearances seem to betray him. True Love never distrusts.

And so I discovered another key to a peaceful life.

I have never mistrusted the Friend with a capital F – Sai Baba – from the moment He entered my life. He says: *"God is the only friend without egotism"*.

I was not going to make the same mistake I'd made when I was young, shutting my heart on Him (Sai Baba is God to me) at the age of seventeen, believing I was on my own.

According to the western culture, doubt is considered as a sign of intelligence. Nonetheless, I fully agree with what Sai Baba states in this regard: *"Doubt is a source of fear, anxiety and insecurity and it expresses obscurantism. Doubt, like arrogance, ostentation of superiority and distrust, is a manifestation of a disturbed perception of oneself!"*

It was not possible to have doubts about Him. Over the years, I experienced His friendship so many times. I trusted Him completely.

I finally left for my seventh journey to India.

This time I stayed at Puttaparthi for a month – all I wanted was the Divine Master's friendship and not that of the world. My choice was final. What scared and discouraged the vast majority of people appeared to be the source of major impetus for my inner search.

Final decisions, especially if they entail great sacrifice, are often subject to hesitation for many spiritual seekers. Still, if we think of God as our nearest friend – under every circumstance, unceasingly, more than any person or thing could ever be – all fears and hesitations fade away.

Sai Baba says that *"feeling united with God is the only happiness"*.

When we think we are alone, we really *are* alone[62], even though God is always present, like a silent observer, discreet and respectful of our "freedom" (so we can make all the mistakes we want), loving us all the time. The free choice granted by Him, from the instant we become part of the earthly world, is nothing but the freedom to choose between the righteous way, the one that leads back to Him, and the way of mistakes, taking us from one life to another, in the dual world of matter, suffering and death[63].

During that stay I realized that whatever happened was only and without exception for our own good. God never wants anything bad for us and, at the end of the day, evil does not exist except as a trial, for the purification and redemption of mankind.

Therefore, regardless of the circumstances, we should always be thankful and grateful to God, whether we understood it or not (which is the case most of the time).

The way back to what I considered as the Father's home was always deeply emotional for me, as I felt expressly called by Him. Every single trip was taken in accordance with His wish and each time I received clear and unquestionable evidence of that.

Those trips have always represented moments of growth, insight, joy and immense love – a rainbow in the inner sky I cherished in the heart.

Feeling at "home" in a place so different and distant from where I lived made me realize that true home was where we found peace of mind, the joy of living and the strength to give our best.

Sai Baba helped me go even further, until I understood that the real home was the heart, the abode of the divine essence, and not an external place. With this clarity of perception and depth of comprehension, we will eventually reveal that the real shelter is a place within, where our being as the divine essence (Atma or the true Self) resides.

We were given life in order to give in return. That is the deep meaning of our coming to earth. Nonetheless, to come to understand that, we should delve deep and rescale our ego – with its persistent requests for gratification, continuously focused outward and off the track, in pursue of satisfaction.

It became clear that whatever was cerebral was not vital. There is no vitality in the people who keep rationalizing, splitting their hair in four to keep their feet firmly on the ground (so they say). They will actually stay on the ground and miss every opportunity to redeem themselves from matter and the slavery to the ego.

Only what comes from the heart (or those who speak from the heart) is life-supporting, connecting us to the cosmic energy we are immersed in. In order to be vital, we have to open the heart to other people and to life and allow ourselves to be guided by intuition that operates when we are in tune with the whole environment.

This insight strengthened my belief that, when it comes to drawing the balance of our actions, what counts is not the quantity, or our share in the activities in life.

The quality often remains neglected when we remain on the surface. We ought to dig deep in the heart and interpret the intentions enclosed within.

The inner voice asserted that the moment had arrived to leave my assignment at the Sai Centre to take care of the "centre" in my heart. The conversation with Sai Baba during that stay took place only within me and His approvals arrived through His radiant smiles, generously given each time our eyes met.

I was back in Italy with a clear mind and with plenty of hard work still to be done. A feeling of alienation from whatever surrounded me was settling in and I was not happy about it at all. My decision to withdraw, announced upon my return, left many of my close associates stunned and disoriented. Some of them thought I was going through a mystical crisis, while others said I'd changed and become a different person.

I went on, believing that our work with others and for others should not stop us from being faithful to ourselves. And so, I minded nothing but my own intuition. Although I loved every one of my associates from the past three years, I felt that that particular stage had come to an end.

I had to move beyond and that was not easy to explain to those who preferred going through life by sticking to the same old pattern, despite their frustrations and lack of satisfaction, besieged by the fear of a possible change. I, on the other hand, have never been afraid of change.

I've read somewhere that correcting is not the same as "punishing". Correcting means getting rid of whatever keeps the ailing person far from his or her life-giving source. That was the purpose of my effort: not merely to "correct" myself to attain liberation. It was not enough. Certainly, others could benefit from my experience – by reflecting upon it, reflecting upon their life and "correcting" themselves in the light of the new vision of things.

I continued to note down all my thoughts, impressions, received messages, dreams, the words uttered by the inner voice, the teachings of Jesus, Sai Baba and other enlightened sages, which reinforced a new, renewed vision of life and prompted my coherence.

A friend of mine told me one day, having noticed the change in me, that I had to face further twelve years of work. What did that mean? Strangely enough, the deadline coincided with the one from the dream experienced shortly before. In the dream, I went to the Italian Consulate to withdraw my passport and discovered that I'd obtained a visa expiring in 2007 – precisely twelve years later, when I actually reached the level of awareness enabling me to be given a new name by the Divine Master – *Yor Glory* – marking the beginning of a new life, lived only to sing the Glory to the Spirit.

This time, however, I was not tormented by the idea of dying – my continuous self-investigation and the streamlining of the ego started yielding fruits. Never again was I obsessed by this thought the way I had been in the past decade, although, admittedly, the obsession had been in the function of my transformation, as it forced me to make the most of my time and live in the here and now, moment by moment, without taking Pindaric flights to a non-existing future, of which I had been convinced at the time.

I was aware that talking about God and writing about God was an arduous task and that everyone preferred to have a direct experience. According to Esotericism, those who knew Him did not need to hear others speak about Him, while those who did not know Him could not comprehend the grandeur of what they heard or read. I, though, could only speak or write about Him. Years later, during an interview, Sai Baba told me the following: *"Write only about Swami"*, indicating the best way to proceed (still, in that particular occasion, His command disoriented me).

How I wished that my marvellous experience could fascinate others, too and, by some miracle, to sweep them off their feet and make them embrace the cause of the inner awakening, to return to the Kingdom of Heaven, to the Father. Only God can realize our dreams, as I witnessed so many times. Only He can make us shine and I (like many others) was the living proof of this Grace. I could not keep that Light to myself, or the Knowledge of the key to the realization of those dreams: unconditional Love.

At Christmas, at the end of my mandate at the Sai Centre, I withdrew, although aware that I would face another difficult period. Loneliness is sometimes more dangerous than the confusion of the world, as other people are indicators of our inner balance. Nonetheless, I had to run the risk of being my only judge. Somebody stated that, after all, living without taking any risks was the riskiest way of all.

It became apparent that our only true judge is we ourselves. Present circumstances stem from our thoughts and actions from the more or less distant past, from our multiple lives.

It is impossible to compromise with evil. Our incorrect behaviour with respect to the original plan, stipulated for each one of us in the moment of incarnation, is consequently paid in the form of illnesses, incidents, existential crisis, depressions, and the like.

We suffer from the outcomes of the ills of life we cause. They do not exist autonomously, in their own right, i.e. they are not independent from those who generate them.

Jesus said: *"Those who raise themselves above the others will be humiliated and those who humiliate themselves will be raised"*, because haughtiness attracts resentment and humility attracts love. As I said earlier, man attracts positive or negative effects upon himself, depending on his behaviour. The outside world is just a stage, ruled by fixed laws. The way to expansion passes through retraction and vice versa.

I started dreaming of starry skies, stars moving in aggregate in most varied geometric forms, with sinuous, orderly movements, as if they were shifting positions. I did not know the reason of that celestial commotion.

The untameable will to understand the deep sense of life did not relinquish.

Having accompanied me to the threshold of my fiftieth birthday, that desire appeared like an unrealizable dream. I trusted I could make it with the help of the Divine Grace.

I lighted the hope in my heart every day in order to satisfy my thirst of infinity and eternity which could be fulfilled only by the dimension of the Spirit.

It often occurs that the will becomes an obstacle, instead of being a medium. This is because, when the path becomes impassable and less attractive in terms of immediate results, there is a risk that we might abandon it. Our contrasting emotions become difficult to master, yet this is the only way for us to continue aspiring to a heightened awareness.

As I proceeded in my scathing work of self-research, I realized I had taken off a worn out dress and was waiting to receive a new one. I felt naked in the interim, slightly lost and at the mercy of occasional spells of depression and incoherent decisions.

Finding myself once again in a world which had once been familiar was tough because it had become utterly alien meanwhile. It was a moment of pause. I expected to be launched into a new, still unknown and intangible reality, without any idea of how long this condition may last. In this spirit, I welcomed my forty ninth birthday and the completion of twelve fruitful years. There was nothing else for me to do except to be patient and wait for the situation to develop further.

In a month's time, I heard I was called to India again.

A man's strength is measured by the capacity to master and sublimate strong desires and transform them into increasingly subtle, divine energy, like the one coming from the desire for God – the divine obsession. In this sense, I felt my strength and determination growing stronger every day.

A year earlier I'd dreamt of attending the Festival of the Peacock, at Puttaparthi. I year passed before the wish to understand the deep significance of that dream was fulfilled. I was revealed that the dream referred to the attainment of Cosmic Consciousness, defined by Sai Baba as "Constant Integrated Awareness".

Precisely a year from that dream, I became pervaded with waves of light and fulfilment, enlightening the intellect. I could "see" beyond the barrier of reason.

A sublime Spirit sang: *"Man, you are not alone; everything sings about your gloomy sadness, everything in nature sings, caressingly, about your rebirth"* and further: *"I asked silence and the night. I sang, suffered, and prayed. The music sung in the oppressed soul frees depressed thoughts – it is always different, yet always the same!"*

I believe those verses address every human being.

Haven't you ever felt emotions like those stirred in the heart by the above verses, claiming that we are all at one, in suffering and joy, if we learn to share and open ourselves to others, to life and to whatever befalls us, albeit against our will, to supporting and loving each other?

Adversities discourage only those who lack the firm will to find themselves and to view themselves the way they really are. Temptations, disappointments and dejections dishearten those who refuse to put their belongings at stake to discover what they are, stripped of their limitations and faults and without the mask that has made them forget their real face. However, those who are willing to engage in their inner transformation and be reborn do not come to terms with the obstacles. The awakening, obtaining a full degree of objectivity of consciousness and the ensuing peace and bliss are priceless. We can savour the full taste of freedom when we discover to have an unutilized permanent inner centre of awareness, connecting us to the Universe, or the Absolute. We are oblivious to it, even though it is right within our hearts.

Sai Baba says: *"Absolute Love is holistic, pure, it is the true liberation!"*

If only we started thinking of it as being the real nature of a human being, and take it seriously so that it can manifest, it would suffice to plant a seed of real Knowledge: the Knowledge of the divine essence (the true Self) within us.

Jesus said: *"The Kingdom of Heaven is within".* The Kingdom of Heaven is a state in which the heart is ruled by Christ Consciousness, i.e. the awareness of being divine.

There is only one obstacle, albeit with a thousand appendixes, between our individual consciousness and Cosmic Consciousness. It is the individual self or the ego (in terms of fear, guilt or doubt). Whenever its power and dominion are in jeopardy, it strikes back with an ancient, lethal weapon: suffering. Who doesn't know suffering? From the cradle to the grave, it rages in our lives, without any way out, symbiotically tied to pleasure. We never get tired of seeking pleasure, oblivious to the fact that intense pleasure is never satisfied (or negative pleasure). Therefore, pleasure and pain are like two pans on the weighing scale, going up and down, depending on the weight of emotions dictated by the ego, influencing the mind and the body. And so we flutter between one and the other, until death.

But the scale has a golden beam – coated with plumb (the ego) – which is the spiritual heart, the only safe hideout from the tempests of life (emotions) and the seat of awakened consciousness, with its three gifts: peace of mind, self-mastery and devotion to the Master.

The God I know resides there – the God who does not demand any prayers, rites or sacrifices. Love is all He wants. The only sacrifice He willingly accepts is that of the ego, of the little individual self, to imbue us in the true, universal Self.

Only in this way will He reveal to us in His infinite harmony and allow us to catch a glimpse of the wonderful plan connecting the entire creation in a continuum of coherent perfection.

The Spirit is revealed only to the Spirit. Only by turning on the light in us, that is, by recognising our divine essence, can we be the Light and hence see the Light we are immersed in.

As long as we pursue the pathway of the world and the emotions linked to the ego (with its incoherence, unreliability, instability, etc.), the Spirit remains invisible and silent.

I knew that perfect joyfulness (bliss, according to Sai Baba), as Saint Francis (the greatest interpreter of the Holy Spirit) used to call it, was often manifest when we acted contrary to "common sense".

I experienced the presence of that celestial condition when the decision was taken by the Spirit (in the sense of intuitive intelligence) and not by the rational mind. In actual fact, this was the case with all the major decisions taken over the past ten years, perhaps even earlier. I was unaware of it at the time, though.

True devotion, as the direct flow of unconditional Love to God, or the river of Love, was dragging me with its current of spiritual life upstream, against the flow of worldly life, at an unstoppable pace.

I could not and did not want to go back because the moments granted to me by the divine essence were so sweet and full that they alleviated the long months of suffering on the inner battlefield of my personality.

Perfect joyfulness, or beatitude, was not a stable presence in my heart hitherto. However, experiencing it in some fleeting moments, sporadically, was significant enough to make me proceed enthusiastically on my path. Those mystical moments revealed that the Holy Spirit expected one thing from us: to stop wanting and asking. Once we do, He would give us everything. It may sound paradoxical, but this is the way it is.

The following verses by an Anonymous author explain and sing about the Love for the Holy Spirit:

"I love You because You see me the way I would like to be, because You understand what I could not express, because You know intimately what I feel, because You are the source of renewal."

I was leaving for India with those verses in my heart. They sounded familiar, as they perfectly expressed my most hidden and deepest sentiment.

When it comes to the journey to the Spirit, the departure is more important than the arrival, since the journey itself is the goal. The enthusiasm of this revelation triggered a powerful inner tension and the understanding of this important verity greatly facilitated the travel from the West to the East. There was a sense of uniqueness there and then, which funnelled all my areas of interests – Astrology, Metaphysics, Comparative Religions, Gnostics, Esotericism, Numerology and the Symbolism of Colours – into God. Under the guidance of the Spirit, they became the beads of a single necklace, whose thread had constantly and indissolubly been made of Truth and Love. Someone stated that authentic mysticism was trans-cultural and boundless.

I found in the West what I had learned in the East, not in religion but in mysticism and in the parallel drawn between the teachings of Jesus, in the Gospel, and those of Sai Baba, in His speeches.

I realized that the Spirit manifested unexpectedly and spontaneously, independently of any effort, to simple and sincere souls, without exception.

Experience taught me that angels roamed the earth in the form of human beings, with the mission to help the distressed souls resume their journey to the light, in this dark age.

The lasting union with the Divine takes place if we definitely renounce all earthly desires and attachments, since dependency and inequality are alien to perfect and divine Love. Likewise, I realized that the gift for creativity correlates with the sublimation of desires.

The Universe is engaged in an eternal and harmonious cosmic dance (in Hinduism, it is the dance of Shiva) comprising everything. I joined that dance and was constantly backed up by the Spirit and occasionally comforted by angels.

I could say without hesitation that I knew God, His angels and their behaviour, which represented the source of optimism and trust. Despite all that, I was not completely unattached from the world and this made me wonder, now and then, why I, and not someone else, was offered such an incredible possibility: to "see" (intuit) and hear the inner voice.

Having read so many books by numerous spiritual seekers, I could immediately tell if the author had known God or if he hadn't really been interested in searching for Him or in finding Him. The latter type failed to stir my attention.

My desire was to serve God by narrating my divine experiences, expressions of the redeeming value of His message. He had rescued me from the slavery of chronic suffering and the fear of death, perhaps because I was a simple soul, like those to whom the Spirit had been announced unexpectedly and spontaneously in the past.

I was permanently absorbed in the reading of spiritual books. I sometimes wondered why I was drawn to this type of mental, almost compulsive activity. I reckoned that, not being able to confront myself with the thinkers in question in flesh and blood, this was a way to compare my experiences to theirs, as they had been on the same path. I wanted to rescale myself through this pseudo-scientific method, perhaps also to seek a semblance of normality that might justify what at times appeared to be an abnormal life (according to my ego).

Through this continuous confrontation, I came to understand that many Spirit seekers from the past who had come to know God had been stigmatized as being mad. As a former psychiatrist, I knew that society had very little generosity and clemency for those who were labelled as "different".

Sai Baba says: "*You cannot deny that I am always with you, like the air you breathe, like the food you eat and like the water that quenches your thirst.*

I am your brother, sister, mother, friend and lover. Look for me and you will find me everywhere. Call me and I will answer, pray to me and your prayers will be heard. If your faith is total and all-inclusive, you will see Me everywhere you go, through the eyes of

Love. I will be everybody. Love yourself and you will love Me, trust yourself and you will trust Me".

I had experienced each word within me and felt confident about my faith in God above all, but could not discuss it with other people. I could have done it with those who shared the same sensations, but where were they?

Whenever I let a hint or a phrase slip out of my mouth, I immediately noticed I was seen as a woolgatherer or, worse, as a know-all. Having heard about some of my experiences, a friend of mine made the following, admittedly benign statement: Are you perhaps a saint? In this regard, Sai Baba says with disarming simplicity: *"When we put into practice Sathya and Dharma (truth and righteousness), life becomes sanctified".* We could all sanctify our lives if we wished to do so. On another occasion, a friend said in a slightly ironic tone (on my statement that I no longer needed to look for God because I had found Him.): 'You certainly do have a high perception about yourself!'

Viewed from outside, my self-confidence might have seemed like exaggerated pride, or a frenzy of omnipotence. As a matter of fact, I was simply experiencing *Swami's* words within me. He reminded me every day, in my heart, that we all had the Divine within. But when I pronounced it, it sounded almost like a provocation to the ears of those who refused to hear or were not listening with their hearts.

This may have been the reason for feeling more akin to the Indians than to the Westerners. Like me, they could easily see the Divine everywhere and perceive His presence[64] all the time. That was part of their millennial spiritual culture.

And so I stopped talking once again, unless I was asked. On the other hand, occasions for conversing came to a minimum due to the life of withdrawal I was leading. Until one day, through a friend, a message arrived which helped me understand the stage I was going through. It said: *"Surely, the possibility to go on a journey with astral energy is not that far away. As it is, your Spirit gets into contact with the subtle, invisible world once in a while. You call them dreams but they are not dreams. You are allowed to know, in those brief instances, what surrounds the Universe and the dimension separating matter from what is invisible.*

Only the few chosen ones know this world. Do not speak to anybody about the things you will be able to understand, feel and see with time. Those who know this reality will get close to you and will introduce themselves. You will be able to understand them, as they are children of the vivifying Light.

Your task is to make others realize the importance of the small things in life and to bestow the flame of Love – with clarity, wisdom and long-sightedness - which has imbued the depths of your being from primeval times.) Humanity has been given the Light – light, purity and the wisdom of the primordial soul. The work done by superior creatures trying to trigger Love in the hearts on earth is a lengthy one. The most receptive ones will take in the message that has always been communicated by Eternity. Assist those who are similar to you to get out of the self-centred shell of the ego. All Humanity belongs to the infinite ocean of God. Make it clear to as many souls as you can that a moment to make a choice is approaching. In a short while, the last train[65] will arrive on the tracks of this age. Those who manage to catch it will approach the rise of a new age. Those who miss the train will continue being inferior beings, subject to the guilt they have to pay for. The memory of the Universe is not a fairy tale. Everything is written down and all actions will twist back as good or bad, depending on the circumstances. Pray, sisters, for your brothers to open their souls to Love and find blissfulness, for the hatred covering the surface of your world to be transformed into the light of goodness, for the suffering distressing the poor little brothers, sons, fathers and mothers to turn into happiness and serenity.

Once you were in Paradise. If you wish, you can evoke it now with the full strength of your love. To them and to you it will then appear the way it had been at the beginning of time. Peace and Love."

Prophets and mystics, east and west, have transgressed the vow of silence for the sake of those who were searching for God, for the sake of their understanding. They were consequently stigmatized either as visionaries or lunatics. In that period of my life, they became a fundamental point of reference and a confirmation of what I had heard and seen. The truth of their words challenged time, space, culture, history and science. It remained incorruptible and is still topical.

The Spirit is the life of here and now, the present which is the eternal becoming, the only time which is truly ours. It invites us to grasp Its beauty without wasting the sacred moments bestowed upon us as we return to this earth over and again. Its presence is as simple as it is extraordinary and it is up to us to seize it and nourish the seed of wisdom and Love.

Those who fail to live up to their beliefs eventually discover that they actually do not believe and that they have not lived their lives to the full. What a bitter revelation in an age abundant with Divine Grace, thanks to the presence of God who appeared in the world in human form (Avatar).

Sai Baba says: *"All of you are sparks of My divinity. Therefore, share your Love with the creatures around you, as I share My Love with all of you. In this way, you will also be divine. When everybody starts following the Holy path of the Spirit, the world will undoubtedly reach peace and prosperity. Leave ignorance behind, illuminate the inner lantern of wisdom and finally give yourself up to the Divine. Develop Love. Only through Love you will be able to nullify the mind, only through Love you can cure all illnesses. Only Love can eradicate the diabolic qualities in you. Therefore, Love everyone".*

The lessons to be learned were many and at times they seemed too much for me to put into practice.

Although things were at times hard to comprehend, I didn't draw back. I preferred the truth, cost what it may. The year commenced in solitude and so I went on, thankful to the

Divine Master for the gift of intuition, which increasingly illuminated my inner search, knowing very well that without the mediation of the Spirit, I would still be in blind ignorance.

Mine was a life of study (having obtained a degree and the specializations) but I knew that all that academic culture, an expression of official science, was insufficient to know the meaning of existence and, most importantly, to reveal its divine essence.

Only Sai Baba made me realize the truth about myself. He made me understand clearly that to really know ourselves and the world, we must primarily be limpid within and clear away whatever is superfluous and ephemeral. To me, the capacity to see clearly, or better, to intuit the essence of things was a gift of Divine Grace.

Aurobindo said: *"The offering of the self must be total and it must embrace all the parts of the being....without rebelling about anything and without rejecting anything....If you offer only one part of yourself but keep the rest....it is you who drive away grace."*

Sai Baba says: *"I want your entire heart and you will be given everything."*

To remain lucid in a society suffocating under the weight of sham respectability and hypocrisy, we must courageously put up with being considered "different", selective and at times even extravagant.

God speaks and nobody listens, miracles of life happen every moment, but how many people see it and acknowledge it with gratitude?

To come to understand the Truth, we must "close the circle": the child turns into an adult and, as he becomes old, he returns to being a child again.

I was probably getting old and was going to go back to being a girl. In fact, my experiences with God were growingly similar to those I had as a child and later as a teenager. I spoke to Him in a fairly natural way, without being surprised.

He was the friend I could talk to about whatever mattered to me, such as love, peace, harmony, trust, loyalty and respect. Back then, my mates were thinking about getting married, whereas I saw Love as a resonance between two souls in the Universe.

I had nothing against marriage *per se*, it was the way people approached and experienced it that was distorted, artificial and driven almost exclusively by material interests. This horrified me and it drew me away from that "institution". It was hardly treated as something sacred and, to me, Love was sacred.

The sacrament resides in Love and not in the rite, said Jesus. I learned, years later, that Sai Baba claimed the same. According to Him, there can be two types of marriage: that of the eyes, i.e. the physical one between two people, and that of the spiritual eye, i.e. of insight. The latter one is the spiritual (mystical) marriage between the soul and the true Self (Spirit)[66] which makes us complete and divine.

The marriage consecrated by God is that between two souls and not between two bodies. The true Spouse is Love and Truth and a marriage can thrive only in Love and Truth – in respect, faithfulness, the spirit of sacrifice and sharing. Otherwise, in the presence of ambiguity, there is only adultery, or convenient habits, false certainties, illusory pleasure and thirst for power (to control and manipulate the other), albeit legalized by religious or civil rites.

In my youth, I noticed that people often played unauthentic roles, wearing a mask suitable for every occasion, to the point of forgetting their own, genuine face.

I could rarely express the uneasiness I felt when faced with hypocrisy. All the more, I was criticized because my face revealed everything, like an open book. I was taught not to judge or hurt other people. Had I spoken out, I would have hurt, more or less consciously, the people barricaded behind a wall of hypocrisy. This would have made me feel even worse and so I generally kept quiet about what I saw.

The moment arrived to break that silence because Sai Baba's teaching was based on Truth. The time came to tell everyone that the lack of authenticity and spontaneity was one of the gravest problems tormenting humanity and the source of many evils in its own right.

It is well-known that Truth is often viewed as something dangerous. Still, the remedy proposed to us by *Sathya* Sai Baba – the divine personification of Truth descended down to earth – is Truth and the behaviour founded on it. He wants to illuminate us on its inestimable value, help us understand that it is the way to salvation from all the evils afflicting the soul, preventing us from seeing the Divine, from feeling Him, breathing Him and experiencing Him. Paradoxically so, we are already completely imbued in Him.

Only Truth can make us distinguish the real from the ephemeral, for us to take an active part in our lives – not as marionettes of our little individual self or ego, bringing forward decisions and projects related to an "illusory reality" that ends quickly in a physical death, but like creatures who have come to earth to re-conquer the lost awareness of their true, divine essence.

For thousands of years, the great masters have kept coming back to earth to teach the rules of the Cosmic Game which is human life and to ensure victory in the final battle against the darkness of ignorance.

The "obstacle race" we are here to run has its own, precise rules and a very specific scope and award: liberation from slavery to the ego and the return to the Kingdom of Heaven, to Immortality.

The major part of humanity obviously ignores the rules of this "game" and can't remember the meaning of the "race", believing it was created only for the sake of running – to suffer or to enjoy, depending on the impulses we receive. We imprecate against the obstacles on our way because we see them merely as impediments and not as lessons to overcome our own limits and weaknesses.

And so, most people keep on running without even knowing why, in a constant and repetitive bustle, aimed at *doing* and never at *being*, as if there were no time for *being*.

Looking around, I saw tired and tense faces, dull eyes, lips without a smile, if not in a stereotyped manner. Life was fleeing, taking along joy, peace and harmony, but there was no time to notice it, as there were so many things to do.

Sai Baba, like Jesus, came to bring the "sword" of Truth, to restore the rules of the game, the *Dharma*, the righteous way, and re-kindle the light in us. We are sparks of His Being, of the Absolute.

So why not allow ourselves a contemplation break to look inside instead of outside and start being honest with ourselves. Change is possible and it is within everyone's reach. Evolution is by no means a painless process, but at least in this context suffering is aimed at its own destruction. In the mundane realm, even what seems to be pleasant eventually feeds suffering, making it additionally difficult to bear.

The above considerations were the fruit of my reflections during my stay in India. They anticipated a period rich with highly vivifying experiences that opened my heart to unconditional Love.

NOTES: CHAPTER VIII

59. This may have been the "precious gem" contained in the case (I saw in my dream): the secret of my initiation.

60. When it comes to character, a friend of mine, a hermit, used to say that there was no such thing as open or closed, beautiful or ugly character. There are only self-centred and other-centred people.

61. Semeiotics: a branch of Medicine studying (the causes by interpreting) the symptoms or signs.

62. I knew it from the personal experience, it happened to me when I was seventeen.

63. Angels have no free choice because they operate only by the will of God.

64. In India, even one-year-old or two-year-old children stop and pay respect to the sacred images they see in the street, without being told to do so by adults.

65. Sai Baba often reiterates this in His speeches.

66. This type of marriage transforms a person into an Androgynous, or divine creature. Sai Baba claims that He is the Androgynous. Indeed, God created us in His own image and likeness (as the Bible says) – not in our physical form but in our essence.

IX

Do not criticize me, criticize only yourself. If you see my flaw, improve yourself.

Groddeck.

Finally, my introspective ability was given the green light (the ego was making less and less resistance). It was the beginning of a new phase in life. I was trustfully considering the new role in making the world a better place – witnessing of the Absolute, or the divine essence within. Once we have experienced what it's like to be in contact with the Spirit – so intimate and remote at the same time – we can never forget it. What remains is a full, intense, new taste of life. Cannot be compared to anything.

I dreamt of being in Australia. I bought a magazine containing a coupon for a free stay in a Buddhist monastery.

I wanted to mail it, but I could find neither the coupon nor the magazine and so I decided to buy another copy. The enclosure of the other one was a box of incense and a hand in miniature, made of gold, and the overall price was considerably higher.

A friend of mine encouraged me to buy it anyway, because the gold hand, allegedly, would be useful for me in a future journey to the East. I would place the gold hand at the entrance of a cave and something useful for the spiritual growth would come out.

The dream reminded me that I was given the opportunity – provided I paid the price (discipline) – to write about Him from my heart (the cave), in order to serve God. The reflections I had put down on paper would raise my awareness (the result would be useful for my own spiritual search) and I would be constantly guided by God's hand that would become at one with mine (the gold hand).

I felt compassion (the greatest of all the virtues), the highest vibration I have ever experienced, whenever I transcended myself with the distinct perception of the divine essence in the heart, as pure Love. Ultimately, the supreme pleasure consists in sacrificing ourselves for the benefit of others.

Writing about God was perhaps a way to express gratitude for this grace. I had been doing that for years when it comes to my own needs, but this time I was going to do it in a more articulated and harmonious manner.

The journey to liberation is in effect the journey towards the fulfilment of the heart. This endeavour would help me reach that goal.

In this "journey", the difficult part was not to understand but to accept the inanity of everything (and the world seen as an illusion) and let go not only of the fears but also of the hopes in order to put ourselves exclusively in the hands of God and His Will out of unconditional goodness, for the wellbeing of mankind.

Indeed, God is present in everything, but only those who act by His Will can reveal Him. I was trying to move in that direction and be primarily and constantly focused on Him. I realized that the true Self or the divine spark, present in everyone, belongs to all humanity, as energy uniting all into Oneness. The ego, on the other hand, is connected to individual consciousness. The true Self therefore is the bridge between us and Cosmic Consciousness.

I found the words "inner awakening" and "Cosmic Consciousness" incredibly fascinating, although I was still unable to grasp their intrinsic meaning. We come to realize it when we reach a higher level of awareness.

To be awakened into the Self means reaching our centre, or the heart implied in the spiritual sense of the word. Until we are stabilized in the heart as the seat of awareness, we keep wondering and roaming about.

Setting someone free from this slavery first of all implies freeing the Spirit from the realm of emotions. This unleashes the energy necessary for the transformation of the state of consciousness – from individual to collective, and eventually to Cosmic.

An awakened consciousness is the necessary presupposition for the new man who will live in the Golden Age Sai Baba has come to herald.

I was invited unexpectedly by a few devotees to visit the caves of P.B. (consecrated by Shiva) in northern India and the *ashram* of Brindavan (Whitefield). Purportedly, only those who visit the place by the will of Sai Baba actually manage to arrive there. I sensed that the engaging proposal was coming from Him.

It was the first time for me to consider visiting a holy site other than Puttaparthi (or any other *ashram* of Sai Baba). At any rate, I was certain that the plan was designed by Him and that evidence of it would arrive soon.

That was a period filled with grace for me, I could perceive it in every cell. I felt in perfect equilibrium with everything around. The balance (constructive perception generating harmony) helped me to follow the right track or the *Dharma* (the righteous way) and carefully choose what was right instead of what was merely pleasant for me to do.

Pleasant things are not always beneficial – most of the time it is quite the contrary. And the consequences for our destiny can be enormous. By following the principle of pleasure, we quickly move away from the true scope of life and the possibility to reach the awareness of what we really are: divine sparks (parts of the Absolute).

However, those who follow the principle of righteousness can hope for a more sublime destiny, that of the realization of the true Self. Others will pursue the perpetuation of the human species in the cycle of births and deaths (*samsara*), under the constant weight of suffering, illnesses and death, until they are offered better opportunities for redemption, in the future.

It is good to keep in mind that pleasant things can block the spiritual development in subtle, apparently harmless, almost imperceptible ways, redirecting even the best intentional individuals towards seemingly more attractive shores. Frequently, a moment of "pleasure" is paid off through years of pain. It is like signing a blank bill.

Power and wealth, sex and beauty (implied as seductiveness) are expressions of the ego. If that is our dream, then struggle, fatigue, suffering and death are guaranteed.

An enormous quantity of energy is wasted to reach those goals which fuel our most negative qualities and turn off every visible light or potential.

Who do we unite with every day? Jesus said that birds of a feather flock together. In the same way, the ignorant (those who ignore the true scope of existence) unite with the ignorant and the bigoted with the bigoted. The Spirit seekers are after the Truth and the purity of heart, but it is tough to find companions in this small category. Yet, the two virtues – Truth and Purity – are indispensable to recognize the true Self and live a life worthy of living.

Sai Baba says: *"Look for good company, or else you will remain on your own. Love only Me. God is the best company."*

Those who are determined in their search for the Spirit make sure that their wisdom is not obscured by their desires. They do not want to displease God. Man is free if he can accept those two forces (pleasure and pain) as expressions of the law of nature, without being dominated or controlled by them. One of the first steps in the search for the real Self is to master them with the intellect. Thus, the greatest fortune includes a devoted heart, peace of mind and self-mastery.

Through a friend of mine, I received the following message:

"Let all those who lend their ears know that the situation in the world is going to deteriorate.

Tell them that humility and Love will be the keys to open the gate of the new age. The ego will have to disappear and the Love for our neighbour will have to prevail.

How many times have I said: Love yourselves like you love your neighbour.

Now ask yourselves, sincerely: 'How do we love ourselves?', and, 'Do we really love ourselves?' If you love yourselves, then you love Me and if you love your brothers and sisters, then you love Me. Do you love them? Your criticisms are arrows aimed at My heart. You rebuke your children, trying to teach them the true path, for them to be happy one day. Are you doing it with your heart, does your motherly or fatherly love make you do that? A loving severity is the right way to forge your children's personality. I now tell you, once again: I have not brought the divine message for it to be dispersed in your cities. Open your hearts and your homes to those who hear My voice. The Truth is one and it leads only to Me."

That was a benevolent but strict call to become aware of our task on earth. But whom could I talk to? I had no idea.

The day I went to collect my ticket for the upcoming trip. I met a few fellow travellers and something extraordinary happened. We were waiting for a person to join us when a friend told me that I still lacked two keys, without adding anything else. He knew about the five keys I had been delivered the year before. I didn't pay much attention to what he said, until the person we were waiting for arrived, presenting me with two keys. He claimed he had just found them in the street and felt like giving them to me.

I was taken aback and perplexed. Was it really a peculiar synchronicity orchestrated by the Divine Hand, only to express His approval to me regarding that trip?

The more subtle interpretation of that gift was yet to be found, now that the code-reading was extended from the initial five to the existing seven keys.

The healthiest and most appropriate attitude to life is to expect nothing, remaining even-tempered and equidistant from the ups and downs of the life of duality.

That was the lesson I learned from that experience and it surpassed any possible fantasy.

To live in duality, or in the world of matter (the 3rd dimension), ruled by the most oppressive laws (compared to other dimensions where the laws are fewer) is a tough trial for a mankind that keeps ignoring those laws and hence is automatically sentenced to perpetuating the life of errors.

Why have religions and state enacted rules of behaviour or laws? To regulate and contain the behavioural disorders of those who are not in harmony with themselves and the world. Those who don't steal do not need any laws or commandments against the disgraceful act of stealing, and the like. Speaking of this, Sai Baba reminds us we should never resort to human courts, even at the cost of paying for something we have not done.

This means that resorting to the law is disgraceful in its own right.

Wrong behaviour generates further errors and, one error after another, we build the so-called "civilized" society.

Courts, prisons, institutes of correction, police, asylums, hospitals, orphanages, barracks, nursing homes, casinos and brothels are places where they try to contain or correct the errors of a sick society. A special place is reserved for the churches and parallel institutions scattered worldwide.

It is not the society that is sick, really, but it is us who are sick in the souls, minds and bodies. The disease is called egotism.

The above institutions (and many other) have no sense to exist for people who live in balance with themselves and the environment because they are their own doctors and priests.

Shortly before my departure, I dreamt of two cobras[67] gazing at me, motionless. The huge one was staring at me, straight into my eyes, and the small one remained apart. Was it my ego getting small in the presence of the true Self, or cosmic energy focusing on me, looking through those burning eyes?

The sign propitiated the wish for the inner renewal by overcoming the individual self (ego) and acknowledging the true Self as cosmic energy in me.

Thinking about the trip I was about to take (to visit the largest cave in India, consecrated by Shiva), my thoughts returned to the gold hand from my dream. I associated it to the entrance of the cave. Things coincided perfectly.

I knew that getting there was quite a complicated enterprise. From the rational and practical point of view, the plan seemed to be rather 'crazy'. We were supposed to cross the entire territory of India, from the North (the border with Tibet) to the South, find the cave and pay homage to Sai Baba – in no more than ten days (the time we had set aside for the trip).

We carried along one thing only, to give us strength, calmness and determination: our devotion to the Divine Master.

Eventually, everything turned out wonderfully and I was in a state of absolute grace all the time. We had a unique and unrepeatable time.

The Divine went out of its way to present me with a great opportunity which compensated for all the efforts I had made to obtain the insight and the capacity to "see" with the inner heart. I had certainly not reached perfection, but I was doing my very best to eradicate my bad habits and proceed in the right direction.

I was given the possibility to experience perfect balance, albeit for a short while, as the optimal condition for every person of good will, living by the rules of the Cosmic Game.

Sai Baba says: *"Hear good things, see good, do good, think good. You will then have the Grace of God, since all evil tendencies will be uprooted."*

Putting God first means choosing Unity instead of duality, Love instead of hatred, Truth instead of lies, good instead of evil, choosing to fill the heart with Him, as the only Love, Truth and Goodness, and win back the lost dignity as divine creatures, or the reflection of God, made in His own image and after His likeness.

This leads to mutual love and respect and to loving God and humanity. This is the true Love Sai Baba talks about. He says that even a mother's love for her child is not love but affection and that even the love of a husband for his wife is not love but infatuation. Essentially, they are forms of attachment. Only the Love for God is true Love.

At the departure, I surrendered to God completely, confiding myself to Cosmic Consciousness, more than to the individual (limited) one.

My luggage was very light and it did not include a map (I knew I didn't need it). The rest of the group did the same. We ate bread (brought from home) for four days, so we did not have to stop along the way. I was not worried about the distances, or the climate. I was just following the call of my heart, sending me continuous confirmations of the divine protection. We arrived at the cave in record time. During the several thousand kilometres covered by an unsuitable vehicle (we were six including the driver and, although he was Indian, he didn't know the way) we were put on trial several times and even risked our lives. It was as if an invisible hand had saved the car miraculously from the impact at the very last moment (four times).

After he somehow managed to avoid a frontal collision with two buses (the fourth incident), the taxi driver stopped at the side of the road and lay down on the ground, panic stricken. We never lost our God given composure; we were simply grateful for His help. True Grace is the happiness of the heart – feeling well and peaceful under any circumstance.

In Delhi, the second day of the journey, there was a moment of impasse. Then I heard the inner voice saying we were about to arrive to our destination, telling me the precise hour of our arrival and so it actually happened.

The Divine was the only safe guide along the way.

We had arrived in India in May, when the moon was full. For Buddhists, Wesak is the sacred night when all the great masters (Buddha, Jesus, Sai Baba, and the others) meet in Heaven to bless humankind and to assist them in their evolution towards the light.

We were finally at the entrance of the magnificent cave. It was the 5th May, a Monday[68]. Everything was propitious – the sky and the earth. We entered what represented the "*Shivaloka*" or the world of Shiva, where the symbolic union of Shiva and Shakti (his spouse) takes place. The energy of the Absolute (hidden), or the Creator, merges with the energy of creation (manifest), the masculine and the feminine become one, realizing Cosmic Consciousness.

I was told I would be able to reside near Sai Baba owing to that experience, in the sense that I advanced well on the path of Knowledge, having turned my back to worldly knowledge.

As a matter of fact, letting myself slide into the pitch dark, perpendicularly, supporting myself with an iron chain (the tunnel was slightly wider than my hips) was like passing through a symbolic initiation passage. It was like returning into the womb of the Great Mother Earth, to get out renewed and revived into a new consciousness, from darkness into light.

Before departure a friend of mine had foretold me that I would never be afraid of anything after the return – and so it was.

There, in the cave, immersed in the semi-darkness, familiar words echoed in me and I kept repeating: *"knowing the Self means knowing the All"*. The All represented creation, which corresponded to number seven. I felt the Holy Spirit (which is the true Self and the All, at the same time) present within, more than ever.

The keys I had were seven. Was that the confirmation that I was about to get a glimpse of the knowledge of the Self, or the inner Master, or the Holy Spirit in me?

I remembered where this number reoccurred in nature: the colours of the iris were 7, the musical notes were 7, the days of the week were 7, the chakras in the human body were 7, the gifts of the Holy Spirit were 7, the esoteric dimensions (of which the 7th corresponded to the Inner Master) were 7, the valleys on the mystic path were 7, the steps on the mystic stairway were 7 and the planes or centres in a human being[69] (physical, ethereal, astral, inferior mental, superior mental, spiritual soul and spirit or divine spark) were 7.

The Harmony of creation was unfolding before my inner eye (the so-called third eye or the heart's eye) which was finally beginning to see.

Back in the light of the day, outside, I felt relieved and weightless. Three eagles were flying in the blue sky and you could see mountains all around, against the horizon – we stood in awe looking at the Himalayas stretching out in their stupefying splendour.

Those timeless landscapes made me so ecstatic that I almost lost orientation. I was no longer in a geographical place but in a dimension of being. In those days everyone kept quiet about their interior experiences and in this way the perceived sensations grew stronger. The only interlocutor (in my continuous inner dialogue) was the Divine Self, letting me know that the awareness and the light were gained in proportion to the daily effort to live the Truth.

The Divine Hand (gold) continued to lead us until we reached the beloved *Swami*. Delhi, Bombay and Bangalore. We had the impression we'd passed from one city to the next in an instant. Five days went by, but they could have been five centuries judging from the intensity of our experiences.

When we arrived to Whitefield, I had a celestial vision: before my eyes, the entire *ashram* was embraced in an immense circular rainbow and I could see the slender, minute figure of Sai Baba in the distance, welcoming me with open arms. I learned later that the vision of the rainbow was symbolically linked to the realization of a yearning desire: that of the opening of the third eye or the vision of the heart (once we have won the battle of the worldly ego) and inner peace. This interpretation asserted what I'd felt in the heart as I came out of the cave in P.B.

On the same day, during the afternoon *darshan*, I touched the feet of Sai Baba when He stopped before me and smiled. It was His welcome, as if telling me: you are finally home.

I spent a sleepless night because I was tense and had a splitting headache. A flow of thoughts, situations, events and images were relentlessly chasing each other. I was lying on a mat on the ground, surrounded by women of various nationalities I was sharing the room with. They were all asleep and I was awake without knowing why. There was so much joy in me that I could not contain it yet I couldn't share it with anybody. I finally decided to get up. It was four o'clock in the morning and I headed for the temple to pray *Swami* to calm my mind. I had a vision of Him telling me: '*Come on, do come along*'.

I remained there until the *darshan* hour. At seven o'clock Sai Baba called us for the interview. I did not want to get up from the ground (I was sitting), still stunned and confused because I was tired, until one of my travelling companions urged me to come along. At that moment I remembered the words He'd whispered to me only few hours earlier: He had foreseen my hesitation and urged me to take part in that meeting with Him.

It was Thursday, the day consecrated to Sai Baba. When I passed through the gates (Were those the gates of Knowledge opening before me?) of His residence, tears of deeply felt gratitude were rolling down my face. I had never passed through those gates before, as I had always been received by Him at Puttaparthi.

His house was surrounded by a grassy carpet. It was a pink building, shaped like a lotus flower, with swans and fallow deer all around to soothe the landscape – so much so that it seemed celestial. When He arrived, God was Him and I felt in Paradise.

At the departure, a friend of mine had given me a book with a prophetic title, *Self-Realization, the Knowledge of the Absolute*. I had it with me and I showed it to Sai Baba, who wrote His blessing on it. I returned home with a feeling of lightness. I could almost fly, as my feet were hardly touching the ground.

The final part of the journey and the interview with Sai Baba were the confirmation that everything happened according to His Will. Sentiment was perfectly in tune with Him.

A few days upon my return, my inner voice communicated a short, enigmatic phrase: *"One must have faith and forget, one must have faith and withdraw."*

The volcano of emotions concerning the most recent experience, still live in me, was stirred up again.

Those words echoed in me for weeks, causing bewilderment and confusion. I'd been "cutting the ties" with the world all my life – with my work, with material gain, friendship and the Sai Centre. What else was there to forget? Where was I supposed to withdraw?

I realized that attaining Unity with God did not require "adding" but "subtracting". In other words, it was necessary to leave behind all sorts of attachments. And so I started thinking that I had to relinquish myself as an individual (or ego) and withdraw into the spiritual heart, or the Father's abode, or the Kingdom of Heaven, to get in touch with the true Self.

That was the real awakening but I didn't feel ready for it yet.

It was always like that. Whenever I thought I was holding victory in my fist, the Spirit would confront me with another inner battle I had to win in order to conquer a new target. I could see the outlines of the "target". But the ego understood it and it did not wait a second to come up with its sophisticated defence mechanisms.

Jesus said: *"Unless you reject your father and mother and your brothers and sisters, unless you give up of all your possessions for good, you cannot be my disciples."*

Someone told me many years before that I had been one of the disciples of Jesus but at the time I found the statement bizarre, a sort of exaggeration. There and then, the words expressed by the inner voice recalled that particular statement.

Sai Baba also says we should annul all the material, sentimental and egotistic attachments (self-indulgence and spiritual pride) – the three zeroes – in order to attain the true Self.

I prayed the Divine Mother and the Divine Master to illuminate my intellect and that of every human being with the shining light of the sun of Awareness and to fill every heart with divine, unconditional Love.

That message bounced from my heart to every cell of my body. The test of my attachment was waiting for me, as the only way to reach the "I" (as divine essence) I had always searched for.

The circle was closing up. I moved from childhood amazement to the boredom of adulthood and was now looking at the age when I was given the opportunity to know the amazement of the awakening of my individual consciousness into a vastly greater, all-inclusive Cosmic Consciousness and wisdom of the heart.

A man's original and natural exigency was not to belong to someone or to be loved but to be free to love, in the Christic, or cosmic sense of the word.

Sai Baba reiterates that we shouldn't let anyone block our spiritual growth. Indeed, the only positive relationships are those that assist us to progress in the awareness of the true Self within.

The wisdom of all times and cultures came down to the same point: withdrawing within is the only freedom.

My intention was to realize with my heart what I had taken in with my mind, as the result of my search.

The origin and the aim were at one, beyond time and space, beyond any illusion of good and evil, pleasure and pain. But I felt that there was still much work to be done to reach this state of awareness. My search was not finished yet.

And right then, a letter arrived from a friend in India. She sent me an unexpected gift, a photo depicting me while touching the feet of Sai Baba. She had found it in a bunch of photos shot at the temple[70] at the time, before it was banned to make photos, and so it became a historic snapshot. The Divine Master wanted to assure me that I wasn't alone in those moments of hard inner work.

In the constant scrutiny of thoughts, words and actions, I became aware that my choices were often limited by emotions. Divine obsession made me fear I would become spiritually proud, knowing that it was the worst, albeit the last, foe of the spiritual seeker (the third zero I had to attain).

It did appear like a perverse game – the more I worked on myself to affirm and experience Truth, the stronger and freer I felt and the more I was exposed to the risk of becoming proud, strengthening the ego instead of debilitating it. We run this risk quite often, as long as there is a crumb of ego (that vanishes only when we realize the Self) or pride for the objectives reached or for being so refined in our perception and seeing beyond the appearances.

Having learned from experience, I was watching against falling into this trap. It is hard to notice if you have fallen into it. I've seen many people slipping in, in spite of their positive intentions to do good, confident of being on the path of realization, if not already realized.

Thank God I have learned there is no wisdom without humility, as an essential indicator to discern between those who have fallen victims to their individual self and those who are enlightened, i.e. who have transcended it. However, I have had the possibility to meet few from the latter group.

I went on with my self-investigation, trying to align the different bodies (physical, mental and emotional) by practicing coherence of thoughts, words and actions. It helped me develop discernment and intuition.

Sai Baba says: *"The life of those who live driven by egotistic scopes is in the hands of others, whereas the life of the selfless is in their own hands."*

I could clearly distinguish the decisions driven by emotions (which I tried to avoid) from those driven by inspiration (intuitive), subject to a higher will. On the outside, however, the difference was not so evident. My behaviour was at times misinterpreted and considered bizarre and disconnected from common sense. I was sometimes accused of listening to no one but myself, although in reality I was trying to listen to my true Self within. My judgement was based on the outcome or on effects of my thoughts, this being the only way for me to make sure that my sensation was right and, by God's Grace, I never had to wait long for the confirmation to manifest.

The most recent test for my perception was the journey I had just returned from. By choosing to follow the path of Truth and mindfulness (I will never get tired of reiterating this), we can model our destiny because, although things are predestined, according to the law of cause and effect (the law of *karma*) we can rewrite "our own page" in the book of life every day, with our thoughts, words and actions, thus modifying what was written previously, thanks to the intervention of Divine Grace.

I believe that only this Truth, nothing but this Truth can explain the arrival of the Avatar and other enlightened Masters. They have been coming time and again with a single intent: to bring Light, Truth and Love where there was none.

Otherwise, how can we explain why Jesus arrived two thousand years ago or why Sai Baba is here in our days. Their teachings are congruent and still topical, defying the weight of the millennia. What would have been the use of those teachings had there been no possibility of change for mankind and had everything been predetermined by eternity?

The law of cause and effect, as the natural or divine law, regulates the world of matter. Despite our wish to go against it or to ignore it, the law is established in our favour – provided we can abide by it, following the teachings of the Masters. Then we can transcend it.

Jesus said: *"Do not resist evil"* and added, *"...but turn the other cheek."*
Sai Baba says: *"Respond to evil with goodness."*

Non-violence has and will always be the ultimate expression of Love as Compassion[71].

We should unrelentingly and tirelessly draw from compassion to neutralize evil, primarily in us and then around us. This is the (behavioural) key to open the door to true life and defeat all the aspects of disharmony, discord and violence.

Over the years I had some direct experiences which provided evidence (in the 4th dimension, beyond time and space) of a cosmic record (in Hinduism it is called *akashic* record) of all the events concerning planet Earth and its inhabitants, probably from the time when they first appeared on the planet.

I cannot elaborate this topic, but there is certainly no shortage of testimonies by enlightened personalities, authorities, saints, eminent scholars of esotericism and mystics. I would like to invite the reader to check my words by reading up first and then experiencing it personally.

All Holy Scriptures claim that man can become the master of his destiny when the intellect and the Spirit, in that order, take control over the emotions, the thoughts, the senses and the needs (or what we consider as such). We must bear in mind that the Holy Scriptures are holy precisely because of the Truth revealed by the Absolute, which is irrefutable at the end of the day (for the believers). Accepting this Truth is the first step towards Self-realization.

The second step, based on the eternal Truth, is man's task to understand and accept the ideal path to realize this Truth within. And here is where we are assisted by the teachings of the great Masters.

The third and most important step is to put those teachings into practice in our daily lives and verify, day by day, the achieved results.

That is the procedure which I have followed in the past ten years and the results have always been positive. Without exception, every step of the way to Spiritual Knowledge, numerous confirmations arrived and lighted the days of my inner search with enthusiasm. Things sometimes seemed almost incredibly simple.

In effect, there were certain essential requirements I had to observe carefully, apparently impossible to overcome – but not quite so.

To obtain the possibility to rewrite your personal story, first of all you have to purify your heart by setting it according to the will to do good. Then, you have to get rid of all your addictions and attachments and, lastly, act unconditionally.

The basic requirement for a makeover is to make choices that are coherent with the above said points. We should choose a model of behaviour and check the outcome according to the resulting transformation.

Everybody has the possibility of accepting the challenge of this fascinating and liberating metamorphosis – from being a slave to being a master of your own destiny. Without a doubt, the price to pay in terms of surrendering the ego is high, but, as we all know, valuable things are pricey.

Clearly, things would be much simpler and more convenient if they were just the opposite. Everyone would yearn for a better life, without much sacrifice, but the Spirit is unyielding. Generally, It remains invisible and silent when we don't meet the basic requirement: choice comes first, followed by transformation and "harvesting".

A pure heart, freedom from ties and addictions and acting unconditionally are the three elements of a "clean" channel through which the Spirit can manifest into the awakening consciousness, becoming increasingly sensitive to higher and higher frequencies, until one becomes a body of light.

From that moment on, consciousness can contemplate the Will of God and Divine Grace starts operating visibly in order to change the puzzle of life and our own destiny for the better. I have experienced it personally, day by day, year by year, from the beginning of this journey of Light.

Sai Baba says: *"You are the cause of your ruin and your good fate. The instruments are in your hands. You can learn[72] the skills. You can break the chains and evade. But if you crawl with your chains and ties, who can save you? Do not blame fate for the condition you are in."*

I could clearly see I was approaching a turning point, announced to me (by a number of people) in the past as a moment of radical change. My inner sensation was indicative of what was going on not only with me but also around me – I was writing a new page in the book of life. To me, all this was just another opportunity offered by the Divine Master to alleviate my *karmic* debt, to improve my destiny on the evolutional plane and, in a broader sense, give a positive contribution to the evolution of mankind[73]. A small light is not the sun, but it is surely better than nothing; it is a small contribution to reach the Light.

However, things were not running smoothly. I was constantly stuck in problems, concerns and difficulties, but my attitude changed. I could notice I was calmer, more serene and tolerant than I used to be.

Out of devotion for Sai Baba and in the constant search for my true nature, I set off for another journey. It was the third trip that year (the tenth in total). It served to experience serenity and equidistance and to learn to discern between divine inspiration and a desire of the ego.

Shortly before my departure I had a revealing dream. I was going to buy a tracksuit for excursions into the mountains and was offered a gold tracksuit. It happened that I was going to celebrate my forty-ninth (49th) birthday in the same year and 999,9 (that is, 4 times 9) was the symbol of sublimated, pure gold (9 is the number attributed to Sai Baba, the Divine, perfection within perfection, unity within unity, order within order and Heaven[74]). Number 9 appeared in a subsequent dream in which I saw nine stars in the sky and a voice told me I was one of them. I thought about the Divine Mother in the dream and its cloak studded with stars and identified it with Heaven.

Symbolically, the number that recurred in both dreams represents, in the mystical sense, the supreme stage of the pathway – beatitude guiding the individual towards annulling himself in the totality, drowning his personality in Universal Love. It was a good omen for the realization of the goal I was hoping to achieve.

Number 9, in its redeeming essence, is also associated with Jesus who, according to the Gospel, was crucified in the third hour, started to agonize in the sixth hour and expired in the ninth hour. It is the end and the beginning, as the last number of the manifest universe. It opens the phase of transmutation and expresses the end of a cycle – the completion of a course and the closure of a ring. To me, this was the meaning of the experience I was about to have at the initial stage of the imminent transmutation of plumb into gold.

I received an invitation to travel to Mount Kailash, the sacred mountain of Shiva, in Tibet, close to the northern Indian border.

I was fascinated by the adventurous aspect of the journey, but quite unclear about my strong drive to climb the 5600 meters high summit (as a matter of fact, its very peak may not be climbed, out of respect for the holy site).

I was perhaps attracted by what it symbolized. In the Hindu tradition, Kailash represents the source of divine, cosmic energy (Shiva – Shakti) and the spiritual heart of man and the world. I accepted the invitation on one condition: provided we first went to Puttaparthi to receive Sai Baba's blessing.

Over the time, I came to realize that I should have been alerted by the fact that divine inspiration was lacking (in the previous journeys, it had been the sole driving force).

When we arrived at the *ashram* at Puttaparthi, I had an outburst of rebellion, like never before, or after. It was a mark of incoherence and I was going to pay for it dearly.

I kept repeating within: "May Your Will be done", accepting everything God was giving me, but it didn't work. The ego came up with a tough trial, causing an "implosion" (a deep discomfort mixed with impatience), followed by an explosion of rejection.

I found accommodation that being the only possibility, in a shed with about 300 beds. I had gladly accepted similar accommodations in the past, even for several days. I have no idea why I refused to stay there on that particular occasion. I left the *ashram* to go to a nearby hotel.

There was something wrong within me and around me and I could perceive it with disarming clarity. My rejection was due to impatience.

That awkward accommodation apparently helped me understand that I was not fit for the kind of journey I wanted to make. However, the actual obstacle and my real concern was not my physical condition (prior to departure, my friends had advised me to give up, considering me physically unfit for the strain). My pride was hurt thinking for a moment that I could not cope with the hard conditions and hence the entire plot was concocted by the ego. The Divine Master signalled indirectly that the impetus was simply based on a desire, it was a fruit of the ego. A few days later I received the confirmation.

I spent three days and three nights in "agony", until I took my backpack, left the hotel and returned ("May Your Will be done" implied accepting everything, even an uncomfortable situation) to the *ashram*, where I asked to be accommodated, making it clear that I was going to leave in a couple of days.

The man asked me why, which was pretty uncommon under the circumstances and I replied I was going to travel to Tibet. What followed was a clear sign for me not to go. I was told it was not advisable to venture into such travels, since the roads to Tibet were dangerous[75]. Besides, it was useless to seek the consciousness of the Self so far away, while it was right there in front of me, like a mirror of my spiritual heart. Sai Baba was there. I was eventually invited not to follow other people's minds because in that moment I had to keep my own mind under control, so that I could follow it afterwards, and find my fortune.

I felt Sai Baba was addressing me through the elderly devotee in charge of the welcome service. I was given a very comfortable room. Having learned the hard lesson, my heart did not need any other evidence. All I needed was tranquillity.

It was the festival of the Guru (Master), or the *Gurupurnima,* one of the most important holidays in the Hindu calendar.

That year Sai Baba stated that only those who lived in harmony were real human beings. Modern man abandons himself only in the few moments of pleasure, instead of cultivating serenity. He talked about friendship at length and said: *"Take your time before you make a friend. Consider his background and the friends he sees. Do not be a person without character, avoid bad friendships and stay close to the fire (good, spiritual people). If you stay close to the dust (people who are not spiritual, slaves to the ego), you will be corroded. Choose the right friend. He or she must be a pure person, that is, whose thoughts, words and deeds are in mutual harmony[76]. That is a true human being."*

Sai Baba talked extensively about the value of harmony and specified that *"When we realize the Androgynous[77] within, we will be able to reach the state of harmony that will allow us to see God"* and that He was the Androgynous (personified Harmony). He went on, saying that: *"brass[78] and gold look the same but brass only looks like gold. It is worth nothing. Gold keeps shining, while brass becomes darker with time. Become human beings in the content (in practice), not only in the form (in theory). Do not live an artificial life, but a real one. Be the gold[79] in this fake world, do not be the brass. The real meaning of God is Light and Truth. It manifests in solitude, by focusing the mind on God. Don't let your mind wander away, following your thoughts about the body or the family. It must be tied to God."*

He concluded by saying that we should have a pure heart, white[80] as milk and other-centred, and that the process of purification could last an entire life. It is never too late to start doing the right thing.

Obviously, the natural law of cause and effect (*karma*) serves to understand our true task (certain goals require many years of searching). If we come to understand it and move in the right direction, the game of repeated births and deaths ends and the lesson is over. Once we have learned it, there is no more sense to repeat it and we can finally transcend our own destiny.

This statement may sound other-worldly, but it is plain truth for me.

The devotion in the heart and the tenacious will to practice the teachings of the Divine Master enabled me to really master my destiny and realize that the sense of vulnerability afflicting us was the poisonous fruit of our negative thoughts. If you have experienced real joyfulness or bliss, even for a brief moment, you know you cannot be affected if you are united with the Spirit. "Gold" is a metaphor of being perfect, nourishing only positive thoughts.

Gold is the symbol of the Spirit. If the thoughts, the words and the behaviour are positive, we enliven the Spirit in us and life becomes worthy of living because it is lived for a good scope and in goodness. This does not necessarily require taking a vow (of a religious order) or belonging to a church (even a priest can lead a non spiritual life unless his life is dedicated to good deeds).

Considering ourselves as believing souls simply because we belong to a religion or a church would be just another common mistake. However, how many of those who profess their belief can say that they verily believe in God and that they are not pretending?

Having access to the Spirit and God entails a pure heart's devotion, in harmony with all the forms of life – unconditionally and without attachment.

Sai Baba says: *"Follow the Master, your conscience and your Dharma[81]. Unity is Purity and Purity is Divinity."*

The Master is Love (as devotion), Consciousness is discernment (as knowledge) and *Dharma* is righteous behaviour (as service). Those are the three keys to feel God within and to no longer feel alone.

Loving, Knowing and Serving are the stages along the way, in discovering our true, divine nature.

Man often feels alone and this loneliness does not imply strength but annihilation, because he is not at one with God. There are two kinds of loneliness: being on our own with God is divine, whereas being on our own with the ego implies depression and fear.

God or destiny are not to be held accountable for our condition of malaise because it stems from our choices, our actions, words and thoughts, from one life to another, accompanied by our credits but also our unsettled debts, whether we liked it or not and whether we believed it or not.

It often happens that we look forward to change, but we haven't got the courage to make the right choices, blaming God even for our lack of character and daring. God has nothing to do with it. Changes come about when we make the right choices and hence draw divine protection and Grace upon ourselves.

Sai Baba says: *"invest part of your time to understand what God commands you to do and the rest to put it into practice. This is total surrender."*

That is always the primary task, but during that particular stay it was revealed as one of the most important "obligatory passageways" towards overcoming the ego and transmuting brass into gold.

I felt egotistic solitude and bewilderment for three endless days because I distanced myself from the Divine Master, erecting a wall of impatience and hurt pride (alas!) between Him and me, dictated by the same ego that had induced me to take the wrong choices. Indeed, the ego is always a bad advisor.

Heeding desires drives us off the true path of devotion, away from the Spirit, because they too are bad advisers, being an expression of the ego.

Sai Baba says: *"The ego always takes and forgets, while Love always gives and forgives."* The former is the night and the latter is the day of the Spirit for someone who hasn't found the inner Light yet.

Joyfulness and happiness are characteristic of the true Self. Unhappiness is characteristic of the false self, or the ego. Appeasing desires (expressions of the ego) results, sooner or later, in unhappiness (expression of the ego), i.e. we go from one expression of the ego to the next, in a vicious circle which can be broken only if we become aware, in a lucid and determined manner, of having fallen into a cycle of death instead of life. Consider for example sexuality, originally the expression of pure (divine) energy. When it is manipulated by desires and experienced without due holiness – or without an affinity of souls, without unconditional Love, when it comes down to power games – it becomes a sterile experience of death, producing only attachment, perversion, violence, confusion, fear, anxiety, apathy, diseases and more death. Again, if man has not been able to open the heart to unconditional Love which is life, he transforms vital energy into a tool of self-destruction for him and the other. The ego makes life difficult, but it makes death difficult too because it prevents us from seeing beyond and attributing the right value to this unavoidable phase – that it is the source of a new life.

On the other hand, the true Self, unlike the ego, facilitates life and death and makes them natural by allowing us to get familiar with their essence.

Detaching from the body is simple and natural if we are aware that the body is an instrument, allowing us to go through the many experiences in the world of matter, of which this is merely one. Only the Spirit is unchangeable and eternal.

Life is enshrined in the Self (the divine spark or Atma) that guides the body through the soul. Therefore, the true Self exists prior to birth and after the body disintegrates. It is immortal and incorruptible. It is pure, sublimated gold, or the Divine residing in us.

During the Festival of the Guru, the inner Master, individual consciousness encountered Cosmic Consciousness. The divine spark (*Atma*) was in the presence of the Absolute (the *Paramatma*) and darkness was dissipated by the Light. The Master (the *Sadguru*) resides in the spiritual heart of every person and His essence is pure awareness, or Divine Knowledge revealed, or eternal wisdom.

On that journey I learned a necessary, albeit hard lesson: the more we are tied to something and the more we suffer when it is taken away from us, although it is for our own good, for us to be set free. The painful lessons are the most profound and indispensable for our growth.

After I'd overcome the inner crisis, I realized that the divine spark (*Atma*) was omnipresent – in the sky, in the mountains, in the trees, everywhere and that Sai Baba was Shiva and Shakti (the divine Mother and Father), the source of energy and energy itself. He was the Creator, He was also Mount Kailash, or the Creation.

Dawn breaks after the dark hours of the night, announcing the start of a new day, just as a tempest is always followed by clear, calm weather. I recognised the danger and stopped myself in time, wisely deciding to remain on my own at Puttaparthi and give up of the journey to Kailash.

Evidently, spiritual ignorance separates us from our true nature, or the divine essence, or the true Self. When we behave egotistically, we betray and deceive ourselves. When we don't love and give freely, we prevent the true Self from manifesting.

To get rid of ignorance, we must know ourselves. In other words, we should primarily discover the real Self within. Truth will then set us free from ignorance and reveal who we really are.

The wisest thing for me to do was to stop in time, instead of persevering in my error and getting confused by discordant relations. It was best to be focused on the irreversible, i.e. the Spirit, and listen to Its soundless voice, the inner voice of the spiritual heart.

We should pause at this expression: listen to our heart. It has become a platitude. Which heart? Certainly not the heart that starts pounding at the slightest emotion or makes us sigh and cry when we experience disappointments.

To hear the voice of the heart, we need to have balanced at least the first three chakras[82] of the body, linked respectfully to the desires which destroy devotion unless we moderate them, anger, which annihilates wisdom if uncontrolled and greed, which poisons each action if uncontained.

The fire of true Love can dissolve those flaws, so common to the entire humankind, and free us from desires, anger and greed.

Three are the powers we can develop to nourish the necessary strength and discover the true essence within: willpower as devotion, the power of discernment as wisdom and the power of action as service (in esotericism: will, power and duty). Again, three are the keys necessary to recognise and feel the divine essence in us: Love, Knowledge and Service.

The *Vedas* (holy Hindu scriptures) describe three types of people: those who don't care about spirituality, defined as animalistic and demoniacal, those who care only apparently about it, defined as human, and those who experience it substantially, defined as divine.

Sai Baba says: *"a greedy man's faith is like a water container with holes in it"*. *"Those who refuse to get rid of greed while pretending to be devotees, can never quench their thirst."* He therefore warns not to fake devotion while avoiding to make concrete sacrifices that would bring a deep transformation.

We were born to 'spend' ourselves for the sake of others and not to 'spare' ourselves , that is, to 'give' ourselves and not to 'receive'. Loving the world is a form of attachment. Loving God is devotion.

The logic of the Spirit is the antithesis of the logic of the world to which our mind is unfortunately subdued. Our education has uneducated us and our culture has made us ignorant. The only truly educational books are those that help us find ourselves again and retake the reins of that 'horse' that got lost and shies occasionally. 'Taming' ourselves requires inner strength, courage and tenacity which can come only from our faith in God.

Sai Baba came down to earth to encourage us, show us the way to salvation and for us to gain or regain our trust in Him. He became flesh, to be part of the visible and tangible reality for those who, blinded by the glittering world, believe only in what they see, but what else can He do for us if we keep ignoring Him?

I was back with a new baggage of experiences to reflect upon, with a renewed trust in the Divine Master, and so I dedicated myself to my study, search and self-inquiry. The experience, although difficult in many ways, strengthened me considerably and revealed the 'direct line' with Sai Baba. My dreams proved to be precursory of His teachings, specifically designed for the pathway I had chosen, even if their meaning was not explicit.

I received confirmation that divine intention was always beneficent and that light and darkness, good and evil, were the two sides of the same coin, teaching us how to unite with the All.

Even the natural law of cause and effect (*karma*) shows that unity is at the end of a man's vital cycle (and of all other forms of existence on earth). Death is the same for everyone and no one can know the place, the date and the modality in which their earthly life will end. No one has ever learned in time "how to deal with" this unique lesson. At the end of the day, it is the same for everyone. We continue to witness that unrepeatable event by attending funerals – at times unwillingly, at times tragically involved, depending on the modality of participation: courtesy, duty, love or affection, but without learning anything.

Death can be a touchy topic and so people avoid it as much as possible.

Devotion, discernment, non-attachment, liberation and Self-realization generally sound like words taken from a mysterious crossword puzzle, without much sense or connection. And yet, this kind of ignorance is paid with life – real life.

Although spirituality has become fashionable, it remains difficult to talk about it. It often provokes reservedness, mistrust, impatience and annoyance.

With whom could I talk about Sai Baba being the conqueror of death, without stirring perplexity?

No one at all. And so I continued writing silently about my mute, sad cry expressing the pain of a mankind that sadly turned their deaf ear to His call.

Sai Baba came on tiptoe, in His humble modesty, yet so majestically impressive to those who recognize Him in their hearts, because He did not want to intimidate us, or arouse fear, giving everyone the possibility to approach Him, without distinction, without asking anyone to renounce their own creed.

Some people commented: How can one think that God descended to earth again, incarnated in this short, dark-skinned man?

The same thing happened in the time of Jesus, although He was neither short nor dark-skinned.

I thought: if only they could see Him with the eyes of the heart, they would see His inestimable and immense beauty and splendour. The "physical" appearance of the Divine can mislead those who reason with the mind, whose heart is kept silent.

He taught me that the energy permeating man, released in the form of sexual energy (the fire of *Kundalini*, the Spirit in matter, according to Hinduism), activating the seven chakras (7 is the number of the Holy Spirit), is the divine expression of the Holy Spirit in man, as Love, Life and Self-giving.

At last, I could clearly see the significance and value of energy sublimation, otherwise consumed in sexuality and in the overall complexity of relationships and the close relationship between non-attachment to the senses and the widening and awakening of consciousness, in the light of spiritual growth..

The Universe, as the creative expression of the Divine, has a moral agenda we are fully unaware of, which does not overlap with human morals.

In essence, man has been and will always be free. Still, he will enjoy this freedom only upon resuming his celestial life. He has been and will be present here on earth as essence harnessed by the matter, with the possibility, depending on the status he has earned, to live a more or less acceptable or bearable life.

My contacts with the Spirit were not illusory fantasies but spiritual and real experiences of knowledge, or presence, revealed with Love, out of Love by the Divine Self in me and I was most certain about it.

There is a part in the *Vedas* that recites: *"You understand and I understand, my dear mind... – regardless of anyone else's understanding or lack of it – that my experience of Infinity is fulfilling and real."*

I often experienced this fulfilment as a sign heralding the encounter with the real Self or the All-embracing, supreme reality.

I learned that the knowledge of the Self stemmed from acts of Love and in my heart I knew my task was performed out of Love. Therefore, I looked forward to receiving signs of approval from the Divine Master before each step on the path, to be certain that not only I would benefit from my writing (in a larger scheme of things, I did not count much).

Meanwhile, I reassured myself, if I was only a medium, a tool to be tuned up in the best possible way, an empty vessel, the Spirit could act through me.

The Bhagavad-Gita[83] reads: *"For the gold flame to burn and provide a constant light, the lamp must be put in a place well protected from the winds."*

My wish was to prevail over the great illusion of the ego, not only for my own sake, but also to testify that this apparently impossible endeavour could be a success, a small flame with a stable light.

I hoped I could give my contribution by following the example of the chosen souls of all times, whose huge task consisted in dissolving the darkness of human suffering on earth.

Truth, or "Eternal Harmony", was a necessary tool. It gave me the confidence to continue my search for the invisible omnipresent. It helped me release my creativity, especially when I was true to myself.

Thinking back about my journeys to India that year, I realized they had a taste of non-attachment, as a prelude to the detailed, secret plan the Divine Master had in store for me.

This statement of fact created a certain foreboding that disturbed my inner peace.

I wanted to be limpid, even at the cost of being tough with myself. I would never treat anyone else like that, however. The Divine Master says: *"Truth must never hurt anyone."*

My not-always-harmonious thoughts ranged from feeling unworthy of so much grace to being worried about the unpredictability of life, or that I would not be up to who-knows-which task, or that my writing would come to a standstill due to my inner unease.

I was well aware that the Absolute was immutable and stored everything in its memory bank. I had always known deep inside that I would be asked, sooner or later, to sacrifice the personal at the altar of the impersonal. Truth illuminates all, even the darkest corners.

I had offered my life to Sai Baba and His cause, the noblest of all causes: salvation of mankind. There was nothing else for me to do but to wait for His call.

67. In the Hindu tradition, the snake symbolizes *Kundalini*, i.e. the energy connecting man to cosmic energy. Associated with Vishnu and Shiva is also the royal cobra or the golden snake symbolizing knowledge, life, divine youth and fertility, that is, the inspirational soul and the intelligence fecundated by the Spirit.

68. Monday is the day dedicated to Shiva and 5 is the number of Shiva. In Hinduism, every day of the week is dedicated to a specific divinity.

69. According to the Gnostic school of thought, the first 5 must be in balance for the inner work to yield fruits and for the person to have access into the two higher realms.

70. Made by the students, not by the devotees.

71. Sai Baba maintains that women are incarnations of power and strength, because there is more devotion in them. Men are more violent (in terms of anger, jealousy, passion, etc.)

72. Sai Baba reminds us that we "can learn the skills" and therefore it is in our power to learn and transform our lives.

73. I am going to explain this part later on, speaking about the "hundredth monkey" effect.

74. Avicenna says that "Every number or any number is but a number 9 or its multiplication, plus a surplus, because there are only 9 digits and values, plus the 0."

75. At the time, Kashmir was in a state of war.

76. Having a pure heart means living in the harmony of thoughts, words and actions. In other words, being coherent.

77. Union of soul and Spirit: to understand this phrase, I would have had to search and think for an additional period of 4 years.

78. Brass represents the ego, whereas gold represents the Spirit, or the true Self.

79. Of course, it is about the gold tracksuit mentioned in His speech.

80. I recall the white Lingam made of light He offered to me in my dream.

81. A behaviour appropriate for a certain role, which varies from one person to another, depending on the person's blueprint of destiny.

82. The 7 chakras are the following: the Root, the Navel, the Solar, the Heart, the Throat, the Third Eye and the Crown chakra.

83. The most important Holy Scripture in Hinduism, the same way the Bible is in Christianity.

X

There is no place unknown to Me because I am omnipresent and nothing can be hidden from Me.

Sai Baba.

A Telugu[83] saying says: *"No one can feel the desire for freedom without having experienced other desires first."*

This comforted me because it meant I was on the list of candidates for freedom, although it was not my major concern. I understood the importance of accomplishing the task of my life – serving mankind – and put the rest in the hands of God.

It is necessary to heave up anchor from the physical body, emotions and thoughts, to become absorbed in the Formless space and savour the "infinitude" of life.

When our heart and mind are no longer drawn back and tied to the past, the Spirit intervenes to guide us, until we break free from the slavery to illusions.

The Spirit is the "Spiritual Knowledge" that transcends individuality and so, as we progress on the path, the ego has to give in and can no longer see itself as the champion of anything because it is the Spirit speaking, acting and thinking in us and for us.

It was impossible to look back without the risk of turning into a statue of "salt."[84]

I was offered imperturbability in exchange for a conscious detachment from my habitual points of reference, or better, attachments hitherto.

Although I was confident that I would eventually conquer fear, never to feel unconscious pain again, I was still restless: the ego, undefeated, was in effect the only thing I had to relinquish because God, or Sai Baba, says we should "renounce" the ego and nothing else.

When we love God, we are given everything we ask for with a pure heart. I knew in my heart that the Spirit was listening to me all the time.

Well, the decisive moment of realization was approaching. Sai Baba told me *"Yes"* while He blessed the book on Self-realization, during the last interview. We cannot cheat or hum and haw with the laws of Heaven the way we do with human laws. God's response to my prayer was His inner call.

Coming back from the previous journey, as I got off the plane, the sky welcomed me with a beautiful rainbow, as if to convey God's message: "I am with you all the time. Welcome home." My home was wherever I could feel Him, without any specific geographic references. He resided in my heart.

Rainbows symbolize the restoration of Cosmic Order and the gestation of a new cycle, but for the Christians it is also a sign of the alliance between God and man, Heaven and earth, a sign of permanent grace, the iridescent circle of divine benevolence, the symbol of the New Age personality, the expression of the Holy Spirit.

I often repeated in silence: "The more you KNOW (Translator's note: in the original language, Italian, the author uses the word "SAI", meaning "you KNOW") and the fewer needs you have" – "KNOW", in terms of Knowledge but also in terms of the presence of the Divine, or Sai Baba within..

Apparently, it was necessary to go through a stage of "sheer folly" prior to reaching the inner essence. Was that perhaps God's folly, mentioned by the mystics in the past and auspicated by Sai Baba to make the world a better place?

Due to a series of family vicissitudes, my patience was constantly put on trial. I felt oppressed and deeply embittered and misunderstood by my son. Still, I was supposed to understand him, as a mother.

The flame that ignited my inner light appeared whenever I turned my thoughts and heart to the Divine Master, intensely and passionately. It was not a paradox. It really takes "the passion of the Light" to overcome the most difficult and tempting obstacles of everyday life. My intent was to divide "the grain from the husk" every day and the task was neither easy nor painless most of the times.

I would cheer myself up: Come on! Only the strong persevere in the realization of their destiny. You are strong. You can make it. One day you will be at His service, in His Kingdom. Don't be afraid of loneliness and introspection – don't forget that wise people consider it as a gift – it would be foolish to consider it deceitful. The gift (that's how I considered solitude) was indeed useful for my inner growth, albeit not always just as pleasant.

Sai Baba says: *"Leave behind every fear and every hope."* I had not managed to cancel the word "hope" from my personal vocabulary and was definitely not ready to do it yet.

Upon careful consideration, I didn't have any specific expectations, but my thoughts sometimes roamed, accompanied by chimerical ideas. My fantasy wandered aimlessly.

These renegade thoughts distracted me (I was aware of this) from my commitment. In order to write, I had to be in perfect tune with the Spirit – otherwise I was blocked.

To attain fulfilment and not to feel empty, Sai Baba, as the Holy Spirit, urged me to raise my awareness (the dream of the feast of the peacock enlightened me on the power of creativity in defeating the power of the senses and instincts) and to consciously detach myself. Having got rid of my attachments, I would be able to love appropriately and be useful to others and to myself.

Will and desire are expressions (higher and lower) of the energy permeating man in his totality. This energy can be managed by the Spirit, as awareness, or by the body (ego), as individual consciousness.

The *Kundalini* energy, or the energy of the Holy Spirit the rainbow, with its original function (subsequently distorted) of assisting the development of the higher consciousness i.e. the energy, which is the Spirit, yearns to return to the Spirit, tends to merge with Cosmic Consciousness, the drop that merges with the Ocean, after it has transcended the harnessing of matter.

The power of the will to Love (expression of the true Self) sets us free from the desire to be loved (expression of the individual self or the ego). This power is an intuitive faculty released in us by devotion, the Love of God, and the wish to help humanity, after we have helped ourselves, because we cannot assist anybody unless *we* are in harmony. It was necessary to undo the partnership with the ego to finally unite with the true Self, but water flows slowly at the source and it takes time for it to reach the light and become a torrent and finally a river.

Likewise, I felt the source springing from my heart very slowly. The true Self as the Spirit was imprisoned in the body. Once the resistance of the ego was subdued, It would enter His Kingdom through the door of balance. There it would become, according to the Hindu Holy Scriptures: "a sweet, soft and mature fruit for other people's pain and a hard and resistant kernel for one's own suffering."

This is how the passions of the ego are conquered and the diamond[85] soul awakened, for us to be able to discover new realms, besides the physical, emotional and mental ones. We then reach the realm of the Spirit, with all its dimensions. In the dream about Sai Baba, when He talked about the new world, He anticipated this moment.

When we have subjugated the ego-subservient disposition, we can create our destiny and serve the Absolute. True freedom consists in knowing how to direct our own nature towards the primordial source: the Goodness which is for the good of everyone, as the only positive direction of existence.

I was pondering on this when I dreamt of Sai Baba again. He entered the room and put, on the bed, a rosary, or *japamala* (with 108 beads), with large beads, like gold nuts, tied to a pendant of gold and enamel, in three colours – blue, red and green. It was marvellous, shiny and regal. I immediately said that it can't be for me, as it was too precious. Two friends came to my mind and I wondered which one of them it was for, but He disappeared without a reply. I couldn't figure out what He meant. As I woke up, I started investigating the meaning and symbolic value of that holy object. According to Hindu symbolism, the thread which ties all the beads of a rosary symbolizes our divine essence, Atma or divine spark, on which creation, all manifest things, is fitted. They are respectively the expression of the Spirit in terms of spiritual essence and the Spirit in terms of created matter, i.e. the Union of the Creator's static energy and Creation's dynamic energy, united together as divine Love, and Will, in Hinduism *Shiva* and *Shakti*, *Purusha* and *Prakriti*, respectively masculine and feminine energy permeating the entire Creation[86].

I learned from the theory of the sublimation of sexual energy, common to all religions and all esoteric and Gnostic schools, that the energy of the sexual impulse, related to the instinct of procreation, is deviated through the procreative channels into the creative ones, so as to enrich the five senses of an ordinary person with a sixth sense, that is, intuitive vision, defined in the eastern culture as the eye of Shiva, the third eye, corresponding to the chakra on the forehead. If the third eye is not open, metaphorically speaking, we cannot perceive or approach God, or Goodness, or Cosmic Love.

In the esoteric anatomy of man's subtle bodies, the third eye, the sixth sense corresponds to the sixth (*Ajna* or frontal) chakra. The person who intuitively understands or discovers something without reasoning that escapes practical objectivity is generally defined as 'having the sixth sense'.

Intuition is the expression of pure intellect (or *buddhi*) and it anticipates the faculty of clairvoyance.

Once it has been purified of the limitations of physicality (the senses) and transformed into compassion, sexual energy, *Shakti-Kundalini* in Hinduism, balances desires and purifies the heart.

At this stage, we can speak from the heart, feel with the heart, see with the heart and listen with the heart. In other words, we go into the essence of things, to the Truth, and faith is experienced as the Knowledge of God.

Life is no longer a mystery. It is beautiful and its splendour manifests with every breath, breeze and sunray, as we are grateful to the Creator of all things, visible and invisible.

I repeatedly thanked the Divine Master, guiding and enlightening me on the mysteries of life, day after day, without break.

The inner toil continued due to my intense desire to clarify things and maintain clarity – not due to the hesitations or doubts on the path. I was certain, despite the occasional moments of dejection, that I was on the right path to the Light.

I managed to give sense to my suffering whenever it emerged and this helped me control and defeat it, even transform it into joy a few times, having discovered that, by changing my attitude to pain, it could turn into a positive feeling. It was about shifting from pessimism to optimism and seeing the glass half-full instead of half-empty.

I hadn't fully mastered my emotions yet (in esoteric terms, this state is defined as "eyes that do not cry"), in the sense that I would sometimes feel inadequate and distant from the environment. At the same time, I felt as if I'd lost something, or an imminent bereavement blocking me. Fortunately, I managed to completely forget about myself and my "troubles" whenever I was intent on listening to someone, which was often the case. Helping others helped me as well.

I couldn't express to anyone what I felt inside. How to explain that I was aware of being in transit, when I did not know where I would end up, or where I would be called to go to.

That year I organized a birthday party for my friends (it was supposed to be my last birthday) and I prepared for the guests, like a propitiatory rite (I didn't know the meaning of), many little green cloth bags and filled them with some Indian rice. I tied them with two ribbons, red and blue, as an association to my last dream of Sai Baba (the gold *japamala* with a tricolour pendant).

I was forty-nine but I felt as if I were a thousand. I was going to start anew. After all, I had been reborn twice already – after my illness and when I met Sai Baba.

How many rebirths was I supposed to celebrate? But it was better to celebrate the daily life, its every dawn and dusk, from what I'd learned from the Divine Master.

More and more frequently, my nights were like an intensive course to revise what I'd learned, visualized and intuited during the day.

To me, the triumphant unification of Divine Love and Divine Will is the mystic matrimony, the realization of the "Androgynous", the complete man. Its symbols are also the Cosmic egg (Lingam), the pentagram of Pythagoras (3, the masculine, or creative, + 2, the feminine, or receptive, = 5, the complete, or realized person), but it is also represented on paintings depicting sacral images, in the oval (almond) light encircling the body of Jesus, as the mystery of light, or that of saints, symbolizing immortal glory. In a nutshell, the Androgynous expresses the union of Heaven and earth, of Spirit and matter and of the positive and the negative, which have transcended the duality in the harmonious union of the body and soul and the divine spark (the true Self or Atma).

Sai Baba is the living incarnation of the Androgynous. He invites everyone to reach His level of perfection. It is not a utopia – it *is* possible to renew oneself and be born again into a new life albeit in the same physical life. Love and Will are the most supreme expressions of the Divine presence within a man. When united, they unleash invincible power and strength. It is the sole power that can defeat the fear of death.

The gradual withdrawal from the world was certainly not aimed at hermitage but at nourishing the awakening of consciousness. I wished to "be" in the world – awakened, lucid, alive and aware – and not asleep like most of the people (defined by Jesus as "the living dead").

The initiated define a soulless physical body as an "empty house". Up till then, I was unaware of the existence of "soulless people", or inhabitants of empty houses – people who were dead in the eyes of God.

My wish was to live guided by the true Self and not simply to survive, dominated by the ego.

I was increasingly fascinated by the knowledge of the universal sense of life. That path required forgetting about the distress for not feeling the ground under your feet, so to say, and daring to leap into the dark, although the impetus to break free and fly was still instable – it came and went.

Sai Baba says that He first reaches out to those who have been waiting for Him, since they have been preparing to meet Him for a long time, i.e. in more lifetimes. This, along with the law of cause and effect (*karma*), explains the apparent preferences in the way He relates to us when we are in His presence, in India, or when we are away from His physical form.

I could firmly claim that I had worked hard until the age of 43 "to find Him", to pave the way for Him to appear in my life. It happened much earlier for some people, or later for others, or never (in this lifetime).

I felt like doing something for those who had never heard about Him and for those who had not recognized him. The gift I had received from Him was too big and priceless and I had to try and share it somehow with the less fortunate brothers and sisters. There was nothing else for me to share, if not my experience and the time of my life spent with Him and for Him, in terms of Spirit of life.

The gift of Love and Truth, enlightening every thought, action and word, served to illuminate me on the meaning of life as the Divine Game, where destiny was but a strategy, to help us untie the knots and settle the debts accumulated in the present, or in the previous lives. Otherwise, we create new debts. It was either freedom (from *karma*) or slavery (to *samsara*, i.e. the cycle of rebirths).

I wanted to use my time to testify a life spent striving, not always successfully, to be a tool of the Spirit. Was it too little compared to what the Spirit had given me? It was all I had.

I asked the Divine Master to make me forget about myself. My aim was to reduce my needs while I was tempering my flaws. Again, the only "prompt" was Love, in terms of comprehension, forgiveness and tolerance. As the relationship with the Divine was gradually reinforced, I felt these feelings consolidating in me and, the more Spiritual Knowledge I had, the more grateful I was to God for this new heart He helped me reveal. I was finally capable of Loving because I could feel, albeit inconstantly, the fullness of the contact with my true nature, as the matrix or the source of Love.

The fruits of the Spirit are many and luxuriant for those who discover the garden of life, made of Love, peace, joy, patience, benevolence, loyalty, self-mastery, meekness and humility. At times I felt so loved by the Spirit that I perceived its domination. My concern was that it might be blasphemous to think about Him in this manner, but that was really how I felt. It was both sweet and incumbent to hear an inner voice telling me: *"You are mine. You belong to me, just as I belong to you. Love me, as I love you. Honour me."*

In this regard, I would comfort myself by reading the messages of Sai Baba and the Holy Scriptures, containing precise references, similar to what I perceived, which confirmed the sacred origin of my sensations.

The time of the Spirit had come, just as the Holy Scriptures predicted. I lived in a unique and precious age of transition, at the turn of the millennium. Mine was the best possible condition – close to God, Sai Baba, Whom I could always feel by my side and in my heart, Who had come to announce the New Age, despite the prevailing catastrophic attitudes, and indicate a path of salvation to the world and to mankind, declaring to be the Androgynous, or the incarnated Holy Spirit. His voice repeated what He had previously expressed (during my first interview), which did not differ from what He normally communicated to the rest of humanity: *"I am in you, on you, beside you and behind you"*. The Spirit of Truth talked to me.

For us to learn to love again, we must feel loved by God, because it brings joy, confidence, peace and self-acceptance. A child grows up well and is serene only if it feels the closeness and is loved by its mother or whoever it is raised by.

Hence, I was wondering: Why was man born to love and not to be loved? If this was so, were we meant to be loved only by the Spirit within? This spiritual truth could sound like a paradox, but it is not. In fact, we can obtain happiness, fulfilment, peace and accept ourselves only if we feel loved by God, as the Spirit in us, that is, by being in tune with our divine essence (our real nature) or His presence in the pure, "spiritual" heart. Then we can love without expecting anything in return, unconditionally, just as during deambulation – we must first recognise the importance of the use of our legs and then train them, so that we can finally walk. Those who experienced disability in their adult age and had to regain control over their limbs know what I am talking about.

Other manifestations of love (fondness, infatuation, passion) that are not considered divine are, according to Sai Baba, merely attachments. They imprison and limit us, creating dependence, and they certainly fall short of providing that peace, happiness, confidence and self-acceptance we really need.

I felt free to confide with the Divine Master and talk to Him with a boldness I had never known before. The reason was that I let go of myself to Him trustingly, without reserve or condition.

I often reiterated to Him: "Your Will be done, and not my will", like a mantra (sacred invocation of the Name of God), and in that case His name was Will.

I firmly believe that, if mankind opened their hearts to Love and Truth and experienced the downpour of Light inundating them when they open up to God, we would become one single heart (in one single body of Light) – the heart of Jesus, Sai Baba, God, the Absolute or the Universe[87].

If the material needs of mankind were sublimated, nothing would separate us again and, united in the Spirit of Love and Truth, we would become a new humankind, looking forward to a new future – the age of spiritual knowledge.

Sai Baba knew how sincere my feelings were when I addressed Him freely and He replied almost spontaneously, infusing me with the courage to go on.

This intimate dialogue with Him librated me from the bonds of worldly morals and laws. Those who depend on the Spirit are accountable to the Spirit, by the Divine Law of Love and Truth. The Spirit expects us to do good and abide by the Divine Law.

Jesus said: *"If you remain faithful to My word, you will really be my disciples, you will know the Truth and the Truth will set you free."*

I felt more and more that I belonged to the Divine (as the Spirit of Love and Truth), that I was His disciple, less and less limited by earthly ties.

I remembered one of my first dreams of the Divine Master, in which I knelt down before Him, declaring my smallness, and He revealed me the treasure I did not know I possessed in the heart. It was devotion, or Love for the Divine. From that moment I started to "learn" through the Spirit, which awaked me into true life. I recalled this oneiric episode from the past because the same year, on Easter Monday, I visited a priest with a group of friends, at the convent where he resided. The elderly holy man was sick. An assistant taking care of him could comprehend his softly pronounced words, and so he interpreted the priest's words for us. I entered the small room with a few people and we were asked to take a large rosary and recite some prayers. I happened to be holding no less than the cross[88].

When my turn arrived to talk to him, he said I was very lucky (in the spiritual sense of the word) because I was holding the cross in my hands (symbolizing suffering as self-sacrifice) – I had picked the best part.

I had another encounter the same morning, for reasons that did not concern me. Again, during the initial rite of prayer, I ended up holding the cross, for the second time.

I came up with an explanation for the inner travail of my life, illuminated by the wise and loving light of the Spirit in the more recent years: my "double fortune" consisted in the second chance, given to me in my ripe age (I had missed the first chance, in my teen age), to subdue reason (mind) to the divine will by sacrificing the ego.

When you know unconditional Love, you live coherently, with discernment. You can immediately see what's true and what isn't. Everything becomes crystal clear – the mind is no longer obscured and the eyes are wide open.

Everything other than true Love is immediately viewed as pettiness, incongruence, instability or as some the many facets of egotism, arrogance, hardness of heart, possessiveness, seductiveness, mistrust, abuse of power and presumptuousness are but a few. If we have discernment, we can spot them at once.

A striking example is service done conditionally, to gain worldly gratification. Unlike true, altruistic service, it serves the ego. In fact, there can be no real service without Love and Wisdom.

True Love illuminates the secrets of the human heart, without leaving any space for shadows. Its strength resides in the readiness to give, which ultimately prevails over any kind of resistance, alibi or any other showing off staged by the ego to oppose it.

Those who are unable to surrender to the Spirit are destined to a life of hard-hearted loneliness – sterile and frustrating.

I wasn't sure whether I could define the experience I was going through as "mystical", but I knew that time mattered less and less to me. I felt out of time in the ordinary sense of the word. It was important to flow along with life, with a calm and serene comprehension of all things, trying to be in communion with my surrounding, so much so that nothing seemed impossible in the light of Oneness. Everything seemed perfect, including the apparently imperfect things.

Clearly, one cannot get rid of desires by continuing to satisfy them. That was the first seed of light planted in the mind, which germinated and bore fruits over the time.

We cannot invoke change if we are not ready to make our choices, get rid of the limitations and stop fulfilling the desires we are addicted to, because those attachments and addictions will keep coming back and inducing us to take self-destructive decisions. They will never allow us to make lucid, responsible choices.

Peace, Power and Light derive from our balanced poise in the spiritual[89] heart (the divine essence within), which implies awareness and emotional non-attachment.

Incredible but true: the golden gate of Knowledge was wide open and I was soon going to receive a message confirming it.

Before the end of the year, a sweet surprise arrived from the realm of invisible assistants (angels) and I was deeply moved by it.

Walking down the street, shortly after Christmas, a friend of mine picked up two small golden angels with trumpets. I was struck by this. Childishly, I also wished to be as lucky, to be "kissed by the angels".

A few moments later, my inner voice guided me down the street, until I found the first and then the second tiny golden angel with a trumpet, identical to those my friend had found. I was in the seventh heaven.

I could not believe my eyes. Love was a safe guide and I was overwhelmed with joy due to this Love token.

Spiritual evolution is the only opportunity life offers to man to redeem himself from his condition of slavery and transcend the law of cause and effect (*karma*) which determines his destiny inexorably, as I said earlier.

To overcome and conquer the fear of loss and death, man must inevitably learn to renounce the wish to possess (attachments, greed, craving, passion, jealousy, envy, etc.). This is the back side of the "coin" – its front side being the fear of loss and death.

The opposite of Love is not hatred or antipathy, but attachment. This should discredit the cliché according to which there is an ambivalence of Love and hatred dominating all human relationships.

If there is real Love, there is no space for ambivalence, or hatred (in other words, evil is nothing but the absence of goodness), as Love belongs to the dimension of Oneness. It is the presence of the Spirit within us (I shall discuss this further on, with regard to the 5th dimension) that has nothing to do with duality. It is all about unity.

Dichotomy is characteristic of humankind and is well marked in the clinical picture of psychiatric pathologies, the "maniacal-depressive psychosis", where both aspects are

196

present in an exasperated manner and they manifest clinically in their particularity – the fear of loss and death emerges during depression, whereas excitement, extreme desire and omnipotence emerge during the maniacal phase.

What we should take into account, from the given example, is the fact that the primary core of this pathological picture is again the fear of loss. Omnipotence (the maniacal aspect) is just impotence (depression) in disguise.

It is good to clarify that renouncing the desire to possess does not imply renouncing the pleasures of life, but abandoning "egotistic" enjoyment, i.e. putting our own pleasure and our own needs first and thus ignoring or even violating the right of others to enjoy life.

Egotism is sacrificed on the spiritual path. It is not a life of sacrifice, though. Attaining harmony allows us to experience Divine Love. This makes us audacious because our fears, worries and suffering are removed. We can finally enjoy life.

Now is the time to see ignorance[90] as the only obstacle to approaching the source of Goodness. We should not waste any more of our precious time.

We are unaware that we create our own reality, that we are responsible for what we are. Thoughts model the character, actions model the circumstances and angels and demons are destiny's agents created by our positive or negative thoughts, respectively. We don't know that we are fundamentally free in our divine essence. This knowledge, as it gradually consolidates in the conscious mind, sets us free from the chains of illusion and helps us discriminate and discern what is real from what is unreal, for us to build a new character, day by day, in the awareness that we are working for eternity's sake, as immortal beings.

When we establish inner balance, we do not abandon ourselves to the storms of life, blindly and lazily. Balance stems from coherence and freedom to do good, which is the Divine Will to act unconditionally, without being concerned about the fruits of our actions. This is the sacrifice (*sacrum officium*, or sacred action) of the ego (from worldly attachments).

Actions done without attachment, aimed at accomplishing our life task, bring the knowledge of the Divine within, or the awareness of the true Self.

Therefore, Love, not pain is born from sacrifice[91], as we have created the optimal condition for the divine seed (*Atma*) to germinate. It resided in the heart, waiting for the opportunity to sprout.

The divine seed of the Spirit in our desire or will to be at one, is common to everyone. This seed is the bread of immortality, or the 'daily bread' we ask from God, to bring us back to our eternal abode, or the Father's abode.

Sai Baba says: *"Do not deceive yourself. The entire world is suffering, I have created it this way, so that man can search for and return to Me."*

In my case, the Divine Plan worked perfectly. What prevents others from coming back to Him?

As far as I know, nothing but spiritual ignorance.

Unaware of his true, divine nature, man altered the natural order of priorities and lost the original harmony. We must put God, and not the ego, on top of the list, followed by society, family and finally by ourselves. In this way, we allow the true Self, or the divine essence in every human being, to manifest.

With the new year, the time arrived to return to India – my eleventh journey – and pay respect to the Divine Master (the source of every knowledge, being the Spirit of Truth and Love) and learn new things.

When I arrived at Mumbai, while waiting for the next flight to Bangalore, I found a small Indian key on a seat next to mine. There was an inscription in Hindi and I was curious about its meaning. I sensed the importance of the message, considering it as the eighth key, delivered to me by the invisible assistants of the Spirit.

Eight is my destiny number (being the sum of my date of birth) and it appeared quite often in my everyday life.

Number eight symbolizes infinity, comprising everything and therefore God and Love as well. It is the number of Paradise, transformation and rebirth; it is the number of stages of the evolutional path in Buddhism; Christ resurrects within us as Christ Consciousness (as the birth of the New Era) on the eighth day; the eighth door is a kind of Holy Grail we must discover to become divine; the Essenian star or the star of the soul has eight points, like the subtle anatomy of the human body, as the sign of spiritual Love; mankind will develop the eighth chakra, as the chakra of the spiritual heart, in the Golden Age. In the Tarot, it is the card representing Justice.

When I arrived at the *ashram*, I showed that small key to an Indian volunteer who was in charge of the welcoming service, asking if he could translate the inscription. I was really amazed when he replied that the meaning of the Hindi word was "Love". Sai Baba says: *"Open the padlock of the ego with the key of Love. As soon as the bolt of envy is lifted, you will enter the Father's abode."*

As soon as I laid my foot on Indian soil, I was presented with the key to open the door of my heart to Love. I was hence given the final supplement to the seven keys I had received earlier. My task was to persevere on the path and continue deserving the abundance of the Spirit's loving care.

The very frequent coincidences, retrievals, synchronicities, signs and received messages were windows which opened into the inner world, showing me the radiant presence of the Spirit within, convincing me more and more that He was holding me by the hand.

Indeed, "Life is a poem written by God. Man can read it and laugh, cry or remain impassive.", but I would like to add: it is also a beautiful poem.

The only way to avoid the ups and downs of life was to earn the wisdom of imperturbability with the awakened consciousness. I yearned to realize it, to secure mental and emotional stability and keep evolving.

Spiritual Knowledge helped me grasp the profound meaning of events, enlightening them with the light of Truth. There was no more room left for doubts. Conflicts melted down, like snow under the sun. Love is warmth and Knowledge is light in spiritual life. They are the great gifts the Holy Spirit bestows readily upon every person willing to renounce the ego.

In that period, enthusiasm was perhaps more useful than intelligence and will. To kindle its flame, we must first know what we want from life, what to fight for and what we want to obtain (hence the importance of clarity of mind).

I worked hard to gain clarity and I succeeded in eliminating most of my fictitious needs.

I had lived my life to the full, albeit with suffering. My desire for maternity was fulfilled when I gave birth to my son. Likewise, my wish to be useful to others was satisfied through the profession I had chosen. I have never wanted to be rich.

My wish to have a companion with whom to share my life remained unfulfilled, but only up to the age of forty, when I started believing I should find completeness within me. Life showed me that, like a proper idealist, I had been looking for the sublime, for perfection and harmony in a love relationship. Those ideals are difficult to reconcile with human nature and its limitations. Had I been looking for an extraterrestrial, a soul-mate or something unattainable?

I think that all human beings, without exception, long for completeness and failing to find it is one of the major causes of suffering or, if viewed positively, a strong impetus to evolve by getting rid of the ego. The latter was my case.

After the age of forty, with the radical change caused by my physical mishaps, having experienced the disability of my illness, with the withering of premature aging and the spectre of death, even this desire faded away or, to put it better, changed its scope as I came to know what I was looking for.

I could have failed meeting my soul mate – the one who belonged to my monad[92] – due to my lifestyle. But on the other hand, I realized that, being a woman, I had a great responsibility to lead the evolutional movement which would guide that monad back to God, in the final union of soul and Spirit.

To a woman – more than to a man – spiritual progress is of fundamental importance to reveal the lowest (the demon) or the highest (the Angel) aspect of the original ring.

Sai Baba says: *"A woman brings a hundred men to God, but a man is unable to bring a single woman."*

I accepted a huge responsibility – being a woman – by choosing to follow a spiritual path.

In the parable of the Virgins who guarded the lamps, waiting for the Spouse, Jesus does not speak about men but about women. It is the woman who is given the task to guard the "light" to illuminate also the man's way and lead him back to the home of the Father. Feminine qualities, when prevailing, bring peace and wellbeing into the world. On the contrary, when a woman does not accomplish her vivifying task (when she takes off the garb of the "Angel of the hearth" to wear the garb of "Eve the temptress"), humanity is condemned to violence and deterioration (Sai Baba speaks about this quite often).

A woman should first surrender to Divine Love because it is much easier for her to leave behind the masculine qualities of the ego such as pride, ambition, abuse of power, passion, authoritarianism, hard-heartedness, anger and violence to incarnate unconditional Love as "self-offering".

Hence, I decided to turn another page and make a quantum leap. I was going to seek completeness within and God would be my companion, always by my side. He demonstrated His continuous presence, especially in the darkest moments of my illness.

I was fascinated by the choice, so unique and special, but the commitment was great because it implied that I would have to "merit" this special companion every day of my life.

Initially, I thought that what I expected – from others and from myself – was too much. On the other hand, what did I have to offer to Him, in return for His Love? I had no idea yet, but I was soon going to discover that all He asked for was Love.

I worked very hard, with tenacity and perseverance to evolve and gain Spiritual Knowledge, awaken my consciousness, refine the feeling in my heart and finally obtain a permanent awareness of the inner Self.

I came up with an explanation for having shunned marriage three times in my life: I was destined to experience illusion or delusion only to see that I was not cut for that and to proceed on my way. I didn't know where to go from there, though. I had no idea and any attempt to discover the destination assigned to me by fate failed.

But I had to move on, trustingly, without wasting time.

Sai Baba says: *"Time is God, so waste no time."*

The eleventh journey, after many years of study, clarified the meaning of marriage. I realized that the only *true* marriage was that of the soul to God, or better, the *true marriage* was the Divine Love in the union of soul and Spirit.

I was suddenly convinced I would meet "The Spouse" meant for me, albeit late in life. Again, it was my mind and not my heart that understood it, which meant that I had not reached the coveted completeness yet.

Anyhow, I was now sure that I had identified the point on which all my expectations converged and this gave me the strength and boosted my enthusiasm.

Knowledge alleviated the suffering once more, as I understood that, being a woman, I was "condemned" to search for a spiritual counterpart (i.e. completeness). It seemed impossible for me to find it on the earthly plain, so I had to search within. On the other hand, men were doomed to experience transitoriness, that is, the fear of losing their possessions.

Experience showed me that desires were not to be fought against. Instead, we should identify them first and then ignore and overcome them. If we fight them, they will become stronger and stronger, until we subdue them. It is therefore understandable that Jesus and Sai Baba recommend: *"Do not fight evil."*

According to Esotericism, a "mystic" is the one who is immune to the charms of the world and not the one who is fighting them. A mystic is the one who eats to stay alive, who makes love to cooperate in the process of creation with the Absolute, the one who is no longer addicted to the pleasures of the senses, not because they have been repressed but because they have been transcended. He does not depend on possession, desires, ego or carnal love, but on the dimension of being, on the will to do Good, or unconditional, substantial (spiritual) Love.

The effort to dispel the infatuation of the material world increased, but it required less and less strain and this was a positive sign. I was on the way to freeing myself from the slavery of the limited ego. Being exempt from having to act for quite a while, I started to see the outlines of what the Divine Master expected from me: to dedicate my life to Him, intuit His Will and put it into practice We express Divine Love only by offering ourselves.

I couldn't help reciprocating the Love that filled my every cell, every breath and every thought. That stay was yet another purifying bath to wash away the illusions and delusions of everyday life.

I spoke to Sai Baba only once during the *darshan*. In that occasion He said He would soon call me (but time was non-existent for Him). He did call me, as a matter of fact, nine months later, during the next trip.

I returned home with a raised awareness. I had another key and a very important one. It was in my hands, or better, in my heart – the eighth key, the key of Divine Love. A few days later, in the street, I noticed an invitation to catechesis near a church consecrated to the Sacred Heart. It read, in large letters: *"God Loves You"* and my heart started beating with joy. I opened the invitation card and read: *"God loves you and would like to meet you. He was incarnated in His Son Jesus Christ, to offer you, today, His victory over all the causes of your suffering."* I read it the way one reads a message from the Beloved One. It was about Him offering me His victory, for me to overcome the illusions and delusions and get rid of suffering[93].

The Holy Spirit announced that It was ready to offer Itself to me. In other words, I was gradually approaching the encounter with the Spouse. It is always useful to remember that everything ends and passes, except Love and Truth. They are eternal and immortal.

I could feel the presence of the Spirit more and more, with each passing day.

I only wished to concentrate on Him, for my heart to become His temple (precisely a year had passed from the dream of the Peacock Festival, symbolizing the purity of heart). Indeed, getting in touch with the Divine was so intoxicating, more than any other thing in the world.

The words dictated to me by divine intuition expressed the timelessness of Truth. I felt I lived in the age of the restoration of Cosmic Order, although signs of discordance and destruction of human values prevailed everywhere in the world. I took in that we were like many a small OM[94], or particles of energy broken off from a common matrix with a precise task (Divine Game). Once we realize this, we return to the original matrix and become pure awareness, or Cosmic Consciousness (the consciousness of Oneness), that does not make any distinction between good and evil or light and darkness, but manifests as pure energy.

Shackles must turn into wings for us to fly towards freedom. To reach it, the paths are different, according to unconfirmed evidence, but the values and the rules we must observe are the same for everyone because we are all One.

Jesus used to say: *"You are of this world, not me. When I go away and prepare a place, I shall come back for you to take you there. The angels will summon the chosen people from the four winds, with a loud trumpet call."*

Christ is back with us; He has come to take us to the place promised by Jesus, two thousand years ago. This is the meaning of the arrival of Sai Baba – the Messiah of the third millennium, the shower of Love pouring the gifts of the Holy Spirit into our hearts, so they can blossom into eternal life, in this Messianic age.

I dreamt of a night sky illuminated by four rhomboidal formations of stars, moving slowly across the heavenly vault, from east to west. It was a marvellous spectacle. I invited other people to take a look, but the magnificent spectacle didn't raise much enthusiasm among the bystanders.

When one becomes aware of his divinity, he becomes both the star in role and the director of his destiny. He is no longer trampled on. He starts creating his own reality.

My personal experience testifies of this.

The *Avatar*, Sai Baba, descended to earth to show us how to gain awareness. The path to salvation is the path of *Dharma* (the righteous way) which brings unity, joy, peace, harmony and serenity.

Opposed to this is the pathway of the ego, whose "landing place" is always spiced with discordance, bitterness, distrust, restlessness and fear. We all get involved in the battlefield which is human life and we are familiar with this treacherous and unsafe landing place.

I dreamt of Sai Baba offering me "pieces of truth" in the form of candied fruit, wrapped in silver paper.

I met a friend of mine in those days who started speaking, out of the blue, about what the task of an "apostle" consists of. We were walking down the street and arrived at a crossroad. He said an apostle was supposed to offer the oil of Love to alleviate the pain and the wine of Truth to eradicate the primary cause of all human suffering. Who spoke through him? I couldn't help thinking about the Holy Spirit. He added that those who had been miraculously healed, like me, could be granted the ability to heal others. They became the channel of the Holy Spirit, which was supposedly operating through me. I would thus be able to give for free what I had received for free,.

This made me reflect for a while on the contact with the Holy Spirit I had already perceived within, the kind of contact we could all activate if we really wanted or, in other words, if we longed for it passionately.

A couple of days later, on my mother's birthday, I had a strange dream. She had passed away more than twenty years before. I saw her coming my way, astonished at what she saw on my face. Moved by curiosity, I turned towards a mirror. What an amazing sight! In the middle of my forehead there was an egg-like protuberance, irradiating a myriad of rays. I remained speechless in my dream – without knowing what to do or what to think of this.

I woke up concerned about the vision of the "solar seal" on my forehead, which left a sour taste of differentness.

I tried to comfort myself thinking about the "chosen ones who would be marked on the forehead" in the Holy Scriptures, although I did not believe I was one of the chosen ones. I rather saw myself as a sinner[95], trying hard to improve myself, so as not to miss the target. Disoriented and unable to grasp anything, I put my dream on the back burner and continued to contemplate a new centre point in my heart. I wanted to concentrate on that stable abode, channelling all the energies in one single direction – the Spirit.

Words like 'Love' and 'sacrifice' of the ego echoed in me in that period, to reinforce and keep my attention focused on the voice of the Self – the soundless voice speaking in the spiritual heart of the human being. There were three requirements to gain access to awakened consciousness, or the "spiritual heart": devotion to the Master, peace of mind and self-mastery, a man's greatest fortune.

I could count on the first requirement, but there was so much work for me to do to learn to manage the power I had. At times, I worked until exhaustion, oblivious of my vulnerability.

I wanted to get rid of whatever was superfluous or disturbed peace of mind and put all my effort in mastering my self and offering Spiritual Knowledge at the service of others.

The *Avatar*, Sai Baba, has come to offer liberation to those who are ready to burn their entire *karma* in this lifetime. There were still trials and sacrifices for the ego to face, but, having accepted the challenge, there was nothing more for me to do but to keep on, with courage and determination.

His message was clear: *"leave everything, detach yourself from everything and follow me. Go and bring My message to the world[96]."*

Many people get frightened when they hear those words. In a sense, I was also touched by their inappealable intransigency.

Nonetheless, people did not seem to be frightened of being continuously "blind" to real life, in constant denial of the Spirit. The humiliating everyday life they live creates more victims than wars, natural calamities and epidemics put together.

Like drops carving a hole in a rock, habits and repetitiveness create a hole in a human soul, unconsciously and almost painlessly. As we get used to it, this type of death doesn't scare us. And so we lose our ideals, imagination, creativity, gratitude, enthusiasm, spontaneity, freshness, brightness, the ability to daydream, enjoy life and share – this is the euthanasia, the good death of the Spirit, if I may use this euphemism.

Three months passed from the last trip, when I realized I had to return to the Divine Master. I went to Whitefield and did service in the kitchen. This *ashram* is smaller than the one at Puttaparthi, but volunteers are needed all the same.

My eyes met the eyes of the Divine Master a few times – they were coloured with kindness, as if telling me: *"remember that patience matures inner strength and courage and courage attracts God's Love."*

One night I woke up deeply moved. I dreamt of Sai Baba allowing me to read from the "Book of Life". I could not remember anything else when I woke up. His reference to something so great and sacred made me wish to delve into the topic. Strangely, it has been rarely addressed throughout the centuries. I believed it foretold an imminent event and that was as far as I could go. Later on, the inner voice returned to the issue to clarify it further.

In the course of that particular stay in India, during the *darshan*, Sai Baba asked me where I came from. Although I knew He wanted me to reply in different terms, I replied in a logical and rational manner, by mentioning my hometown, just as I did in the past.

When He walked away, I remained mortified, contemplating the fact that I was not "ready" yet. I knew I would be able to reply from my "heart", the way He expected, when my heart was wide open.

As the years went by, Sai Baba seemed to select, one by one, the people who stood by me to help me learn through thick and thin.

Particularly during those months, He picked wonderful, angelic people who conveyed lightness, although it wasn't the time to "fly" to Him yet. There was one more task on earth and, considering my suffering brothers and sisters and the commitment taken in their regard, I knew I had to sanctify myself before being able to help the others do the same.

I remained in India until *Corpus Christi* Day, when I saw the Divine Master passing by in front of me, smiling. That was the last time I saw Him prior to my departure.

Shortly before the beginning of the *darshan*, a *sevadal* volunteer enabled me to stand in the front line, so I could see Him from close up and grasp His smile, to cherish it lovingly in my heart. The Holy Spirit, in the person of Sai Baba, blessed me with His smile, on Its festival.

I've learned we can feel privileged even if we suffered, provided we are aware of the cause of our suffering.

My intent was to write for those who suffered, lacking the awareness that could set them free and redeem from an adverse destiny, an issue for the majority of mankind.

Experience taught me that, the higher my awareness was, the easier it was for me to accept suffering, which characterized most of my life.

A few months earlier, a numerologist analysed my date of birth and confirmed the adversities in my life. Mine had been a destiny of loneliness and pain.

At that point, I understood the words of the elderly priest, not long before, concerning the cross I held in my hands. The "choice" had been made before I came into this world, as part and parcel of the destiny my soul had agreed upon in order to evolve quickly and pay off the *karmic* debts as soon as possible. The "cross" would change my path from horizontal, or mundane, to vertical, or spiritual. By relinquishing worldliness, I was supposed to free the divine essence imprisoned in me.

This was why I met, in the midst of my life, the *Avatar* Sai Baba – to cancel my distant and not-so-distant past[97] definitively. This connection was described to me in the reading of the *Shuka Nadi,* on the day when I touched the feet of the *Avatar* for the very first time (what an unforgettable coincidence). I had come to this world to free myself. I was not ready to understand the meaning of that phrase then and so I didn't give much weight to it.

I carried a talent and perfected it through numerous lifetimes, always doing more or less the same thing – listening to others with my heart and not with my ears, intuiting the truth in them when our souls touched each other, "seeing" with the heart's eye instead of my physical eyes, even things others occasionally refused to see or didn't know they possessed within. In this way I understood their pain, anger, fear and the most intimate and unavowable suffering.

The sixth sense, the described ability is defined as such, was actually not the fruit of my university studies – it was mine from birth.

When I was working at the hospital, colleagues were often surprised by how quickly I came up with a patient's clinical picture, grasping immediately the core of the problem.

My ability to "hear" the patients did not develop from clinical practice. My personal suffering made me recognize immediately the taste of their suffering because it "tasted the same". It is impossible to understand, unless from one's own experience. Indeed, in a sense, I was a born "psychiatrist". I did not become one and I mean it in terms of spiritual assistance and not in the academic sense of the word.

A couple of days after my return to Italy, I dreamt of being in India, at Whitefield. I had just been there. A friend of mine came to pick me up at the *ashram* to go and do some service together. We were supposed to accompany some patients to the *darshan* of Sai Baba. All of a sudden, it started raining and we all took shelter under a porch. There were many tall, enormous trees in front of us. A gigantic eagle with dark feathers, a white chest and a yellow beak was perched, motionless, on top of a very tall palm tree. The bird was so huge that I thought (in the dream) it couldn't possibly be real, it had to be an optical effect, it was the size of a building. The eagle, as if in response, turned its head towards me and looked straight into my eyes. I was now sure it was not my imagination but a real eagle.

It was an unforgettable spectacle and, as always, I woke up with a thousand questions.

I immediately investigated about the symbolism of the eagle and came up with meanings that explained many aspects of my situation at the time.

The eagle is the king of the sky, celestial and shiny at the same time, symbolizing the direct perception of the Light of the intellect, "the eagle looks straight into the Sun's face and one can look at the light of eternity only if the heart is pure", contemplation and communication with Heaven, Christ's ascent to Heaven, the winged word, the Word, power and courage, bringing messages of the Heavenly or Divine Will. It is related to the "eye that sees everything" due to its penetrating look; it is the bird of Light and Illumination; it is the symbol of the apostle John whose Gospel starts with the knowledge of Logos (Christ, Light); it is the inflexible and devouring will; it indicates a marked tendency to freedom and the overcoming of revelatory family issues.

The last mentioned aspects of its symbolism perfectly reflected my issues. I wanted to shed light on my affections and express myself openly within my family, at any cost.

A few days later I had another dream which brought me back into the realm of work. I was accompanying a girl in need of psychiatric treatment to a psychiatric ward where I met a head physician I knew.

He greeted me, in a friendly manner, with the following words: 'Hello! Christ reigns! Welcome! We were waiting for you. I called you forty times.' He asked me to come back and work there again.

I immediately replied that I had cancelled myself from the medical register (which I actually had) and therefore could not resume the job. This trivial justification was supposed to conceal my rejection for the profession.

I woke up very confused, as I understood that this world, visited in my dream, did not correspond to what I had really left behind. It was a parallel dimension (the 4th dimension) where the same things took place as here on earth. Some of the colleagues I met in the dream had passed away years before.

It could have been an astral journey, but there was no way for me to check. Anyway, what was real was the fact that my "dreams" often anticipated, even years ahead, events which eventually took place.

In this regard, a few months later I had the umpteenth confirmation of the mechanism, of consciousness, the mind cannot relate to yet.

NOTES: CHAPTER X

83. The language spoken in Andra Pradesh, the state in which Puttaparthi is located, is Sathya Sai Baba's native tongue.

84. Referred to the episode in the Bible about the destruction of Sodom, when God forbade those who fled to look back at the city in flames. The wife of Lot infringed the divine commandment and was transformed into salt, while her daughters and husband managed to save themselves.

85. Sai Baba says: *"May your love for the Divine be brilliant and strong, like a diamond."*

86. In Hinduism, the cult of Rada Krishna and Sita Rama symbolizes Love, sublimated into Divine Will. Spiritual couples depict the unity of positive and negative energies, implied as polarities.

87. Years later, I heard the following words spoken in my heart, while Sai Baba was walking by during a *darshan*: *"You are in My Heart, the Heart of the Universe, together with all others...."*

88. The symbol of the Universal Logos or Christ or Cosmic Consciousness.

89. The Spiritual Heart corresponds to the eighth chakra in the subtle body of the "new" man who will inaugurate the Golden Age. In Sanskrit, "*hrudaya*" (heart) means "place where compassion resides".

90. A simple but eloquent example of spiritual ignorance is believing that jealousy is an expression of love. The opposite is true, as a matter of fact, because jealousy is a sign of attachment and lack of trust – not love.

91. Paradoxically so, the greatest pleasure stems from sacrifice.

92. According to Esotericism, it is the original, primordial core; couples of souls originate from it, incarnate on earth and unite in the moment of liberation, only to be absorbed again into the Divine Light, in the ultimate fusion, or the matrimony of souls and the Spirit. The inner voice mentions it further on.

93. Many years later I received the confirmation, when this actually happened (the end of suffering).

94. OM: the sacred primordial sound from which Creation originates, according to Hinduism.

95. In Hebrew, the word 'sin' means "to miss the target".

96. The same words were repeatedly communicated to me by the inner voice in the years to come.

97. Those words were prophetic in the light of what was confirmed through the revelations of the inner voice and in other messages, but also by Sai Baba personally, years later.

XI

Misfortune is something big but man is even begger than misfortune.

Tagore.

What I experienced in the last decade made me see the world in a totally different light. I started viewing life, the surrounding reality and myself from a new perspective.

Death, time and space do not exist for the Spirit. Death is only a new start, pain is just a balm.

By accepting to be incarnated, I accepted once more to die to the Spirit and be born in a physical body, like everybody else.

The discovery that I could obtain what I wanted, with my own strength and with the help of God, was a great revelation. What I was looking for was within me.

Seen from this angle, the world with its tragedies looked more like a comedy. And my tiny mind was trying to comprehend it.

The language, therefore, was no more that of the world but that of the Spirit and I wanted not only to understand it but also to get a good command of it. To do that, I had to reawaken the consciousness into the Spirit. Mind and individual consciousness no longer prevailed, although they continued to thrive and lay claims.

I had to dismantle ideological traps humankind developed over the centuries. I'd had enough of taboos, obligations, rules or pseudo-moral constrictions.

Freedom means relying on the consciousness awakened into awareness, not on individual consciousness based on common moral. In brief, we should feel with a "pure" heart, being at one with the true Self, instead of reasoning with the mind, contaminated by the ego (individual self).

If you feel with the heart, there is no need to follow rules. You obey only God, as the Spirit of Life, or the Supreme Order and His Law, which is pure Harmony and pure Love.

It was a relief to realize that evil was an immature aspect of goodness and darkness was the absence of light. In the mind of God, there was no room for evil or darkness, although It comprised everything.

Considering the soul as energy, connecting the mind and the Spirit, brought me to a natural conclusion that the most common illnesses of the past century, namely neurosis and cancer, derived from the loss of the sense of life. In this regard, obsession, as a neurotic condition, is the mental equivalent of an auto-immune disease on the physical plain. It is the origin of various pathologies, including tumours.

Everyone should ultimately return to God and so our primary task is not maintaining a family, ourselves or paying taxes but finding ourselves, or the true inner Self. In order to find the lost sense of life, we must be able to differentiate the eternal from the ephemeral, even if this entails moral disobedience or disregard of human laws, which are also ephemeral. It is important to acknowledge that by ignoring the eternal, divine and cosmic law governing the universe, we generate the ill-being of life, diseases and death. When the heart is cured from the illness of egotism, the mind and the body heal automatically. The panacea of all the diseases is discovering the "spiritual heart" within, which opens the door into a universe of Light or cosmic energy, into the new world or the Kingdom of God in us and the Kingdom of Universal Brotherhood.

I woke up one night and heard the inner voice say: *"I shall help you to interpret the Book of Life."*

The messages (or orders) were at times hermetic rather than synthetic, but I nevertheless felt honoured by His attention. I had already heard something similar in India (in a dream about Sai Baba).

I spent the rest of the night meditating and contemplating the possible meaning of that phrase, but as usual, I had to rely on the will of Divine Intelligence. It was the wisest thing to do.

A few days later I dreamt of floating, in the form of thought, above a multitude of Indian women and children moving all together, in a flux. High above, I met a friend (he had died long ago), also floating, who said: 'You'll see, you shall float in the air more and more often.'

When I woke up, I had a distinct feeling that it might have been another astral journey (into the 4th dimension), like those that had already taken place in the past, when I discovered magic, surreal landscapes, such as mountains covered with pink snow, yellow skies, white salt lakes, turquoise seabed with mountains raising to the surface of the water to become islands – they all seemed like landscapes of another world.

In our world, the "colours" of nature are not as vivid.

We live in an obscure age, when obstructing forces adhere to the more vulnerable. Only the strong, who live in Truth, can really face and repel them by the Divine Grace they earn.

We should learn to ignore the temptations or provocations coming from the advocates of obscure forces. That is the only way to prevail in the conflict between darkness and light. We defeat hatred with love, falsity with truth and violence with peace.

I was aware that, each time I returned from India and resumed my western-style daily routine, I eventually rescaled my priorities in favour of the more ephemeral aspects of life. At the *ashram*, God was the priority and all the rest followed. The same was true for the vast majority of people who went there and followed the order of values of the *ashram*. However, when they were back home, those people were again primarily concerned about the ordinary issues (work, family and entertainment). They dedicated time to God only if they were not too tired.

Whenever we returned from Puttaparthi, most of us were "enlightened", but, in a few weeks (the less fortunate in no more than a few days), the light would "gradually turn out".

No one seemed to understand the reason for this shift, but the explanations people came up with were symptomatic of the degree of mental aberration of the consumer society we were fully immersed in, unfortunately.

The experience made in India was generally sold off as illusory and chimerical, like some fairy tale one has just been told. Then, one returned to his or her usual occupation, which was considered as something real and inevitable.

Every fairy tale is in fact a meaningful story conveying important underlying messages. Likewise, visits to Puttaparthi, or to Whitefield, offered a great teaching encompassing all other teachings. Everyone who went there gave priority, more or less consciously, to Sai Baba – the expression of the Divine on earth – with respect to worldly issues. This is why people returned home "enlightened".

I would compare the *ashram* of Sai Baba to a university of the Spirit. One is imbued with the Grace of God (*conditio sine qua non*) while attending intensive courses of Spiritual Knowledge. They require a full time, 24/7 engagement. A whole person.

The evaluation of the acquired Knowledge of the Spirit, or the "exams" passed upon the completion of the "course", can be based on the state of awareness (in terms of peace, bliss and the like) attained by the student. Even without having realized that he, or she, is in the presence of the *Avatar*, i.e. a Divine Incarnation (like Jesus, Buddha, Krishna, Rama and so on), that alone would free the mind sufficiently for His Grace (pure energy, or Love) to manifest.

Unfortunately, if we carry along the entire baggage of thoughts and desires, with our attachments lying in wait, as soon as we move away from the physical presence of the Divine Master, they return in bulk, fill up the mind and control our conscious attention. Everything is back to square one.

Sai Baba says: *"You ask for many things but no one comes to ask Me for what I have come to give you."* Like Jesus two thousand years ago, He has come to offer the freedom from the slavery of the ego and the cycle of rebirths, *samsara*. Are we going to listen to Him this time? Who knows? I was doing my best.

In reality, it is not even necessary to ask for what He has come to offer because He gives it anyway, for free, as soon as we stop asking, clear away the mind of whatever is ephemeral or superfluous, open the heart and offer our life to Him, in terms of time. That is the only thing we actually possess, albeit in its inevitable passing. Nothing else is ours in the material world, however hard it may be for us to accept it.

Offering our life (in terms of time) to Him does not mean "losing" it, as many people fear, but "illuminating" it with the Light of true Spiritual Knowledge and warm it with the warmth of true Divine Love (human love is a "compulsion"). We fail to understand this irrefutable reality because we ignore the Truth.

In this regard, Jesus said: *"Those who look for the Kingdom of Heaven will have the rest in addition."* Hence, respecting the right order of values – God as Love, followed by humanity and the individual – is the recipe for becoming a beacon and not a turned-off lantern, short of oil, that is, Divine Love.

People who couldn't follow the same priorities back home turned off after a wile, unavoidably, just like a lantern that has run out of oil. Sai Baba is the oil of Divine Love, or Sai Joti (the light of Sai).

There is so much ignorance, confusion and incoherence in the minds of people when they fear God, instead of fearing the mistakes and ignorance they fall victims of, so much so that they can't understand His words. He is there to give continuously, without ever taking anything. When He says: *"I want your entire heart. Make Me your priority"*, He invites us to fill up the hearts with Love by putting Him, as Love, on top of the scale of values, for us to be richer – not poorer.

He affirms His Love for us, souls in exile, who can't find their way back home, to our real dwelling – the house of the Father.

When He says: *"Come one step closer to Me and I will come a hundred steps closer to you"*, He means that if we make a single step towards Him, He will give us much more than we need.

When we give priority to Sai Baba or God, we put unconditional, Divine Love before all the rest and Love implies living a joyful, serene and rich life, with the fullness of the Spirit – Love and more Love.

So, only by giving preference to Love can we see everything through the eyes of Love, know the divine essence within and realize our common origin. We are all children of Light. We belong to the same family of humankind and we have the same Father – God, the Absolute.

When Love is placed at the top of the list of priorities – the pure and unconditional Love Sai Baba talks about – everything is done out of Love, in terms of righteous conduct. Righteous behaviour (*Dharma*) can put us back on the straight and narrow path – the right path for each one of us – with out the risk of getting off the tracks again, unless we decide to do so.

The upright path brings peace of mind. It is homebound, leads us back to our Father. We then discover that we are "Love".

Therefore, considering God as Love, or Sai Baba as Love and the utmost priority, implies that we are Love. We become aware of the inner divinity and overcome the differences. We become part of the All once again.

The ancient Greeks claimed: *"Know thyself and thou shall know the Universe."* To this day, this has been man's major task. The sooner we realize that we are the children of the Light, the sooner we find the path home, to that oneness we are all part of.

This fundamental and unfathomable Truth is God's visiting card.

Sai Baba Says: *"God is Love. Start each day with Love, spend each day with Love, fill each day with Love and finish each day with Love. This path leads to God."*

Love means letting go of the fears, leaving hypocrisy behind and ridding ourselves of unhappiness, grudges from the past and obsessions of the future, to express divine energy in our thoughts and actions, here and now, in the personal mission that is specific for everyone, but always aimed at finding ourselves. No one else can do this in our stead – we heal ourselves. This search is strictly personal, individual and suprarational, in the sense that it transcends the mind and utilizes other abilities, more or less developed, such as intuition, telepathy, metaphysical perception, clairvoyance and the like. We investigate the unchartered universe of our inner world, consisting of several dimensions penetrating each other, we thought we knew. As a matter of fact, we discover that our knowledge of ourselves is much inferior to our knowledge of the Moon, or Mars, for example. I arrived at this conclusion with much humility and compliance (with the Spirit), fully aware of its implications.

Scientists are convinced that life holds few secrets in store for man. They plan, mathematically, the duration of a human life in the coming centuries. They have cracked the code of the human genome, the DNA, probably to use it for some future mass cloning (of human beings), freezing corpses with a promise of a happy awakening on a day that might never come, freezing embryos, ovules, spermatozoids for all kinds of purposes, and so on.

A kind of selective distraction prevented science from seriously addressing death as a passage to other dimensions. On the contrary, it has tried to find ways to avoid death, or delay it as much as possible, as if physical health and its conservation were the only scope of human life (in this regard, you might want to investigate artificial insemination, transplants, genetic engineering, etc.).

Scientists could object to this by saying: "We deal with what we see and therefore we study life on earth. Someone may think about death as an interim process, but no one can establish there is anything beyond this life and investigating in this direction would be a waste of time. No one has never returned to report on it."

In reality, those folks are not aware that, in this way, they actually work in favour of the ephemeral because they neglect the other side of the only coin called "man" – his spiritual part, the divine, immortal and eternal essence.

Time is precious – not for the scope of something which is limited to forty, sixty or eighty years of earthly life, but to gain eternity and immortality, to return home.

Those who invest time in the Spirit – not in science – work for eternity. They consider the Spirit as the noblest part within, in the heart, permeating the entire Universe – not as something external.

Spirituality is within, religion is outside. Religions divide people, with their different creeds, but the Truth is One.

By turning the heart's key in the sense of Divine Love, we earn our freedom. By turning it in the sense of egotistic love, we remain enslaved. Life goes on, but we continue to believe in the "right" to choose between good and bad. Ordinary people refer to "goodness" in terms of material wellbeing, pleasure, wealth and sexuality, while "bad" represents the absence of all that. This limited and limiting vision stems from ignorance. Indeed, good is not always what is pleasant and bad in not necessarily the absence of pleasure. Contrarily, what is pleasant can be bad and the absence of (egotistic) pleasure can be good. Sai Baba says: *"Unless you put an end to your desires, you will put an end to your life."* This is an unpopular truth hardly anybody is prepared to listen to, yet it is the basis to access Divine Grace, true Knowledge and true Love.

A person without awareness searches for his or her lost completeness in sexuality. At the end of the day, he, or she, is looking for the union with the true Self, the Spirit as cosmic energy within. A heedful person realizes this, having learned to discern 'being' from 'having'.

A person lacking awareness will seek to appease his or her frustrations in all kinds of drugs, trying to expand his or her consciousness. An attentive person knows this can only be attained if we are aware of our divine nature, of being at one with the All.

Therefore, evil is an immature form of goodness. Spiritual Knowledge is our source of strength and power, disclosing the ultimate Truth of things: All is Love. The union of the soul with the true Self and the awakening of consciousness as stable awareness in us is the only true goodness we should be after. It is not out there, in the world, though. Sai Baba says: *"Turn your back to the world and you will find God."* This affirmation is not an invitation to forget about others, but to love them in a new, divine way. Turn your back to the world of "having" – fictitious goodness most people believe in, oblivious to the fact that they have chosen a surrogate of goodness. It comprises partial truths, attachments, seductiveness, greed, pride, ambition, arrogance, anger, abuse of power and competitiveness. You will find the world of "being" – real Goodness comprising peace, truth, harmony, sharing, compassion, non-violence, joy, bliss, fullness and Light.

Finding God means experiencing unity with our inner, divine nature, aware of being part of Him and realizing that we are at one with the entire Creation, as individual consciousness awakens into the collective, Cosmic Consciousness.

When we learn to discern the realm of being from the realm of having, we awaken into Cosmic or Christ Consciousness. We discover that our separateness from the divine stems from the disconnectedness from the original blueprint for which we were born, or from the inner imbalance. Once balance is restored within, we can "see God" (the divine essence we are all made of) again in our heart and in the heart of our fellow men.

Sai Baba says: *"I am the Androgynous. You can be like me if you become aware of your essence. When you discern the male and the female inside, you will attain the harmony that will allow you to see the Divine."*

Harmony – the greatest Goodness (along with freedom) I have always yearned for –
enables us to see and recognise the Divine within and without. This was a sensational
discovery, although it generally does not cause a sensation at all.

After years of contemplation, I realised that the masculine principle was referred to the
Spirit residing in every person as the divine spark (or the true Self). The feminine principle
was referred to the soul and the body hosting it.

Those fantastic revelations enriched my perception but I could not compare my notes
with anybody, if not with the Spirit – always present and showing Its solid and timely
support and loving approval.

I dreamt of being at the *ashram* at Puttaparthi. Sai Baba was walking towards the main
gate of the *Mandir* (which was open), His initials inscribed on it: SSSB (Sri Sathya Sai Baba).
All of a sudden, He stopped, turned to me and greeted me with a smile.

I intuitively interpreted this gesture as a signal that I was advancing well. The message
must have arrived from Him. As a true friend, He came to earth to assist me (and to assist
us). We could experience Him again as the Spirit of life in our consciousness, as reawakened
beings.

Dreaming about Sai Baba filled me with peace and joy, beyond comparison. It was a
sacred happiness, a special one. I felt safe, loved and honoured and I was infused with self-
confidence and trust in Him (within me).

No one else could protect me in this way – all the time and everywhere. It was a support
par excellence (according to Him). No one else could guide me to freedom. He saw my
sincere heart and was moved by my loneliness. He approached me, person to person,
allowing me to recognise Him the first time I touched His feet, when He stopped in front of
me, smiling, years earlier.

I dreamt of Him again after several days, intent on teaching[98] me. Unfortunately, upon
awakening I could not recall the content of His lesson.

I did not feel I had mastered myself and so I obviously could not assist others if I was not
even useful to myself.

I had to "experience" the healing process myself before I could suggest it to the others and
testify to its effectiveness. I was my own, or God's guinea pig – or of the Self operating
within me.

While considering how to proceed, I couldn't say my search was chaotic. Whatever I was
doing in terms of self-investigation, was carefully guided, moment by moment, by the
invisible hand of the Holy Spirit, or otherwise I would not have been able to always find
the right thing in the right moment and it occurred constantly, every day. I moved in
harmony with a profound feeling, which was getting increasingly refined.

I did not have the possibility to compare myself with someone with the same, parallel
experiences and a common goal. Without this opportunity, I was forced to ask the Spirit
(my best friend) to help me and He replied: *"See every difficulty as a challenge. Life is a*

challenge. Face it. Keep moving, don't stop, and know that the answers to your "Why's" will be revealed to you if you persist and persevere."

The Spirit expected tenaciousness and devotion from me. I knew I possessed them and this awareness was my main driving force. It said: *"Be strong and courageous, encouraged by the certainty of success, whatever happened. Time is running out and you will have a role to perform in the global plan."* But, what plan was He talking about? That I couldn't know.

I recalled the new world from the dream of Sai Baba, the seven keys plus the eighth one found in India. Was that perhaps the key of the Kingdom? And what about the golden angels with trumpets, what did they announce, stepping into my life in that strange and unusual manner?

I knew well that happiness belonged to incorporeal realms and dimensions (the 5th and the 6th dimensions etc.). In our world (the 3rd dimension), there is only pleasure and suffering. I wondered when harvest time would come, but I saw immediately it was not the right attitude towards the Spirit. Instead of nourishing expectations, I was supposed to surrender to His will.

We should choose a path paved with principles and forge our character by living up to them. This implies coherence, daring and honesty.

We are spellbound by everyday life. We accept its incompleteness – form without substance. I felt more lonely every day, sometimes happy and other times thoughtful. I wanted to persevere in my search for impartiality (detachment from the illusory aspects of satisfaction and suffering) until I re-established the connection with the Self.

My experience of the family was not that of value, at least in the terms society (represented by people who were neither free nor aware) defined it. On the contrary, I considered it obsolete and without values. It was a fighting arena – to evolve, in the best of cases, or to involve, in the worst case.

I did believe in friendship though, as self-giving, or unconditional, loyal, sincere and free Love. We cannot belong to anyone, if not to the Absolute.

Perhaps suffering paid me occasional visits to leave little space for spiritual pride. Suffering forges a wise person if there is joyfulness in the heart. Otherwise, instead of soothing, it causes illness or death. There is the risk of becoming intoxicated with our own presumed superiority when we start "seeing" that the world is full of "blind people". The ego strikes back and gains corˑrol, wearing a new mask this time – wanting "to be free".

I simply couldn't contemplate salvation and abandon my brothers and sisters, unaware of the danger as they walk across the mine field of "desires". I had to do my best to help them with my testimony, at least to indicate the "mines" I could easily spot. Wasn't that the most natural thing to do?

Most of the time, life is like a journey and we fail to see the beauty of the landscape if the mind is troubled by passion. As we approach the destination, the predominant impression is fatigue.

I was more and more convinced that evil was oblivion of Goodness and therefore only true Knowledge could help us advance towards the Truth. Even the use of "free choice", understood as the possibility to choose between the good and the bad, is based on neglecting true Goodness, or the awareness of our divine essence.

If man really knew, if he was aware of what was good and what was bad for him, what would be the point in making a choice? He would do the right thing every time. Sai Baba says: *"Free choice is just a chance to make a mistake."* Of course, at our own expense.

Man builds his future day after day, through the choices he makes in the eternal here and now. Destiny can be remodelled continuously, by awakening the consciousness and raising the awareness, with true Knowledge. Otherwise, we cannot avoid suffering. I believe this is clear by now.

It makes no sense to blame God if things do not proceed well because we are the cause. We are ignorant and life is the school we attend. Unless we study hard to master the entire program, it is useless to find fault with the school. Our failure is evidence that we don't understand its true purpose.

As for me, joy (fulfilment) came and went, like waves crashing on the beach, (at times) washing the heart with kindness – and so the heart learned to recognize the taste of true Love.

I met a friend who confirmed a message I'd received. In a few years I would be given a task as a spiritual aid, but she couldn't say more. She said there was an elevated spiritual entity by my side, protecting me. Sweet is the day and tranquil is the night to those who love God and make themselves an instrument of His will, for the benefit of others, because the Grace of the Holy Spirit is with them.

I had two strange dreams in the same period and I wondered if they were astral journeys.

In the first dream, I crossed the sidereal spaces in the form of thought, knowing I had to take part in a pilgrimage to somewhere. I travelled at a frightening speed and stopped myself with my thoughts, realizing I was in a vortex of bright particles, like sparkles, which formed an incredible arabesque of flickering light.

In the other dream I witnessed the end of the world. Fire rained from the sky and nobody seemed to be spared from it. I looked for a shelter with a couple of people, in the tunnels in the snow, which seemed like coffins. I woke up still a prey to the horror of that scene.

In the silence, the inner voice told me: *"Learn to live beyond yourself, relying on your forces and abilities, so that those around you can see, with their own eyes, that I work through you, so that faithless souls can come to know Me – not through your words, but through your deeds that put My Message into practice."*

Loneliness is God without form. Silence is God without sound. Both are His supreme expression and most difficult to put into practice, unless experienced in perfect harmony with Him. They were my daily bread in those days.

I dreamt of a shooting star, crossing the sky in my direction. I felt it was a good omen. In fact, destiny had something marvellous and incredible for me in store.

I had been reading the story of *Avatar* Krishna (the *Avatar* of Love[99]) for several days when a friend of mine invited me to an *ashram* of the devotees of Krishna in Italy. They were celebrating His birthday in the company of an Indian master who had arrived there for the occasion, from Kashmir. He was a hundred and ten years old and was considered an enlightened soul.

In general, I avoided meeting large groups of people because I preferred staying on my own. However, on that occasion, the inner voice suggested to me to accept the invitation and so I left, without thinking twice about it.

After six hours of travel, we arrived in a place of peace, surrounded by forests and hills, inhabited by a small spiritual community. I felt as if I had arrived in India. Everyone was already gathered in a small temple, ready to sing sacred hymns in a silent, celestial atmosphere. In the semi-darkness, near the altar, I could make out the hieratic figure of an elderly man, wrapped in a spotless, white robe, with long, white hair and a long, white beard, sitting in a lotus position, eyes closed. He seemed to belong to another dimension.

The more I was looking at him, the more I sensed something familiar about him. In a few instances, my heart started beating. I was looking at the old Indian sage from the dream made precisely three years earlier, in which he gave me a case containing "the secret of my initiation".

I was deeply moved by that amazing discovery. Not being able to contain my emotions, I broke down and cried with joy, in a soundless and liberating outburst. Was he the shooting star coming towards me, in my dream?

I waited patiently for several hours until the chants were over and then I went out and waited, just like everyone else, to greet Him.

The Master was the last to come out. My heart started beating again when I realized that my dream came true. The elderly man in front of me was about two meters tall and very thin, exactly the way he looked like in the dream. His elegance was statuesque and he seemed to shine his whiteness and the emanating light on everyone around in the dark night.

I asked if I could meet Him the following day and was granted permission. It would have been tough to leave without that promise. So I spent a sleepless night, meditating and contemplating the event.

I was definitely convinced that the holy man had been announced by the shooting star coming toward me in the dream, the previous night.

I met Him the morning after, with an interpreter who translated from Hindi. The gift I was going to receive was huge, beyond words.

He asked me if I had been initiated by a master and I replied that my Master was Sai Baba. I then told Him about the dream I'd had three years earlier.

He said that, if the dream turned into reality, it was a positive sign, meaning that I'd made the right choice in life. Being privileged, I had to work even harder. If I wanted to be initiated, I had to put myself totally in the service of My Master, that is, to follow His message full time, give up of my personal life and offer my whole heart to Him.

Sai Baba told me the same thing. The elderly sage left, reminding me of the importance of being always compliant with the Divine, also by going to pilgrimages to holy places because "to taste a cake was different from looking at it or imagining it." I fully agreed with him and my frequent visits to India, visiting Sai Baba, served that purpose.

I remembered saying to myself, in the dream, that I knew I would not be initiated by Sai Baba, in His physical form, but by a Master sent by Him. But first I had to find the treasure hidden in the "case" from my dream. I was convinced it was detachment from illusions and renouncing egotism. I gave much thought to those issues upon my return. It had been my twelfth trip to India and it was, actually, characterized by non-attachment.

I sensed that the next journey would be about renunciation. Everything was inter-connected – it was going to be my thirteenth[100] visit to India.

Referring back to the idea of the university of the Spirit, the number of lessons during each one of my trips was related (to my mind) to the specific issue I elaborated throughout the stay, facilitated by the Spirit.

The Spirit had spoken through that holy man. I was inundated with Grace and at the same time immersed in a solemn atmosphere which troubled me, as the investiture had confirmed an incontestable truth, again so much bigger than me. My dialogues with the Divine had not been sheer fantasy. I had dreamt about Him, questioned Him, received His messages and written and read about Him.

The Divine revealed itself through that Guru (Master), in His sacredness, presenting me with a unique and unrepeatable opportunity. He left his body the year after and so I had taken the last opportunity for me to meet him.

Before departure, I took part in a purification rite with fire (typically Hindu) which concluded this borderline adventure. With increasing awareness, I was approaching the solemn moment of the nth turning point, anticipated a long time before.

I was setting about to take the decisive trip to India, to gain more clarity about the said encounter, to conclude a phase in life and start a new spiritual adventure of liberation (as Sai Baba confirmed to me shortly after).

During the flight to Mumbai, I asked the captain if I could admire the starry sky from the cockpit. I was immersed in the vault of heaven, joyously excited, as if I'd been in one of my dreams (or astral journeys), wandering with the stars in the form of thought (without my physical body). Inundated by unexpected and overwhelming delight, I wished to be annulled and become pure, formless essence once again. The captain brought me back into reality, showing me planet Jupiter and the constellation of Scorpio. It was an unforgettable and marvellous spectacle of divine magnificence.

It was the first time for me to go to India in that period of the year. It coincided with the holiday of Ganesha, the elephant with the human body (Hindu symbol of discernment) that protected and propitiated everything and removed obstacles on the path of redemption, towards the realization of the true Self.

I kept repeating silently, like a mantra, the various stages of the realization of the "Inner Spouse", or the true Self, namely devotion, discernment, non-attachment, liberation and realization.

Four are the guardians watching over the "door of Knowledge" that opens into the road of liberation, namely peace, Self-search, acceptance and the company of the sages.

Only Sai Baba could tell me how far I got on my inner journey. He is the greatest shining mystery planet Earth has hosted for eighty years and I was bestowed upon the huge grace of living in His age, in the hour of Truth.

In Him I recognised the One who had been announced by Jesus two thousand years earlier. I had been present then, by His side – a part of me (my heart) was certain about it. I read and heard many people claim that the Essenian Community, which had existed in the time of Jesus, returned *en masse* at the end of the second millennium to welcome the arrival of the Messiah, incarnated in Sai Baba. I received messages of confirmation and a number of evidence. In some of my dreams set in that age, my emotions, above all with respect to the figure of Jesus, left an indelible mark in my heart.

The world has no beginning and it has no end, it was not born and it will not die. Or rather, it was born from our ignorance and it will die when we become aware that everything is energy, including matter, imbued with divine essence.

The new world I was attracted to was the inner world of the Spirit and I was there, at Puttaparthi, to find a shortcut.

Ten days later, Sai Baba invited our group for an interview.

The night was dark and stormy. At four thirty, when we went out to join the *darshan*, it was pouring with rain and it was cold (which happens rarely in India). There was a blackout and so the lights were off. The lanes were flooded by torrents and water was almost knee-deep. This is characteristic of the monsoon season. For an instant I thought that the *darshan* might be postponed, considering the terrible weather, but I was wrong.

When we entered the *Mandir*, soaked to the skin and trembling with cold, we waited for the Divine Master's arrival

Sai Baba walked through the crowd at seven o'clock and called for us. My friend and I looked at each other's eyes, deeply moved. Five years earlier, at the end of an interview, Sai

Baba parted from us declaring that He would summon us in the morning next time, when the air was cool. Indeed, we could testify of that.

Over the previous five years, I had returned many times and had other interviews. However, for my friend it was the first visit in five years and the first opportunity for us to be together, in His presence. As always, Sai Baba kept His promise with the precision of a Swiss watch.

During the interview, although we did not raise any personal issues, except for a couple of questions about my son, He came up with an unpredicted statement (because I did not formulate a single thought in that moment): "I will take care of your liberation!" It was His present for my imminent birthday – I was going to be fifty soon.

In His presence, the issues of the last months slipped my mind, but He, who is always present and never forgets anything, reminded me of them. He was always with me and within me, whenever I repeated in my heart the various stages of the journey to liberation and Self-realization, like a mantra.

I always dissolved like snow under the sun in front of Him and my relentlessly hyperactive mind would calm down completely. What I could remember though were the requests and thanks I was asked to convey at His feet and nothing else. I knew He could read everything about me directly from my heart. I had therefore made a note to remind me to ask for an approval to write a book about Him. He took the piece of paper but did not reply immediately. He invited me to come back two months later, in November. I interpreted His invitation positively. That was His Grace, His Greatness and His Divinity.

Sai Baba says: *"If he is overpowered by inner enemies, how can a man successfully defeat his eternal foes? Burdened by laziness and inflexibility, how can he attain wisdom? Only balance and impartiality can bring Peace and Harmony."*

Peace and Harmony are the face of God. He is Peace, He is Harmony. The smile is His expression because God is joy. We are divine only if we are joyous. Peace, Harmony, Love and Truth are synonymous of God.

Whenever we are not joyous, we are only human. True joy is revealed when we recognise and honestly accomplish the task we were born for. Knowing why we are on earth is synonymous of awareness.

Sai Baba's words seemed to conceal some arcane mysteries, larger than me, lying in wait in my daily routine. I remembered that Cosmic Law established that destiny (*karma*) could not be avoided. It can only be transcended through upright conduct and overcome by Divine Grace.

In the course of my permanent self-inquiry, I saw that my mood was undergoing a heavy, apparently inexplicable bending. I wanted to understand the underlying causes to avoid repeating the same errors over and again. The will and determination to change myself were not enough. One must understand and reveal the mechanisms behind our repeated mistakes.

As a matter of fact, there was something extraneous about the ups and downs, uncharacteristic of me and yet absorbing so much of my energy.

So I discovered that, when we insist on helping someone, while we'd better refrain from doing it for some reason (related to their destiny), we automatically burden ourselves with their load.

In a nutshell, we'd better stick to the tasks in line with our destiny, instead of carrying on, albeit well, other people's duties or replacing them. Having clarified this brief premise, this subtle *karmic* mechanism, I would like to point out that this does not mean that we should not assist others. But before we do it, we'd better be aware of the consequences of our acts and handle the situation with a certain non-attachment and objectiveness, maintaining our balance as a useful asset in dealing with the possibly ensuing crisis.

This might be one of the reasons why Sai Baba invites all those who arrive at the *ashram* to remain focused on Him and avoid acting as the "good Samaritans", trying to help everyone in need there.

At times we risk hurting others instead of helping them if we provide for their needs too diligently or too generously, simply because their needs are not necessarily realistic. We should learn to discern and "see" to be able to serve others.[101]

To learn to discern also means to understand to what degree the suffering we feel is intended for us and vice versa. The point is that our suffering should be experienced with awareness. We should also figure out to what extent our "intervention", at times indiscriminate, stems from a genuine urge to assist others, or if it is an expression of our need to feel useful, or to be the heroes of the day.[102]

However, in my inner turmoil, I could recognize something which was not supposed to be neglected: I hadn't fully accepted the fact that I was a "stranger in the world" (most people found my choices scary).

The Holy Scriptures and Esotericism had warned me: people are afraid of those who know themselves and those who search for Knowledge.

I returned home on the threshold of my fiftieth birthday, no longer disturbed by the future – and that was really a great accomplishment.

With serene humility, I accepted that I belonged to the Spirit and to His Will, knowing that lasting joy and peace stemmed from the realization of who I really was.

I thought about Sai Baba's words and the fact that I didn't yearn for liberation *per se*, but I considered it as an obligatory phase to realize the true Self, fully convinced that it was the best way for me to be useful to humankind (a bee in my bonnet since childhood).

For my birthday, I received a card from a friend of mine. He seemed to have read from my heart when he wrote: *"In this lifetime, we don't have to withdraw ourselves. Likewise, in the next life, upon liberation, we won't have to be reincarnated, unless from a higher need to perform a prearranged task".*

I was relieved by the message. It sounded familiar and reminded me of Sai Baba's words. It implied that I would succeed in transcending my destiny and defeat my ego one day. It was no longer an arcane mystery but the announcement of a victory. The mere articulation of that hypothesis sounded like a dream. But expressed by Him, it turned into inconfutable Truth.

Coming back to earth would no longer be a burden – if that was God's intention. It would be a return to a divine life, by His Will. In this manner, it would not entail the settling of debts in this world of separation, disharmony and discord, where material duties and sensual pleasures mattered more than loving God. I found and recognised my adventure companion in the Spirit – the golden Friend with whom I forged an accord of indissolvable alliance.

Gandhi, the Indian apostle of non-violence, claimed: *"When you dive into the river, the desire to dive disappears. Likewise, when you find yourself face to face with God, the desire to see Him cannot exist anymore."*

For me it was the same. I kept returning to India to deepen His teachings because to see Sai Baba was an extra gift – no longer the overwhelming wish that had characterized the first few journeys. Performing my task with gratitude in the heart, with non-attachment, without thinking about what I would gain from it, brought me peace of mind.

Back home I started to harmoniously reorder all the material I'd written over the years of contemplation. In my inner world, the emotional tempest calmed down and the air was clear. I came to understand that loneliness helped me master my destiny. Hence it grew less and less painful or bitter.

I dreamt about a myriad of luminous formations furrowing the sky, gathering slowly to form an immense cross made of light[103]. I witnessed this together with many other people, dumbfounded by such an extraordinary celestial phenomenon, on a square. Everybody fell down on their knees in prayer. The vision announced the beginning of the end.

I woke up in the middle of the night, baffled by the touching essentiality of the images I witnessed in my dream.

In the morning, as I was riding my bike across a downtown park, my eyes caught a sheet of paper, laid on a bench. I stopped to read it carefully, my curiosity stemming from the urge to do that. It said: "Will this world survive?" I read it at first as a disturbing query, considering the dream I had just had, but, remembering Sai Baba's words in this regard, I calmed down.

In the Divine Game of life, seen as an obstacle path, what makes the difference between winning and losing? It is the existence and application of free choice. If there was no possibility of making a mistake, it would no longer be a game.

Since everything in the world of duality is governed by the law of cause and effect, I cannot help thinking, basically, that the life of goodness corresponds to Paradise and the life of evil (or mistakes) corresponds to the Hell depicted in the Holy Scriptures.

Those two possibilities are open every day, on our planet, possibly in other parallel dimensions as well, where our journey continues after we leave our physical body.

The positive energies created when we behave correctly attract and emanate beneficial influences. Negative energies, developed by incorrect behaviour (going against true Goodness), attract and emanate harmful influences. This is based on the law of attraction according to which similar energies are drawn to each other on the subtle planes of physical matter. When it comes to the coarse plane of physical matter, opposites attract each other.

Angels have neither sex nor free choice. They are fulfilled, as they are at one with God in their respective dimensions (the 5th dimension?), beyond matter. Human beings, on the other hand, in the physical (bisexual) dimension (the 3rd dimension) seek fulfilment and completeness in the union with the partner.

Inner peace or conflict will be the award or the punishment, the victory or the defeat we sentence ourselves to, depending on how we choose to play this game. And so, if it is human to err, to persevere becomes diabolical. Man has a thinking mind – a faculty to comprehend his own mistakes. With the right information and true knowledge, he could avoid the repetition of mistakes, of course aided by his good will.

Those who err by ignoring true goodness are not sinners, but simply ignorant. Sinners are those who continue making mistakes without the intention to change. A "recalcitrant" behaviour is the most dangerous a man can have, being totally deaf to God's call, totally blind to His presence and hard-hearted. There is a thin line between that condition and feeling unsatisfied, downhearted and useless. We end up underrating ourselves and wasting our sacred, God-given time, lifetime after lifetime.

It is like serving a life sentence. Under the circumstances, that is, without the warmth of Divine Love and the light of Spiritual Knowledge, life inadvertently becomes a real self-inflicted punishment. It is tough because we don't know how, when or where it will end. Indeed, no one knows how, when or where he or she is going to die.

This dual-reality game (matter-spirit), triggered by a "virtual" freedom, can be steered towards victory if we choose the path of Goodness, Light and Harmony.

Sai Baba, Jesus and the great enlightened sages from the past delivered the message of Love which is nobody's property. But it can be experienced as Harmony, Grace, or as a gift. When the lesson is learned, the debts paid off and the *karma* undone, the game is over. Divine Grace is proportional to the human effort to master his or her own destiny. *"When the heart of stone cracks open, human sins are put back into it."*

Divine Grace intervenes only when we long for true goodness and intend to act according to God's Will. In this was we elicit the power to transform something impossible into something real.

At times, as I rebelled against appearances and searched for the essence of things, I couldn't stand myself and refused to give myself a break. But I knew I would find peace of mind as soon as I had what was still missing in me.

I thanked Sai Baba all the time for standing by my side, as I tried to work and improve myself and become His messenger. I wished to serve Him with Love, with every cell of my being.

To overcome emotional blocks and material obstacles, we have to become independent and self-sufficient – materially and emotionally. We get stuck if we depend on others because we lack courage and willpower. Therefore, before we start searching for the real Self, we should first recover our small individual self (ego) and master it.

I prayed the Holy Spirit to instil those qualities in the people, to put an end to the enslavement of mutual seductiveness, exploiting palatable concepts such as sex and pleasure, money and power. Seduction, spiritual ignorance and emotional dependence are expressions of the major and most widely spread violence – past and present. Those are the fierce enemies of the Spirit, or Love and Truth. But beware, this violence manifests in an occult, subtle and covert manner.

Spiritual ignorance prevents us from seeing the innate destructive potential of seduction[104] and seductiveness. Worse than that, most people believe that those qualities should be cultivated, instead of being eliminated together with other faults. Most people are fascinated by the "success" of seductive people, without realizing that they are often victims of this "success".

It is a trap in which, sooner or later, we all fall a prey to. Our society functions like a mouse trap. It puts a piece of "cheese" under our noses, to distract us from the invisible cage that surrounds us, with its invisible door that shuts the moment we "take a bite". The "cheese" is pleasure, the cage is slavery and the door is addiction that cuts us off from any possible search for freedom.

This is why we need all the courage and willpower to win the invisible enemies of true Freedom, Truth, Harmony, Peace and Life. Our enemies are forms of death.

One day, I was leafing through some magazines when I ran into a striking headline: *"Living on her own, a choice written in the sky."* What a coincidence. I had reached the same conclusion quite a while ago. The same day, I opened a drawer full of letters, notes and photos and picked up, without any particular reason, a small envelope yellowed with age. Inside the envelope, there was my mother's letter to my father, dated more or less when I was conceived, fifty one years before. I had never read or seen that letter. To my utter surprise, I realized that that day and month – of the discovery of the letter – coincided with the day and month on the letter.

I felt the presence of my mother (her soul) beside me. Perhaps she wanted me to find that special letter. Where did it come from? It was a mystery. How could it have remained unnoticed for so many years? I had raked up those papers each time I moved from one place to another over the years, but it never came to light.

Excited and happy, I started to read it: my mother replied to the questions I had raised myself. She presented me with a lesson of life on self-esteem and love, considered as timeless commodities.

I cried with joy and honoured her memory with thoughts of gratitude. I wanted to share my joy with her – the joy is not real unless we share it, I told myself.

When we understand our task, we will be able to accept it with true joy. We will then be capable of enjoying life and it will no longer be a punishment but a gift, the gift of the Holy Spirit.

I learned that the Spirit was like an ocean. To know how it tastes, we don't have to drink all of it. In other words, we can sense His presence in our daily life, as ordinary people, sparks of the Absolute, if we recognize ourselves as such and not only hear others speak about it.

Sai Baba says: *"You are here to know that you are a spark of the Divine Fire. You will realize very soon that others are also sparks of the same fire. So, how can hatred, anger and envy thrive in the shining light?"*

When we recognize our nature, as divine creatures, life can regain that fresh, light, sweet, delicate taste we shall never get tired of. We shall be intoxicated by its goodness, without any bitter, sour or heavy aftertaste.

The return of the Cosmic Christ, or Universal Consciousness and the arrival of the brotherhood of Light, have been announced in a number of sources. Sai Baba's arrival testifies of this Truth through the awakening of the hearts into Divine Love. The realization that we are all sparks of the same fire, the fire of the Spirit, allows us to rediscover the divine within, as mankind awakes into Divine Love, in a collective awakening.

In this age of renewal, the main task is renewing ourselves, or deciding to change our lives positively by acquiring a new Knowledge – the Spiritual Knowledge of the heart.

This Knowledge invites us to overcome whatever blocks the flow of divine energy (which is Love), namely fear, anger, doubt, hatred, jealousy and greed and practice sincerity, patience, forgiveness, balance, harmony and tolerance.

We should learn to recognize what is immortal in us – the divine essence that participates in the Spirit of the All – and be dedicated to own spiritual growth. At the same time, we should never hinder other people's development - that would be a serious mistake. Sai Baba says we should be very careful and warns us against putting ourselves between man and God. *"Woe betide the one who acts as an obstacle on a person's path to God."*

The new consciousness of the Spirit can be synthesized in the five human values Sai Baba stands for: Love, Truth, Peace, Righteousness and Non-violence.

He has come to convey what Jesus announced two thousand years ago: only those who were born twice shall see God, such as the humble, those with a pure heart and those who were reborn in the Spirit and reawakened into a new state of consciousness allowing them to see God as Divine Love in every person and creature.

Hence, instead of surrendering to the illusions of the world, we should try to improve and open ourselves to Spiritual Knowledge. We should be the living examples of Truth, bearing in mind that we can only change ourselves and no one or nothing else. That is all we can do for others.

A profound personal change can influence other people and the surrounding environment positively. Don't we agree that optimism is infectious?[105]

We are the brotherhood of Light and Sai Baba is the Cosmic Christ within everyone of us, the divine sparkle. We should be bold enough to choose to "dare", to make the quantum leap (within) for the sake of "eternal" life. But we must hurry up. We are running out of time for this inner make-over.

While driving on the highway, admiring a rainbow[106] heralding the end of an autumn storm, I had a flash of inspiration. I realized I was again a "sparkle of Light", after two thousand years. Like many other souls at the end of the second millennium, I was contributing in the restoration of that Christ Consciousness Jesus had announced, shedding His blood, as if to saw the seeds (i.e. Spiritual Knowledge) for this new, collective blossoming of souls in the garden of the Spirit.

I felt close to God, or Jesus, or the Holy Spirit then, just as I feel close to Sai Baba now.

Jesus said: *"Before this generation passes, the signs of the end will become visible."* Did He refer to my generation, the generation at the turn of the ages?

Only God could tell and so I kept the question for myself. I was patiently waiting for His sign to approve the work I was carrying out: humility was the passport for His Kingdom within me.

The commitment undertaken with God many years before was clear and essentially identical to that renewed with Sai Baba, in the first interview He conceded to me. I no longer lived for myself – I lived for Him.

The commitment healed me, first the body and then the soul because we are the disease, but we are also the miracle. Jesus would say after every miracle: *"Your faith healed you.",* and further: *"Your sins have been forgiven."*

God is mankind and so to serve others means to serve God and ourselves because, remember, we are all One.

The message I found in those days is still valid for everyone: *"You should only allow things to happen. Come out of this chrysalis, this space limited by the restrictions of your mortal mind, and allow yourself to be transformed into a beautiful butterfly[107]. A new freedom, a new world is waiting to open up for you as soon as you leave behind the old ways, thoughts and ideas and transform and renew yourself."*

NOTES: CHAPTER XI

98. My intensive course continued in Italy, full-time.

99. Of which Sai Baba is the reincarnation.

100. Number thirteen in the major arcana of the Tarot represents "death", i.e. the transformation from old to new.

101. Hinduism maintains that the *satvic* (pure) man does the right thing in the right time, to the right person, unconditionally. Therefore, only those who are pure in the heart can know how and if it is appropriate to do something for the others.

102. This behaviour is typical for the *rajasic* and *tamasic* man (victims of passion and indolence, respectively).

103. Years later, I realized that that dream had announced the passage from one life, characterized by the cross – implied as interior suffering – to another life, characterized also by the cross, but implied as the divine light within.

104. Here is the definition of the word "seduction" in the Italian Dictionary: seduce, drag into evil by means of flattering, allurement and deceit; flatter, allure, deceive, attract, charm.

105. In this regard, the so-called effect of the hundredth monkey is enlightening. It shows how the evolution of an individual can trigger (in a way which is still unknown to science but not to the mystics) a domino effect and bring about the evolution of all the members of the same species, regardless of time and space.

106. For me, a rainbow also symbolizes the presence of God. The Light decomposes into colours, to become more visible to human beings.

107. Years later, those words were also confirmed through a peculiar event I witnessed. I found an exotic butterfly in the street (in my neighbourhood), in late December, rigid with cold and dying. It was revived in my hands and it flew away. Later on, in India, I was given a photo of a butterfly identical to the one I'd found, which had flown away mysteriously, with the writing "Happy New Year". I had found the butterfly on the 28th December, the previous year.

XII

The awareness of the Self manifests when delusion vanishes, or rather, when the delusion that this dreamworld is real vanishes.

Sai Baba.

I felt a slow but steady inner transformation taking place, more and more distinctly. Over the year I had acquired more balance, which testified to the gradual increase of impartiality towards joy and pain. Although my equanimity was not stable yet, I hoped to master it soon.

On the spiritual path, we learn we should never count our chickens before they are hatched because we can make the wrong move at any time. The ego keeps encouraging us to take "alternative roads" because, as long as we make mistakes, it means it has not be defeated yet. It wants to stay with us till the game is over.

The alternative to unconditional surrender to Divine Will, filling the heart with peace of mind and true happiness, is the imprisonment of the ego, characterized fear, guilt and doubt. It is either God (the path of the Spirit), or the world (the path of the matter). There is no other way.

Christ, or the Messiah, in the figure of Sai Baba, assisted by thousands of "apostles" scattered around the world, is with us already. He is calling those who have not forgotten Him to do their task for mankind, for Him.

I could feel it in my heart, although my mind demanded explanations, precise dates, facts and evidence.

I realized that intuitions and coincidences were not dictated by chance but by the sacred content transmitted in us over the centuries, by that which connects one lifetime and the next, one experience and the next one, namely the Divine Light (essence) which never fades, albeit concealed by our imperfections and ignorance, maintaining its fixed residence in the heart.

The search for Harmony, as Truth, stems from a divine need and makes us evolve. On the other hand, when we are not in Harmony, the discomfort is generated by incorrect and ambiguous behaviour and every effort to evolve is fruitless. We are unhappy because we are unable to satisfy this divine need. It is always alive in us, even when we are oblivious to it.

If we decide to ignore this Truth, our illusions will inevitably crumble down, sooner or later.

All of a sudden, just as on in many other occasions, the day of the departure (announced to me two months earlier) arrived. It was going to be my 14th [108] voyage (and the 4th that year) to India. I left with a group of a hundred and twenty devotees. We were going to work as volunteers in the kitchens of the *ashram*. Sai Baba says: *"Two working hands are more sacred than the praying lips."* It was my first experience of this kind.

My activities were mostly intellectual and so I decided to put myself to the test by doing manual work. I made myself available for the night shift (2:30-5:00 a.m.), to prepare breakfast. To be more specific, I was supposed to cut papayas and pineapples.

I would never have thought I would be able to keep up with the pace[109]. Surprisingly, I never missed a single shift and was never tired. I was supported by the divine energy magnificently and my endurance exceeded all expectations.

During those weeks I experienced the umpteenth manifestation of "Grace". I felt like a leaf swept away by the wind of Divine Love, strong and light. I was His instrument. As a member of the human race, I felt like the "most wonderful materialization ever created by the Divine".

A few days passed before Sai Baba called some of us for an interview. It was the fifth time for me to receive this huge gift – to be close to Him, to be able to touch His delicate hand and talk Him. I held His photo and a pen in my hands. I asked Him, from the bottom of my heart to sign the photos, as a signal that I could continue writing about Him. He silently took the pen from my hand and signed that photo. He then commented that I was worried because I didn't know if I should continue writing. He added, firmly: *"Write it and I will bless it."* I had not uttered a single word on the subject to Him.

During every interview, I managed to find a place to sit close to His armchair (on the left, like His ally). I was delighted beyond words at being so near Him, albeit for such a short while, because time stretched into sweet, immense eternity.

He asked me for the first time where my husband was. I replied by kissing His left knee and His feet, delicate like rose petals, while He laid His hand gently on my bent head: He was my Beloved.

He confirmed it with that loving gesture and a blessing.

I finally asked His permission to go to Tibet. Shortly before my departure to India, I was invited to go there to do some voluntary service. He replied resolutely not to go there, as Tibet would come to me. I was puzzled by that grandiloquent, enigmatic reply.

He conveyed certain profound concepts in those few minutes that should otherwise require months or years of elaboration to be understood by a small mind. The heart took them in with immense gratitude. I was fulfilled, confused and dazed at the same time.

Sai Baba stated that the three main guidelines for all mankind to transcend delusion were:

Do not forget God.

Do not believe in the world as true reality.

Never be afraid of death.

We should keep God in our thoughts all the time and let Him accompany us in all our actions. We should dedicate everything to Him, without considering the material world as the only reality, without succumbing to its flattering and seduction.

According to Sai Baba, the worlds awaiting us are quite different. Jesus foretold the same thing two millennia ago, when He spoke about the return to the house of the Father.

Instead of fearing death, we should learn to "experience" it as the dawn of liberation, or a passageway to real life. When the body dies, the physical casing - the prison we are so much fond of - ceases to exist.

Our true nature is to be eternal, immortal. We are the divine essence which continues to exist, forever.

Sai Baba's birthday was approaching and so I was called to work during the day, too. I was in the group preparing floral decorations in the temple and around the Divine Master's residence. The experience was celestial – to say the least. I felt I was already in Paradise.

While I was busy arranging garlands of flowers along the railings under the windows of His home, I was deeply touched as I shared immense joyfulness with a work mate I hadn't known. I let out the phrase that we were under the windows of God. Amused and surprised, he replied he was a film director. His film about Sai Baba was entitled *Under the windows of God*. What formidable synchronicity. I wasn't sure if I was dreaming – reality was so fantastic and marvellous in its perfect harmony.

Days passed in a state of complete fulfilment – thoughtless, without concerns or problems. I was totally blissful.

Time acquired a magic dimension of the everlasting present while enjoying the privilege of working in the house of God, placing flowers, fruits and gold angels of all sizes within the *Mandir* (the temple).

This sacred place is like an island out of time and space. Its colours are soft and delicate – rose-coloured, light blue and ivory. One can be there only during the *darshan,* or the *bhajans* (twice a day), to sit on the floor in silence and meditation, waiting for Sai Baba. Only volunteers may enter it and move around with extreme reverence and composure.

I felt like one of them because I had free access to the temple at all times, taking part in the preparations for the holiday.

Those people dedicated their lives to Sai Baba to be able to enjoy this privilege and I wished to do the same. I had already promised it to Him. I worked night and day and felt increasingly charged with energy.

I had an incredible vision during a break from work.

It was midday and I was in the room, lying on the bed for a few minutes, eyes closed, to relax. I saw a sky with a myriad of bright, whirling comets. They joined to form a large cross of light. From its centre, the Divine Mother, Our Lady, came to me, dressed in light. I heard the inner voice calling Her: "Mother of Light".

Immediately afterwards, I floated in the air in the form of thought (without my physical body), admiring surreal landscapes, while formations of multicoloured lights continued to whirl in the sky. Forests, lakes, rivers of indescribable beauty stretched beneath me. I knew I was in another realm.

I opened my eyes and got up, bewildered and deeply moved, surprised of being in India and not in Italy. Over the previous few minutes, I had moved from one dimension to another – too quickly to realize it was daytime and that I wasn't in my bed. It was twelve thirty – half an hour after I'd lain down on the folding bed, to catch a nap.

Again, life showed me it was made of the same stuff as dreams. It was hard to believe that the wonderful scenery I had witnessed a while earlier (in the presence of the Divine Mother) was less "real" than my stay in India, in God's residence, so far from everyday reality – which was also dreamlike.

Perhaps, if we could all view our daily reality as daydreams, being the spectators and the actors at the same time, we would find the strength to distance ourselves from the world and its illusions we consider to be so real – but is it really so?

Sai Baba says: *"Day-time or night-time, whenever they arrive, always be kind to people. Hurt never, help ever."*

Being kind to everybody and feeling the divine presence within leaves no room for sadness or discontentedness. Day and night, we should be open for His message and experience it around the clock. The Holy Spirit[110] (Sai Baba) can consequently answer our prayers because we establish a harmonious union with the divine essence within (through cosmic energy).

During that stay at Puttaparthi, I experienced a deep sense of inner freedom on the path of the Spirit, with the understanding that this unity, the state of Oneness, had always been there, albeit ignored, and that nothing in the world could ever undo it. It was irreversible.

The freedom to be what I really was – pure, divine essence – awakened in me a childish feeling for the marvel and the fantastic, mixed with amazement, with an intimate sensation of absolute harmony with the All. It was no longer the decision of the ego but of the Divine Will, implemented through me, under the direction of the supreme director – God, or Sai Baba. He guided me every step of the way and relieved me of the responsibilities. I wished to be a leaf dancing in the divine wind. Indeed, I have seen that, if we allow ourselves to be guided by Him, He carries our burdens for us. This is how every moment of your life (belonging to the Divine) should be lived, with enthusiasm and by letting yourself go to the cosmic dance of Shiva (God) – according to the Hindu representation of creation.

The magnificent vision I had in my room made me think that when the cross, symbolizing worldly life (of suffering), "becomes bright", i.e. allows itself to be illuminated by the Spirit, the Divine Mother manifests in us in the form of light, transforming human life into divine life. In other words, my subtle part was transmuted.

For years, I gave as much importance to such experiences as to those that occurred in my waking state, because they enriched and integrated the Knowledge of the Spirit.

Sai Baba is the Father (*Baba*), the Truth, and the Mother (*Sai*), or Love. He is Brahma, the Creator, Vishnu, the Conserver and Shiva, the Redeemer. He is the Son, or the Christ who came to redeem humankind. He is the Holy Spirit who has come to comfort us and give everything we need.

In His youth He declared to be the Son of God and 'as an adult He declared to be the Divine Mother and the Divine Father. Today He claims to be the Holy Spirit.

In this Messianic Age of the Holy Spirit, unless we rouse into the "Sun" of the true Self, we will not see God as the Holy Spirit among us and within us. We will keep giving value to the "Moon" that is, to the ego, or the individual self (mind). Consequently, we will not be able to transcend duality and benefit from the Grace of the Holy Spirit – the awareness of our divine origin.

I ceased to feel sorry for myself quite a while before. I comprehended that all the fortune and the Divine Power resided within me. They were in every person. Permanent happiness stems from this awareness maintained all the time in the heart, as Sai Baba stated, when He summoned the entire group of a hundred and twenty people for an interview in the *Mandir*, shortly before our departure. He spoke to us for almost an hour, lavishing caresses, smiles, sweet and enlightened words, *vibuthi* and much, much Love. He told us: *"Although it has many names, water always remains water"*, and invited us to find unity in diversity and overcome analysis with synthesis. He said that true Knowledge was the knowledge of the *Atma* (the Divine Self) and invited us to repeat *"I am Divine"*, I am the true Self, instead of *"I am a human being"* (while pronouncing this phrase, He mimed a miserable, curled up being). He added that energy was matter and matter was energy and demonstrated it by materializing in the air a cross and a gold necklace He put on a devotee's neck. He said that God is the Holy Spirit, it is Cosmic Consciousness, it is *"Sat – energy, Cit – consciousness"*, and that the entire Universe is conscious energy and conscious energy, awareness, is *"Ananda – bliss"*. He went on saying that the level of consciousness varied from the lowest level (mineral world, rocks) gradually to the highest (plants, animals and human beings).

The body, being matter, possesses a level of consciousness of a very low vibration frequency. When it dies, what remains is the immortal essence which neither dies nor mutates. When it moves away from the body, interrupting the vital and vivifying connection with it, it can cause the illness or the death of the body. He said: *"Atma (divine essence) is omniscient, omnipotent and omnipresent and energy is Love, Love is Power (the greatest Power), Love is Light and Love is God"*. He specified that He was speaking about Pure Love, free of egotism, and not about human love in terms of sensual or emotional attachment (between husband and wife or mother and child). He said we should not mix up the matrimony of the I, as the true Self, with the matrimony of the eyes (ego). The former is the true matrimony (spiritual matrimony of the soul and the Spirit) and the latter is the physical matrimony of two people (bodies)[111]. He reiterated that matter was energy, that it wasn't our ears that heard, it wasn't your eyes that saw, it was not our nose that perceived scents but the energy passing through the physical organs of sense, just as electrical power passed through the bulbs of the temple (the *Mandir* was illuminated by hundreds of light bulbs).

While He spoke, I looked around, ecstatic, enraptured, trying to fix into my memory every single visible detail of that holy place, knowing it would not be easy to return in there again.

Sai Baba continued, assertively: *"Love is life. It is energy. Love gives life. It enlivens us. Every cell is Love".* He spoke about realization and I heard Him define it for the first time as *"Constant Integrated Awareness",* that is, being permanently concentrated on the true Self. He said there is concentration, actuated by the senses, contemplation, actuated by the mind, and then there is meditation, actuated neither by the senses nor by the mind. A true *sadhana* (spiritual discipline) consists in serving others and the Sai organization should be only Love and unconditional Service to others, the true sat-sang (good company) is that of Truth and company of God. He then exclaimed: *"I am God, I am the true Self. I am below and above, around, in front and behind you. I am Love. All is Love. Concentrate on the breath. 21500 times a day man is born and dies.* He repeated: *"So-Ham",* miming with his hand the movement of the wave: *"life enters (oxygen) and death exits (carbon dioxide)."* He went on: *"There are no human values without the coherence of the three Hs: head, heart and hands. Honesty, correctness and focus on God are necessary to avoid mistakes and wrongdoings. Love is the language of another dimension, beyond time and space. God is the Sun and the mind is the shadow (or the Moon which relies on the light of the Sun to shine). If there is Love, there is also Peace of mind and unity. No conflict or duality. There are many people in the world, but few values. The world is full of characterless people. When you move in the direction of God, the shadow is behind your back. When you move in the direction of the world, the shadow is in front of you (if we turn our back to the world, we face God). The divine nectar is in the glass (body), but the glass cannot taste its sweetness. The straw (the mind) used for drinking cannot taste it either. The same stands for the tongue (the intellect, the buddhi) which cannot discern the taste. The nectar must arrive into the stomach (the heart) where everything is digested. Only the heart knows and can savour the flavour of the Divine".*

Sai Baba concluded this unforgettable discourse with the words: *"Say good things, do good, hear good things. First understand, then be determined and finally act."*

That river of Love (His speech) was a divine song which pervaded us completely. We left the meeting ecstatic, walking on air.

As He walked by, I kissed His feet three times and He put His hand on my head again.

He returned to the crowd of His devotees patiently waiting for Him, in silence, the crowd I usually made part of, outside the *Mandir.*

I had just been hosted in "His temple". What an incredible gift!

His last words resounded in my head: *"Only the heart is able and knows how to savour the taste of Divinity."* (the pure, spiritual heart, awakened into awareness) and the last divine recommendation *"First understand, then be determined and finally act."*

Again, in His message I found evidence that Spiritual Knowledge was fundamental for the awakening of awareness.

We should first defeat ignorance, then nurture determination and choose Goodness and Truth. At that stage, our acts will represent a genuine service to others (not to the ego), that is, to God.

I left India in a state of grace, filled with peace of mind and bliss.

On the way back, on the bus from Puttaparthi to Bangalore, I fell asleep, exhausted, and this is when I received the last gift in a row. I dreamt about a multitude of elephants surrounding me, wondering where Gita, Sai Baba's elephant (accompanying Him during all solemn ceremonies), was. Sai Baba appeared in that instant. Coming towards me, He asked *"What is your name?"* Naturally, I replied: "Divine."

I woke up and looked around: the elephants were gone. I was at the airport.

When I arrived home, I finally started experiencing in my heart what I had contemplated, spoken and written about for such a long time.

Like good wine maturing silently in the barrel, waiting for the moment of transformation, I felt I had reached the level at which I could consciously perform the task for which I had been born and Sai Baba bore it out by making me feel like a "queen" in the Kingdom of God during that stay.

I was intent on re-savouring, with my heart, the sweetness of the experiences I'd just had, representing a stable force, in order to maintain the balance between the Cosmic Mind and the individual mind, like a bridge between the Spirit and the body, an antenna between the earth and the sky, and take part in the life of the entire Cosmos. That is when I dreamt about the end of the world once again. The predominant danger this time was not fire but the inclination of the axis of planet Earth. It was inclined with respect to itself and nothing was the way it used to be any more. Everybody was trying to run away, stricken by terror. Then another peculiar dream followed. I was at Puttaparthi, taking part in a procession. Everything was enveloped in golden brightness – there were golden houses, streets and people. I interpreted its symbolism as the healing of humankind and the victory of the Spirit (gold) over matter: a new Jerusalem.

I finally understood the origin of my pain: it was the separation from the true Self – not the separation from others – which had caused so much suffering in my life. How come I hadn't seen it before?

I came to realize it at the age of fifty because that was when I managed to detach myself (but I wasn't free yet) from the slavery of the ego and stopped identifying myself with the physical body. In other words, I was no longer my own enemy, or the enemy of the true Self. We were about to become friends.

No doubt, it is fully up to us whether we shall end up in Paradise or in Hell.

I realized that the multiplicity of Oneness – infinite forms constituting the visible and invisible Universe – depended only on the different vibratory frequencies of the electromagnetic energy permeating the Universe. This interpretation of reality gave me peace of mind.

When we offer everything we do, think, say, eat or write to God and His Glory, it gets purified and our inner vibratory frequency is elevated. We can perceive God's call to tune in to Him. This was the great lesson of that journey.

I revealed the divine energy's power of "transmutation", as part of our original nature. If we are purified, we are given the possibility to transform ourselves and change, to consciously attain the 4th dimension (astral) of the psychic realm (we reach it unconsciously in our dreams) and, subsequently, the 5th dimension (of pure awareness, of the bodies of light) of the spiritual realm. That is the path to connecting with the entire cosmos.

I realized that the "Spouse" was the Spirit, the path leading to Him was Truth and pursuing that goal was the greatest dream of all – the realization of the true Self within.

Precisely a month passed from the last interview with Sai Baba when the inner voice woke me up at 3:30 a.m. (Christmas was approaching), with a disruptive message: *"You will follow God in Heaven with your whole being and you will leave behind all others."*

I cannot comment on that message, but I admit that I was obsessed by it for the following three years. Not a single day passed without my thinking about it.

It announced a new life or an interim phase into another world waiting for me, but when, how and where I did not know. I had to trust God completely.

The unity with the Divine, with the Spirit, is not attained without strain. However, once there, there is an immense award in store for us, a real treasure – the awareness, which includes the following gems: unfathomable peace, self-fulfilment, inner voice (of silence), intuition and completeness in solitude.

After a few days, I dreamt of being asked since when I had been married to loneliness, implied as the Divine Spirit. I replied I'd got married to it ten years earlier. In the dream, my body became insensitive to sensory stimuli. Was it a new stage of my journey? I had no idea.

I dreamt of being at Puttaparthi, during a *darshan*. After the interview, Sai Baba approached me and I kissed His hand. He invited me to follow Him into the temple. As we walked side by side, He asked what I was by profession and added that I would come and live close to Him, in a very comfortable place. He went into the house and came out carrying two plates of blessed food (*prasad*). One contained seeds and the other sweet rice flakes. Deeply touched, I bent down and kissed His feet. We ate the *prasad* together with another lady who had joined us in the meantime.

I was stunned and embarrassed for the familiarity Sai Baba treated us with. He went back into the house and brought us two photos. He gave one to each of us, but the other lady passed her photo to me. Then Sai Baba had a long talk with me on things I already knew and others I knew nothing about.

All of a sudden, the other lady started crying, because He would die one day and leave us. Sai Baba answered sharply, looking her straight in the eyes: *"I will never die!"*

I woke up at 3:30 a.m. at night (that hour is called 'the hour of the Brahman' in India). I often had similar dreams at that time of night, when I received messages from the inner voice.

After that particular dream, a different 'study plan' developed and took shape in me, to help me improve the Spiritual Knowledge through my dreams (or astral journeys).

The change of evolutional level entails a change of tasks.

Up till then, my task had been to learn, study and know. From that point on, I had to implement (and write about) the long journey of the soul in search of the Divine Spouse.

I spent Christmas Day on a mountain, in the midst of a white landscape covered by a sparkling blanket of snow, illuminated by the sun: it was a blanket of light, peace and silence. I had to focus and organize my ideas before I started to revise the collated material. I knew I could not exempt myself from doing what a part of me had asked to do, something Sai Baba had promised to bless.

For several long months I felt as if I'd been put with my back to the wall, dreading that I wasn't up to the task. It was yet another game of the ego. As a matter of fact, I was not supposed to think of the outcome of what I believed to be my task.

From the rational standpoint, as I leafed through the notes, my fear was that I had embarked on something totally insane. I kept telling myself: 'My beloved Swami, my life is in your hands.' So I kept my spirits up and continued writing about what I felt in my heart and stopped thinking about the results.

I dreamt of finding myself in a surreal world, where flaws were overcome in a new way. Each flaw was transformed into a different kind of flower. For example, envy was transformed into lotus flowers that filled up all the fountains and decorated the city. Perhaps the revolutionary Spirit of early Christianity was rising again, but without rites or dogmas (to reinforce faith) – a Spirit that would reinstate man's self-confidence, the power of self-healing, a harmonious relationship with nature and God and so each person would be his/her own priest?

Nature is divine and it does not allow voids: water fills every hole it encounters on the way and the wind reaches all the free spaces. Man shall also find self-fulfilment. The greatest dream is about to become reality: the void is being filled up.

Sai Baba says: *"Those who know their own heart well cannot be tricked by the illusions of the world."* The one who knows his/her own heart also knows the heart of another person, since we all make part of one single heart.

There is no better way to receive than by letting go of yourself. This means slackening your hold on what is illusive, unreal and earthly, to allow yourself to be inundated by Light. You find yourself again, your essence, as the only thing that is worth looking for. You are what you are looking for. However, if you don't know what you are searching, how can you find yourself?

I finally took this truth in through the knowledge of the heart. I saw that the middle way was the way of the heart, but also that – right between recklessness and faint-heartedness – courage was the right, indispensable means to find God.

Sai Baba has come to offer us liberation, before we leave our body. The Spirit of the revolution of Love has come to bestow upon us the Grace of consciousness, the awakening into the awareness that we are pure, divine essence – here and now. It belongs to all of us indistinctly and irrefutably (just like Love), because the Kingdom of Heaven is within each of us and among us.

He has arrived to cancel two thousand years of ignorance, to indicate the path of salvation from physical and mental illnesses, to decree the end of sorrow and human sadness and to offer protection from all the perils in disguise. In turn He asks us to trust and surrender to Him and to open our hearts to Love – the major force in the Universe.

The Grace He has come to bestow upon us, in turn for our openness to Him (by practicing His message), as the requirement for attaining equanimity and a balanced heart. It is the guarantee that our connection with the Divine will never be undermined again.

I spent the whole night listening to the voice of my heart, sweetly reiterating: *"Welcome into the home of Sai, welcome into the home of Sai."*

Sooner or later we shall see that God is our only, or our last – but not the least – resort. We'd better stop wasting any more of our precious time and realize it, because this is not the time to be tepid or hesitant.

Sai Baba says: *"I need you to be ardent and fully dedicated to Me and My work, ready to implement My will, whatever the cost. I ask for everything and only when you give me everything, you will receive everything. Nothing will be denied to you and you will find out that what I have is yours. Therefore, love everything you can lay your eyes on, love everything with the awareness that you are at one with the entire creation."*

Jesus expressed the same thing: *"Leave all to have all."*

The Divine Will revealed itself to me and there was one task left for me to accomplish – to accept it obediently and devotedly, continuing with the self-inquiry, prayer and meditation and being more and more receptive.

I had not reached "impassiveness" yet, but in any case I always opted for the Light.

We have all been credited a spark of cosmic energy in the heart (to give and to forgive always) to manage as the capital owed by the Absolute. In this sense, mankind is a divine concession to planet Earth.

Life is joy, but also service to God through our fellow men and women. Service is giving ourselves. It starts from us and comes back to us. And this is why we should be grateful to those who give us the possibility to serve others.

The inner voice kept inspiring me, day and night. My writing was swift-winged, like the wind. But, like the wind stops all of a sudden, my critical attitude (fuelled by pride) would stop me, unexpectedly. The fear of criticism or a hypothetical failure would block me for seemingly endless periods of time.

Agonizing weeks went by. This was clearly my only task. I knew that Sai Baba (the Spirit) never gave two tasks at the same time. Only when the first task is brought to the end, the next one comes forward (I knew that from my own experience). This observation contributed to my further annihilation. And so I established that there were still some rough edges to knock off in me.

The first months of that year passed in a relentless search for the stability of mind and the purity of heart. I was comforted by the timely revelation that periods of "crisis" were given for those who are on the pathway of the Spirit. All the more, they are seen as obligatory stages, so that we can rest and regenerate the forces before resuming the "climb to the top".

At any rate, going through those states, with their disturbing intensity, was certainly not an exhilarating experience, especially when the ego made its cutting remarks to convince me that I was not up to the ideals I aspired to.

One of those days I came across one of Sai Baba's messages, so appropriate for my situation: *"Obstacle forces attack the weakest. The true battle is won by ignoring the provocations coming from the mouthpiece of those forces."*

Well, I was still weak, but not weak enough to surrender to the ego. Besides, I was prepared to surrender only to God. He was always there and, even if I sometimes could not perceive His presence "loud and clear" during the day, I could feel it during the night.

In that difficult period, I dreamt of the Divine Mother, Our Lady, with the blue veil covering Her from head to toe, all studded with golden stars. It was as if She held all the vault of heaven in its place, with Her gentle power. Next to Her there was an elderly man with white hair, his arms stretched out to me. He said: "I don't want any rejection. I want openness, affection and a heart full of Love." I was deeply moved by the sweetness of his voice and by his words. I woke up serene. The storm was over.

The crisis made me realize another very important thing: speaking of trusting ourselves, the subtle reference is not to the individual self, or the consciousness of the mind which is again subjugated to the ego. The reference is to the true Self, the divine essence, the Atma, or the spark of cosmic energy within, as the expression of God in us, which ultimately means having faith in God. And this is why Sai Baba says that, unless we regain our Self-confidence (i.e. faith in the true Self), we can neither have faith in God, nor can we see Him. Individual consciousness is limited, misleading and illusive, so how can we trust illusion?

Indeed, when God takes you to another place, it is just to teach you some "new steps" of the...cosmic dance, Shiva's dance, the dance of the creation of life, in the various realms that constitute the entire Universe. In this regard, Sai Baba says: *"Only I know the agony of teaching you every step of the dance of life."* He is with us more than ever when we suffer, although suffering prevents us from seeing Him, being the expression of the ego. Again, this shows how the presence of the ego hinders the realization of the Divine.

I dreamt of being in an immense cave with white walls. It was a holy place, an underground temple with gigantic stalactites hanging down its enormous vault, like exquisitely intricate chandeliers.

At the far end of the cave, there was a blue lake with many white swans – some floating, others sleeping along the banks. I noticed that some of the swans ducked into the water to catch something but could not figure out what it was. As I woke up, I felt as if I had visited another dimension, as I did on some other occasions in the past.

A few days on, I received a message through a friend of mine, saying: *"Hear My admonishment. Do not be distracted by those who are fond of confusing others. Fog closes in upon the mind of those who do not believe in the energy of the Absolute. Now more than ever, the disciples of the light must be vigilant and firm in their mission. Try to stay united in the name of Love, so as to overwhelm the monkey that wants to slip into your mind. The Sun is above you and you must bring it down into your heart, until your bodies become bright lanterns. The Light that will emanate from you will be the light of many small Suns. Therefore, new flowers will blossom and your path will be in bloom."*

I realized that, as long as we inhabited this planet, nothing was permanently conquered. The doors of Paradise and Hell were always wide open, for every one of us.

And so, what matters is discipline, perseverance, the tenacity in pursuing the ideal of the true Self and to interpret every possible standstill in the search for the cosmic fusion with the Absolute as part of our evolution – and not involution.

Everything arrives to those who can wait patiently. In this instance, obviously, waiting does not imply lack of action or fatalism but a vigil and conscious waiting.

I had to be patient and trust the Spirit. The state of grace and its familiar sweetness and fullness was bound to return to me, as I felt I was fulfilling the mission I'd been born for. Sooner or later, it would lead me to the fulfilment I had always pursued.

There was nothing else for me to do except to continue in my effort to harmonize the inner realms of mind and emotion, to establish calmness and impartiality allowing the direct contact with the Divine and to live in peace with the entire Universe. Outside that harmony, any kind of fulfilment was uncertain.

Through the inner voice, Sai Baba made me understand that being restless did not fit into His teachings. To overcome it, I simply had to trust Him and bravely face the challenges of life. I had never been short of courage. The more I renounced the ego, the easier and smoother my life was.

That tension and restlessness stemmed from the perception of the major changes outlined against the horizon, albeit in a somewhat elusive, vague and hazy way.

I couldn't expect to know when the Spirit would come to talk to me next time or what was going to be Its next message, could I?

The only path for me was to surrender to Him completely, as no one else could help me find the answer to those voiceless questions. There was no one to talk to about those pressing issues and I experienced a tide of climax, close to breaking the banks of tolerance.

I knew it was my mind's game, but I still was unable to leave my emotions out. It seemed as if there was no way out, my back was pressed to the wall.

I came to a conclusion, with much objectiveness, that, after each and every wave of grace bestowed upon me during my stays in India in the presence of Sai Baba, a period of tough inner struggle started as soon as I returned home.

And that was the proof for me that all the games of the mind were orchestrated by the ego. It certainly had no interest in our development, that is, our liberation from its dominion, let alone in our inner peace that would decree its ultimate exile.

To maintain my strength, I prayed God with all my heart, immersed in the study of the symbolism of dreams and searching for evidence of my good intentions to hang on.

The dream of the holy cave, entirely white, with the blue lake inhabited by swans, could represent the initiation into a new state of consciousness, enriched by discernment. The swan symbolizes purity, the Androgynous[112], discernment, the knowledge of the true Self, the Heavenly Virgin and the return "home". For the Alchemists, it is an emblem of Mercury, the hermaphrodite, the union of opposites in the Oneness. It is the solar light (masculine) incarnated in Apollo (according to Greek mythology), whose birth was attended by seven swans, who flew seven times around the island of Delos, their native land. It also represents the force of a poet and poetry; it is the symbol of desire; it resides in the "*bindu*", the atom of sound (according to Hindu mythology). It is the assumed form of the majority of entities in the Other Kingdom, representing higher states of being in the course of the entity's liberation and its return to the Supreme Principle.

A lake in Hindu mythology is an emblem of Shiva and "the lake of the heart" for a Yogi. Those swans floating in the blue lake reminded me of my yearning to emerge from spiritual ignorance to the Spiritual Knowledge of the true Self, so as to attain mental stability. Through the purity of heart (swans in the lake) and a balanced mind, I would reach self-realization that is, I would come back home, to my purified heart (white holy cave). With that dream, the true Self was offering a new impetus to help me move on.

In the following days I came upon Sai Baba's message: *"The day when you comprehend that what I am taking away from you is for your utmost joy, will be the day of your arrival....home."* (to your heart or true Self).

In effect, the moment we become aware that happiness does not depend on external circumstances, but exclusively on us, we are mature enough to know what true happiness is – giving Love, without expecting to be reciprocated, without demanding Love from others, or trying to dominate them.

The Divine Master continued to teach me, day and night. A dream (not only mine but also my friends' dreams; they used to call me to report on their dreams) is the easiest, most immediate way to create a contact between the Spirit and the soul, skipping the obstacle of the mind. However, in the more recent period of crisis, in the waking hours, the mind was busy complicating things instead of simplifying the work of self-inquiry.

The only thing which never betrayed me was my intuition. In fact, it came to my aid whenever I needed to clarify things. It was such a great and irreplaceable gift, growing stronger each day. I could comprehend previously incomprehensible things. The seed and the shoot from the earlier years grew into a thriving plant.

This evidence of our divine nature, our intuitive intelligence, encouraged me during the not-so-bright moments, illuminating the toughest trials I had to face with wise farsightedness and tolerance.

My "inner persecutor" (that was how I called the Spirit in moments of profound crisis) suggested that God wanted us to sacrifice what we loved most to Him. I knew it was He highlighting the smallest mistakes in my interpretation, or behaviour, adding weight to it until it felt heavy, like a rock. Without exception, it was for my benefit, that is, for the benefit of my inner progress.

But that was not enough for me. I occasionally prayed to God to allow me to take upon myself someone else's suffering. To my mind, I could heal more easily from other people's illnesses, because they were not intrinsic to me, and, on the other hand, the other person could take a breath of relief after years of suffering. Over the many years, I had not managed to correct this attitude of sacrifice. I used to formulate this kind of prayer in childhood.

Intuition and awareness were the keys to the Spirit and the Spirit, being Truth, was nourished with purity, coherence and humility. Therefore, to be able to perceive and experience His presence, I wanted to cultivate the attitudes that stimulated my intuition and awareness. I discovered how to maintain contact with Him.

Peace and fulfilment experienced when least expected, signal the contact with the true Self, perfect joyfulness of the heart and the fullness of nothingness. I could finally let go of myself (in tune with Cosmic energy) to openness, gratitude, benevolence and surrender again. Love and Compassion made their way to me, within me. Grace was back to embrace me tenderly, protectively and reassuringly.

As I observed my life, I saw that, just like everyone else, I could live a life of a master, or that of a servant, depending on the way I utilized my mind – positively or negatively, that is, by accepting to be accountable for my own life and for my own mistakes, or by considering other people responsible.

The main road to securing the mastery (of my destiny) was that of the Spirit and not that of the ego, or desires. So, that was the meaning of Sai Baba's often repeated line: *"Turn the key clockwise and you will have God, turn it counter clockwise and you will have the world, or, in other words, it is either freedom or slavery"*, adding: *"When you are focused on God (Rama)[113], there is no more room left in the mind for desires (Kama)[114]."*

As on earlier occasions, the people He allowed me to assist in turn guided me unknowingly on my way to the Light. The beauty of this pathway lay in the possibility to transform the unknown into the known, inside and around us.

The Spirit wanted me to acknowledge that everyday reality was ephemeral, that everything was an elusive dream, to understand that there was no time to rest. I had to realize the new vision of the world at once.

I felt dazed and then, slowly, as if anaesthetized, I distanced myself from everything else, without any enthusiasm and dumbfounded.

My days were filled with an enervating wait for the confirmation that my intuition was right and that the inner voice was of a divine nature. Was I going insane or simply progressing on the path? I observed lucidly that the mind, although part of me, worked against me, fearing the beginning of its own end, sending me signals of fear and doubt to stop my inner progress. I was merely going through some trials to steel myself and strengthen my faith in the true Self.

Our life can be renewed only through our decision and will. My will was firm and determined and the decisions taken many years before were unyielding. I was not going to take any other path, at any cost. I kept repeating that to myself – perhaps God wanted to hear me say precisely that.

I realized unmistakably that, to conquer the freedom from the ego, we were not supposed to be influenced by other people's desires. We had to follow our own. It was of utmost importance not to identify with other people's expectations in our regard.

It was difficult to stay out. I had always been ready to identify myself with another person's suffering. I could understand it better by sharing and helping the other overcome it. My discernment had to be polished further, to distinguish better what was mine from what was not – if I wanted to avoid succumbing to it spiritually.

My favourite pathway to God (Sai Baba or Holy Spirit) was that of devotion and compassion. Surrendering to His Light unveiled the secrets of the Universe but also blinded the mind. Having learned that Mystic Love, experienced without discernment, may reduce the mind to chaos, I did not want to mistake the "siren voice" (the mind) for the "voice of God".

Notwithstanding my emotional turmoil, I remained convinced in the heart that the voice I heard belonged to Him, the Spirit, and no one else.

Again, my ego came forward to mock, provoke and weaken me with thoughts about unworthiness, inadequacy and incapacity.

The awareness that I was working for Him (the Divine Master) cancelled all my negative thoughts with a stroke and everything went back in its place. I could see with the heart's eye that renunciation meant getting rid of the burdens of life, that lightness brought joy and peace and that illusions would never trick me again into removing myself from the project of banishing the ego.

I found an interesting line and took it in as a personal message. It said: *"Do not take another person's karma – you haven't undone yours yet. The task is being done, but it's not easily accomplished."*

Seeing with the eye of intuition and accessing the three worlds (physical, subtle and causal) requires discipline and austerity. The true Self transcends those three worlds. Was I ever going to attain the "Formless" realm? That I didn't know.

I dreamt of St Leopold Mandic, whom I didn't know at the time. He gave me a gold Bible and announced that a treasure, yet to be discovered, awaited me at the bottom of my heart so as to put me in touch with cosmic energy.

A few days later I dreamt of Sai Baba. He came towards me, smiling gently, took my hand and put a watch on my wrist. I didn't know how to fasten but He showed me, patiently and lovingly, another opening near the quadrant. There were two fasteners but I could not figure out their meaning[115].

I dreamt of Him again two days later. We were together with some of His Indian students, standing on the staircase of a great white Victorian building that might have been a University. Sai Baba was the Divine Master everybody referred to. A middle aged elegant man approached respectfully and asked if He could help his dying father. Sai Baba answered He could not assist because He was not supposed to interfere with the will of someone who wished to end his life. The man's father wanted to die.

I intervened, saying: "They are trying to lay the blame on You, *Swami,* since they don't understand. They should be angry with themselves, as a matter of fact. A man is responsible for his own destiny."

He turned to me and looked at the wrist watch (the one He had presented me with in the previous dream) and asked His students what they saw. No one seemed to notice anything. I intervened again, saying that the hands were turning counter clockwise. Everybody remained speechless.

I was surprised to find myself being the only woman among the students of Sai Baba. Particularly because He was so friendly with me.

In India, Sai Baba lovingly spends much of His time with the students who represent, as He says, the leaders of a future humankind. He tells them: *"I give ¾ of my time to you and ¼ to mankind."*

When I woke up, I recalled that, during the last interview, by a strange play of fate, I sat down in the men's part (within the ashram, the two sexes are separate in the public places and in the temple). Sai Baba looked at me and made a sign to move from there, adding: "Next life". I understood that He hinted to my next reincarnation as a man.

At first, I felt deeply disappointed and humiliated, but then I realized that that too was a game of the ego and accepted that possibility with pleasure, hoping to return only to serve and assist the others.

Going back to the dream of the watch, I noticed it took place exactly on the anniversary of my father's death. Apart from that coincidence, something hampered my interpretation of those dreams, especially the part that appeared like a countdown (the hands turning counter clockwise). I gave up because there was nothing I could do about it and decided to wait patiently for further clarification.

Then I dreamt of being in India. My son was also there and he couldn't fall asleep due to the bright light shining directly on his eyes. In that period he actually was in India, at Puttaparthi. My son woke me up the same night, at four o'clock in the morning, with a phone call (it was 7:30 a.m. in India). He told me joyfully that he had just come out from the interview in the course of which Sai Baba had taken his face in His hands, drawn it closer to His and looked straight into his eyes.

Again, I arrived to the conclusion that life was but a dream in a dream. It was so evident if you lived in the company of God.

I understood that the light shining on my son's eyes was the light of the Divine Master illuminating him with His gaze, in actual life.

I was grateful to Sai Baba for having welcomed my son (His son) into the awareness of His Divine Being. It was a double grace – for him and for me. I received a tangible proof of the Heavenly protection of his spiritual transformation.

I found further evidence, in that same period, that the inner voice was the voice of the Spirit, or the true Self, or the "Guardian of the threshold" guiding the disciples of the Light, on earth. It is the Light shining in the darkness, heralding the destiny of the hesitant, dormant consciousness that will be fulfilled through the changes.

We erroneously say that, when we can't make our choices, destiny makes them in our stead. But, it is always us – the part that is more elevated than the individual consciousness moves in a certain direction to make things happen. In other words, an event does not befall us, from Heaven, but it is us who allow things to happen by behaving in a certain manner.

Nevertheless, the real solution to our problems can arrive only if we are fully conscious. The solutions of the unconscious mind are merely partial solutions.

Well, the true Self made itself heard more and more often, preparing me for yet another makeover, a radical one, that would turn my life (already eventful as it was, the inner one in particular) upside down.

On the other hand, the true Self had already expressed itself earlier in my life. For example, when I was thirteen it had announced that I would have a son at the age of thirty and that the road would be uphill all along. Or, when I was fifteen, that I would soon hold my dying father in my hands, or when I was twenty five that I would have to go back to Sicily due to my mother's death – to name but a few most important instances, leaving out the rest.

I was absorbed in those thoughts when I came upon a photo of Sai Baba. I read on the back side: "Surrender to the will of God." I fell asleep that night, reassured by His presence. After many restless nights, when I was wondering how to proceed, this one was going to be calm.

I dreamt of flying, bodiless, above a great lake covered with lotus flowers ready to bloom. They were still green. The next day, riding my bicycle, I soliloquized with the Self on the solitary life I lead due to my choice (to seek the union with the Spirit), when my eyes caught huge black letters on a white building wall. I read: I LOVE YOU,...and my name followed. It was He who had drawn my look in the direction of that wall. Tears of joy were rolling down my face. A message of love exchanged by youngsters became His message of Love for me, in the very moment I was thinking about it. So powerful is the omnipotence, the omniscience and the omnipresence of the Divine Self. And so, when you recognize the path, you cannot get off the tracks any more. As we grow, accept and get to know ourselves, we become co-creators in the Work of God. We are constantly under His protection.

As children, through family relations we learn to love in a more or less distorted manner. Unfortunately, this determines all our future choices in life – unless we overcome spiritual ignorance.

This could induce us to believe that destiny cannot be escaped from.

Yet, we can overcome this almost obsessive and compulsive modality of repeating the same mistakes, because, at the end of the day, this is the real issue. How many of you can go back into the past and see that the so-called "unavoidable" choices were made more than once, or that the same mistakes were done repeatedly, in spite of the sad consequences?

The drives or desires that push us to behave in a repetitive way will cease only when we withdraw the "ideal images" we project on the objects of our desires, with the awareness that all we need is already within us.

This means that only one thing, or person, or situation, is not more desirable than the other *per se*. In our mind we construct (based on the modality to love acquired in childhood) an idealistic image of the so-called "object of desire" and then try to fit in people or situations that come into our *karmic* game. What must change is not other people or situations, but our point of view or perception of the surrounding world, since the more or less profound attachments to the most significant aspects of our existence stem from our projections on the world. From life to life, they make us come back to earth, in conditions of increased slavery, depending on the degree of our emotional involvement.

In this perverse game, objective reality is always eluded or removed at the detriment of truth and replaced by utterly illusive fantasies, for the game to be perpetuated. For instance, we do our utmost, believing we are giving all of ourselves in a relationship, without ever attaining inner peace, without feeling well about it. We call this love and refuse to admit that we have wasted a lifetime in a perverse power game.

In plain words, we kid ourselves to carry on, until we become "intoxicated" with habit. We end up believing in the fantasies we built up, mistaking them for reality, while the truth of the matter lies in the subconscious mind, like a drifting mine that is triggered and blows up in a moment of "crisis".

A frustration or a provocation or a threat or something like that is enough for the mine to explode. Facing existential failure, a person is invaded by a sense of guilt, or panic, anxiousness, fear of abandonment or loss, angst of living or fear of dying.

It is imperative to discredit the common belief that destiny is unavoidable. The major mistake is failing to look for the Truth within, or failing to give it the right value once it has been revealed.

If we are open for the truth about ourselves (our limits and flaws), we can understand the true meaning of certain situations and bonds. We can see if we have been involved in relations of love or power, dictated by emotional involvement and directly related to the law of cause and effect (*karma*) that determines our lives until we transcend it.

We must always bear in mind that true, unconditional Love is liberating. It never enslaves or causes addiction. The thirst for power, seduction or domination camouflaged as love, affection or passion deprive us from our freedom and neutralize the soul and expressions of life such as joy, peace, creativity, imagination, intuition and fantasy.

You might wish to know how to discern what holds together two people in a relationship – whether it is love or attachment (thirst of power). It is easier than what you may think. When a relation, any kind of relation – romance, friendship, marriage or family – is characterized by true, unconditional Love, there is complete wellbeing and constructiveness. People feel good because it is about sharing, respect, trust, openness, (inner) growth, clarity and honesty.

When it is about attachment or thirst for power, the relationship is destructive. It is dominated by confusion, narrow-mindedness, lack of satisfaction, apathy and inertia – symptoms of an incomplete relationship. It lacks the aforementioned positive attributes and so its evolution is hindered.

In this age of "liberation"[116] rather than redemption, we should know that the ego cannot be redeemed. We either extinguish it, or it will extinguish[117] us. The time has come to clarify things and ban any ambiguity, meanness or compromise with the evil forces.

Emotional investments unsupported by True Love and its subtle, pure and limpid vibration, are destined to succumb as "investments at a loss". We lose our inner peace, safety, Self-confidence and Self-esteem and we end up being disappointed, anxious, afraid, insecure and self-contemptuous.

Sai Baba says: *"Be an instrument in the hands of God and let Him use you for any scope He prefers."*

I often turned to Him in those terms, saying: "Make use of me the way You consider best." Each time I would end up being in the right place at the right time, doing something in His name, as if to testify of His presence when or where it wasn't obvious.

Sai Baba is the Holy Spirit that guides us with the Light of inspiration, sustains us throughout the change, the transformation of our hearts, whenever we turn to Him with Love. He will help us break the chains of constriction, if we really want it. He has come to call us, to awaken us from the dream of ignorance and make us His messengers, or better testimonies of what we are – pure, divine essence (sparks of that Light) – so that we can illuminate the world and convey this truth to mankind.

NOTES: CHAPTER XII

108. In the Tarot, it corresponds to "Temperance" whose symbolism is related to the Androgynous and the age of Aquarius.

109. We went to the *darshan* at five o'clock and so we slept few hours at night.

110. ...this is the Spirit of Truth and Love.

111. The "I" and the "eye" refer to the spiritual Self and to the physical eye (the ego), respectively.

112. Expression of the mystic matrimony of the soul and the spiritual Self; it is feminine in its contemplation and masculine in its action.

113. Rama is the *Avatar* of righteous behaviour (*Dharma*), that is, God as righteousness.

114. *Kama*: means 'desire' in Sanskrit.

115. One was probably of the mind and the other of the heart.

116. Sai Baba says that: *"Many people ask for freedom without knowing what it really is. There is freedom of physical illnesses, of the senses or of the mind, but the real freedom is that of the cycle of rebirths. Man should redeem his present life to earn the freedom of the cycle of birth and death"*.

117. Let us bear in mind what Sai Baba says about desire: *"We either overcome it or it kills us"*.

XIII

He who is immature cannot understand the condition of the mature.

Rumi.

One thing is certain: man cannot identify himself only with his physical body because we are not the body. We are *also* the body, though. Relevant to this, we should consider our origins for a moment. What we are is not the consequence of our choices. Looking at our current life or our birth, we haven't had the possibility to choose our parents. Neither have we been given the possibility to choose the modality or the time of our physical death. We cannot actually extend our life, not even for a fraction of time.

As soon as we realize that the spiritual heart is the most important temple, that we are essentially the "Spirit of Love", there will be no more need to strain or delude ourselves, nurture false expectations, hide flaws or deceive ourselves and others. We shall be able to improve and change our destiny. Sooner or later, our common aim will be the perfect purity of the Light.

Sai Baba says: *"In this false world, only God is Truth and Love. Be Love!"* It is an invitation to unite, to recognize ourselves in the divine essence uniting all mankind. The same essence resides in each one of us.

We belong exclusively to the Spirit. It is our only partner – all other bonds are illusory. They are not dictated by true Love, pure and spiritual, but by various expressions of attachment (of the ego).

In extreme terms, the "homeless", the "scientist", the "entrepreneur", the "artist", the "politician" or "the man in the street" are equally divine. They just play different roles in the illusive reality. No one is better or worse, they are merely different and this heterogeneity is overcome when the awakening to the awareness of the true Self allows us to see Oneness in everybody and Unity in diversity.

The only true task is to seek, find and unite in the Spirit, or Oneness[118], and restore the original unity of the Universal Brotherhood. Every person's primary objective should be to come to know himself, or herself, to find and accept himself, or herself, to unite with the Divine and realize the true Self.

If we believe that we are accomplishing our task in the world, but still feel bad, we should take cognizance that this task is "fictitious". It is not true. Why then persevere in the error?

Fictitious tasks and needs are born from attachments or illusory dependences on one or another bond, like the family, the roles we play, work, religion, institutions, organizations, our nation or race.

Actually, we belong only to the Spirit, as children of one Father and one Mother, the Spirit and manifest Nature, united in Love. The seed which generated us contained the imprint of Oneness. When we find this imprint again, we will be able to reawaken into real life and be reborn into the Spirit.

Jesus said we had to be born twice to be able to see God and enter the Kingdom of the Father. The second birth takes place with the recognition of our divine essence – it is the birth into the Spirit.

I dreamt of reading a book on sacrifice (surrender to God) and liberation from slavery to the world. At the time I was writing about those particular issues.

In the same period I attended a course in Gnosis delivered by a group of people.

That experience, although brief, helped me clarify many obscure points regarding the various realms and dimensions we move and live in, without being aware of them.

They, too, spoke in terms of "death of flaws" and "sacrifice of the ego", referring to modalities to stick to Truth and be reborn into the Spirit, as our second birth.

It was the first time for me to hear, in the West, such clear explanations on how to address and overcome flaws of character on the practical and theoretical plane.

Modern man appears to have forgotten that character flaws cause suffering and are the origin of all evils inflicted upon him. Sai Baba says: *"In the past, man held in due consideration primarily character, then health and lastly money whose loss was not considered important at all. Nowadays, values have been inverted and so people's primary consideration is money, followed by health and character. Nobody gives much importance to character any more, undeservedly, and so true human values gradually disappear."*

I learned that the "Sacrifice of the self" implies that a person is removed from the profane (mundane) use of his/her nature to reinstate its sacred use through service to humankind. The scope is to reinforce the inner power and propitiate and thank the Divine for the gift of life.

This example was set by Jesus and is set by Sai Baba today.

To sacrifice "ourselves" means making our lives sacred. That is obtained by offering our lives to mankind, for instance to communicate true, spiritual knowledge which helps awaken the consciousness to higher vibration frequencies, for everyone to tune up with the True Self with the power and potential latent in us, free from the ego.

Sacred work consists in "Christizing" consciousness, i.e. transforming individual consciousness, through collective consciousness, into Christ or Cosmic Consciousness by awakening those energies which lie dormant in every human being – once the flaws are overcome because they block manifestation, knowledge and implementation.

When the lake of the heart is calm and limpid (pure), it reflects the divine light. If it is rough or dirty (impure), the divine light cannot be reflected (I remembered the dream of the lake with the swans).

One day, I was sitting at the table and writing, as usual, when the following phrase came to my mind: "The Lord is always in front of those who can see Him". In that precise moment I saw, through the window, the automatic gate opening slowly. I was alone at home and so the switch can't have been pressed by anybody else. I leaned out of the window and, amazed at my own words, I simply said: "Welcome" to the Spirit manifesting itself in that extraordinary, symbolically eloquent manner.

When we are on the path of the Spirit, we must be prepared and not be surprised by anything because for Him everything is possible. We should remember that.

I kept softening my "flaws" to reinforce my character. I felt like an athlete, training incessantly, to be ready to make my utmost in the coming competition. However, I had no idea what major grace was in store for me.

From the study of the Astrological natal chart, according to *Karmic* Astrology, and from what I had been foretold, I had learned years earlier that this lifetime's *karmic* task was to lead others back home. I hadn't been able to understand the subtle meaning of that phrase for a long time. But then I started realizing that, perhaps, I might help others to rediscover their true home – the spiritual heart. As they went through the stages I had gone through, my experience (as a direct testimony) could guide them in the discovery of the true Self, true certainties, true joys and a true life.

It was a sudden intuition. I could not prevaricate any longer when it came to Sai Baba's invitation to write a book on Him. I had to be more determined in my commitment. Many years passed before I managed to bring that task to the end with the last turn of the screw.

My attention was continuously captured by inexplicable facts and incomprehensible dreams and my mind required more clarity to undertake the serious work of synthesizing the material gathered over the years.

As if Sai Baba was trying to tell me in my dreams that He had arrived in this age to reopen the "door to the heart" for us to reveal our inner world – just as Jesus had arrived two thousand years ago for the humankind that, unfortunately, hasn't made much progress on the pathway of the Spirit throughout the many years.

In the more recent dream, Sai Baba drew my attention to what was going on with the watch. To my mind, it was referred to our age, in its cyclical becoming. The hands were turning backwards, yet no one seemed to realize it, as if mankind was unaware of having "gone back" into living in a messianic age, like that of two thousand years earlier. At any rate, this was my free interpretation.

After the dream with the golden *japamala* (rosary), in my dreams I saw other rosaries made of crystal, rose-coloured quartz, sapphires and emeralds. Each of those dreams announced something beautiful.

The last one announced a visit to a shrine of St. Michael. Situated in a wonderful setting, the sanctuary is an example of sacred Medieval architecture – quite austere, dominating the valley from the top of the cliff. I was struck by an inscription on the portal at the entrance that read: "Confine yourself in solitude and I will speak to your heart." I had come the way up there to read those words.

I realized I had stopped writing. My justification was that I had to work on myself further and continue with my spiritual retreat.

As I contemplated the words of Jesus, I saw His message of Love as the universal fountain of life we should all drink from. I could clearly see the difference between True Love and attachment in my daily life.

Life is Love. It is about self-giving. When we love (when we are thirsty of giving), we are alive. Those who are alive will never die because they share the immortality of the Spirit owing to the divine essence within that connects us to the cosmic energy – the inexhaustible source of life.

But when we are attached (when we are thirsty of having), the ego prevents us from drawing from the universal source – Love. We thrive on other people's vital mental energies. On the mental plane, this mechanism manifests when we control others, induce dependence or steal others' souls (the worst expression of control).

Due to this struggle to "come into possession" of other people's energies, human beings are incomplete creatures. Being dependent, we are unable to integrate the remaining complimentary part, obscured by our ignorance. Although constantly present, it is unusable in that state.

This integration is beyond reach if one is still in the state of dependence. Every effort to evolve is blocked until we master our senses and our individual consciousness. We must know how to manage the ego (mind and emotions) before we venture to climb the true Self.

The completeness we yearn for consciously or unconsciously is attained by reconciling the opposites (the masculine and feminine qualities, present every human being), that is, by harmonizing inner masculine and feminine[119] aspects, in the final union of the soul with the divine essence (*Atma*), that is, in the realization of the true Self.

As long as we are driven by the polarity of the opposites, we cannot reach Christ or Cosmic Consciousness and unite with the Divine. I kept repeating this until it became an integral part of me.

Before we learn to make a difference between True Love and attachment (thirst of power) and finally choose between those two opposite modes of behaviour, we survive (not live) as " living zombies" and lead miserable, unhappy lives. In other words, we remain incomplete.

When Jesus said: *"Let the dead bury their dead"*, who did He refer to? I think He was talking about people who lived without acknowledging the Spirit, without reawakening the consciousness of the Divine, instead of *living* – in the spiritual sense of the word. People who have not awakened the consciousness to the Light cannot enter His Kingdom of Light, the one that Jesus prepared for us and Sai Baba invites us to attain. They will have to reincarnate and return to earth and wait for the crucial moment to arrive for them, too, when they will dispose of their ego.

We are not aware that, even though we live in the 3rd dimension, we are also immersed in the 4th dimension (astral or emotional realm, the most refractory to the development of consciousness from individual to universal) and we can reach the 5th dimension (of pure awareness, of the bodies of Light) through our spiritual growth.

In this regard, Sai Baba announced the beginning of the Golden Age (2012?)[120] in the first decades of the third millennium and the transition of one part of mankind (the spiritually prepared who will reach the awareness of the Self, or a higher vibration frequency) who have attained the Christ Consciousness (of which He is the utmost expression on earth) into the 5th dimension through the etherealization of matter.

The remaining part of humanity will reach the 5th dimension with the arrival of the next *Avatar*, Prema (Love) Sai, in the south of India around 2030, who has been announced as His future Incarnation. Although insensible of the change, the late comers will be able to join in thanks to the more elevated group – those who have reached the awareness of the Self – as they will have raised the vibrations in the surrounding world enough to trigger the Sathya Yuga, or the Golden Age.

As I gathered more and more information on the symbolic meaning of my dreams, or astral journeys, I discovered that the illuminated cross in the sky – like the vision of Our Lady, the whirling stars, the rosaries, the vision of Jesus and the rainbow – announced the arrival of Christ, or Cosmic Consciousness. The cross is the symbol of Love in our actions, heart and thoughts.

All those dreams foretold the arrival of the Golden Age. Being able to testify to something so magnificent (the world of dreams belongs to the 4th dimension) was fantastic.

Sai Baba says: *"Be with the Truth. Be with yourself, with the essence in you and put it into practice."*

I understood the deep connotation of His invitation to maintain my withdrawal from the world.

I dreamt of being at Puttaparthi, giving a lecture on human values and the possibility to live a balanced, harmonious life. In that context, I explained that to feel the Divine within was so stirring that we reached mystical ecstasy.

I had a stupefying experience on the way back after visiting some devotees. We dwelled upon Sai Baba all day, remembering the trips to India we'd made together. At dusk, I was in the car with some friends, homebound, silent and intent to converse with the Spirit. I silently asked if the time was ripe to talk about Him in the book I was writing, above all if the moment had come to announce His return among us as the Messiah, or Sai Baba, or the Holy Spirit. In my heart, I was waiting for an answer, or a sign.

Out of the blue, I asked my travelling companions about the probability for us to see a rainbow in the sky, in that weather. I thought, if only I could see it, it would mean that the Spirit replied positively (my friends had no idea of my speculations).

There had just been a thunderstorm, the sky was still covered with dark clouds and the sun seemed to have already set. Their logical reply was that it was impossible.

In a few minutes the sky cleared up and not one but two rainbows turned up. One was right above the running car and the other on the asphalt. They said the rainbows had appeared for me. My heart rejoiced – the Spirit had answered not only immediately but, more importantly, affirmatively.

The incarnated Holy Spirit lived in India, so I decided to leave to meet Him. I was going back to my beloved Sai Baba again.

When I arrived in India, I was told He was in Kodaikanal, in the mountains (where I had been twice already). My travelling companion and I decided to test our luck. No one could tell us how long Sai Baba was going to stay there, but we departed anyway. Our wish to see the Divine Master again was so strong that time passed quickly as we drove 600 km.

The next morning, we were off. The women's queue, always very long, stretched as a serpentine along the lake shore where the *darshan* was given.

When I arrived, I realized I was literally at the end of the queue. I said to myself: 'SAI RAM'[121].

I was preparing myself with my eyes closed to catch His look, when I felt someone pulling my arm. I thought it was a beggar asking for charity. It was a *seva*[122] inviting me to hurry up and go to the front. That part of the queue was chosen to be the first to enter Sai Baba's residence (a large country house).

I quickened my pace, once again deeply touched by so much Grace. I found myself in the front line, waiting for Him. It was like hearing, in my heart: "I have been waiting for you. Welcome!"

Sai Baba passed through the crowd and stopped in front of me. I touched His feet with my hands and handed Him all the letters I had been asked to deliver. He smiled and went on.

That direct contact, sweet and unexpected, filled me with joy and peace. My task was accomplished for that trip (among those letters there were some requests for help due to severe health problems). I could return home but I obviously remained – there were more lessons to learn.

There was a surprise in store for us in the afternoon. Sai Baba went back to Whitefield (His ashram of Brindavan near Bangalore).

And so we took a taxi and ground along 600 km on the way back. He had given us a unique, marvellous *darshan* in that charming place, suspended in the clouds, among eucalyptus trees. It was Paradise on earth.

The festival of *Eswaramma* (Sai Baba's mother who had died many years before) was approaching. From analogy, she is also the Divine Mother. For the occasion, Sai Baba gave a very poignant speech (at times even hard), saying that: *"Man today is diabolic because, instead of loving God and fearing sin, he loves sin and fears God"*, and that *"The diabolic features of doubt block the knowledge and those of fear block the will."*

In those days we met a strange character who introduced himself as "SAI RAM"[123] which was a rather extraordinary name, considering that it was the common greeting exchanged by the devotees in India and worldwide.

He was young and elegant and he wished to know if we were healers. He then went on and revealed many details (some of them personal) on me and my travelling companion, regarding our past and future life. He then left, again in a strange manner, saying that in case we needed him, it was enough to look for him. Then he disappeared. But where would we look for him?

We reckoned that the character was no one else but Sai Baba who had come for a "private" interview under this unusual guise.

In many parts of the world, not just in India, Sai Baba appears to people to assist them, disguised in a variety of ways as individuals beyond suspicion and disappears after accomplishing His mission.

That short journey (it lasted only nine days) was very important. It helped me shed light on certain not-so-clear matters on my pathway. I succeeded in clarifying, once and for all, the "obligatory transition" relevant for my inner work. There was no one to discuss it with, also because most people are hardly willing to tackle certain topics.

I realized that, by choosing chastity, we did not automatically reach spirituality. However, if our thoughts were chaste, or pure, we distanced ourselves from the kind of sexuality which was an end in itself (seeking mere physical pleasure[124]) and could elevate the energy of the Eros to more sublime and creative levels. This sacred energy can connect us with the entire Universe when it unites the body and the soul with the Spirit. I learned that, if we were optimistic, creative and animated by the joy of living, all the chakras and all the bodies (physical, ethereal, emotional and mental) were in harmony, in particular the solar plexus, or the third chakra. Being the door through which we access this energy within, it had to be unblocked, to allow cosmic energy (*Prana*) to navigate through the body. If this chakra is blocked, primarily due to accumulated negative emotions, the individual's natural expansion is prevented. The person becomes gloomy, depressed, plaintive, inclined to somatising and predisposed to colitis and backache, which is unfortunately quite common in our society. Eventually, one is unaware of the nature of his/her suffering. Unless we reveal the real illness, the healing processes cannot take place.

Sai Baba claims that all illnesses originate from the mind. They are caused by mental conditions loaded with negative thoughts and emotions (passion, desire, envy, jealousy, fear, anxiety, resentment and so on) but we unfortunately refuse to see or acknowledge that. He condemns hypocrisy more than theft, and explains that, by showing our aspirations to Him while still attached to the world, family or wealth, we deceive Him.

It is actually self-deceit, since we are aware of being in disharmony with ourselves, feeling empty, useless, confused and indecisive.

He therefore asks for our whole heart, so it can be filled exclusively with Love – not with deception, ambiguity or compromise that pave the way of salvation of our worst enemy – the ego (desires, attachments, flaws and fears).

There is only one thing we must give up - our faults. To live a healthy and peaceful life, there is only one thing we must renounce - the ego, or egotism. Whatever the illness, devotion and honesty (Love and Truth) are the remedies.

This is the only way for us to walk with the Divine, cooperate with Him, feel strong and free and be what we really are – divine sparks. When we become aware of our faults, we gain the courage to kick the self-destructive habits which are typical of a misleading, non-*dharmic* life.

Awareness is the gift of the Holy Spirit, or Divine Love, Divine Mother, Sai Baba (all of them being Oneness) to the people of good will.

The Holy Spirit had been but an abstract name for many years, a grandiloquent term applied so extensively in popular pet phrases that its profound meaning got lost over the time. Since childhood I had heard people speak about things occurring "as the work of the Holy Spirit" referring to something unexplainable. The time arrived for me to start comprehending who the Holy Spirit really was. Even in the paintings, a veil of mystery had always hidden Its true and authentic meaning from me. I discovered that the "tongues of flame" (of the Holy Spirit) that descended on the apostles and subsequently on the disciples of Jesus, represented the gift of inspiration and transformation of the Self.

My wish was for all the brothers and sisters in God, especially those who suffered most, to gain more and more Spiritual Knowledge and consequently plenty of strength and peace of mind, just as I did.

Summer arrived and one day, as I was walking along the river bank, intent on gathering ears of wheat and fleur-de-lis, I saw two swans swimming in the green stream near me. I was thinking about the reflection break my creativity had obviously taken (my mind could not stabilize on a plane of equidistance from everything around me). All of a sudden, the inner voice interrupted the magic of silence and the following words thundered inside, like a biblical command: *"Wake up and follow me"*.

An emotional earthquake shook my thoughts: it was an ordinary day, an ordinary place, in a wheat field and by a river, when destiny manifested itself (through the true Self) with an affirmative, lapidary and unambiguous command.

That imperative and stern revelation was similar to the one I had received a few months earlier. I had never received such powerful revelations up until then. It did not give me a moment's respite and it removed, once and for all, the veil from my personal story and my surrounding environment.

In that instant I interpreted life like a business trip. I was here, on earth, to finalize a well specified mission. Upon completion I would be summoned back to base. All the rest was just a pile of illusions. On the spur of the moment I realized that faith was a gift and if we misapplied it, or failed to apply it, it was taken away from us. Only the strong could face their own destiny, patiently, because they had a firm inner, divine confidence.

Clearly, my permanent effort to improve myself so as to be useful to others in the future (for them to obtain the knowledge of themselves), gave me the right to isolate myself from the world. What I was going through was just an interim period, necessary to foster my inner makeover which had already begun. Consequently, I would accomplish the task of writing the book.

That voice, soundless and faceless, commanding me to start living again (a true life, that of the Spirit), awakened to the Holy Spirit.

The Spirit brought me back into the world of awakened consciousness, just as Jesus said *"Talita Kumi"* (stand up, walk) to Jairus' daughter and resurrected her from the dead to real life (two thousand years ago), awakening her to the Spirit.

Jesus returned to earth as Christ Consciousness. How come *I* felt it instead of everyone else? How come the surrounding space was empty and I found myself floating on a deserted island, beyond time and space, in the sea of humankind who continued dragging its heavy yoke, apparently oblivious to this major event?

Then I understood the meaning of the dream in which Jesus patted me on the knee[125] and said: *"Leave your pride aside and strengthen your will. This is the time to act. The immense treasure you have revealed cannot be kept locked in the case of your heart. You must draw it out and offer it to everybody."*

The battle with the inner enemies (flaws of the ego) was not over yet. Although I risked wasting my precious time and despite the command of the inner voice, I kept telling myself that I was not ready for the task. I had not sacrificed the ego completely yet. I knew I had to empty myself of every thought, feeling, or personal intention and become the channel of the Spirit. Those were the terms for Him to act for us, speak for us and think for us. *"Confine yourself into solitude and I will speak to your heart"*, the inscription read.

Sai Baba says: *"Turn your back to the world and you will find yourself face to face with God. Peace of mind, perfect delight is beyond possession or renunciation. When we are no longer attached to anything, we are not scared of renunciation. Thus, those who are attached to the physical, worldly life and its illusive pleasures are afraid of losing his/her life or dying."*

Fear and attachment prevent us from seeing, knowing, savouring and experiencing the most precious asset in man's possession, or better, man's only possession and I wanted to testify to that – of the divine presence of the Spirit within, called *Atma*, spark, or essence.

Addictions and desires preclude the awakening to the awareness that brings freedom and the ability to see the only reality we belong to, enabling us to discern the real from the unreal. The bond with God sets us free. A beam of light comes from the Sun shining on us and we realize that we, as "light beams", and God, as the source of Light and Love, are one thing.

When we live our lives with Love, being Love, each of us represents a light beam that stretches endlessly in a permanent communion with all forms of life in the Universe, visible and invisible. We vibrate in unison, playing the notes of the eternal music, the origin of all things – the harmony of the Universe.

The beam of light is the divine essence. As our awareness rises, we can identify our flaws better, so we can correct or get rid of them.

I learned that the world of the Spirit was not subject to the natural law of cause and effect (*karma*). My study of Evolutionary Astrology revealed the same thing. The astrological natal chart is not valid any more if we transcend our destiny. As I said, destiny (*karma*) can be transcended only by the power bestowed by the Grace of the Spirit, i.e. the power of Love.

The daily renewal I was experiencing left no space or time for second thoughts. Its pace was firm and resolute in order to free my inner energies and allow them to express themselves with awareness through the task I had been called to perform.

I was meditating with a friend of mine one day when I had a vision of a *tulsi* plant (sacred in India; symbol of sacrifice; a devotee of Krishna transformed herself into a *tulsi* plant to express her love for the Divine) whose intense scent recalls that of basil. I interpreted that vision as a good omen. I found out afterwards that a *tulsi* plant symbolized a pure heart, filled with devotion for the Divine and that was not all. There was a sequel to this story during my next journey, a few months later.

I kept repeating the name of Shiva (one of Sai Baba's names) in my spare time, day and night.

Let me remind you again that Sai Baba claims that repeating the name of God (in whatever way we preferred to remember it – as Jesus, Krishna, Shiva, Sai Baba, Rama, Buddha or Allah) is the easiest way and the greatest opportunity given to humankind in this dark age (*Kaliyuga*) to redeem ourselves from the power of the senses and conquer the way of liberation. The Divine Name makes all our good wishes come true (I verified this innumerable times over the years).

I felt increasingly connected to Heaven and increasingly disconnected from earth, but I did not forget that I still had a task to accomplish.

When you consider mankind as a family, you care about everyone's salvation, not only that of your son, wife, mother, father or best friend. I was very grateful to God for helping me understand and feel this from the bottom of my heart.

I dreamt of being at Puttaparthi. The floor of the temple was paved with blue marble. I said: we should be glad and thankful for being here, in the presence of the Divine Master, Sai Baba.

After a few days I really left for India.

When life demands our change, due to our discontentment or uneasiness to live, we should not resist it. After all, the transformation is for the better. We should be prepared to get rid of well entrenched ideas and convenient yet harmful habits and make room for new things in life.

Generally, we find it difficult to give up on the old frameworks, prejudices and convictions, even after they have become obsolete.

And to think that great revelations are just waiting for the possibility to come into the open. But a full glass cannot be filled. It has to be emptied first, as I said earlier.

If we are still attached to the old patterns, refusing to leave the prey, we cannot "enter" a new state of consciousness and, subsequently, a new dimension. The inner voice was telling me: *"Change and do it fast."*

I was back in India for the sixteenth time in eight years. Upon arrival, paradoxically so, I felt more confused than the first time I came here.

Actually, every trip had its own theme, but that time it was different. Something inside me was different.

I left with a group of eighty people to do service in the kitchen, like the year before. I was accommodated in a dormitory with about thirty women (whom I did not know) but that had already happened in other occasions and therefore did not justify the confused demeanour I experienced and manifested.

As usual, I made a resolution to put myself in the hands of the Divine Master and accept whatever happened, serenely.

All I had was a folding bed (on some other occasions I slept on the floor, on a mat) and my suitcase which functioned as a bedside table and wardrobe. During the night, bats flew skimming my head but, strangely enough, I was not disturbed by that. As the days went by, I felt like a queen (within) and regained the familiar demeanour from the past.

After a couple of days I was in the front line and I touched Sai Baba's feet. That contact made me happy and I did not ask for more. Being lulled by the waves of His Love sufficed. I was unexpectedly summoned by Him for an interview, together with twenty other women who had never been in an interview. This was uncommon, but I paid no attention to it at first. When I was in the interview room, sitting by His side, near His armchair, He took my face lovingly in His hands, held it firmly and materialized plenty of white *vibuthi* for me, telling me to bring it to my mouth (on other occasions I took it away for other people and so He specified that it was for me). He asked me about the book and I replied that I was proceeding with difficulty. He urged me to write only about "*Swami*". He then invited the group of women who were there for the first time to join Him in another room (He invited other people too, some Indians we didn't know).

I remained seated, believing I was not one of the "novices", but He beckoned me to follow Him. And so I followed Him to the other room and sat down by His side, again, near His armchair.

By asking me to join the group in their first interview, He highlighted my initial feeling of confusion which reflected a new condition, due to my inner transformation over the previous months. I was a new person compared to the person I had been during my previous journey, a few months earlier.

It was as if I'd been there for the very first time, but also as if I'd always been by His side.

When He sat down, I kissed His left hand with infinite gratitude and devotion, holding it tightly between my hands. I couldn't let go of it. He remained still and allowed me to stay like that throughout the interview, with all the people in the room.

As I write about what happened on that day, my feelings are so deep that they still testify to the joy and amazement of that experience. It was so extraordinary that it sounds incredible.

I kept holding His hand. He occasionally drew it away to extend it to those who wished to kiss it and gave it back to me, holding my hand firmly and caressing it with His thumb. Tears of joy, a river of Love was gushing from my eyes for Him, the Beloved Divine Master.

I learned later on that tears of joy at the sight of the *Avatar* express the purifying contact between the soul and the Spirit.

During those never-ending minutes, my mind could not believe it really happened. I was where I had always wished to remain forever. I could melt down in my own tears to flow into Him, into the ocean of Love comprising everything. At the same time, I asked Him in my heart to show me that I wasn't dreaming. His heart perceived the silent question coming from my heart: "Is it really you, the Divine, who is holding my hand?" He replied by squeezing it firmly, in an affirmative and reassuring manner.

My mind finally stopped and I could no longer hear the conversation (which went on) between Sai Baba and the people in the room. When I woke up from my reverie, I realized that they too were deeply moved and shared my joy. Love was in the air we breathed.

Krishna Day arrived and, on that holy and propitious day, Sai Baba made everyone attending the *darshan* promise that they would come back on His birthday, in 2000 (the 75th anniversary of His mission on earth), with a present: a pure heart and a stable mind. An endless procession of Indian women walked past Him, each dressed in traditional costume and with a *Tulsi* plant on her head, symbolically offering a pure heart.

My thoughts went back to the vision of the great *Tulsi* plant I had shortly before my departure. The Divine Master had anticipated this moment through my vision.

I realize every day, for the umpteenth time, that we experience God in His fullness only by putting our ego aside. Only altruistic service brings us closer to the Divine. However, when the desire for gratification is still present, the ego and nothing but the ego is at play.

The body is but an instrument in the hands of the Divine. The divine essence giving life to it is God itself, residing in us. By dissolving the ignorance that makes us believe we are nothing more than a physical body, we discover we are immortal. I will never get tired of pointing out that unconditional service and total surrender to the Divine is the main road to Him. He knows very well how, when and why to send us what we need to evolve, once we have decided to put ourselves at His service.

Sai Baba says: *"Worldly happiness is a moment between two sufferings. It does not stem from success but it comes and goes, like success."* We find lasting happiness only in God, by accepting His Will and learning to be equally distant from joy and pain. When we realize we are pure, divine essence, the world is transformed into Heaven on earth because the Kingdom of Heaven is, in fact, within. Our real name is *Atma*. At that point, the grace of the Divine Master (i.e. the Inner Master) allows us to connect the inner Divine with the Divine around us through the spiritual heart, functioning as the cosmic antenna for Universal Love.

In his infinite humanness, Sai Baba becomes a child when with children, man when with men and God when on His own, offering Love to those who don't love, Peace to the restless and Braveness to the fearful, providing the instruments of completeness and authenticity and ridding us of the burden of incompleteness. He states that we are living temples because the Spirit (God) resides in everybody's heart. We are vortices of cosmic energy pulsating with the entire Universe, although a vast majority of mankind is in the dark about it[126]. Everybody is striving to be loved instead of loving, to be understood instead of understanding others.

Sai Baba descended to earth to help us reveal the Eternal Truth within. He suggests: *"First serve God, then serve others and eventually serve yourself. While helping others, do not think about your own problems. In that way you will help yourselves."*

I have always followed that sequence, also in my psychiatric work, before I met Him.

We have to live in Truth to approach the Divine within, because when we are insincere, our mind is more attached to the body.

The mind comes and goes, it is here in the waking hours and it goes away during sleep. The Spirit, on the other hand, is always present within, even if we are unaware of it. The Spirit has no destiny, it comes from God, it is God and it goes to God (as pure Love).

The path to the Spirit is the path of Truth and Love, in its different phases. In the first leg of the journey, we are messengers of God (of the Spirit), then we discover to be the children of God and finally we realize that we are at one with Him, fully aware of our divinity. Having reached that state, we stop being "victims" of attachments and desires pushing our mood up and down and depriving us of our peace and wellbeing.

This is the stage when we start glimpsing the true reality, or the reality of *Atma*, the divine essence. It is the stage of the "witness" *(Turiya)*, when we realize that we are not our bodies or the ones who act, but just instruments of God. That is the fourth stage, preceded by the three stages: waking (first), dream (second) and deep sleep (third).

Speaking of those who distrust everybody, Sai Baba says: *"I have no intermediaries, I alone come to rouse you."* Why? Because they have not gained the ability to discern and would not be able to tell His true messengers from the fake ones.

Still, addressing those who can discern (with awareness), He states: *"We are all messengers of God. We see God in everything and in everyone. The entire Universe is our Master".* Through the inner voice He heralded the arrival of many of His messengers who helped me in the task I had to carry out.

The Golden Age or the Age of Truth (Sathya Yuga) will come when we surrender to Him trustingly. Surrendering or letting go of ourselves does not imply that we do not act. Remember, it implies unconditional acting, free of charge.

Sai Baba talks to us like a mother. He is the Divine Mother and as such She relates to Her children depending on their eating abilities (She feeds newly born babies with milk, older babies with baby food and children with solid food). Thus, He approaches us differently, depending on our capability to take His message in.

We should not be surprised when we read seemingly contradictory messages in His speeches. Again, it is our mind playing games to induce us into a mistake, because God never contradicts Himself.

He came to rouse the will of good in us and invite us to transform our lives into His message: Do it – don't merely try to do it.

After my very first interview, my son wrote me a letter to congratulate me for being picked out as the messenger of God. I found that phrase very strange at the time. Who inspired him? During the recent stay I remembered that sentence and reflected on the state I found myself in, suddenly and unexpectedly. I was a new person. I was the daughter of God and, like a devout daughter, I sat by His side, next to my loving Father, hand in hand.

I was entranced, free of any type of suffering and in my heart there was only space for love and happiness. His divine power made me dream of a radiant future when I, His spouse, would be at one with Him, the Spirit.

Let me reiterate, the path of God, unlike that of the world, is initially arduous, because the trials involve larger and larger responsibilities. Nonetheless, the strength, the courage and above all the awareness of dealing with the trials increase at the same time, so that understanding and knowledge lead to the awakening of consciousness, as the enlivening growth in the light of the true Self. "Going on" becomes easier and easier and trials become sweet and mild as we achieve the task for which we were born.

The pathway of the world, on the other hand, looks very attractive and pleasant at the beginning, with its immediate and tangible rewards (on the level of senses). As we go along, thorns start coming out - problems, frustrations and the inevitable disappointments – and so "getting on with life" becomes increasingly difficult. As we face the trials of life (diseases, deaths), we feel increasingly weak and confused, until life is gradually emptied of meaning in the absence of true knowledge and consciousness. We end up feeling nothing except an unbearable burden, which becomes the "malaise of life".

Shortly before leaving India, I attended a conference on Sai Baba, depicting Him as the *Avatar* who is here to wake us up. The statements reminded me of the command of the inner voice, telling me: "Wake up and follow me". For me this was yet another confirmation that the messages arrived from Him, the Divine Master.

It was not the first time for Him to talk to me by means of situations or very disparate individuals. Whenever others spoke about Him, intuition, like an antenna, picked up everything originating from Him, addressed to me – messages or simple instructions (even if others were not aware of being channels of the Divine).

This can happen to anyone who listens with the heart. We can all hear the voice of God, if the heart is pure, and catch the frequency in which He "transmits" His voice, His waves of Love.

We are what we pray for, says Sai Baba. I had prayed so much for the rebirth into the Spirit and I finally felt I had crossed the threshold. Something in me had awakened. I had spent some heavenly moments, hand in hand with God-Sai Baba. I could no longer be what I had been before. My tears had dissolved the many layers of encrustation in the soul and opened the heart to His Grace.

The time finally arrived to "lay down arms" and put into practice what I had learned. The "weapons" were the books and I had devoured hundreds of them.

It was time to stop investigating, studying, contemplating and summarizing. Free from fear and hope, refusing to understand, yet wanting to understand everything, I wished to humbly put in writing what I had learned up till then, without waiting any further.

Sai Baba says: *"Give up on understanding, do not ask to understand. This uncertainty is something I want and I don't make mistakes. "*

The Golden Hand, that of the Divine, continued to guide me on the right path. I trusted Him blindly, more than my own mind, and allowing Him to manifest through me was enough.

The chains of constraint and illusion were finally broken and I felt ready for the destiny of a mistress, no longer enslaved by the ego. I knew it would mean being more alone than before, though. I was going to be more alone, but with Truth and God in the heart.

Even the most jarring note was useful to recompose the music of my life and this discovery made every moment extraordinary and gave sense to everything. Even what seems insignificant is useful in a certain way when we begin to see, conscious of the events we get involved in.

Sai Baba made me feel at one with everything, teaching me that the union with the divine essence extinguishes all desires, generating a state of fullness that replaces the need for anything else, except to give myself to others and unselfishly share the bliss I experience.

Having returned home, I found a message from a friend of mine, telling me about the twelve numbers of the clock, like twelve steps indicating the surrender of the devotee's heart at the lotus feet of the Divine Master through various unspecified disciplines. In fact, Sai Baba says: *"I will hold tightly, close to My heart, with Love, the aspirant who takes the steps shown on the clock to reach total surrender to Me."* I thought about the dream with the clock whose hands turned counter clockwise, as if to say that everything came from God and returned to God, the eternal source or the Absolute. The twelve disciplines reminded me of the corresponding number of Hindu Holy Scriptures (the 4 Vedas and 8 Puranas), whose knowledge is the guideline to the worlds beyond beginning and end, birth and death (perhaps the 5th dimension and beyond).

He says that the Trinity (in Hinduism: Brahma, Vishnu, and Shiva) is present in every individual in the form of three attributes: action (*Rajas*) purity (*Satva*) and inertia (*Tamas*) Moreover, we should attain three principles to achieve bliss:

1) Know that the world is unreal and its nature is transient.

2) Give up on the delusion of considering real what is unreal.

3) Attain a single goal, that is, go back to the original source – the Atma.

I felt that the last point explained the meaning of the dream with the clock. These three principles enunciated by Sai Baba reminded me of the three esoteric principles, namely will, power and duty:

1) Mystical death, that is, elimination of defects.

2) The second birth, or the awakening to the awareness of the Spirit.

3) The mystical marriage, which is the union of the soul with the Spirit, or Self-realization.

Self-realization is followed by the sacrifice for humanity (*'Wake up and follow me'*), i.e. the spread of true spiritual knowledge, the work for the Sacred, that is, for the Spirit.

At that point I understood in my heart that the cross symbolized mystical marriage, the alchemic wedding transmuting lead into gold (having eliminated the ego, the soul weds the Spirit).

I could occasionally feel I was on the finishing straight and feared the rising of spiritual pride. I also wondered if such positive deliberations were a bad joke of my pride (ego).

There was no one to discuss this with freely, without running the risk of being regarded as a fanatic or a fundamentalist or plain crazy. I heard people say more than once: you talk like a priest, and I was puzzled because, in general, no one listens to the priests speaking in their language standardized by indoctrination (incomprehensible, if not obscure).

I had to keep talking to God, the Spirit in me, about experiences that could lead to the liberation from the ego and the awakening of consciousness, from my own angle.

When we open ourselves to God and consciousness is awakened to it, we can comprehend the secrets of the Universe, enclosed in a single word, the Word, or Divine Love.

Soon after that, I abandoned the conflicting logic with its opposing dualities (light - dark, good - evil, life - death, etc.) to experience the peace and the fullness of the Oneness I had already discovered. It was part of me, since I had surrendered to Him.

I dreamed about the end of the world for the third time. After the destruction by fire and the Earth's upheaval due to the inclination of its magnetic axes (north - south), this time I saw water having flooded everything: it was the great flood.

I got this message: *"Elevate your consciousness and realize that you are ageless, young like this day, old as eternity. If you live fully, here and now, in the eternal present, you will always be young, like the present. Be constantly reborn in the Spirit and Truth: you cannot remain static in this spiritual life".*

The Spirit gave me no respite: it was an invitation to progress faster towards the goal, with persistence and determination, contemplating and meditating, to review and modify every little aspect of life that was not in harmony with His message.

Just like the vision of the *Tulsi* plant, after a while I had a vision of a branch full of almonds, all ripe and ready to be picked (with a split shell). Symbolically, the shell and the almond represent the relationship of the phenomenal world and the spiritual essence. Years earlier I had dreamt of an almond tree that soared lonely, full of flowers, on a green hill. It finally bore its fruits and they were ripe now.

The almond tree is the emblem of Christ, whose divinity is hidden by His human nature, just as the fruit is hidden by the shell. It symbolizes the mystery of Light, the secret of inner enlightenment. According to the Book of Revelation, it corresponds to the rainbow, another symbol of the opening of the third eye, i.e. inner enlightenment. For the Jews it is a symbol of a new life, overcoming the duality of matter and spirit, water and fire, in a balanced unity. The almond is the halo of Light around the images of Jesus, the Divine Mother (Our Lady) and the saints.

That vision was a good omen: I felt that my efforts would one day yield success, not worldly but spiritual, thanks to the divine intercession of Sai Baba who had lifted the *karmic* burdens from my heart.

The life of withdrawal outwardly appeared to be limited and limiting. It seemed miserable externally but what looks miserable for the world is pleasing to God who confirmed His constant and loving presence in me.

He tells everyone: *"Be happy"* and keeps reminding us who we are: *"Prema Swarupa"* (or embodiments of Divine Love). Those are the opening phrases whenever He addresses humankind. He calls us "Embodiments of Love".

When we run short of external expressions of love, we discover that the source of Love is within us. This is the most surprising discovery that a man can make in his entire life, realizing that what seemed to come from outside is the reflection (projection) of our Love on the other, reflected back on us![127]

That is why spiritual progress is the only real progress (and the top priority task) of every person of good will. When we overcome the duality of spirit and matter thanks to our own progress, the last attachment will also cease: the Love for God (who is the only one we can hold on without affecting the realization of the true Self), because at that point we will be at one with Him.

As I said, by learning to master the senses, the mind and emotions, we become stronger, more powerful, intuitive, aware, our own masters and masters of our lives. I've experienced it myself.

Exponents of esotericism say, *"As long as sexual energy is used to satisfy the pleasures of the senses, it does not ascend to the top of the head to fertilize the higher centres in charge of creativity and intuition. The brain cells are still numb and are content to ensure the smooth operation of the lower functions, nothing more"*.

Due to their scarcely evolved consciousness, most people believe it is impossible to live without sex, or without eating meat. The common belief is that such "abstentions" weaken the body.

Human life is full of erroneous beliefs. Most people are unaware of the fact that the principal disease is actually their obsession with the body.

I dreamt of climbing a crystal wall. I struggled until I reached the top and I held myself firmly, to remain in that position. Then I burst into tears. It was as if the joy of conquest merged with the bitterness of the loss of the illusions of the conquest itself. Those tears betrayed a certain apprehension about the changes in prospect. The detachment was not total and I was not at one with the Spirit yet.

The dream gave me an important lesson about an aspect that should not be overlooked on the spiritual path: we shouldn't create illusory expectations that bring only pain because when we reach the top we discover there is no goal to achieve, everything is already within us, the goal is us.

Once the illusions of imaginary spiritual successes were behind me, I clearly saw that the realization that everything I ever needed was already inside me would bring me inner peace.

One morning, half asleep, I saw a notice written in English which said: *"If you win your emotions, you will reach serenity through equanimity."* It was a confirmation that the interpretation of the dream of the glass wall was correct. I still had to free myself from the illusions in the realm of emotions. My thoughts flew to India quite often, whenever I saw a white trail of a plane in the sky. I would turn eastward, with an irresistible attraction to the Beloved, despite the closeness I felt. He helped me understand that the initial impetus, the enthusiasm and the will were not enough for the completion of the work. I had to get rid of the unnecessary load through constant discipline.

I delved on the relationship between the cure and the service rendered to others, in terms of self-healing. The teaching of Sai Baba reminded me of my personal experiences from the past, at the time of the illness.

Health is given to us to serve others, not to think about ourselves.

Accordingly, since I was healed (functionally), life (health bestowed upon me by Grace) was no longer mine, that is, it did not belong to the ego any longer, but to something higher, to the Spirit, the true Self (the same spiritual essence we all have within) – and therefore it belonged to others.

Hence my choice to contribute to making the world a better place (born from the heart) led me to become one of the children of the Light and collaborate in the accomplishment of the Work. But I didn't know these things at the time. I was still unaware of the real meaning of life.

That choice, which opened my mind to intuition and the creative power of the Divine, allowed me to write and give my contribution to the Work. I received all kinds of supports through signs, symbols, dreams, holy scriptures, the teachings of Jesus and Sai Baba. Having said that, I conclude that true healing is the healing of the soul.

That was how I learned to know the pathway assigned to me by fate, with its various steps marked along the way and the tasks I was entrusted from time to time. As I gradually accomplished the tasks, my confidence and trust in the Spirit grew. The original pessimism vanished and the vacant space was taken by optimism. The steady improvement of my quality of life allowed me to implement what initially looked like a farfetched project. It became a living reality, easily demonstrable in the face of evidence. Why did I consider it important to write? I was aware that not many people had the time, the opportunity, the ability and bent for studying, investigating and inquiring on the subject I had been working on for many years. To keep for myself everything I had personally discovered and verified seemed unacceptably and deplorably selfish.

Nobody could stop me from thinking that I was destined to perform that task to testify to the experience (but also to benefit from it personally). Spiritual Knowledge is a wonderful gift from God that no one can keep for themselves without losing its intrinsic and priceless value.

The only thing I could do was to put myself at the service of the Divine Master to help with my testimony, in the dissemination of His message. I saw no other way to express the gratitude I felt, if not by loving everyone and everything, unconditionally.[128]

I felt that doing something for someone we didn't know was the best way for us not to expect anything in return, apart from the joy for being able to give part of ourselves. Sai Baba says: *"Love does not seek rewards. Love in itself is the reward."*

Moreover, to write means to build beyond the dimension of time and space because a writing can go anywhere and last forever, if it has value.

I continued to write, convinced that true knowledge was a means to heal the body and the soul (whereas spiritual ignorance remained an instrument of death). I could see the seed of Christ Consciousness grow, getting ready to blossom in me after an unexpected "frost" (the death of my father) had blocked its ripening, early in life.

I felt a constant and powerful presence of God in me and this gave me clarity and confidence. I thus realized that the real help to the sick soul could arrive only from the light of Love and true Knowledge, and not from psychiatric drugs or psychotherapies. Truth as an expression of Divine Love can heal mental confusion and cure.

To obtain Divine, Universal Love, we must first restore fraternal love and see humankind as the Universal Brotherhood, with one Father and one Divine Mother, that is, God and Nature, united in the divine, omnipresent energy of the Holy Spirit (as "Son", or Love, or Christ Consciousness within us).

Indeed, we can re-establish that world, made of Love and Harmony, the Paradise we lost when we went to the dimension of "having" from the dimension of "being", and consequently triggered the duality of matter and spirit and the logic of conflict, discord and desire. The time is now ripe for this quantum leap.

Jesus said *"Love each other as I have loved you"*.

Brotherly Love is the first essential step towards the realization of Unity (in diversity) of mankind.

The true Self, present as *Atma,* or divine spark, in every one of us (the candle at hand to light up and illuminate the darkness, according to Lao Tse) is at the same time One for all of us, in all of us. Through this spark each of us takes part in the unity of the whole, in the true life, in the Spirit.

The dark age of ignorance, exaggerated individualism, domination of the ego, recklessness and disharmony will end soon and make room for brotherly Love, understood as offering ourselves to the brothers and sisters.

In the Golden Age, human creative potential will be completely developed and man will be fully aware of his divine essence, for the good of all mankind. We can begin to awaken to it right now.

Sai Baba says: *"In the entire Creation, only man is eligible to reach Ultimate Joy. What a tragedy that he disregards this right and goes here and there, looking for small pleasures, worthless frills. He plays like a child with dolls and puppets and calls them elephants and horses. He is seriously absorbed in that game and, in his ignorance, he imagines that the objects of the world are real. But that does not make the Universe of Illusion less unreal"*.

I dreamt of being in front of an elephant, all harnessed in gold[129].

I felt ready for the discovery of new worlds, that is, to continue with the transformation of consciousness and start a new phase in my inner life. A favourable period of further opening to the world of the Spirit was coming my way. Someone wrote: *"Fate is sometimes so generous to allow us to probe the imponderable, if only for a few moments, and find out that the imprint of our original unity is eternal, just like life itself."* This concession of our divine essence (i.e. the Holy Spirit in us) is a powerful evolutionary thrust towards the liberation from the ego and the realization of the true Self!

NOTES: CHAPTER XIII

118. The three S stand for: self-confidence, self-sacrifice, self-knowledge

119. Respectively, they are predominantly masculine (action) and feminine (contemplation.

120. The dates may vary.

121. In other words: Thy Will be done.

122. Indian volunteers involved in the ushering service (*seva*).

123. Sai Ram: means "homage to the Divine in you."

124. Sai Baba says: *"Pleasure is a moment between two pains."*

125. The knee, in the anatomy of the subtle symbolizes will, but also pride.

126. Lao-Tze says: *"Instead of cursing the darkness, light a candle."*

127. I've already written about the projection of the ideal image on the other person, which leads us to mistakenly think we cannot live without this or that person, which makes us unhappy and dependent.

128. This task was later confirmed to me by the inner voice.

129. In Hindu mythology, it is Airawat, the elephant of Paradise (*Indra Loka*). I discovered it much later. In India, the elephant symbolizes discernment and good luck, both useful for removing obstacles.

XIV

Knowing without doing is useless.
Doing without knowing is foolishness

Sai Baba.

One day I walked into a church, driven by an inner call. I found an inscription of Jesus on which I had been pondering over the years: *"Blessed are the pure in heart, for they shall see God"*. That was what I wished for: a message from God for me[130].

Freedom, lightness, naturalness, spontaneity were the things I loved most in life, in people, in the writings, as an expression of the language of the heart. It was not easy to assess my own progress. Always guided by the Inner Master in me, I sometimes came upon some bench marks in books and that was useful. In this regard, I discovered that the first initiation implied the mastering of the physical body, the second one of the astral body (senses, emotions) and the third of the lower mental body (mind). My tolerance, will power, concentration and understanding were reinforced in the recent years of self-investigation. I was about to face the most difficult stumbling block – the mastering of the mind (or so I thought). After I'd crossed the bridge connecting the bank of ignorance with that of awareness and found myself here, I felt supported by the true Self in this sense.

I dreamt of so many bridges over the years. I crossed them all – the longest one and the most inaccessible one made of knotted rope – and always arrived to the other side safely, in spite of all. This, for me, has always been a confirmation of my inner progress. When it comes to everyday life though, I noticed that, while I was writing, I no longer lived in the habitual dimension, as if enraptured in another realm. But as long as I was immersed in the normal daily routine, I couldn't write any more. It was quite a dilemma to choose between the two conditions, so I let myself be guided by the inspiration of the moment and, since what can't be cured must be endured, I transformed my defeats into victories. However, "renunciation" remained to be the greatest "transgression" for the ego, paradoxically and, as such, it cost me dearly.

Indeed, initially the ego does forgive us for the restrictions we dare to impose despite its resistance. So I went through moments of sublime fullness and creative inspiration, alternated with dark and sinister spells of frustrating inactivity. Being inactive was really not typical of me but it was the price I had to pay for the rebellion of the ego against the discipline I'd imposed on it. I knew that by then. Discipline, pain and effort are essential for us to evolve (although I am not happy about this statement). They are, actually, the most effective medicine to put out the ego[131]. We should remember that, in order to awaken the consciousness to the true Self, without this "awakening" becoming risky, we must completely master the little individual self (ego), or otherwise the flame of Truth can burn instead of illuminating.

That highly challenging year in terms of inner work ended with a visit to the Divine Master – my seventeenth trip.

On arrival, one night at 4:30 a.m., while I was on my way to the *darshan*, I saw an astonishing spectacle in the sky. It reminded me of some of my dreams, in which the stars danced in the sky (coincidentally number 17 in the Tarot deck is the arcana "Stars")[132].

As usual, I looked at the sky, when suddenly one by one the stars began to shoot. At first I thought I had a vision, or that I was hallucinating. Stars were really showering but I learned about it only the next day, when I phoned home (Italy). I witnessed, unknowingly, the celestial dance of the "Leonids", the meteor shower caused by a comet that had crossed·the sky in the northern hemisphere, the year before.

The following night I dreamt (or was it an astral journey?) of the same, amazing spectacle. Upon awakening, I remembered something important from the dream. I was told that I had achieved independence (which the inner voice confirmed when I returned to Italy).

During that stay at Puttaparthi, I had the opportunity to consider an aspect (still unclear) of the natural law of cause and effect (*karma*) and I will briefly explain it. Considering that free will was essentially an illusion of the mind and whatever happened, happened for the good of man (because God is always benevolent), I wondered how come bad actions could weigh upon or worsen one's destiny. I discussed this topic with an elderly devotee who had lived next to Sai Baba for over forty years. He explained that, since the physical world was illusory, complicating one's *karma*, or destiny, was an illusion of the mind as well, as the law of cause and effect was related to the physical world, i.e. to the body that belongs to the dual world of matter, and not to the true reality, that is, the Spirit.

True reality, that is, the Spirit, is not affected by anything, much less by the law of cause and effect. Hence, it cannot be subject to any complications. God cares about the spiritual and not for the material salvation of humankind, that is, He only wants our welfare, in the sense that He wants us to reach the so-called 'Kingdom of Heaven" as quickly as possible. He wants us to attain the highest dimension we can reach, the 5th dimension of the creatures (bodies) of Light.

Our real welfare is therefore our spiritual evolution and not the physical or material wellbeing. What really counts is the Spirit, not the body.

That's why the law of cause and effect, self-generated in the bosom of matter, does not care about the suffering and disease it inflicts upon us, as they are remedies for our inner growth and the redemption from the bondage of the ego. This interpretation, which may not be convincing enough for the most stubborn to detach from the ego and worldly life, is nevertheless in my view highly reliable.

During the journey I experienced once again the *karma* of the group, namely the duty to deal with the problems and trials that may not be ours but pertaining to others in the group, that we however have to address personally, being part of the group.

On His birthday, Sai Baba made a speech on liberation, in terms of absolute non-attachment, and on God, in terms of pure Light. He urged us not to be dazzled by any illusion and remain firm as a rock. Non-attachment and discipline lead to eternal bliss (the realization of the Self in us).

I had always been attracted to magic thought, understood as sacred participation in the harmony of the All.

In India, the environment greatly facilitated this vivifying participation. I let myself go to the Divine Will and my life became a beautiful daydream, experienced as a well articulated metaphor of the origin and the conclusion of life. Being physically close to the Divine Master and His impenetrable mystery, His Spirit of Grace and Light elevates common everyday reality to the highest degree of mystical experience, when experienced with the heart.

God is interested in our most noble, spiritual part, the divine essence, or "the spiritual heart". When we offer it to Him, we have the possibility to return to the original source one day – the Kingdom of Heaven, or the Kingdom of the only Goodness.

I returned home on Christmas Eve. After a few days, the inner voice conveyed to me a victorious message: "I have healed you completely".

The soul was healed, as anticipated in the dream experienced in India, telling me that I had achieved independence (perhaps from the bondage of the ego). Had I finally managed to dominate my emotions and mind? I hoped I had. I woke up in the middle of the night, moved and stunned by those words, still unable to grasp their profound meaning and priceless value.

With regard to my inner progress, I noticed (without placing too much emphasis on it) that I'd acquired greater emotional stability and become more patient and forgiving with others.

God, in the person of Sai Baba, had ordered me to write. He guaranteed the ability, strength and courage I needed to complete the task I had undertaken, and so I stopped worrying about the delayed progress of the work. Surely, it would have been enlivening to exchange views with someone else regarding my deepest feelings, but it happened rarely. So I maintained the inner dialogue with the Divine Master, night and day. At night I often stayed awake for hours (meditating on my experiences with the Divine), but this did not compromise my performance during the day. I was always fresh in the morning, despite everything.

I reached the conclusion that there are generally three modalities in which we come into the world and depart from it. The first mode is *"satvic"* or pure, stemming from true Love, creating the union of two souls rather than two bodies. It is extremely rare and it distinguishes the most harmonious and positive destinies of highly evolved souls. The second mode is *"rajasic"* or passionate, stemming from the union of two bodies rather than two souls. It is the most frequent mode, distinguishing tormented and restless destinies, lacking harmony, characteristic of less advanced souls. Finally, the third mode is *"tamasic"*, coming from the union of two bodies but based on deception or abuse of power (rapes, incest, desire for possession, etc.). It is violent (fortunately less common)[133] and it distinguishes the most hostile, destructive and completely disharmonious destinies of souls that are hardly or not evolved at all. The last mentioned is the most miserable condition, which does not allow the person to experience power without guilt, or love without doubt. In short, it is a sentence to a hellish life. I think this picture briefly depicts the life of all mankind and hints at the importance of the degree of evolution of the parental figures' souls – and while we are at it, of the souls of the unborn as well - for the more or less auspicious fate of every single individual, starting from birth.

Through the evolution of consciousness, Spiritual Knowledge enables aware choices of birth into optimal conditions of selfless Love, that is, conditions that attract down to earth equally evolved souls, based on elective affinity. This enhances the spiritual evolution of all humanity.

Accordingly, the advent of the Golden Age and Spiritual Knowledge starts taking shape for a mankind that will see the restoration of the primary value of unconditional Love, over passion, attachment and any kind of violence. Only unconditional Love can yield Love and more Love. Therefore, working on our inner development is the main task of every human being, since it is for the benefit of the entire humanity, for eternity. The evolution of consciousness is the only real, lasting asset that man can possess (inherited from life to life, in all incarnations) until he reaches the ultimate goal – the return to the Absolute, to the Light.

I was convinced that, prior to birth, every soul (or perhaps only the more developed ones) chooses the next incarnation, in agreement with the Spirit, and hence the future personal Heaven, Purgatory or Hell, the reason being that the Spirit (as I was explained during my last trip to India) is not bothered with suffering or evil, but cares only about the soul's growth. Thus, an ill fate could be chosen to evolve faster, provided that, once embodied, the soul chooses, on the basis of free will, the pathway of evolution and not that of involution, that is, the way of the

Spirit and not that of the world. In summary, man is the architect of his inner peace and joy, or his troubles and punishments.

Acceptance, as the ability to recognize the *karmic* game and break away from its consequences (implicit misfortunes or fortunes), becomes an essential tool for developing the awareness of the true spiritual reality. Only impassiveness can prevent pain. Accepting either luck and success or failures and misfortunes with equanimity and impartiality is the proof of Love for the Divinity that gives us everything and takes everything away, guiding us back to It, as the source of all things. This is surrendering (letting yourself go) to God.

Surrendering to God is the only way to pull all the destinies together under a common light, that of Divine Grace, because to surrender to God is to give Him the luggage and allow Him to lead us to the promised land. Sai Baba says to leave our "burdens" to Him and travel light. This means offering every action, every thought and every word to Him.

The words of the inner voice heralding my complete healing (body and soul) opened the door to the promised land.

Eleven years back, my body was healed (it was a physical healing). But I was now foretold that I would be healed spiritually (it was the healing of the malaise of the soul). What had I done to deserve so much?

Perhaps it was devotion that invoked Divine Grace on me.

It all seemed so simple and amazing at the same time. I found myself to be the protagonist of a covert, charming story. Everything became increasingly clear and bright under the illuminating rays of the Divine Light, I stopped wondering, "Why me, why on earth me?"

I joyfully accepted the gifts bestowed on me by the Spirit, with all my gratitude. The reality I was living in filled me with a fulfilling calmness, physicality acquired a certain lightness and my mind was clear as it never was before after I had offered everything to the Divine Master.

I started the new year the same way as I had finished the previous one, in solitude and meditation, as always placing everything in God's hands.

A friend had once said that my life would have been empty and desperate had I not found God, and I absolutely agree with him.

Since what cannot be cured must be endured, having accepting my fate, I surrendered to God with deep devotion. I found a great treasure inside me, patience, tolerance, humility, determination, intuitiveness, insight and compassion, as I learned to view things through the heart's eye, through the lens of Love.

I knew that the same jewels were stored in every heart. They were invisible because they lay buried beneath layers of spiritual ignorance. Even the most educated people are not exempt from these "layers". Academic culture and scientific knowledge, unfortunately, does not help to reduce that kind of ignorance.

In my life, darkness turned into Light, even though outwardly almost nothing seemed to have changed. It was an inner modification that gave me a new vision of the world. Actually, the transformation subtly affected everything around me, imperceptibly, and so the quality of my life (even of those who lived around me) and my relationships progressively improved.

The "misfortune" of being on my own (in the eyes of the world), finally switched to good fortune, because I found myself alone with God.

I often met people who came to visit me to have a chat or to ask for advice.

When they took leave (more relieved than before), they generally said: 'Lucky you, you're so lucky to live alone, to have time for yourself and for what really interests you,' (which was God). "Alone" meant "unmarried" (I lived with my son at that time).

They believed I was privileged because I was serene. Whose merit was it – mine or God's? I eventually stopped questioning myself, as I reached the conclusion that I was Him and He was me. We were One. In other words, it was to the credit of the Self or, if you wish, of the divine "seed". It is present in everyone and allows all those who really want it (everybody – sooner or later) to be born for the second time, but this time to the life of the Spirit which is Love, and become children of Light.

The wind of spiritual renewal was gaining momentum early that year. Those who know its power know that nothing can stop it and no one can escape His Will to transform because, once it gets going, it can be very risky, and it may cause illness or even death.

I learned a prayer of St. Francis and I often repeated it to the Divine Master: *"Please give me the serenity to accept the things I cannot change, the courage to change what I can and the wisdom to know when to do one or the other."*

I've never let any opportunity that might serve to awaken the consciousness to the awareness of the Self slip. At times I seemed to recognize a Greek heritage in my veins – so shrewd was I in collecting the signs and the omens[134] that life was offering me on a silver platter.

The inner Master instructed me to study the meaning of the Word of God, as the tool I had always used with the intent to serve others. There was still so much to learn on this subject if I wanted to be of service to mankind. Indeed, I realized that we reach intuitive perception if we master the senses, the thoughts and the words.

I promised to Sai Baba, a year earlier, that I would offer Him (for His birthday, in 2000) a pure heart and a stable mind. I did not realize then that the promise entailed the above mentioned three initiations (I don't know if someone else realized it at the time).

At that point, everything was clearer. I still had a year and a half, but, considering the huge endeavour, the time seemed very limited and only His Grace could preserve me from failure.

Guided by the Spirit within, I learned that the appropriate use of the 'Word of God' determines the distribution of the power of Love throughout the Solar System, and that preserves, strengthens and stimulates life itself. The ability to maintain the strength is based on refraining from speaking. Hence the importance and value of silence.

As humanity progresses, the love between genders, in its many expressions, will be moved on a higher level by the language of Truth. The current expression (emotional and erotic outpourings) on the physical plane will be replaced entirely.

True Love that unifies those who are engaged in the service and aspiring to God will then be realized. It will be the new glue that will unite the couples of the future Golden Age.

Vital energy will thus be elevated from down below (the 1st and the 2nd chakras) upwards (the 5th or Throat chakra), all the way to the centre regulating speech. The gifts of the Holy Spirit will then manifest in the renewed humanity as three aspects of Divinity:

▪ Love and Wisdom, relative to the 1st initiation (mastering the physical body, i.e. Spiritual Knowledge).
▪ Will and Power, relative to the 2nd initiation (mastering the astral body, i.e. renunciation of illusions).
▪ Light and Intelligence, relative to the 3rd initiation (mastering the mental body and uniting with the Divine).

When the motive behind our actions is not selfish and personal, when it is selfless and impersonal, our service will be real service to humankind and only then man will resurrect. It will manifest as understanding, appreciation and putting into practice the words of Jesus Christ: *"The Kingdom of God is within you, you are Gods"* and of Sai Baba, *"You are embodiments of Divine Love, the Atma. You are divine".*

The Golden Age (the Age of Aquarius, Spirit, Love and Truth) will mark the transition from individual consciousness to collective consciousness, and subsequently to Cosmic Consciousness. Service will be the expression of the Will of Goodness to implement Unity in Diversity or the Universal Brotherhood of all mankind.

Whether I was happy or sad, the journey into the inner world continued. Clearly, everything came from God, as His gift and His Grace.

I knew what I had to defeat if I wanted to find peace and stability of mind: the impurity of heart, unwanted thoughts, which popped whether I wanted it or not, from time to time, into the conscious mind. This was an obstacle but it represented also an advantage, as it prevented me from claiming victory ahead of time and becoming proud.

I was not able to completely eliminate the causes of suffering, but I learned to recognize them quickly and clearly. This reduced the emotional agitation to a great extent, because I was emotionally less involved. Once again, Spiritual Knowledge proved to be the most useful antidote to soothe and heal the pain. I witnessed, not entirely fair-mindedly (hence the suffering!), to the death of some parts of me. They were replaced by new ones as a confirmation that I was going through a new birth, towards a new life. In this context of renewal, I inevitably advanced through the storms triggered by the ego, constantly maintaining the goal of calmness, inner peace and awareness. On the other hand, we inevitably go through the process of worshiping the form of the Divine, until we land one day in pure, 'formless' Love (something that Sai Baba had long urged in me and urges in all of us.)

This made me realize the magnitude of the sacrifice of Jesus two thousand years ago and that of Sai Baba nowadays: they descended to earth as Divine Incarnations in physical form – the First one, with His mystical death, and the Other, with His divine life. The First one was embodied as the Holy Spirit and the "Son of God", while the Other was embodied as the Divine Father and Mother and also as the Holy Spirit (which in fact represents the Trinity of Father, Mother and Son), for the salvation of humankind.

Both of them came to show us the path of salvation, for us to choose between the two possibilities offered to man on the basis of free will: the path of the "world" – of the cross of suffering – or the path of the "Spirit" – of the cross of Light. The pathway of the world (of seduction and power) generates confusion and violence, and consequently, ignorance, death and the fear of dying, whereas the one of the Spirit (Love and Non-attachment) generates peace and clarity, and accordingly the courage to live, real knowledge and "eternal life".

Ordinary people are purportedly not eager to find God, thinking they can fend for themselves – except when they are in despair. At that point one can, and sometimes must, revive the idea of God that had been set aside. I too had behaved that way in the past until I reconsidered the value of consistency in the pursuit of the union with God.

Only when our behaviour is consistent with our thoughts, words and actions, we can develop discrimination and awareness.

On the staircase leading to the awakening of consciousness, all the steps are connected. We should skip none if we want to continue our ascent. In my case, consistency meant having nothing to ask from the Divine Master after I had offered Him my life. I just had to quietly accept what He, or rather the Self, or the divine essence in me, found appropriate to offer me to facilitate my journey. I learned that the first initiation animates the heart centre, the second animates the throat centre and the third initiation animates the centres of the head (third eye and crown chakra). As we continue on the spiritual path, the whole personality is flooded by the Light pouring from above. From then onwards, the higher mind (the star of the soul), or the immortal part of man, guides our life, enriching it with clairvoyance and clairaudience.

There is also a fourth initiation, the great sacrifice (the sacrifice of life, when it is offered to humankind, of which Jesus Christ has been the major example). Released from his role on earth, man turns into a Solar Angel and returns to his Heavenly abode, that is, the world of the Sun or Spirit (*Suryaloka* for the Hindu), where he connects with the spot he emanated from – the very source of Light. After the death of the physical body, the life contained in it as *Atma* (or divine spark, pure energy, spiritual essence) seeks its source and ascends to the "Heavenly Father", or the spiritual Sun (the Spirit), in four stages:

1 - withdrawal from the physical body, 2 - withdrawal from the ethereal body, 3 - withdrawal from the astral body, 4 - withdrawal from the mental body.

These notes taken from esoteric literature and the writings of Sai Baba made me consider the dreams, the revelations of the inner voice and the messages I'd received up until then from a new perspective.

When you attain liberation from worldly attachments, you activate the 6th chakra[135], or the third eye (the eye of intuition), and reveal the hidden jewel which is then transferred to the 7th chakra (of the crown). From that moment we actuate the return to the original monad (the fusion of *Atma* with the Oneness) as the union with the true Self.

The jewel is the divine spark in us, the spiritual essence, or *Atma*. The case is the 6th chakra. I recalled the words of the wise old man, offering me the case with the secret of my initiation. I was constantly seeking help from the Divine Master to reinforce the spiritual will in me, not only spiritual curiosity. Not by chance, a little later I found out about a course of meditation that was to start soon. It was the answer to my prayers.

In the past I had practiced Zen meditation (briefly), then the Meditation on the Light that I still practiced (intermittently, due to ignorance, not having understood the importance of continuity in the practice). Meditation is an extraordinary tool to transform the desire into spiritual will. I accepted this holy gift with gratitude, having learned to appreciate its intrinsic and unbeatable value. I wanted to come into contact with the true Self and never abandon it again. Since that time (twice a day) there's always been a sacred, inviolable time, dedicated exclusively to the contact with the spiritual essence connected to cosmic energy, mind-independent, continually focused on Him, the Spirit of Life. I gradually perceived the awakening of a growing awareness. I accepted solitude (just like suffering, much earlier), with serene equanimity. It becomes the permanent companion of the Divine and thus a privilege – not a punishment or a sentence, as most people commonly think and as I used to consider in the past. Truly, there are two sides of the coin to everything, depending on whether you look through the eyes of the Spirit or with those of the world. The first perspective belongs to Heaven, the other to earth, one is immanent and the other is transcendent, one is oriented towards eternity, the other towards the ephemeral, one looks inward, the other outward.

But Light cannot coexist with darkness (compromise with evil is unattainable), hence the eternal dilemma of humanity: to choose Light or darkness? The dilemma is too demanding to be addressed, so most people postpone the decision and leave it for a "better" future – if they raise the issue at all.

Sai Baba today renews the call of Jesus voiced two thousand years ago: *"Never put off until tomorrow what you can do today. Do not miss the last train which is departing (it is moving already)".*

Nonetheless, most people prefer not to think about it, because, just as when it comes to death, they delude themselves that the call is not intended for them but for someone else.

Sai Baba says that positive and negative, masculine and feminine, happiness and sorrow, day and night exist in the Universe and in human consciousness alike, which only confirms that the principle of duality applies in the manifest (physical) world without exception.

The spiritual path does not require making a choice between Heaven and earth, which initially may seem unthinkable and even paradoxical, given that we have a physical body as inhabitants of planet Earth, which is also a physical body, that is, we make part of a great body on the level of form. It requires the awakening of consciousness to real life (of the Spirit), for us to understand that these two aspects of reality (matter and Spirit) are not in conflict but coexist until they unite and merge into each other through the fusion of soul and Spirit . That will take place when we are ready to be born again, for the second time (this time in the reality of the Spirit), and realize the Androgyne in us.

At the turn of the millennium, Sai Baba came to proclaim Christ or Cosmic Love, as the royal road to the salvation of humankind at the dawning of the Age of Truth and Love. He says, *"Give and forgive, do not take and forget."* Forgiveness is what opens the door to gratitude and joy.

Jesus said: *"Glory to God in Heaven and peace on earth to men of good will"* and again: *"Thy Will Be Done."* The good will is the Will of Goodness, the Will of God. The most valuable exercise is forgiveness.

The seed of Cosmic or Christ Love cannot germinate unless we are reconciled with the surrounding world, in the harmony of opposites, abandoning all negative ties to the past imprisoning us in the wrongs and injustices made to us or the sense of guilt for the pain inflicted on others. We can discover Universal Love once we have grasped Unity in Diversity.

Forgiveness and sharing are tools of the consciousness awakened to the Spirit. Always keep in mind that shared joy is double joy and shared pain is halved pain. The day of departure finally arrived. It was my eighteenth trip to India, where I could assess the progress made in the knowledge of the inner world and of the divine essence within.

On the first day, during the *darshan*, during the time Sai Baba shared with us, I heard the inner voice say: *"Ask and you shall receive, ask and you shall receive,..."* and so on. I said to myself, ok, I got it, but the voice kept repeating the same phrase. A few days later I dreamed of Sai Baba holding out His hand and I realized what the inner voice had anticipated. The next day I was called for an interview. He was kind, as always. It was my eighth interview, but in that particular situation, there was something special about the familiarity of the physical closeness. It was as if I had always been by His side. I felt at home in that room.

In that occasion I realized the meaning of the words uttered by the voice. I asked if I could have one of His robes for a devotee and one of His handkerchiefs for another one, both of them suffering from serious health problems.

The relationship with Him was so confidential that some people reproached me for the "uninhibited attitude" towards the Divine Master.

I couldn't help being myself and being spontaneous and affectionate with Him. After all, He was my best Friend, Father, Master and Spouse.

Sai Baba asked me again where my husband was and, once again, I kissed His left knee. I was sitting in the same place, next to Him. He knew He was my Spouse, but wanted me to confirm it. Many years later (in December 2006, during an interview), He asked me for the name of my husband and I answered promptly and loudly "Sai Baba", while He caressed my head, smiling. In that interview He spoke of my son, or rather His son (as He had specified during my first interview with Him), predicting a future for him in another continent, where my son was supposed to move and start a new life, with His blessings. Before leaving, I kissed His hands again. He knew that I didn't feel like moving from there, so great was the fullness and joy felt in His presence. He therefore invited me to take leave and said, *"Keep me with you."* He invited me to carry Him in my heart and be Love, that is, to be happy.

In that interview He told us that He was present wherever there was Unity and Gratitude, Harmony and Love. That is when I realized that it was not wrong to ask for something if the request originated from someone else, when we did not ask anything for ourselves.

Sai Baba says: *"How can he who sees Unity in all things be misled or suffer?"*.

Unity in Diversity is the principle to keep in mind in every event of life, not to lose sight of the Divine and to maintain inner connection with Him. God is Unity. It is the Oneness present in all human beings who, thanks to His presence, are at one again when they discover the divine inner essence.

My soul had espoused the cause of the Spirit and I was increasingly aware and honoured – Universal Love was the ocean to which I belonged.

I dreamt of planting a very tall tree, whose branches fell top-down to the ground, full of unknown orange flowers (the colour of Sai Baba's robe). It was a tree of another realm, whose branches were blown by the wind, swaying in a surreal dance. Its fantastic vision and impressive beauty filled me with tranquillity.

Sai Baba says that there are no external enemies. Our (inner) enemies are the negative thoughts (devious and biased), aiming at weakening and impoverishing us, making us feel alone, vulnerable, helpless and hapless. We do not get disappointed or feel bad because of some individuals or things, but due to our illusory emotional investments.

In fact, no man is born without the inner seed (spark or essence, or pure energy) of God and no one is prevented (from outside) from making it bloom. We alone can make that seed blossom and make the flower of awareness sprout in order to express and share what we really are.

I dreamt of being in the Garden of Eden. There were many varieties of tropical plants that enriched the lush and thick vegetation. The sky stretched endlessly. What was unique about the dream was that I found Paradise just behind the corner of my house, that is, it was at hand and in the dream I was quite amazed that I hadn't discovered it before.[136]

The dream may have pointed out that the Peace and Harmony transforming everyday life into Paradise on earth were really handy, around the corner, where nobody expected to find them (I discovered it years later).

I returned from India, again imbued with His Grace, to reflect upon and elaborate the lessons learned during my stay there.

The Divine Master helps us see our mistakes, but He doesn't show us the Truth until we overcome them. And when we realize this, we can share it only with those who have already awakened to a new consciousness, that is, those living in truth, coherence and harmony with God and with others. This was yet another confirmation that, sadly, only those who live in harmony with the Divine will pass into the highest realms of the spiritual dimensions and so will be able to "see".

Through the inner voice, the Divine Master helped me discern what was true from what was illusory, to accelerate the awakening.

Everyone can hear this voice, the voice of Truth, and learn to tune with it in the heart, thus avoiding mistakes and omissions which may cost us dearly in terms of spiritual evolution. The error in itself is never negative. On the contrary, it can indeed be a source of great insight, provided we accept it with honesty and courage and try to fix it by implementing the Divine Will. In this way, we can be sure that the good will manifest.

What is negative is to persevere in the error, blocking the development and the ability to see with the eye of the heart (i.e. with awareness). This prevents us from seeing God as Love and Truth.

I learned that being good was not enough. We should learn to be conscious of our divinity if we want to be useful to ourselves and to others and heal, see and be. All this is possible only if we live in and for the Truth.

If we adopt this lifestyle, we will ensure harmony and the manifestation of the gifts enabling us to know ourselves better, be at one with God and express our true potential.

I kept saying in my heart: *"Thy Will Be Done"*, knowing that the choice that makes the difference is about accepting what fate sends us and renouncing what we cannot have.

On the night of Shivarathri (February of the same year), Sai Baba materialized a golden *Lingam*, or the cosmic egg, the primordial form of Creation. It is an expression of the "spiritual heart" of every being. It came out from His mouth, in front of a multitude of devotees, to propitiate the peace for humankind. The event occurred in public for the first time after two decades to inaugurate a new course related to the Age of Aquarius (or Golden Age) or Truth.

So many extraordinary events marked the time beat at the end of the millennium. The weeping statues of Our Lady, the statues of Ganesha drinking milk[137], the comets, the dance of their meteor shower and the lunar and solar eclipses. All those signs announced a major change, but my interpretations went thus far and so I put everything in God's hands.

I dreamt of being on a beach, with a huge crowd of people. We were all waiting to be baptized in the sea. Then, magically, a large green leaf materialized in the air. On it, arranged symmetrically in a row, on one side there were newborn boys, dressed in blue, and on the other there were newborn girls, dressed in pink.

I interpreted that scene as achieving "Androgyny" through the purification of the body in the sea, as a symbolic expression of the Divine Mother and the Holy Spirit, through the baptism of the Spirit.

At that time I was offered the opportunity to attend a course in spiritual healing with colours, essential oils and crystals (Aurasoma therapy), but above all to have experiences that would deepen the knowledge of a past life that was closely connected with the present one.

For the first time since I'd met Sai Baba, I considered going to a place that was not India.

I found myself in Greece during Orthodox Easter (which came as a surprise) – a magic moment of extraordinary beauty and sacredness. It was simply unforgettable (I warmly recommend it to everyone). To my mind, the Divine Master had perfectly organized that "vacation" for me.

My anticipations proved correct and timely. I received an important clarification on the most significant choice I had made in this lifetime (in terms of responsibility, emotional involvement and existential setup): the decision to have a child, although I was single.

It arrived as a flash of inspiration during a church service in a small Orthodox church, a very old one, located on a promontory surrounded by the sea. An enchanting place.

Easter, the feast of the Will of God and Forgiveness, opened the door on a previous life to help me forgive myself.

What shocked me most, even more than the discovery itself, was the conscious, aware and direct, personal revelation – not as something I'd learned, read or heard – on the "effects" of the law of cause and effect (*karma*).

Shortly before leaving, under the constant guidance of the true Self or Inner Master, I had read in some esoteric books that the solar mysteries were three. One of them was the mystery of the sea – reminding me of the dream of baptism of sea[138] – related to astral light and the law of *karma*. It allows us to address two essential issues when it comes to removing the obstacles on the way to liberation – the reading of Akashic records and the insight into the lives that are significant for the life in progress.

Thereupon, the disciple may work intelligently in the present and start putting her/his *karma* in balance. As the past debts are eliminated, he gradually understands how to undo the *karma* in the three realms: physical, astral and mental. This work is done for eternity, because by clearing *karmic*[139] residues from the previous lives, without creating any new debts, that is, by living in the *Dharma*, living righteously, we lighten the "baggage" of the soul until it can attain Self-realization, or the true Self.

Hence, the dream about the baptism by sea hinted at the key to interpret the "mystery of the sea" of my past lives.

Shuka Nadi had investigated the Akashic records for me in India some years earlier. The flash of inspiration I had in Greece regarding a life lived in that very land made me realize with dismay that a single, innocent wish, if expressed intensely, was enough to force us to return to earth and live an entire life full of tribulations to satisfy the wish forgotten at birth, something we had personally "commissioned".

That discovery frightened and knocked me down momentarily. I was seriously disoriented, even though I had already attained a fair mastery of myself. As a matter of fact, I was able to recover quickly thanks to my self-mastery. The climate and environment was the best possible from all points of view, to support and help me come out of the tangle of emotions and thoughts I was in.

Returning in my thoughts to the reading of Akashic records, I'd had an insight into its content many times with regard to my life. This helped me interpret the meaning behind a few constants in life and I allowed things to happen without me looking for them. In fact, I already had enough material to work on and there was no need to search for more.

This attitude and the constant self-inquiry helped me flow more smoothly with life. I'd say to myself: you should leave behind what is no longer acceptable for your evolution because it does not belong to you any more (not in terms of possession but as being part and parcel of destiny). As a matter of fact, we waste time and energy by clinging stubbornly to the past that no longer exists and can only mortify us by preventing change – and life *is* change.

When it comes to neutralizing the allure of the world, I realized the importance of learning to listen to the inner voice, as the most significant experience preserving us from self-destruction and keeping us on the path of spiritual evolution, i.e. on a vibration frequency high enough to neutralize the low vibrations of matter.

However, when it comes to dreams, it is important to develop the ability to understand and interpret them as messages from the unconscious mind, aimed at removing blocks and obstacles on the spiritual path.

In general terms, man is reluctant to choose the spiritual path over that of the world, considering the Spirit as something alien to him, something that does not imply a practical benefit or immediate gain, something intangible, perhaps even bizarre or non-existent.

Lower joys, those of the senses, the only joys known to man (being ignorant about the spiritual reality that permeates him), attract him more and cause him to lower his vibration frequency increasingly, thus maintaining the energies concentrated on the lower chakras. This facilitates addictions and attachments, eliminating the individual's higher – intuitive and creative – potential, completely erasing the will to do good, or the Divine Will. Inevitably, the soul's development is blocked. Most people are not familiar with these subtle mechanics of the soul's "perdition" and fall a prey to the wolf, only because it is disguised as a lamb.

Those who cannot read with the inner vision of the heart will rely on appearances. They have to believe in what they see with their physical eyes. But physical sight is so fallacious.

As I said, Jesus, Sai Baba, the masters of esoteric schools and the Holy Scriptures of all religions agree that those who persevere in error cannot know the truth, i.e. God, because God *is* Truth. Sai Baba says: "*Truth can only be revealed to those living in the Truth*".

Continuing to write – so as to contribute in the spreading of knowledge and the realization of the true Self – was the only way to help others protect themselves from a certain self-destruction. This is rooted in the fact that they are unaware of the true reality, that is, of the spiritual reality.

More than anything else, I wanted to defeat that ignorance in me once and for all and show others the way to salvation. It was necessary to reach the awareness of the true Self to be able to testify that the goal was attainable.

This thought blocked me and I was unable to advance any further. But then I resumed writing, confident that knowing the Truth without sharing it with others would be a serious shortcoming. Moreover, the task had been confirmed by Sai Baba.

Surrendering the ego to the Divine Will is the most difficult step for a reluctant individual, when it comes to choosing the spiritual path. Still, there is no other way for a man to stop considering himself as the author of his own actions, only because he has a "conscious self" i.e. the individual self, or the lower mind. He can then get rid of the illusion of being separate from the divine essence.

Only by restoring contact with the true Self can we progress in the selfless acts and feel at one with the Divine, thus being the instrument of His Love.

Spiritual growth is nourished by the serenity of heart. In fact, when I was at peace with myself, I could write for days on end. It was an empowering confirmation and a vivifying reality.

My emotional nature assisted me in my devotion, but became an obstacle for the implementation of my task because I would occasionally flare up and didn't feel like writing any more. Fortunately, these episodes were brief and were immediately followed by calm.

After several months, one night, at the usual hour (at 3:30 a.m.), the inner voice told me: *"You will work with the Sun and with herbs, with life and with nature."* Having read the Akashic records, I learned that I had been a healer in my previous lives (with herbs and medicinal plants). However, the message sounded a little odd[140] for this lifetime and so I put it aside and stopped thinking about it.

Regarding the epochal change on our planet, while continuing to study esoteric books, I learned that the increased vibration field (an aspect of this change) on earth entailed fatigue, worries about the future and depression. Besides being personally familiar with those symptoms, I also witnessed them in other people over the years.

I read that the disciple, on his own in his journey, could not ask for help (been there, done that). As we tread along the path, our capacity of synthesis increases (I experienced it more and more often and others recognized it too), and we consequently understand life better.

Some time passed before the inner voice spoke about the transformation of energy from negative to positive. It mentioned the Masters from other dimensions I had recently heard about during the Aurasoma therapy course held in Greece. One of those names stuck in my mind: Nada, meaning "divine sound" in Sanskrit, pointed at the sound that heals.

At that time I kept wondering whether it was proper to interpret the inner voice as the voice of God. Indeed, for me it had always been Him – the One, the Divine Master. With time, I became absolutely certain.

I dreamt of being in India during the *darshan*. Sai Baba spoke to me in the crowd, telling me that I could help others heal only when they become ready to see, in themselves, their noblest part (it was the issue I addressed in those days). I was torn between the realization that people wore "masks", playing the roles the "great Director" (God) had assigned them, without being spontaneous or sincere, and the fact that I had to keep quiet about the insincerity I "saw", since it is unacceptable to reveal what we "see" to those who lie to themselves and to others.

I was wondering how come I could "see" it and for what purpose. Perhaps it served only me to learn to understand and increasingly accept others and this fake world (as Sai Baba defines it). In other words, it might have enhanced the ability to understand, for the sake of my spiritual evolution.

After the first initiation (that brought out the intuitive ability to see with the heart, or with the third eye), in my prayers I asked Sai Baba for the second initiation (opening the heart to understanding). I knew I could not attain the will of goodness, the compassion of the heart and the stability of the mind without His Grace.

Nature was my friend, especially in times of despair. I listened to the wind and felt it on my skin – for me it was the voice and the caresses of the Divine Master comforting me.

Sai Baba says: *"When a breath of wind touches you, it is I caressing you."* Sometimes I almost levitated in ecstatic contemplation, as I watched the clouds dance in the sky: pale, dark, white or rose-coloured. The starry sky, in the evening, embraced me with a thousand arms of light, stretching from every star. Everything sang hymns to the Creator and the creation.

Those who are unwilling to commit wholeheartedly, let go of all their fears[141], abandon the ego and have faith in the Spirit of Life, will never be able to put aside the mind and allow the Angel within to manifest through the body transformed into an empty channel, like a cane, to allow the divine breath of cosmic energy to pass through and sing His Divine Song. This is the " healing sound" mentioned by the voice, inviting me to lovingly trust the cosmic Laws (the macrocosm expressed in the microcosm).

The Divine Song of the Spirit is unconditional Love that fills the heart and helps overcome our negative thoughts and emotions, restoring the original dignity of the beings of light (angelic creatures).

What we retain is lost. When we are not tied to anything, we discover that we have everything. He who seeks happiness for others will always be joyful, but he who seeks for himself will always be unhappy. In this regard, Jesus said: *"He who gives his life, will live. He who keeps it for himself will lose it"*. Sharing, in all its forms, is an expression of the Holy Spirit. Jesus, Sai Baba and all the great souls are His manifestations who come to the rescue of mankind.

I did not know any better way of giving than to share, through my writing, my magical and wonderful experience with God. I recall the words of a friend of mine: *"Who you are is the gift of God; what you do is your gift to God".*

Whenever I got involved in spiritual discourses, all my spiritual pride would come rushing out, so if I did manage to prevail on the dialectic plane, I came out annihilated on the plane of awareness. I had to acknowledge that pride was still alive in me and admit that I had a long way to go to outdo my ego (disguised as pride).

Would I manage to defeat all the demons that lived inside me? The best thing to do was to pray Sai Baba to ensure His presence in His temple in me (the heart), to help me purify it and be worthy of Him.

I dreamt of a procession of falcons in flight. As they advanced, they took off and formed a long dark line in the sky. Around me, a crowd chanted hymns and songs of praise to the Lord. I was definitely in another dimension, because nothing reminded me of earth.

Since I couldn't interpret the dream, I decided to put it on the back burner. As I mentioned earlier, Sai Baba says that this is not the time to act tepidly (referring to those who act out of interest and give in order to receive back). We must pick one side or the other, being either with God or with the world, i.e. being either hot (referring to the pure in heart, those who give selfless Love, unconditionally) or cold (referring to those who don't give at all, thinking only about themselves).

He says the search for pleasure for pleasure's sake is diabolical and hedonism is a form of corruption (like seduction), whereas the pure in the heart live in search of the Spirit, aspiring to God and not to pleasure, that is, the pleasures of the body don't appeal to them.

I learned from the teachings of a great Indian saint, Ramakrishna, that we should engage only in the duties that are commensurate with the degree of the ego's abandonment to God. In other words, those who are not ready to break away from the pleasures of the senses ought to remain in the world until they are available for a change of trend because, following the spiritual path requires the purity of heart and the choice of Truth. One cannot cheat God.

These words are raw but true. They can't be sweetened or softened, which is where Spiritual Knowledge is useful – it provides the strength and courage to accept the truthfulness and the rawness.

I thought about the dream in which Sai Baba mentioned the task He was preparing for me. But I still had to work hard to rid myself of the illusions of the ego, to prepare myself to accept His new gift of Love.

I continued with the self-inquiry, examining the masculine and feminine qualities in every human being, to see my deficiencies and how to make up for them and eventually balance these aspects of my personality. I recognized creativity, decision-making, decisiveness and the momentum of volitionality (in a word, "action") as male qualities. On the other hand, emotional fluidity, receptivity, intuitiveness and sensitivity, but above all surrendering to the Divine (in a word, "contemplation") were feminine qualities. In this regard, the Vedas recognize seven attributes in women and three in men that are useful for their receptiveness to the path of the Spirit.

When I moved in harmony with the Spirit, the quality of my life improved significantly. Everything that is done out of Divine inspiration is holy and the sanctity of a life experienced according to the Divine Will is translated into force and untameable power. In other words, Harmony transforms life into Paradise on earth... and Paradise can be found just around the corner – it is that close. By following the Spirit without hesitation, we learn how to live in a safe Universe, where the ego does not need to build defences that make part of the bitter part of life (fear, mistrust, touchiness and irritability) and are overt expressions of ego's weaknesses.

I realized that the success in eliminating the ego depended on the constancy of carrying out the winning choices, without hesitation or change of direction or gear. This required patience and perseverance.

NOTES: CHAPTER XIV

130. It actually arrived as a message of the inner voice many years later. Nothing happened without being sealed by a divine confirmation, sooner or later.

131. As we know, medicines can be bitter but efficient.

132. This arcane marks a point of no return. When we get there, the devout can only act according to the Will of God and follow the path to mystical enlightenment.

133. Exercising any form of domination over other people, even in a subtle way, is a major expression of violence.

134. This attitude is typical of the ancient Hellenic culture.

135. Chakras: energy centres, located along the spine, connecting the physical body to the cosmic energy that surrounds and permeates it.

136. After several years, I changed home and went to live just behind the corner of the house where I had lived until then. That new "nest" felt like Paradise. What an extraordinary coincidence!

137. Our Lady (the Divine Mother) and Ganesha (the Son in the Hindu Trinity: Shiva, Shakti and Ganesha) are symbolic expressions of the Holy Spirit.

138. This was yet another proof that the predictions expressed through my dreams, messages and revelations were parts of a single, divine plan.

139. Sai Baba confirmed this years later, when He informed me that my past *karma* had been cancelled, by His Grace.

140. At the time, I was mostly aware of the interest related to profit when it came to alternative, herbal therapies.

141. I would like to point out that those who cannot get rid of the fear of loss are, paradoxically, doomed to lose everything on the material and spiritual plane, including the possibility to break free from it.

XV

There is nothing more amazing than the truth – we just need to reveal it.

Author

unknown.

The Hindu Holy Scriptures say: *"Those who accept the glory of the manifest creation as their own, those who realize that the entire universe is inside, are divine, despite the thoughts still playing in their minds".*

These words reassured me while I was striving to stabilize my mind, constantly repeating the mantra: "Om Namah Shivaya". I filled every moment of manual work, or while waiting, while in the street, or driving a car, or riding a bicycle, with this invocation to Lord Shiva, of whom Sai Baba is an incarnation.

This mantra[142] brought me peace of mind and calm, even in moments of great tension.

Sai Baba says: *"Attain Paradise within and your desires will be fulfilled immediately. All the misery and suffering will end.*

Feel beyond the body and its surrounding environment, beyond the mind and its motivations, beyond the thoughts of success and fear.

The real cause of suffering in the world is the failure to look inside, relying on external forces instead".

The final words fully explain the meaning of the painful feeling of incompleteness that has always plagued much of humanity. We feel incomplete simply because we don't look within, but entrust ourselves to others, unrealistically convinced that we can find affection, satisfaction, security and confirmations outside. Yet, inasmuch God resides in the silence and simplicity of thought, He surely dwells in us, too.

He says: *"There is no place without God"* and again: *"You are not one but three: the one that you think you are (physical body) what others think you are (mental body) and what you really are (Atma)".* Atma is Love and Truth. In brief, it is our vital part, our best part. It is life itself that animates us. The Divine Essence is us - it is our true Self.

A few months after my return home, I left for the nineteenth trip to meet the Beloved Goodness.

At that time of the year, the Indians celebrated the Festival of the Guru (He who illuminates the darkness). In His address on this important occasion, Sai Baba spoke once again about the main purpose of human life and the discovery of the true Self, saying that *"Man's primary duty is to acquire the knowledge of the Self. This knowledge, once obtained, makes us realize the purpose of life. It is the only way to find the 'lost wholeness'. There is no other way".*

He continued by saying: *"Love is the most powerful force of all, the pure expression of the Divine in the Universe. When Love, latent in each one of us, is used collectively, in its cosmic form, it becomes Divine (Cosmic) Love"* and added: *"Be embodiments of Love! I want all of you to live in the intimacy of a close relationship and cooperation, like brothers and sisters. I want you to make a vow today: promise Me that you will lead, henceforth, a life pervaded with Love".*

He asked us to make another vow, after the one we had made the year before, promising that we would present Him with a pure heart and a stable mind for His birthday, in 2000.

Due to the decoration works in course whereby the ceiling of the *Mandir* was being covered with gold leaves in view of the upcoming festival, while we were sitting and waiting for Sai Baba during the *darshan*, we found ourselves under a shower of gold blades of straw. This unique situation felt like the advent of the Golden Age, with us experiencing it as protagonists and spectators at the same time. In my continuous delving, I was wondering about the law determining the course of one's destiny, written in the book of life. What turns a positive destiny into a negative one and vice versa?

I answered myself the best I could: according to the natural law of cause and effect (*karma*), when we operate by the benevolent Will of God, anything can be transformed into something positive, as everything done in the name of God and offered to Him becomes sacred. Man possesses the power to turn lead into gold, but his ignorance prevents him from seeing it. Whereas, when our free choice is implemented according to the human will, even something positive could become negative, unless Divine Grace intervenes because it can overturn any situation.

Taking stock of the situation, I could see in every meaningful relationship of my life a *karmic* debt – either settled or being still paid off. This new way of looking at personal history helped me maintain an attitude of equanimity and non-attachment, but it also brought out the ability to accept and the willpower to continue on the spiritual path to the true Self. I understood with increasing clarity that emotional non-attachment did not mean indifference, but the ability to love unconditionally, beyond conflicts, interests, prevarications or entitlements.

I'd collected some information that helped me identify five past lifetimes closely related to the current one and so I could interpret events, encounters, changes and important choices taking place in this life.

Every event slowly gained a deep sense within a larger framework. Hence, consciousness was ripening - the search for Truth was reaching realization.

Nothing happens by chance. There is always a reason behind, whether we see it or not.

Due to our intellectual pride[143], we claim that only what can be proved or documented exists. But we don't take into account that each test is rebuttable, as the person performing the test (who may be a "person of science") always applies worldly knowledge (limited and fallacious). Most importantly, it is the knowledge of the true Self that opens the door to the awareness of being divine.

Without awareness, or the knowledge of the heart, man is blind. To me, science describes a world as seen by a person who turns his blind eye and deaf ear to the call of God. So much remains to be discovered and "seen" with the eye of the heart within us, in the inner world.

The knowledge of the heart – not mundane knowledge – can unlock the mysteries of life through the wisdom of intuitive intelligence. There is no wisdom[144] without humility and respect (fear) of God, just as there is no real greatness without honesty. In fact, the real achievement for humanity is not going to the Moon, or Mars, or finding out how many asteroids (more than four hundred) hover at a safe distance from the Earth's orbit (although it is impossible to determine their trajectory, their motion, and hence the risk of impact with our planet, which could decree the end of the Earth as we know it today), but transforming attachment into unconditional Love, greed into the capacity to give, a desire for pleasure into a desire for harmony.

It is the only way for our soul to move from the dark night of ignorance and see "the rosy fingers of dawn" of a new day, that of the knowledge of the Spirit, to overcome the bitterness and dissatisfaction that have always plagued it and taste the sweetness of peace and the fullness of perfect glee (constant bliss).

I realized I had been paying off the pending debts and was on my way to close the account. I could feel it in my heart.

In this new light, I reviewed the two dreams featuring the wrist watch given to me by the Divine Master. In the first dream I was offered a second chance (a second fastener), to break free from the cycle of rebirths (the watch in terms of time, in its cyclical passing). In the second one, I was given the opportunity to go back in time (hands turning counter clockwise), to past lives, in order to gain a better understanding of the underlying significance of what I was supposed to pay in this lifetime, as *karmic* debt.

Sai Baba says, *"God will spread the gifts of His Grace and protect all those who possess the six noble qualities, namely Enthusiasm, Boldness, Courage, Intelligence, Energy, and Value."*

I started applying all my goodwill to see if I had those qualities. The heart, as my Self was telling me, was the winning road. The pain of lost attachments, habits and customs was slowly replaced by the joy of discovering independence, autonomy, fulfilment and freedom.

I have always carried along two things, since childhood: dark glasses (I thought I was oversensitive to sunlight) and a wrist watch (I have always loved punctuality).

I suddenly realized I could do without them: the sun not only ceased to bother me any more – I even discovered that it energized me. And, I could be punctual every time it was necessary, even without a watch.

Upon my return to Italy, I walked into a church one day. I saw a symbol (an equilateral triangle with rays spreading all around) of the Holy Spirit on the altar and, above it, a blue dome studded with golden stars enveloping the Divine Mother, Our Lady, also dressed in blue.

I recognized Our Lady dressed in blue and surrounded by golden stars from the dream I had, months ago. I thanked God for having inscribed that day in my life.

That visit inspired me to expand the knowledge of the Holy Spirit[145]. I had already realized there was the Father, the Mother and the Son in the Christian Trinity (while in Hinduism, it was Ganesha, Shiva and Shakti). But then, on my birthday, I identified the seven gifts of the Holy Spirit. It offers Itself to man, to become his Inner Master. In my heart I could feel that the realization arrived from Him.

The seven gifts are the following:

○ WISDOM, as the ability to live in the noblest sense of the word, in the Gospel of Jesus. It is the pearl for which we are ready to sell everything.

○ INTELLIGENCE, as the ability to always maintain our ideals high and emerge above the impurities of life.

○ ADVICE, the voice of the heart indicating what is good for us, without imposing it on us.

○ FORTITUDE, the ability to defend Truth with humility and firmness, with faith in God.

○ SCIENCE, the ability to understand and interpret the Divine Scriptures, from which Spiritual Science derives.

○ COMPASSION, the ability to see into the hearts of others and to trust them (so that the Love He instils in us can flow into others).

○ FEAR OF GOD, the ability to respect God and His Glory, observing His Law all the time.

The most evident sign of the presence of the Holy Spirit in a person's heart is Charity, understood in the broadest sense as the ability to offer ourselves, to love unconditionally and share selflessly. This is the highest expression of Divine Love.

Jesus used to say: *"There is no greater love than to lay down one's life for the friends,"* His were not empty words. He gave proof of this truth, by giving His own life for the salvation of humankind, for the salvation of all people.

Sai Baba, the divine incarnation of the Holy Spirit, has been giving Himself for over 70 years, since He started His Divine Mission on earth, at the age of 14. He has been available to His devotees every single day of His earthly life, never keeping anything for Himself. He wears a simple, orange robe, walks bare footed and mingles with us to give us Love, Love and more Love, in every possible form, visible and invisible. All the work accomplished by Him over the many years is evidence and testimony of His Message of Love. He takes every possible opportunity to give everyone equally and those who have visited Him in India have been able to see how true this is.

But His gifts can also reach remote places. Like me, many people can testify to having received them, even at home. They arrive everywhere in the world, at all times, day or night.

Sai Baba says: *"You are the pure, pristine, eternal Spirit. Once you wake up from the dream of attachment, you will understand that mundane life is but a dream".* This is the awakening to a new consciousness – the Christ Consciousness, or the Cosmic Consciousness – the reawakening from the dream of material life into real life, a life in the reality of the Spirit.

When it comes to this subject, literature is so vast and rich that we don't need to dwell on this aspect any further.

Sai Baba says that righteousness (*Dharma*) protects the one who pursues it, but that: *"Today, man's only motivation in life is self-interest. He fills his mind with all kinds of desires and violence has become his way of life, without knowing what he's doing, where he's going and which steps he is taking. And so he throws his life away. With every step he takes nowadays, in his outermost and innermost affairs, he walks away from the path of Dharma (righteousness) and his love is drying ... man stagnates in the ignorance he is immersed into. To expand, Love needs effort (spiritual discipline) and gratitude. Without them, man is unable to recognize that his own ego will cause his fall, destroying his divinity within. He can't stand the truth. Man today does not accept the truth but, with his great ego, he is attracted to lies and accepts them. No matter how educated a mean person may be, his/her negative qualities will never be eliminated through education. You are incapable to understand what the divine commandments are and what God wants. Then, how can a person who does not understand the diabolic nature of desires and the orders of God (divine life) understand the Divine?*

It is not considered to be a 'sin' if a person makes a mistake unknowingly, but if the error is done deliberately, then it is to be considered as a very grave sin. This is the primary reason why we get stuck on the spiritual path. Soon enough, everything will become Divine. Therefore, do not waste any of your precious time because you will never be given another opportunity like this one. The 'satvic', or pure plant cannot grow on contaminated soil".

Once again, it is not enough to be good to heal the ills of the soul. Discipline and honest living are necessary to attain awareness.

Then we can count on divine protection (Grace) and divine inspiration. All that is communicated by the Divine through the workings of the Holy Spirit. I was invited by friends to visit the Shrine of Our Lady of Medugorje. The opportunity I'd been waiting for for years finally presented itself, just when I had realized that the Divine Mother and the Holy Spirit were the same thing. We departed on a night of the new moon. The black sky studded with stars was the "vault" of my church, that is, my heart.

With the first lights of dawn, I caught a glimpse of the sea in its magnificence. We drove along the coast all day, enjoying its many colours and bays, ravines, gorges, beaches and cliffs. Seawater filled every void , gently hugging the islands, large and small, scattered along the Slavic coast.

We arrived at dusk – on time, unexpectedly, to attend the evening celebration on a day dedicated precisely to Her, the Divine Mother: on October 7th. We were unaware of this anniversary, but the Spirit was guiding us wisely to the right place, at the right time.

I seemed to be inspired and realized that the Holy Spirit had given me three gifts, by awakening talents in me. They were: poverty in the Spirit, i.e. the willingness to accept Him and the receptiveness to hear Him, Spiritual Knowledge of the revealed verities and finally discernment – to know what comes from Him and what comes from the world, or the ego.

During the Mass, the officiating priest began to read the Gospel and quoted Jesus: *"Ask and you shall receive".*

I was stunned and upset and burst into silent tears of joy.

They were the same words that the inner voice repeated incessantly throughout the *darshan* of Sai Baba, in the last trip to India. When you address God – the Spirit of Life – with your heart, your prayers are answered. He wanted me to feel His presence everywhere (in the world) and there was no distance between us any more: we were at one.

He, the Oneness, undivided and yet in communion with everyone and everything, renewed His protection, but most of all His caring Love, to welcome me everywhere, all the time.

After visiting the hill of Our Lady's Apparitions, feeling the same divine energy I was already familiar with (having perceived it at Puttaparthi), I returned home. I did not witness the outward phenomena that many pilgrims claimed they did. In the heart, however, the feeling of communion with the Divine and the certainty of being loved were reinforced and this, in turn, provided the confidence to love humankind, nature and the whole Universe.

The downpour of His Love filled the river springing from the true Self with the same pure, crystal clear water that filled, as divine consciousness, the blue lake of the spiritual heart.

Sai Baba taught me that women symbolized devotion and men symbolized wisdom. Thanks to devotion, women entered the "palace", that is, they could reach the innermost place in the heart, while men (wisdom) didn't go further than the "audience room".

Sai Baba says: *"Sai Baba's women Messengers should increase throughout the world, until My Message is spread everywhere. There is only one God and He dwells in the heart. When you understand this Truth, when you develop devotion and surrender to God, there will be only one religion, the religion of Love, and there will be only one caste, that of mankind."*.

I perceived the invisible realms (the 4th dimension), including ours, more and more clearly. I visited them in my dreams or during meditation and always received enlightened lessons on the continuation of the spiritual path. I was grateful to God for all the gifts that opened the door to Compassion and Love. As they overflowed, fears and doubts disappeared.

I felt in my heart that if I could settle my *karmic* debt by the Grace of God, my suffering would end.

I often dreamt of children of all ages. I took care of them lovingly (giving them milk, almonds, a picture of Sai Baba) or saved them from different perils (fire, water, ice, etc.) These recurring dreams may have had a link with a new world or a new task that awaited me, but I was not sure.

Those who seek happiness for themselves will always be unhappy, but those who seek it for others will always be happy. A "small" person is someone who seeks only his own happiness; a "somewhat bigger" person is the one who wants to make his/her family or country happy; a "great" person pursues the happiness of all people. We are what we think, thus thinking big makes us great and thinking small makes us small (I kept repeating it).

Hence the importance of dedicating daily at least a portion of our time and energy to the supreme ideal, instead of being completely and unnecessarily absorbed by the challenges and needs of everyday life.

Sai Baba says: *"Prayer, meditation and the repetition of the name of God, in this dark age, make you realize the Light of God within.*

Listen to the inner voice. Equanimity and Love are rights acquired from birth". A few minutes of meditation a day can radically change our lives for the better. One night, the inner voice told me: *"The rosary is a wreath of blood and peace"*.

Once again, a lapidary phrase full of Christ symbolism helped me understand that renunciation, sacrifice (blood), equanimity and awareness (peace) were essential for a divine life (rosary). Therefore, blood (as the lymph of life, the nectar of the victory over the senses – not as the substance of death) and peace (that cannot be imposed but is experienced as awareness of our own divinity) were harmoniously united into a rosary, as the only "necklace" we carried around our neck at birth, like the destiny (to me, the rosary symbolized destiny).

I gradually came to terms with my fate. My thoughts stopped whirling as waiting came to an end. It was giving-time for me who had already received so much. The next day at sunset I saw a rainbow around the Sun, between the clouds: I was not alone in admiring that marvellous view, other people were also struck by its extraordinary beauty.

The next night I had a very strange dream, with Sai Baba wearing overalls and carrying a heavy suitcase, refusing help.

I woke up shocked: I had never dreamt of Sai Baba unless in His aura of sacredness. All the more, the atmosphere in the dreams was even more sacred than in reality.

I was so disoriented by such an unusual sight that I did not realize it was a stratagem (actuated by Him), for me to understand the message I received a few days later.

I was absorbed in a reading on a spiritual healer (very popular in the Philippines) when the following phrase caught my attention: *"When human beings discover the truth within themselves, they will take off the overalls and start wearing healer's clothes again. Everyone will go back to being his own healer. Know thyself and you will know the universe".*

The word "overalls," confirmed that it was time to take off that "suit" and put on the clothes of the healer. I couldn't help remembering the words pronounced a year earlier, in India, by that strange character called "Sai Ram." He turned to me and my travelling companion and asked if we were healers.

Once again, the Spirit indicated that I had discovered the Truth within me. At the same time, I was busy writing that, paradoxically, to find ourselves we sometimes had to go far away, only to find out that what we had been seeking was within us.

It was as if the conscious part of me had written in order to benignly trick the other, unconscious part. As if one part of me mocked the other. It meant that the ego was still resisting.

Supreme joy is what we get when our desire and the Divine Will fully overlap. The proof of the pudding is in the eating.

I believe that such fortunate circumstances are rare, but one such moment certainly arrived for me.

As if turning up for an appointment with destiny, a rainbow appeared in my heart. I could call it 'Heaven behind the corner'. I finally reached the other bank. I had done my utmost to purify my life and was finally able to honour the gift, that is, the opportunity to write only about *Swami* and finish the book Sai Baba had promised to bless. I was convinced it was a heavenly task and so there was no fear of criticism or obstructionism.

He was the author and He was the recipient. I held the pen but, in my mind and heart, my thoughts and feelings were His and no one else's.

In the world, there are people who "sleep", people who are "awakening" and people who "awakened".

In our spiritual blindness, we ask God to help us choose between one or another path in life. In fact, there is only one true path; the one that leads to Him, that is, to the true Self.

Those who are already on that path cannot renounce it and can only ask God to give them the strength and the will to continue. They want to stop making promises and start keeping them. I was confident about my imminent realization of the purpose of my being on earth. I knew that the hard times were coming to an end – I sensed I had passed the trial, even though I did not know which trial. Was I going to achieve the victory over the ego, in terms of mind?

I dreamt of being in India, with Sai Baba, to distribute some *saris* (traditional Indian dress). Then I went home to get some additional items, as if preparing to move. I awoke fulfilled and serene. It was Sai Baba's birthday and, for the first time after so many years, I was celebrating it away from His physical form.

That evening I went to the Sai Centre to sing the *bhajans* in His honour.

There I met a devotee who came to deliver a message for me. He said, "You have recognized both the Son and the Father, and therefore the door is open for you." That was it. It was up to me to do the inner work and assemble all the pieces of the puzzle, as soon as possible, as there was no time to waste. Before leaving the Centre, the devotee told me that his wife had seen me in her dream, handing out large and beautiful olives, generously. He thought it was a good omen.

The olive tree is the tree of Peace (peace is life, peace is God), Love and Abundance. It is sacred for the Christians. In the Celtic calendar of trees, it corresponds to the day of my birth. In classical Greece, it is the sacred tree of Athena (the goddess of wisdom) and there used to be one in the Parthenon, the temple dedicated to her, overlooking Athens.

I firmly hoped we will soon eat the "fruits of the Tree of Life" and know the age of peace and abundance.

I like to imagine thinking as a bridge enabling the passage from ignorance to knowledge. I crossed many bridges in my dreams, always managing to reach the other shore. Could that be Spiritual Knowledge? I ardently hoped so.

I spent a lot of time thinking, contemplating, meditating and writing. As I delved, I saw the union between the soul and the Spirit as the union between man and the entire Universe and all mankind and I enjoyed that vision.

Each person's complementary half at the level of coarseness (matter), is a person of the opposite sex, but at mental level, the complementary half is about the latent qualities of the opposite gender. For example, if the other half is a man, then it is his feminine qualities in him and vice versa. Finally, at the level of soul, it is the spiritual essence, the divine spark, the *Atma*. In every man or woman, there is a soul, the

Bride, waiting to know the Groom, i.e. the Spirit. The union of man and God is the union of the lover (soul) and the Beloved (the Spirit). The inner voice (the Spirit in me) confirmed it to me years later.

Sai Baba says that, according to the Divine Law, the entire creation is considered feminine and only God – the Absolute, as the creative energy from which everything originates, is male. All creation is therefore feminine. Mankind is feminine, just like all manifest nature.

We all have the Spouse waiting to complete us in the fullness and perfection that human nature has always yearned to know (albeit unconsciously). This is how we become Divine. The Spouse is Divine, Pure, Free and unconditional Love, the Lord or the Spirit of Life.

When this 'mystical marriage' (third initiation, or realization of the Self within us) takes place, we will be able to eat the fruits of the Tree of Life again. To make it happen, a desire to reach the goal is not enough. There has to be a decision to come to God.

Only the right decisions can change our lives, our destiny, and shift it from slavery to freedom.

The third millennium will be the bearer of great global transformations. For example, planet Mercury could be absorbed into the solar orbit and planet Earth (considered as the third dimension for its vibratory frequency) could be absorbed into the orbit of Venus (regarded as the 5th dimension in terms of vibratory frequency). To get an idea of the significance of the vibratory frequencies with respect to human behaviour, consider the fact that depression or negative emotions create low frequencies, whereas joy and positive emotions produce high frequencies; expressing compassion produces the highest frequencies.

Therefore, in that passage of orbit, planet Earth's vibratory frequency could leap from the 3rd to the 5th dimension.

Those who are not ready to make this step will remain on the planet that will replace the existing planet Earth, maintaining the same frequency. This new planet will host the Avatar Prema Sai (Prema means Love in Sanskrit), around the year 2030. Certainly God does not abandon any one of His 'sheep' and so He will return to Earth to save the latecomers' souls.

All this could be the result of imagination, but it is also true that what we sometimes imagine or dream becomes true, as we have witnessed over the last two centuries. As for me, the door to liberation was already opened by means of discipline and sacrifice – or so I hoped.

I wanted to share my joy with all the brothers and sisters in God, for them to be able to recognize the Christ who was back, and be well aware that humanity was one family, united in Him. It was the Christmas wish for the year in which I received so many gifts and surprises.

Sai Baba says: *"Following the Dharma (righteous behaviour), the karma (fate) vanishes. In other words, by following the right path, we cancel the additional trials in life because we have learned the 'lesson'".* I reached the point where I felt in my heart that the life of service was the only life that was spent well.

I learned that considering life as the soul's mission requires a deep understanding of the relationships in this lifetime, in the light of previous lives, since the duration of a relationship and the issues it raises are linked to the lessons we have to learn and the qualities[146] we have to nourish in the current life.

If we can make an honest and sincere introspection, we can investigate aspects of our inner life and know ourselves better. It is the first step towards the knowledge of the true Self that deserves to be taken, even if only to improve our daily lives.

Two years elapsed since the inner voice had sent one of the most disturbing messages. It was still topical to me – it didn't give me a moment's respite. It often reminded me of the words of Jesus: *"He who is not willing to repudiate his father, mother, children, siblings and his own life cannot be my disciple. Whoever follows me without carrying his cross cannot be my disciple"* (meaning: without having espoused the cause of the Spirit and sacrificed himself for humankind). This was the deeper meaning of that announcement: Jesus Christ, Sai Baba and the Holy Spirit were synonymous, they were the same thing. They manifested through the voice reiterating the same words, two thousand years after: *"Wake up and follow me".* The Inner Master (the *Sadguru*)[147] spoke to my soul. *"Talita Kumi"* (stand up and walk), said Jesus, awakening the daughter of Jairus to the Spirit of Life. Two thousand years after, the miracle was repeated and the Holy Spirit stirred my individual consciousness, making it aware of its divine essence, uniting it with the Cosmic Consciousness.

It was hard to see the faults and equally painful to strive to transform them into virtues. My soul had to endure so many torments to renounce the attractive demands of the ego. On the other hand, I acquired the ability to always recognize the cause of the disturbance I felt and to foresee the effects. I could no longer deceive myself, as I had done in the past, when I was unaware of the divine essence in me and that I belonged to the Oneness, Absolute.

I was getting ready for the "invitation to lunch" I had received years before by Sai Baba in a dream. I remembered the words of Jesus: *"Blessed is he who feasts in the Kingdom of God".*

I no longer cared when that would be – in this or the next lifetime, it made no difference as I knew I was working for the Eternal and for eternity, for what had neither beginning nor end, for Heaven, not for earthliness. Time and space no longer mattered. By then, I had become familiar with the divine food, namely the water of the Spirit – the Truth (the Age of Aquarius is represented by a man holding a jug, pouring out the water of Truth, i.e. Spiritual Knowledge) and the bread of the Spirit – the Will of God or the Will of Goodness.

Jesus said: *"He who believes in me will never be thirsty or hungry".* And again: *"My food is to act upon the will of the One who sends me and to accomplish His work".* I had the same yearning: to stop being "thirsty and hungry" and to accomplish His Work.

I realized that the power of the Divine Will could be exercised by those who had managed to transcend, not to repress, the instincts associated with the senses, that is, to transmute the fire of passion into Compassion and Love for humanity. For years, my efforts were aimed at improving and strengthening the character. It was a winning choice. Sai Baba says, *"Having character is the most important thing; this is why we are human beings and not animals; a man without character is not worthy of being considered as such".*

I passed some difficult tests in life but I have no intention of writing about that, as it would not serve any relevant purpose. The truth is, everyone is given a different "cross" to carry, according to their own fate. However, we should never be afraid of not being up to a challenge, because challenges are always tailored to our forces. A feeling of acceptance could bring us closer together. We should always focus on what unites us, in every circumstance of life, if we are to realize the divinity within us.

I was given a great opportunity to allow my old, obsolete perspective "to die" and give rise to a new way of experiencing life, viewed from the heart's eye, with awareness.

Again, I dreamt of being close to Jesus, holding His hand. What a wonderful dream. There was so much Love in that familiar, loving gesture.

I could share a child's joy and a sick person's pain. My heart was open to the Glory of God.

Most frequently, sublime or Divine Love stems from deep pain, because only when the ego withdraws (and this costs us a lot of suffering if we are attached to physicality), we can finally see that God is Love and Truth.

Sai Baba gave me the keys to open the case (the eighth key, that of Love, was added to the initially given seven keys, and, upon the conclusion of that task, the ninth and final one arrived – that of Truth). He had restored the lost purity, or Heaven on earth. In this way He repaid me for my devotion and dedication to Him. I took a step towards Him, and in return He made one hundred towards me.

I was light-hearted and carefree as never before, as far as I could remember. He had prepared me by sending angelic presences that helped to clean my aura, on several occasions. This interior work served to remove the constricting, unnecessary thoughts from my mind and helped me discern the vain illusions of fictitious desires from the real longing for Love, inner Peace, Truth and Freedom.

Many noble souls inhabit the world in order to help humanity rise beyond the boundaries of matter and more and more of them will descend to earth to fulfil this sacred and unparalleled task with us mere mortals.

Clearly, the time announced by Jesus has arrived – when God speaks to men directly, without intermediaries, when "even the young will prophesy". It is evident. Sai Baba has been using the same words, repeating them over and again in all His discourses over the decades.

I had always felt in my heart that the inner voice was the voice of the Spirit, God's voice, even if my mind (expression of the ego) fought against it and tried to make me doubtful about that profound, compelling and valuable certitude, pulling me back when I wanted to go forward and forcing me to give up when I wanted to persist.

I went ahead and persevered on the path towards the discovery of the richness of the inner world. Ego was not the winner, but I was not claiming victory. I preferred to remain on the alert at all times.

Sai Baba says that the inner voice brings Love, Light, Truth and Life. It has been like this for me.

The inner voice is the Christ Consciousness (Krishna Consciousness in Hinduism), which awakens in us as pure awareness, or the Knowledge of the Divine within.

Sai Baba has come to earth to make the ancient knowledge of the Vedas (revealed Hindu Holy Scriptures, from which all religions have drawn through thousands of years) topical in the world today, to bring us the recipe for happiness, or better for bliss, and to defeat the worst enemies (selfishness and ignorance) of our nature, the parents of illusion (Maya), causing all the ills of mankind.

No misery or suffering remains when one is freed from the ignorance afflicting us, empowering the ego and preventing us from recognizing the inner, true Self.

I used to say firmly: "I will never think that I have lowered myself too much, if what I do serves to raise someone who is unable to rise on his/her own above the condition of servitude. I will never run away from someone who is drowning. I have no doubt about that".

All the brothers and sisters (humankind) were always in my heart, even when it was not obvious, judging from the length of my withdrawal from the world.

In this regard, I had a very special dream (in terms of details) in that period. I was walking along a cliff with a friend and devotee of Sai Baba (with whom I've shared many experiences in India). Suddenly, as we talked, she slid down the slope and I tried to hold her with one hand. I couldn't make it, so I slid down too. I held her close, with one hand, and with the other I clung to the rocky edge. We were both hanging in the air. Soon I realized I was running out of forces and could not cling any longer but I did not want to let go of her. My last resort was to invoke Sai Baba and surrender to Him. I said, "Thy Will be done" while my grip (of the rock) gave

Absolute). They are all synonyms of God. "I", therefore, is the form of Atma, or the form of God".

In India, many saints have attained realization by repeating the name of God. Others must have done that in the West as well. I was constantly repeating it, whenever opportunity arose.

I'd often say: when you find yourself in front of the most beautiful of all pearls (Divine Wisdom), put aside all the rest.

Fate smiled at me victoriously because I moved closer and closer to the goal, to that union that never binds, that sets you free.

The dream of Sai Baba and the gold wedding ring on my finger confirmed that, on some level, that mystical marriage had already been celebrated. It was manifest in the physical reality I was experiencing.

It was so hard to break the veil of illusion, because would ever be the same. The sacrifice had been accomplished, leaving the old behind to welcome the new. In this context, the time I spent meditating was the most precious of the day for the direct contact with the most profound and authentic part of me.

Looking around, I was not surprised that others were struggling to realize the truth about the value of meditation.

In the swirl and din of daily life, it seems almost impossible (and sometimes impractical to most people) to find even a few minutes to meditate on the true Self, while it is considered normal to dedicate all day to what we really aren't, like our body, chasing one thousand tasks and illusory pleasures, until we lose sight of the divine essence in us.

The third millennium was on the horizon, with great promises of a restored balance between the forces of the heart and those of the mind.

I asked Sai Baba for the gift of compassion in my heart and peace of mind, but I didn't know how He would respond to my prayer. I was soon going to discover that.

One night, the inner voice told me: *"The well of St. Patrick is sublimated gold".* The message was that, by sublimating earthly love into Divine Love, the heart would reveal its true essence, that is, unconditional Love, like an inexhaustible gold mine. However, it took patience, perseverance, purity, courage, coherence and trust in God and His Grace "to dissolve the ego", with all its expressions. Luckily, I was fully aware of that.

On the first day of 2000, I strongly sensed a call from India and a desire to meet the Divine Master. He set the departure date for me (had I listened to my mind, I would have left immediately, but it would not have been the right time).

On the same day, like every time I invoked the presence of Sai Baba, a robin appeared in the garden. To my mind, it was one of His messengers coming to confirm that I had chosen the most suitable date. Shortly after that, a devotee told me that, when I dreamt of Jesus in the midst of a jubilant crowd and He patted me on my knee, He wanted me to understand that my hour had come – the moment of Truth (not death!). Moreover, he advised me to stop talking about Heaven to those who still didn't know what earth was and just be at one with the All, in Love.

Indeed, I was not supposed and I couldn't expect people to be able to "fly" if they didn't even know how to walk properly. Provided I was asked for an advice, I could only suggest how to prevent danger, or how to keep away from an existing danger, or how to find a way out of a looming danger. My advice was not always welcome. People sometimes grew suspicious, if not even disappointed. Alas, there was so much misunderstanding around me. Only the Spirit showed understanding because It knew my intentions.

God does not request obedience out of fear but out of Love. He does not want us to obey Him for fear but because we trust Him, doesn't want the law, but harmony – balance and beauty. Thus, when we are aware of God, Creation, in its many expressions, is experienced as infinite harmony.

In His birthday speech the year before, Sai Baba spoke again about the Androgyne (the perfect man), as a symbol of Harmony in man. I contemplated the path of the heart (the middle way) as a way to achieve Harmony and realize "the Androgyne" within.

The heart (the 4th chakra) is in the middle, between Heaven (the 7th chakra) and earth (the 1st chakra), that is, between the masculine and the feminine. The union of these two complementary principles in the heart gives birth to the quintessence, or divine spark in us, or the Spirit as Christ Consciousness (the 8th chakra, the eight-pointed star of the soul, symbolizing awakened consciousness to the Essenes).

Creation is represented by the number 7[150] (the number of the perfect man), God is represented by the number 1. The sum of those two numbers is 8, which is the number of the man reawakened to the Christ Consciousness (symbol of Infinity, the dove of peace, the Holy Spirit, the 8th chakra, the chakra of the spiritual heart [the 4th chakra is that of the heart]). If we divide 8 by 2, i.e. 8: 2 = 4[151], we are back to the heart, or the middle way, but also matter, the monad, which had been divided by the original matrix to manifest itself in physical, human form.

Hence, balance lies somewhere in between, in the heart, in the awareness, and Harmony stems from its achievement (in my opinion, this is the way of the Tao). Once again, I heard the inner voice one night, telling me: *"The goblet should be drained".* It was a cryptic message and literally bitter, in its essentiality. A profound silence engulfed my dismay. I had not finished settling the debts of the past, when I had to face new trials – were I to realize Christ Consciousness, or the fullness of the Spirit, the true Self in me.

I had read in some esoteric texts that, when you are not progressing on the spiritual path, it is because you don't pay attention to the given orders, that is, you pretend nothing happened and keep making mistakes.

The spur to go forward comes from persisting in the chosen discipline. Hence the importance of will and tenacity in following the spiritual path. As if to assist me with a simple and essential hint to attain unity, the inner voice spoke again: *"divide everything in two: good and bad. Then, just follow the good and eventually you'll no longer see the bad".* The inner voice told me to follow the Will of Goodness, the Divine Will, the path of *Dharma*, of righteousness, to simplify my daily routine, without being concerned about the evil or things not proceeding the way I hoped.

Whether by coincidence or as a curious case of synchronicity, I ran into the same words in an esoteric text a few days later. They indicated at synthesis substituting analysis and seeing the Divine in everyone as the only antidote for thinking badly about other people. In other words, Unity in Diversity.

Not to desire anything for ourselves and to be inoffensive were other important requirements for achieving the union with the All. Finally, it said that we incarnate to overcome our flaws (hatred, anger, jealousy, envy, pride, desires and greed). Rebirths will cease when we transform our faults into tolerance, devotion, kindness, compassion and Love. In those words I recognised the message of Sai Baba, Who says: *"Always choose good company to attain detachment from illusions and delusions. We do not care to know if a friendship is right or wrong, although it is essential to investigate this before we start seeing someone. Therefore, Vedanta says: 'Good company brings non-attachment, non-attachment brings liberation, liberation from illusion brings mental stability, mental stability brings liberation from slavery'. If we want to keep all the senses under control, we must do the satsang, that is, be with good people. When we are in constant communication with God (the best company par excellence) our feelings appear stable, optimal, exemplary and immortal.*
It is therefore crucial to understand that the cause of our own downfall are the wrong company". (speech made at Christmas, 1999).

I understood that liberation from illusions and disappointments stems from non-attachment, that being the only way to achieve equanimity. There is also a close link between equanimity and stability of mind, which is what I asked from Sai Baba (inner peace).

At that stage, I had a poignant experience. I read a text on meditation mentioning the eight keys to "transcend the mind," right on page 88 (in that book). It was also the year of the beginning (of the "final" choice; it was also a year whose individual digits totalled 8: 1988 or $1 + 9 + 8 + 8 = 26 = 2 + 6 = 8$) of the search for the Christ Consciousness, also represented by number 8. At that time, I did not know all these meanings related to 8 (also my destiny number).

This told me that all was at one: The Christ Consciousness was manifesting in me. I was presented with eight keys (the 8 keys to meditation). This synchronicity reinforced in me the desire to continue. I was on the razor's edge, between the innermost and the outermost and a ray of gold light guided me in the right directions.

n the same period, I made a startling discovery. Transcribing sacred texts allows us to communicate on an astral plane with the Ascended Masters who authored them. By some divine coincidence, in that week I transcribed entire books dealing with spirituality that I had borrowed, because they were no longer commercially available.

In my life, the Divine Master Sai Baba was, like the Holy Spirit, the indefatigable and ubiquitous protector and adventure-travel companion. Reading esoteric classics, Gnostics and the teachings of Sai Baba with keen interest, I made new discoveries every day.

One thing surprised me: the golden thread, or the bridge between the personality and the soul (the silver thread was the bridge between personality and the physical-ethereal body) was made of the same substance as the path leading to Heaven. That substance was called Love, Joy, Compassion, Wisdom. What a wonderful (and precious) discovery. I had been following that path for thirteen years without knowing it.

I found out that we enter the Kingdom of Heaven by practicing meditation, doing service to humankind and studying occult classics. Then, the Masters take us by the hand and lead us to the Father's abode. In addition to that, the requirements to get in touch with the Holy Spirit were five: purity, contentment, ardent aspiring, studying and surrendering to the true Self.

I knew those words – I had been experiencing them in the heart for years. Delving quietly into those readings, I checked my degree of development with respect to the said requirements: the timing was perfect for the death of illusions and the awakening of consciousness to the true Self to take place.

The trip to India was going to be a test for me to verify with the Divine Master how much I had achieved up till then.

I understood with my heart the meaning of Divine Love, that is, the Love for all people and things, seen as Oneness, without good or evil. Paradoxically so, the real, meaningful, unbroken bond – the safe and powerful bond with the Spirit – is the only bond that sets us free.

In order to "fly", free from the illusions and delusions of the world, and for me to be able to face the Truth, the eternal, inalienable reality, I needed true Love – which was freedom. Clearly, when there is no true Love, there is a need to idealize others. When we feel insecure (and unable to love), we can't find the courage to see others the way they really are, lest to lose our (false) certitudes, which are really excuses to justify our loneliness without resolving the issue. On the other hand, in my opinion, the popular saying *"Better alone than in bad company"* is still valid.

During the night I had a brilliant flash of inspiration: I saw with baffling clarity that all the evil we have done, even to ourselves, was done to the whole Universe, just as each person's joy goes into the reservoir of cosmic energy. That is to say that the good and the bad are reflected on the entire world because everything is connected in perfect continuity, represented by the Spirit and the Spirit is ubiquitous[152]. It is cosmic energy.

This amazing discovery left me aghast because I perceived it in my heart and it acquired an incredible value, very different from what my mind recorded. I saw the consciousness of mankind as it was structured in today's society, in the hands of a lobby who had absolute power on information in general. Developed countries, to increase their wealth, let the developing countries starve. I had always known that, but I had not really realized that the very same countries that had caused such tragedies everywhere in the world, throughout mankind, were politically and morally responsible for all this.

There will never be peace on earth unless we consider all humanity as a single family, whose Father is God as Power, whose Mother is God as Divine Mother, or Wisdom, whose son is Jesus Christ as unconditional Love.

We may not we aware of it, but humanity, physicality (our bodies), the subtle worlds of thought and emotion and the surrounding nature are all closely linked.

Hence, the human values that Sai Baba has advocated all His life are the only way to restore the harmonious balance necessary for maintaining life on earth and avoiding the foretold catastrophe (earthquakes, floods, etc.). Only by changing ourselves and by eliminating our faults can we improve the world, not just in terms of mankind but also in terms of social and natural environment.

The moments I experienced were so perfect that I wished time could stop, so that I could enjoy those instances more and contemplate their perfection. But then, life is not static. It is in the state of constant motion, a becoming through which perfection is acquired, increasingly harmonious and complete in its continuous evolution.

Was the real joyfulness I felt within the kind of permanent inner peace one can feel even in the midst of a storm?

The inner voice addressed me again: *"Add lightness to your actions, depth to your insight and simplicity to your being!"*. It was yet another pearl of wisdom presented to me by the Spirit.

I had a vision a few days later, preceded by another announcement of the inner voice that said: *"These are your friends."* I saw a big house and many people, busy doing the strangest things.

I looked around and thought: But, I don't know anyone here! Was it perhaps an anticipation of a future that awaited me? I had no idea and the voice didn't say anything else.

The eyes of the heart offered a harmonious vision of the world – strangely, even in places where, apparently, but only apparently, there were ongoing conflicts between good and evil. This new vision infused me with strength, courage and tenacity. And I was determined to pursue my task.

NOTES: CHAPTER XV

142. We can bring about an inner transformation by repeating sacred words.

143. A proud person trusts no one but himself, but *which* self – the true or the false one? The answer is, irrefutably: the false self. When we experience the true Self, there is no room for pride. There is only humility. The proud trust only what they see but, due to their limited capacity to see, they end up being dominated by fears and mistake a rope for a snake.

144. What we fail to learn through wisdom and humility will be inevitably learned through suffering and humiliation.

145. I would like to point out that, whenever I mention the Spirit, I imply the Holy Spirit.

146. The noble qualities are: adherence to truth, duty, devotion and discipline.

147. Several years later, the inner voice repeated the very same phrase.

148. Loyalty is the highest virtue in a marriage, as it underscores the free will to give love out of love, like choosing to live with someone because we love him, or her – and not because we wish to satisfy a need.

149. Nevertheless, they arrived a number of years later.

150. Pythagoras loved number 7 for its great spiritual potential.

151. Number 2 recalls the myth of the soul mate – the other half of the monad that will be found again in order for the two halves to be fused into Oneness – but only after each half has found the true Self again.

152. In this regard, let me suggest that you search for further information on the Hundredth-Monkey Effect.

XVI

He who has been freed from suffering must help others break free from it.

Author unknown.

Shortly before leaving for the twentieth trip, I dreamt of being in a magnificent cave, formed by the roots of a giant tree (judging from its size, it couldn't have belonged to this world; it corresponded more or less to a ten-storey building). I was with a friend of mine in that dark place (I had found Sai Baba owing to her ten years earlier and was about to depart with her). I felt calm since I knew how to get round that type of cave and find the way out into the light. She was eager to leave, fearing to remain tangled down there. So I guided her out, comforting her as we walked through a narrow tunnel filtering the sun rays.

I came out first, then pulled her by the arm and helped her out.

That dream showed me that, even though I was still entangled in the fetters of the world of emotions (at times, the rational part of me was afraid of failing), I would overcome every obstacle thanks to my insight, by tapping into a deep, ancient Knowledge of the path leading to the Light, or the knowledge of the Spirit. The next morning I found a strange leaflet in my mailbox, saying: "Assistance needed for a free-lance job."

The phrase seemed to express my own need.

In fact, that is when I felt I should come out of a challenging family situation. I believed there was no other way for me to dedicate myself to writing full-time, to be able to offer the book to the Divine Master on His 75th birthday. At the same time, it seemed quite impossible[153].

I knew that "healing the soul" meant breaking free from all forms of mundane slavery. Predictably so, the inner voice had anticipated that *"The goblet should be drained"*. After the surrender and awakening, the inner transformation required total detachment and giving up of all desires.

I remembered the words of Jesus: *"Do not resist evil. It can be overcome with sweetness, trust and Love, as the gift of the Self. There is no greater love than giving your life to your friends"*.

The greatest gift a man can make is an act of Charity, implied as giving oneself to the others. I kept repeating that to myself, in my heart.

I had to accept adversities with serenity and patience, which was not always an easy thing to do. I knew there could be no real transformation without total acceptance, no real change without a clear vision of the obstacles.

I wanted to love the unwanted features, mine and others', to facilitate the changes – for the coarse traits to fade away and for sweetness and understanding to fill in the vacant space.

Fear is the lack of love, or unrequited love, or the inability to love back. It can be cured only with True Love. My heart had a moment of illumination.

The best healer is the one who was hurt, who suffered and managed to overcome the obstacles (albeit at a high price), and eventually discovered compassion so he can interpret and understand other people's hearts.

We must recognize our mistakes and be impartial, as this is the only way to become the children of Light, capable of creating, healing and serving, to allow the Divine Light, or the energy of the Holy Spirit, to speak through our bodies that become channels of His bestowals (of faith, hope and charity).

Unfortunately, in this world, evil causes more sensation than goodness. There is a saying that goes: A falling tree makes more noise than a growing forest. Indeed, bad news bring high audience ratings.

This "forest" that grows silently in the midst of humanity is represented by the children of Light (the stars' seeds) who will continue to work to raise the awareness of the sleeping brothers and sisters. It is unfortunate that we cannot awaken those who want to stay asleep. But this work will continue against all odds, because the Light will welcome everybody sooner or later, no need to rush. The year 2000, as the year of the unity of opposites (duality contains the seed of unity, if we know how to overcome the differences, diversities and contrasts), invited us to share the joy with everyone, as humanity was entering the third millennium and the doors to infinite possibilities were opening for man to realize his innate fullness of an authentic creature made of pure gold, i.e. sublimated gold (I reckon the inner voice referred to this when it mentioned St. Patrick's well).

The reconciliation of opposites (or rather, complementary elements) would bring about the most important discovery (due to its intrinsic effulgent quality): that we are children of God, belonging to one family which includes not only humankind and the earth, but the whole visible and invisible Universe (together with other realms or dimensions). This is the vision offered by the Cosmic or Christ Consciousness, of the shift into the 5th dimension (pure awareness, or the dimension of the bodies of light).

The transition from the narrow view of individual consciousness to the re-awakened Cosmic Consciousness will not be painless, however. The tower of false security and illusory attachments will collapse and the ego will not find a place to stay. Hence, man will no longer be vulnerable or feel inadequate, dissatisfied or isolated from the world for fear of being hurt. He will trust other people and embrace understanding, tolerance, Love, Peace and Truth.

One night, unexpectedly, the inner voice told me: *"Beautiful being, you are ready now!"*. I did not know what I was ready for.

I thanked the Divine Love for having taken possession of my heart, flooding it with compassion. I finally emerged from the "cave" to return into the sunlight of the Spirit, with the true friend of mine, Truth (the friend from my dream is called Vera) (T.N.: v*era* means 'true' in Italian).

Paradoxically, illumination stems from the Unconscious mind and not from the linear, apparent clarity of mind (which is actually illusory). Experience gave me evidence of that.

I had another very uncommon dream. I was informed of the date of my death (in 2030). Meanwhile, I was given a strange assignment, as a volunteer physician, to extinguish the "human torches". It was a strange period on planet Earth, when collective madness was rampant, driving many people to burn themselves. Under such circumstances, teams of volunteers were activated, ready to intervene wherever it was necessary. I was immediately on the field, operating: I saw about one hundred people for whom there was nothing left to do, as they were almost charred. A terrifying sight.

That dream was astonishing for its "surreal" realism (if I may say so). It made me think once again of a hypothetical future task: helping others to extinguish the fire of desires to avoid being burnt down and succumbing. I stopped making other assumptions and put everything in God's hands, as usual.

While I was getting ready to leave for India, a few people asked if they could join me. And so I changed my mind about visiting the Divine Master on my own. He had a different plan.

Prior to my departure, I discovered something impressive: between the pages of certain books I hadn't opened for many years, I found birthday cards dated a few decades back. One of those was my mother's. It said: "Have faith in God. The real life is that of the Spirit. You will go to Paradise and enjoy it for eternity." The other card had been written by my sister thirty years earlier, in English: "Lead me in Thy truth and teach me".

Just like in some earlier occasions when I made similar discoveries, I didn't remember those birthday cards at all. It meant that I hadn't been impressed by them back then, certainly not as much as I was impressed in that moment. My path had obviously been mapped out well in advance.

My inclination towards the innermost realm always coincided with the love of knowledge, as synchronicity coincides with creativity and Self-realization with peace of mind and the overcoming of all dualities.

Twenty years without the awareness of God was a tough period, but also a great lesson because it served to avoid any future risk of "relapsing".

Sai Baba says that life is the most important school we can ever attend. I was taught to recognize the wheat from the chaff, the necessary from the superfluous and the sublime (I did not call God at the time) from the necessary, but, above all, to ignore the trifles that fill our daily life unnecessarily. The list of examples is too long to fit herein, but if you look around, you will see them everywhere.

When I retired, I abandoned the world of "doing" (outermost and mundane) and entered the world of "being" (inner and spiritual). This was the first great achievement in the adventure journey my life had turned into. I took a risk when I leaped in the dark, but I learned to fly. Only mediocre people act solely when it is safe. The bold risk. Who dares wins, or rather, God helps them, while the tepid, purportedly, like the mediocre, will not enter the Kingdom of Heaven because they have not sacrificed anything for Him – or they arrived too late, with nothing good to offer to Him.

The reason for mentioning this harsh truth was not to stigmatize those who are insensitive to the call of the Spirit, but to renew the invitation for the change of direction, which is always feasible, in my modest opinion. While there is life, there is hope, but it alone does not suffice to change. Besides, those who live in hope, die in despair.

Finally, the day of departure arrived and the eleven of us were the ones Sai Baba wished to see. This gave me peace of mind (having understood that I should act according to His Will) and, as usual when His Will coincided with our desires, the joy was great, intoxicating and almost uncontrollable.

Upon arriving at the *ashram*, I found an inscription that struck me for its simplicity. It said: *"Removing illusions is liberating"*.

After two days, Sai Baba called us for the interview. That call was so unexpected and surprising that we thought we were dreaming.

For me it was the ninth interview (9 is the number of the Avatar Sathya Sai Baba). As I entered the room, time seemed to stop. I sat next to His chair. He materialized for us women some white, fine *vibuthi,* and asked me what I wanted. I was thrilled about being there and deeply moved for the grace bestowed on us, and so I couldn't understand that Sai Baba was addressing me, personally. I was translating from English into Italian for the others, and, referring to them, I repeated to Sai Baba three times that I did not know what they wanted.

I was very happy in that moment because it was the first interview for many of them. I was therefore not focused on myself, also because some of them had high expectations with regard to their health problems (Sai Baba had promised them a recovery in a dream).

It was a dream come true for them, but also for me, as I did not expect to receive such a great gift, so suddenly. On such occasions, the mind is no longer in control and it becomes useless and superfluous, like a flashlight without batteries. Only the heart can come to our aid and it did.

Sai Baba drove me out of the "dead end street" by materializing a gold ring with three diamonds (identical to that which I had seen in the dreams seven years earlier and again a few months before, but I recalled that detail only afterwards). He asked me if I wanted it and put it on my right ring finger (just as in the dream), repeating three times that it was perfect for me.

Then He went on with the questions and answers while I kept translating, although I felt "empty", light, weightless, like a cloud, throughout the interview.

Translating helped me come out of the blissful absent-mindedness in which I was immersed.

Sai Baba confirmed everything He had anticipated in the dreams of two people and materialized for them some objects as a token of His Love.

He finally asked me where we were staying and I replied we had found accommodation in the *ashram* (which is what He always suggests) and He added: *"Good girl"* (He used the same words He had used in the dream I had prior to my departure. Yes, I was a good, a white-haired girl). I kissed His hands and His right knee.

Immediately after the interview, I met a devotee in a lane of the *ashram*. He told me: "A mother's love is the pillar that supports the Universe. Don't ever ask anybody about anything. Otherwise you will just compromise yourself. You should only ask Your Master, with confidence, joy and serenity, because devotion in your heart protects you from everything and everyone." It was an important lesson: we should "Love" without "bitterness," because the heart is the Holy Grail, which should contain only honey – not gall. Therefore, Love should, symbolically speaking, turn the blood (representing sacrifice) contained in it into nectar.

The message hinted that something would happen soon (I didn't know I was going to face a difficult period). Sai Baba had spoken to me through that devotee.

I've learned over the years that, when you meet someone who speaks from the heart, expressing selfless Love (with bright eyes), in that moment you are having a *darshan* with God, you are having a vision of the Divine because True Love is always an expression of God, irrespective of the channel.

And so, I associated those words with the interview and recognized Sai Baba's message. He intervened in time to alleviate an injury in the heart that could have scratched the joy offered by Him for permanent use, for me to remain firm and unassailable by the suffering, because He is Joy, Love – He is All.

In those days I attended a study group on desire. The lecturer stated that we, human beings, were like the well of St. Patrick's (the words of the inner voice re-emerged). We were supposed to contain nectar and not gall – the bitterness that swallowed everything, inexhaustibly, for the simple reason that, the more we satisfied our desires the more they multiplied, like an everlasting lesson of life. I considered them lessons to consolidate what I had learned from the inner voice.

Negative thoughts and negative emotions poison the water of life and transform it into the water of death. It cost me dearly to learn that.

We all reflect in each other. Some people see only goodness, others see good and evil and others still see only evil. In reality, we only see ourselves, that is, what we believe we are like.

It was the Shivarathri festival and you could feel sleep-inducing energy. Everybody was affected by unnatural weariness which predisposed people to sleep even in daytime. During the *darshan* I found myself struggling to overcome sleepiness. At a certain hour, Sai Baba materialized a gold *Lingam* (*Atma Lingam*, dedicated to the divine essence; the previous year had been dedicated to the heart, or *Hrudaya*) amidst a cheering, enthusiastic crowd.

Perhaps that materialization symbolized a whole man, the Androgyne, the new man of the Golden Age. I thanked Sai Baba in my heart. I was grateful for the opportunity to participate in the magnificence of this sacred moment.

He made two very important speeches during the festival, and I am recording it in part, hereafter: *"Embodiments of Love! You are made of bliss. You are creatures of joy. You are truly the embodiment, the authentic personification of beatitude, the metaphor of happiness, but you have forgotten it and so you wonder around, looking for joy and happiness. How ignorant it is to look for joy, while being the true embodiment of all the joys. The focus of spiritual conversion is the understanding of your own indwelling nature .... Five are the types of barrier causing pain, suffering and distress. The first is ignorance, the second is incompetence, the third is pleasure, the fourth is passion for the things of the world and the fifth is anger and frustration. Due to those five obstacles, man is separated and driven away from his Atmic reality. He is unable to experience the darshan of the Spirit and savour the joys of the Spirit. The fundamental reason stems from the fact that he identifies with the body ... ignorant is he who considers the body as something he should sacrifice everything for. There are many annoyances inflicted by the body: diseases, ambitions, sexual pleasures...Pain is related to the body and, if we place it at the centre of our attention, it prostrates us in a state of misery ... Incompetence is the characteristic of those who consider the world real, forgetting about their own innate Self, while pleasure is understood as the satisfaction of the senses. They consider sensual, worldly pleasures as something we cannot live without, like breathing, and that generates loads of oppressing suffering.*

Passion is a kind of burning love for worldly things (wealth, money, comfort). ... You rely and depend on one person. If he/she satisfies your desires, you're happy, but if you are not satisfied, you begin to hate her/him, losing your human prerogative. Many devotees pray to God for their wishes to come true and when this doesn't happen, they lay the blame on Him and start hating Him. It is some kind of aversion which is increasingly gaining ground in the world, between disappointment and frustration. With so much dissatisfaction around, many relationships go wrong – between mother and son, husband and wife, brothers and sisters..."

Sai Baba also talked about dreams (among other things), saying that: *"All the experiences in the waking state, imprinted in the consciousness, are reconstructed in the state of dream. There, experiences become effulgent and are coupled with the Principle that brightens the internal organ of the mind (i.e. thoughts, intellect, consciousness and the ego, illuminated by the light of Atma, contribute to experiencing all the perceptions of the five senses) ... Spirituality means considering everybody equal, feeling equanimity for everybody, recognizing the same Spirit in every living being. Constant integrated awareness is unalterable bliss, true knowledge, the causal form, the supreme causal state, the fifth, following the first four coatings that constitute a living being, namely the first or coarse (physical body) one, the second or ethereal (subtle) one, the third or lower mental (subtle) one and the fourth or higher mental (subtle intellect) one ... When the end approaches, the rules of grammar will not come to your rescue. "* In other words, worldly knowledge is not real knowledge. Awareness and real insight are unassailable by joy and sorrow. At the end of life, nothing else will come to our rescue. All the rest will be totally irrelevant (He showed it to me).

"We should not spend our lives pretending: what we have in the heart should also be on our lips and we should walk the talk. This is how a real man behaves and God is looking for someone like this, not for someone who only appears to be or is dressed like a man. From childhood till adulthood, man's search of worldly matters grows deeper and deeper. Doing research on the earth doesn't suffice. He also conducts research in the sky and on the stars and travels into space in different ways. He has fathomed everything except himself. Man today travels millions of kilometres into outer space, but he hasn't yet entered his own heart. He doesn't trust himself, but the expects others to trust him. This is the first mistake. He must first and foremost trust himself. This trust is called Atma-Ushvasam, because self-confidence is tantamount to having faith in the Self and discovering the bliss of the Self." Sai Baba invites us to keep our minds open, *"If someone asks where God is, tell them: He is everywhere. And if they ask you what He looks like, tell them: He looks like Love.",* adding: *" Do not follow the body, do not follow the mind, follow your consciousness. "* (Shivarathri discourses, 2000).

I returned home, but a part of me remained sort of lingering in another dimension. Something happened there which permanently modified my state of mind. It was a subtle shift, yet so profound and consistent that I felt awakened to a new awareness.

I dreamt of being called back to India[154]. As soon as I arrived there, I found myself in the *Mandir* at Puttaparthi, with a large crowd. I was called for an interview, to the same room where I had been a few weeks earlier, in real life. Sai Baba stopped outside to bless the jubilant crowd.

Suddenly, the crowd got up, gathering by the exterior walls of the *Mandir* and I, who was inside, hearing the growing buzz of people, looked towards the window and saw that the walls were flexing under the pressure of thousands of bodies who wanted to get in. Dozens of faces stood before the closed windows with gratings, to look inside.

I was saddened by the spectacle. Those people had no possibility to enter, no matter how ardently they wished to. They were left out, full stop.

I woke up still dizzy of the inescapable and bitter reality which transpired from that dream. I clearly understood that I had to hurry back to India, against all common sense, because the Divine Master was waiting for me there. I interpreted the episode of the crowd that was left out of the Temple in evangelical terms. I remembered the parable of the virgins – those who were inside had brought along the oil of the Spirit, or True Love, the purity of heart, to wait for the Spouse. The others, outside, had not obtained it in time and so they missed the chance to enter.

This analogy baffled me. I realized I had no time to waste. I had to leave as soon as possible, if I didn't want to be left out like them. In my heart I felt that I was at a turning point. Destiny had paved my way with great care. I had worked hard for many years to reach that point and now that I was there I felt dazed and stunned. On the other hand, my inner strength was ripe and I felt I could move a mountain.

I was given the chance to show God that I was ready to do anything for Him, and to show other people that sacrifice actually lead to true happiness, bliss and joyfulness of heart. Words were not enough. I had to express Truth through actions and creative inspiration.

On departure, a friend told me: "The circle is closing for you, the doors are wide open." For me, there was nothing more left to do, except to dare and take off. I realized that a phase of inner transformation had been concluded and a new one opened up. The trial I was supposed to go through consisted in draining the chalice, like the inner voice had instructed me to do, even though I didn't know what to expect really. I deemed it necessary to respond to that inner call, which was more like a command.

Within days, I finished all the practicalities to meet the deadlines. I organized everything possible for my son, booked a ticket (the first time for me to buy an open ticket), and put my return in the hands of God. It was the only safe thing to do.

My true Self was not telling me whether I would return or not, or whether I would stay there for months or years. I just had to surrender completely and let go of everything, even of my son. God would look after him (as Sai Baba had assured me several years earlier). On the day of my departure, I couldn't help writing him a letter (a spiritual will) which I left on his bed, deeply moved.

321

With that trip, that part of my life was coming to an end. It was the twenty-first journey, but I will elaborate the analogy between the trip and the respective number further on.

This departure, with the open ticket in my hand, had a different flavour compared to the others. It was indescribable because I had never tried anything similar before.

Later on, I realized that all the journeys to Sai Baba had been a constant return to the source. I was moving from myself to myself, because our heart is the true Temple of God.

The heart is the tip of the scale which is life, whose plates (the mind and the senses) oscillate frighteningly, until we come to realize that we are neither the one nor the other. Only then can we stabilize the tip, or the heart, and find balance, stop being swept by emotional storms and, at last, listen to the voice of God, in silence.

A few days after the departure, the inner voice spoke to me again (this time at daytime), while I was absorbed in the silence, gazing through the window at the trees blown by the wind. It said: *"What do you want, that I am not already giving you?".*

That question, made in a booming voice, left me stunned. I immediately felt the need to go out into the open air to take a look at the sky, in the hope that the answer would be written right there.

I found light rose-coloured clouds gently filling the pale blue background of the spring sunset sky. Those were the colours of the *Mandir* at Puttaparthi (rose and blue). So, that was the answer: the union of the rose-tinted (feminine) and the blue (masculine), "the Androgyne" in me. Perhaps I wanted to realize it too quickly. That night I dreamt that I had already arrived in India. I was preparing a great feast, in Sai Baba's honour.

I had read in the theme of that year's solar revolution about a period of decisive transformations. I was going to have an appointment of vital importance to the soul and the mystical union, upon making a heroic choice. To fully enjoy the taste of life, that of the Spirit, we must "know how to surrender". This phrase was appropriate for the time I was going through. If "you can't let go of yourself, you can't enjoy." As I reflected upon these words, so simple and so great because they contained all the perceptible Universe, I had a flash of inspiration. In a moment I realized that the day was made to see where we were, and the night to see and reveal where we came from and where we were heading to.

We have to "let go" of the day with its illusory safety, every night, when we go to bed. We also have to "let go" of the night and the mysterious wandering backward and forward in time and the boundless space, every morning when we wake up, if we wish to rejoice in the completion of the experiences of life. Everything is but a cyclical renewal. If we are attached to the past too much (or too little), we get stuck and are unable to fully experience the present – which actually is the only time we can make use of.

It was the "first" spring of a new life. I was walking down the street when my eyes spotted a newspaper headline that said, "when actions speak louder than words." It was a confirmation of my choice to depart and let my son learn to manage his life by himself. I had full confidence in his ability to become autonomous and independent, although he was still young.

Most acquaintances saw my departure as pure madness. I had just returned and it seemed absurd (rationally speaking) to have to go back. For me, time and space were not factors that could prevent me from responding positively to the call of the Divine Master, to His voice, which communicated me the following message (or better, a declaration of Love) shortly after that: *"I love you. You are mine. I am yours. Love Me and Honour Me"*.

Those words crowned an everlasting dream of Love, even though I had not been aware of it constantly. They meant, basically: be Love! I had been given a new life, so that I could honour and love Him, because Love is God. If you love God, you are God, you are at one with Him, you are Him, you are Love.

Easter was approaching and the following inscription stood up on the facades of churches: *"The Word became flesh and dwelt amongst us"*. This miracle of Love had happened two thousand years ago with Jesus. In our time, with Sai Baba, I was among the lucky ones who recognized Him.

The Divine Master has become man once again, for the ailing humanity, tired of suffering and eager to renew itself into a new life at the dawn of the spring of the third millennium.

As I was sorting out my diaries, I found a note written down by my mother prior to my birth. It was still very topical and just perfect for that moment of separation from my son. It said: *"A mother knows what human flesh is, the clay, the raw mass that must become Light, as she impresses Heaven, the Infinite and the Divine in the soul of her son. The scope of education is attaining a perfect person, divine in grace, eternity and Love. A man without Love is a sail without wind, a container without content"*.

Although late, I realized that my mother had been a teacher of life. She initiated me to the knowledge I expanded later on, throughout my entire life. What Sai Baba often says is true: *"Honour your mother as you honour God himself."* She had instilled a thirst for true knowledge in me. Perhaps that is why my soul had come to her, as mother, when I was reincarnated on this earth. That was what it needed. She had never met Sai Baba, but her words perfectly reflected His teaching, as yet another proof that Truth is Immortal, limitless, beyond any religion or belief. It is God himself.

That discovery drew me much closer to her in that delicate moment of my life as a mother. It was a true gift from Heaven.

The inner voice spoke to me again: *"I'll drive you beyond your body."*

It was yet another confirmation that I was on the right path, which encouraged me regarding the choice I'd made. I told myself that a generous heart loves everyone and has real power (i.e. the desire to serve) and strength (i.e. wisdom and patience), that being the attributes of the Divine Will, the Holy Spirit.

Those were the gifts that the Spirit infused in the heart and I sensed its great ability to Love everyone and everything.

I learned from an ancient esoteric book that only those who were near the end of their human cycle of rebirths could "understand", in terms of comprehension, the mysteries of life. What a coincidence, the last grade of the Virgo sign speaks about the last reincarnation in a cycle and it corresponds to the degree of my sun, at birth.

Life goes on in other dimensions, but without physicality (the inner voice had foretold that I would transcend my body), not the way we have always believed, that is, with a resurrected "body". The physical bodies are formed only to return in the physical dimension, on earth, in the cycle of rebirths. Rebirth (few people know this) entails a loss of power and freedom, in exchange for purification. In other words, it is a "rehearsal" for those who have been sent back to the school of life, because they failed to rise to a higher dimension.

I felt this could be a crucial moment for a full-time commitment to writing the book (the one you are reading), and so I filled two suitcases with diaries (it was my only luggage). I hoped to find enough creative inspiration to complete this work I believed had been commissioned by the Divine.

The day of the departure arrived. I left everything behind, without looking back, with a certain degree of fear and pain due to the confusion generated in me by this extraordinary adventure. I headed for Brindavan (Whitefield) where Sai Baba was at the time.

I realized I had returned to earth because of my emotional involvements developed from one life to another (just like everyone else). I was going to break free of that, but I could still sense all its influence on me.

Sai Baba says: *"Stay away from passion, yearn for Love and Peace"*, because passions recreate and extend the *karma*, whereas Love and inner Peace set us free. Emotional involvements create sentiments and passions related to the instincts of conservation and survival, finding deep roots. This is not about simple, innocuous affections, but about dangerous attachments that burden human destiny until the person loses peace of mind, be it for the ingratitude for what one has, be it for the excessive desire for what one does not have. Ingratitude and desire are both fruits of the ego, remember that, and they generate apprehension and malaise. Ego isolates us from the rest of the world, making us feel lonely and preventing us from feeling and enjoying the unity with the All and therefore tapping into cosmic energy which is put at our disposal by the Absolute because we are divine creatures.

And this is why, if you have God (that is, if you have Love) and nothing else, you have everything. If you have everything but you lack God (that is, you lack Love), you have nothing.

I came to understand this during the period of isolation from everyone and everybody. Still, it was a period of completeness and fullness of being, of unity with the All. I had only Him, the Spirit of Life in my heart, and so I had everything.

As soon as I arrived, I was welcomed by Sai Baba who stopped in front of me, allowing me to kiss His feet. His eyes were telling me: This time, I am going to speak to your heart. And so it happened (from that moment onward).

He let me know immediately that, prior to being assigned a new task, I had to attain inner harmony (and within my family), to be able to spread His knowledge into the world.

I used to go out twice a day to have a *darshan*, and spent the rest of the time writing.

Every time I thought the goal was within reach, the task would get tougher. On the other hand, I could see that I was not going to stay in India for much longer. I had to return home to address (and resolve) the unresolved issues there.

Two months passed when, one day, I felt like asking the Divine Master to instruct me regarding the date of my return. Something extraordinary happened on the same day and this made me reveal the date.

I was aware that attaining enlightenment required deep insight, few words and a lot of meditation.

Only a "realized" soul (he who knows his divinity) knows the reasonless joy (true delight) felt by the heart that meets the Light. When we master ourselves and our senses, the Spirit is free and hence It can guide, inspire, enlighten and talk to us.

Acquiring Harmony (the Androgyne in ourselves) is the only pathway to God as the harmonic vibration *par excellence*. The only way to get in tune with Him and love divinely, that is, unconditionally, is by reaching this vibration.

Harmony stems from the cognisance of being divine. "Realized" souls do not need anyone to feel complete, as they are aware that they are at one with the All. They feel fulfilled and can offer themselves, without fearing that they will lose something, knowing that what we really possess (the spiritual essence) is ours forever and no one can ever take it away.

I asked God for discernment and Spiritual Knowledge (expressions of the Absolute in man) so as to proceed on the path, attain compassion in the heart and stability of mind and to be useful to the world.

He heard my prayers and made me see the aim within me – not with the mind but with the heart's eye (awareness) – telling me (in my heart): *"Do not ask, do not wish.*

All you have to do is Love and I will give you all the rest." True, real life consists of Silence, Harmony and Love. They fill the heart with gratitude towards the Absolute.

The soul, "timeless" and "reasonless", prevails over illusion and hence it *is.* Being the divine essence, it knows it is a part of Oneness.

When you no longer think that there is a beginning and an end, it is a sign that you have arrived, you have acquired the sense of belonging to the All, you have inner peace and no desire or emotional drive. The mind – and, along with it, the ego – has stepped aside. From that point on, God operates within you and you become pure awareness. Your search has reached the end.

Here lies the meaning of the phrase spoken about Jesus: *"Glory to God in the highest, and on earth peace, good will toward men."* Peace is God and God is with those who live in Peace and Love. Good will is Love (Divine Will) and awareness is Wisdom (Divine Mind).

Months earlier, I had asked Sai Baba (when we were inaugurating the year 2000) to grant me compassion of heart and peace of mind. He replied by calling for "non-attachment" and "sacrifice".

I listened to Him and obeyed His call. Consequently, I obtained what I had asked for. I drained the chalice, I emptied it, thus allowing Him to enter my heart and fill me with Peace and Love.

Gall was transformed into nectar and the bitter goblet turned into pure sweetness. I realized that the goblet represented the sacrifice of the self (ego) which, once transmuted into joy (nectar), announced the victory of the Spirit over matter.

The inner voice said: *"follow the path of the angels, that is, the path of devotion and silence".*

I dreamt of Sai Baba asking me what kind of work I wished to do. My reply was rather strange – I told Him that I loved watering plants and bringing them back to life. So, I was entrusted to take care of a garden. Did the garden represent humankind? And what about the "plants" I wished to water? Did they represent those whom I wanted to help restore their true life, that is, be themselves as the divine essence. Would I alleviate their heavy inner burden with words (water of Life, Truth and Love)?

The only sign of the return of the Christ (the Holy Spirit) was the awakening of the heart, the awakened consciousness. Plants represented people He would send to me and the garden of God was His humanness, according to the vision of the heart. I told the Divine Master: "If others could hear you as I do, they would certainly believe that You are indeed God".

I dreamt of Sai Baba again: He came to visit me in the room to correct my writings. We were sitting at a table and He was drawing some symbols which reminded me of the astrological symbols of the masculine and the feminine (Mars and Venus). I thought of the Androgyne (I understood that He wanted me to explain the meaning) and the union of complementary parts.

During the (most recent) interview, He asked me what I wanted, three times. In silence, my heart replied: "I want You, only You, always You", while the mind failed to grasp that He was talking to me. My wish was to love God with all of me, to find fulfilment in the Spirit and realize the redeeming unity.

When I woke up, I could not remember any of the drawings He had made, but I was certain they had remained within me. He confirmed, once more, that the realization of the Divine within was the mystic unity of the soul and the divine essence, the Spirit.

I asked Him for compassion and He asked me to detach myself from emotional ties. I asked Him for inner peace and He asked me to sacrifice all my desires.

I drained the goblet, just like He had instructed me to do through the inner voice. I lost everything but I found Him, the Spouse, Harmony, the Love I had always looked for, since birth.

His living presence in me is the fullness I had always longed for because He is reality, He is imagination, He is the dream, He is the inspiration, He is the work (form, creation), He is the Absolute (formlessness, the Creator).

With His vivifying presence, He was about to transform lead into pure gold in me. He says that, in order to enjoy the indescribable joy of the Spirit, instead of adoring God in the form with all kinds of flowers (ephemeral), we must adore Him in the heart (formless) with the eternal flowers of our virtues, such as non-violence, compassion, charity, sacrifice…and Love.

In that period, spiritual courses (for the students) were organized at Whitefield and Sai Baba used to deliver a speech every a day. He spoke about devotion and purity, saying: *"He who chooses God forgets about the world. He who chooses the world forgets about God. There is no other choice. God is our best friend, our Only friend – selfless and without desire."* He offered us an opportunity not to be wasted because tomorrow could be too late, as the same opportunity might not present itself again. This is because *"Human life is a rare opportunity to evolve."* Jesus said the same thing: *"Never put off till tomorrow what you can do today".*

I found myself so many times in the front line, in His presence. Tears of joy rolled down my cheeks each time my eyes met the effulgent beauty of His gaze which merged with mine. The Self, the Spouse, the best Friend who never abandoned me, lifetime after lifetime, the silent, respectful, caring witness to every event in life, was present when the eight doors (Chakras) opened up, to reveal Himself within me. I could then unite with Him in the perfect, harmonic balance of the impersonal and the personal, of the manifest and the hidden, of the Spirit and the body and soul.

He had me receive the eight keys (and subsequently the ninth one) as evidence of His assistance, support and celestial guidance. How fortunate I was to be blessed by

His Grace. It meant that what I had discovered in some esoteric books was true after all: the Spouse comes for us (the Spirit comes for the soul).

Sai Baba says: *"God seeks a pure man, an authentic devotee who is stable and constant. God is the only omnipresent being, so why go and look for It? In the world today, people are divided by many differences. They are one way inwardly and another way outwardly. Perverted minds whom God does not want, people who laugh instead of crying and who cry instead of laughing. God does not look for hypocrites who are human only in their physical form, but have a monkey mind.*

God wants human beings who behave like human beings and not like quadrumanes. A human mind hosts sacred and pure intelligence. Its qualities must therefore be expressed with natural, pure feelings and not artificially."

I dreamt of being in the company of Sai Baba. He asked me to accompany Him to the home of somebody I knew. When we arrived at a big villa in the countryside, I entered first to show Him the way. But we found some people sleeping in the living room, lying on sofas and completely covered with white sheets.

I was embarrassed and didn't know how to wake them up. Swami was there but they continued to sleep and couldn't see Him. I found it unacceptable, I was bewildered.

I woke up concerned. What was the dream's message? Did I see the whited sepulchres? Was I assigned the task to wake up those who slept even in the presence of God? I found that interpretation embarrassing (and over-resounding) and so I put things into proportion and reckoned that I certainly had to work hard to finish the book as soon as possible. Perhaps that was a way to help reawaken the consciousness of the sleepers.

In the previous dream, Sai Baba drew a symbol that reminded me of the perfect man, the Androgyne (the man consecrated to the Spirit, in the mystic matrimony of the soul and the Self) and the inner voice confirmed that we could become complete and perfect to serve God if we left every bond behind.

The following morning, while waiting for the *darshan*, I saw a rainbow in the sky. It was round and it enclosed and crowned the *Mandir*. I had seen an identical rainbow four years earlier, in a vision, exactly on the same spot.

I remembered that seeing a rainbow in its royal magnificence symbolized inner enlightenment. Consciousness was reawakening and I was going through a magic and sacred period. I tried to sooth all the wounds in the heart by filling it with compassion and I could fly again on the wings of the Holy Spirit, that is, with His support. Sai Baba gave me everything I had asked for from my heart, and much more. Indeed: "When you discover that you are divine, you are at one with God."

I wrote for nearly three months, continuously inspired, when the Divine Master showed me the date of my return home (where I still had some unfinished business to attend to).

To me, the message of the inner voice announced a temporary parting from Him: *"The offer was made many years ago, when you offered me your life that was mine already, but you didn't know it yet. The sacrifice of all the ties and desires must be accomplished through detachment and renouncement, so that the gifts intended for you can manifest, namely discernment and awareness of the divine in you, as Power, Wisdom and Love, as the means for achieving peace and liberation from the karma. I have personally promised that to you, remember? Then, the coarse metal will be transformed into gold and it will be sublimated, pure gold. This is why purification is required – only a pure heart can recognise the pure essence it is made of.*

I am the Holy Spirit, I am the Ocean, I am the Paramatma. You are still a spark, Atma. May your thought be only One: attaining Me. SAI RAM."

Power, Wisdom and Love represent the trinity of the figures of the Father, Mother and Son. Therefore, the Divine Master was announcing to me that the Trinity would soon settle down within me, permanently. I was dumfounded.

Only a year earlier I discovered I was incarnated (also but not only) in this lifetime due to an unrealized wish from a previous life (the wish to have a child). In this regard, the Upanishad say that, fundamentally, there are three obstacles to liberation: desiring a partner, desiring a child and desiring wealth.

Owing to a gift from God (my son arrived as a gift from Heaven), I overcame the last desire (obstacle)[155] during this lifetime. The road was clear and I could finally reach my goal.

Living together with my son was difficult but it helped both of us evolve and come closer to God, or Sai Baba. I realized what the fundamental issue in the "game" of this lifetime was during my journey to Crete. Illusion yielded ground to the reality of the Self. This expression was most adequate as the conclusion of that last trip, when it comes to the person I was never going to be again.

When I left, months before, I felt in my heart that I would return liberated. Sai Baba would set me free to confirm that sacrifice lead to true happiness (not the kind of happiness the world usually intends) stemming from the union with God, with the Self.

My only expectation was given body – the expectation to feel at one with Truth and Love. I wanted to experience the time of God, the eternal present in the temple of God (the heart), to speak, feel and act from the heart. As the saying goes: *"See how a man lives and you will know how he thinks. That is how we discover the value of coherence."*

And now, the circular rainbow appeared in the sky, just like in the vision I'd had years before, to crown Sai Baba's temple and His temple in me – my heart.

How can the river stop flowing into the ocean when it reaches the estuary mouth (Knowledge of the real Self)?

The truest part of me felt I had reached the destination - the ocean.

The true Self was the Spouse I had looked for for so many years, but He was already within me, always waiting for me.

Human nature in terms of physicality (feminine, in terms of created life) came to recognize the divine nature, as the spiritual essence (masculine, in terms of creating life, being pure energy), owing to the awareness received from the Holy Spirit. My inner work was accomplished. In the dream made in India, Sai Baba showed me that the masculine and feminine principles were going to reach completeness in the Androgyne, because perfection leading to the divine man and subsequently to the solar angel (spiritual sun) could be obtained only in the harmonious fusion of the two complementary aspects.

Achieving enlightenment means achieving the Spirit, or the Sun within. By realizing the true Self, we become like tiny suns; we are able to see God, the Light, that is, the Sun of the Spirit.

The inner voice conveyed that I should follow the path of the angels (of devotion and silence). Was I on the path of the solar angel (the perfect man)?

I understood with my heart that there could be no true Compassion or Universal Love without the detachment from emotional ties. Unless we renounce our desires, there can be no real inner peace or stability, since both factors serve to promote the opening of the heart to the awareness of the Self.

Owing to this opening, we speak "all the languages", in the sense that we learn to speak the language of God, that of Truth and Love, as the only language the entire humankind can comprehend. That vision ripened in me.

He who surrenders to the Spirit nurtures no doubts, has faith in the Spirit and is no longer afraid. This was the incomparable truth and I felt I was its living witness.

I left on the day Sai Baba had established for me, since He had me find (the moment I asked Him to show me the departure date) the numbers corresponding to the days of departure and arrival home. I carried back some new, vivifying and intoxicating stuff – the completeness within, the union that no one and nothing could ever scratch or dissolve, the liberating unity, the bond with the Spirit.

It was as if the drop (the divine spark) was about to merge with the ocean, maintaining (in the Self) the "seed" of awareness and union with the All, and become an integral part of that ocean of pure energy. The merging was only a question of time and time had no value at all at that point.

The Avatar Sai Baba is the living expression of that pure energy, the heart of the Universe, the Constant Integrated Awareness (*Sat Chit Ananda*). He descended to earth to reawaken in us the awareness that will open the door to Cosmic Consciousness, for all humankind.

Only by surrendering to Him and by trusting Him could I believe and feel certain that I had spoken, felt and seen God as the Spirit of Life, Love and Truth. Had I stopped at the level of reason (the inferior mind), I would have come to the conclusion that it was sheer fantasy. The three zeroes – overcoming material attachments, emotional ties and self-attachment (ego), in order to see God – were before my eyes and in my hand, in the three diamonds of the ring that Sai Baba had put on my finger to remind me that I could find Harmony and live in the vibration of the divine essence within only through balance and equidistance. We create miracles in our lives. Blessed are those who suffer and will be at one with God one day because they were able to transform suffering into an act of Love. I'd suffered and struggled so much to reach a higher level of consciousness (or a reward) and in turn I was given the capacity to reach the essence of things, discover the deep purpose of life and regain true freedom.

When man receives the gift of Divine Love from the Spirit, he accepts his *Dharma* (destiny in terms of duty and righteous behaviour) with tranquillity and trust. He becomes a new person – according to my personal experience.

I learned that I had overcome illusion owing to my devotion, but I didn't crow over my victory because I was still living in a physical body (I repeated it to myself to keep it in mind at all times).

Shortly after my return home, I found the last key, the ninth one, which fell out from the luggage of my son[156] who had just returned from India. *Sathya* (Truth) was inscribed on it.

Then I dreamt of Sai Baba hugging me with infinite affection, reminding me of the rules of behaviour to follow (*Dharma*). In brief, the rules said: the Knowledge of God is the very essence of life (the essence of True Love) and the identification with the Beloved (the true Self or Atma in us).

The following night I dreamt of a newly born "divine" child. Its skin was bronze-gold and luminous and it was shining in its naked radiance. It was wearing gold bracelets with precious gems around the wrists and ankles and it was rubbing its nose against my face while I was looking after it, showing its superb beauty to everyone. Was it perhaps Bala Krishna (the little Krishna)?

The Spirit was born in me in the form of that divine child – that is how I interpreted that simple and marvellous, essentially sacral dream.

In this messianic age of crucial changes, our task as "human beings" is to obtain Harmony with the All, to utilize the divine potential in us for a good cause, for the Light, continuously balancing every discordant note with Love. In this way we will remain unperturbed and aware that everything is in the hands of God and that His plan is perfect.

In a Gnostic reading, I found an explanation for the parable of Jesus, when He invites us to bring out the child in us to enter the Kingdom of God. Newly born children's divine essence is still clear of all the aggregates (*karmic* debts born from emotional involvements from past incarnations) from previous lifetimes and this is why they are considered pure. Those aggregates are gradually structured until they form, around the age of twenty, the new personality and the mental body (inferior mind), with all the limitations related to it.

Man must be born to the Spirit to become divine again, to cancel those aggregates which have become his personality (essentially made of flaws and desires) and break free from the limitations of the mind. Then he can rediscover, deep in the heart, the divine essence or the true Self.

I realized why the sin against the Holy Spirit (understood as a repeated sin – when a person keeps making the same "mistake", although he has been made aware of it – and a sin against the divine energy, understood as sexual energy) could not be forgiven. The reason is that, since the "mistake" was repeated or misused, the same energy that would have otherwise redeemed the soul, to eventually heal human nature and make it divine, reduced human nature to animal nature.

Under those circumstances, when the low vibration frequency of physicality has no possibility to tune itself with the higher frequency of the Spirit, man cannot invoke the Divine Grace but must expiate his destiny, that is, pay the debt in full.

Again, we and no one else are the creators of our happiness or unhappiness.

The Divine Game of human life is a test-bed to regain angelic purity (lost when we descended to the world of matter) in the union of complementary elements, enriched by the awareness of life's intrinsic value that could be developed in us only through worldly experiences, for us to be able to return to the Light – this time with the "awareness" that the only true life is that of the Spirit. All this becomes comprehensible when we enlarge the narrow vision of the individual consciousness (with its beliefs: one life, the current one, and one world, the one we live in) into collective consciousness and then into Christ or Cosmic Consciousness, embracing the life of the entire Universe, visible and invisible, with its variety of realms and dimensions beyond the limits of time and space.

I dreamt of a long procession of people – among whom I recognized my son, friends and acquaintances and many others – stretching before the Divine Master, honouring Him in the act of kissing His feet.

Did such dreams stem from my desire to take part in the collective awakening of consciousnesses?

Back into my usual environment, everything seemed perfect – including the imperfections. What once seemed like Hell was now Paradise, seen through the pink lenses of the Divine Love.

This is the power of the Holy Spirit, when we rediscover it within.

NOTES: CHAPTER XVI

153. And it actually was so, because the book was completed five years later.

154. This event turned into reality soon after that.

155. I never cared about wealth. As far as the partner is concerned, I found God as the Spirit of Life in me, as the only true friend.

156. He had no idea how it had ended up there or whose it was.

XVII

"Those who have written generously have not written in vain".

Joyce.

Back home, a friend of mine volunteered to type my manuscripts written during the months of my stay in India. Our work in front of her pc continued patiently throughout the summer. I sent the draft to an editor in September, convinced that my task was done. However, as an Indian saint put it: "A truth-seeker's battle goes on day and night and continues as long as he lives." My struggle was not over yet. Moreover, the dream of offering the book to Sai Baba on His Birthday (the next November) was still very much a dream, although on that occasion, during the *darshan*, He made a blessing gesture on the disc I had brought with me. That was my twenty-second trip to India.

From the very start, I had associated the trips with the Tarot cards of the Major Arcana – the symbolism of each card invariably matched, by analogy, the significance of each respective journey.

That one in particular was referred to the last Arcane – "The Fool". In terms of numbers, it corresponded to zero. (in all, they are twenty-two, but the last one represents the zero).

That year was so important for my path. The twentieth trip, in which the mystical marriage of the soul with the Spirit was consecrated, corresponded to the Tarot card no. 20 – 'Judgement'[157].

During the interview granted to our group, Sai Baba materialized the gold ring with three diamonds and put it on my right ring finger. He therefore 'married me'. My travelling companions interpreted this event in the same way and shared the same feelings.

This event triggered the creative inspiration that helped me come up with the first draft of the manuscript, shortly thereafter. In fact, in a week's time upon my return to Italy, I was called back to India for an indefinite period of time, or, for as long as necessary to do the work - or at least to prepare the draft – that was waiting to be done for years. However, I realized that only later.

The command of the inner voice merely informed me that I had to leave, nothing else.

That was the twenty-first trip, corresponding to the Tarot card no. 21 – 'World'[158]. This arcane expresses the culmination of the work undertaken, the completion, the Kingdom of God, it expresses the glory and the victory of the humble, that is, those who recognize and accept in their hearts the Cosmic Order, but also the hardships foreseen by fate, sublimating the pain caused by the defeats in life.

In brief, it represents the squaring of the circle, the philosopher's stone, the awareness of Harmony, or Gnosis, as the supreme reward for the efforts dedicated to the search for Truth.

I couldn't help drawing a parallel between each arcane and the respective journey (the symbolism of the numbers). I was exhilarated about how well it reflected what I was going through. The Divine Game unfolding around me was so perfect.

As always, the course of destiny took care of bringing me down to earth. At this point, the twenty-second trip (the last one in the same year) enters the stage. As I said already, in the Tarot, 22 corresponds to zero and the card is 'Fool'[159]. This was the last secret entrusted to me by the Tarot, which implied a possible beginning of a new cycle, characterized by humility and surrendering to the Divine Will, but also the closure of this cycle which coincided with the end of the second millennium and the cessation of attachments and desires I'd had up till then. It was like: Cheer up and start from scratch!

I was still facing two possible options: all or nothing, i.e. spiritual realization or mundane slavery. I had chosen the first option and that was the occasion when I confirmed it.

To help me understand that the work (the book) was still unaccomplished, the Spirit resorted to a thousand tricks. However, albeit with good intentions, I diverted them every time to other 'targets'.

In the first year of the third millennium, for example, I received several pens as gifts. I thought I had already finished writing my book – pity they arrived too late. I made a mistake because I was unaware of the Divine Master's plan. He was leading me by the hand all the time, towards new goals. The Spirit is incredibly patient with us when we show total blindness for what It is trying to submit to our attention. Despite Its assistance, we are distracted by the ego.

Self-realization or the mystical marriage between soul and Spirit is achieved by giving priority to the Love for the Divine Spirit over any other bond (through non-attachment) or desire (through renunciation). The inner voice confirmed what had happened in the presence of Sai Baba and the ring on my finger was a tangible proof. What happened did not imply my withdrawal in a forest or a place in Heaven. I was not yet exempted from the game of life and its obstacle race. However, I was in a better position than before, as I discovered that the inner dimension of peace was timidly stabilizing in me. I managed to paint pink even the gloomiest landscapes where I found myself immersed in once in a while.

Someone said: *"When you no longer think in terms of beginning and end, you have reached your destination, having conquered the sense of belonging to the All. You have inner peace and no desire. The mind, and with it the ego, have stepped aside.*

From that moment God works through you. You become pure awareness and the search is over.".

In a sense, this is how I felt, but the search was still far from being over. The inner voice dominated the scenery of life for months, lovingly and authoritatively, with increasingly long and detailed messages ranging over diverse and complex topics. My small mind would get stuck, especially when the voice spoke about new, totally unknown dimensions.

I was often told that the sky was my permanent residence, that the *karma* was about to end its sidereal race and that I would return to the stars: *"Try to orient yourself in this world. You cannot imagine how much inner light you have to give, or to offer to those who are alien to Light, being earthly. There are many things for you to do in the future. Just wait and see, they will present themselves. Dear sister, you will draw to you doves of light from the sidereal vacuum. Love Me and honour Me and you will be a sovereign of time when the shadow distances itself from your divine essence. You will be a swift traveller of these unfathomed depths and you'll comprehen the task you have to accomplish.*

Let bygones be bygones, nothing belongs to you. Heaven is your permanent residence, Heaven is your family, where friendly souls await your glorious return. Brighten your steps with the Sun's light. A thousand Suns are nothing in the presence of the light of God. I am your Beloved. Fill yourself with Me. Rejoice, the time has come for you to return to Me.

Gracious wave, the ocean awaits you, it has prepared the place for you. Do not worry. Although your divine Twin Soul is far away, He will join you and both of you will come to Me, for the final union. I should be the one celebrating that great moment, and you should become great with the means I provide you with.

Do not ask, do not beg, I know your heart but I may not talk about things that are yet to be fully realized. Your karma is about to end its sidereal race and you will return to the stars. Your permanent residence awaits you, as well as the joy and love of the One who has never abandoned you, not even for a moment on this Earth, where you have shed so many tears.

It's over, darling, the race is finished. Your son will be with you at the investiture, soon to see you take part in a major design you will take part in, as a valuable pawn in the game larger than you, thus completing the design you have been part of. You will no longer be influenced by flattery or illusion. But do not regret this, as you are now immune to the vile contagion of inert matter. You belong to a larger star and that star is you. On a golden morning, you will find a blue mark on your hands. This will be the time you have yearned for for so long. Never stop to sing My praises and Glory will come to you. Peace and Love".

What I called an obstacle race, in earthly words, was actually coming to an end. Or was I just interpreting everything with my limited rationality?

The messages I received depicted a rosy picture of the future, made of Love and Harmony. I was going to experience joy and the love of the One who had never abandoned me, not even for a moment. Although I still played part in the grand design, like a precious pawn, I was now immune to the 'vile contagion of inert matter'.

At times, I was benignly accused of refusing to listen to the wonderful things communicated to me, such as the reference to a life lived two thousand years ago, next to the Divine Master of the time: *"At that time you loved Me and followed Me zealously. Do the same in this lifetime"*... or when I was foretold that the moment was approaching when I would *"cross the threshold of reason to explore unfathomable spaces, unattainable with the knowledge you presently have". ..."Do not think, let Me guide you. Do not act, let Me move your hands to form new algorithms, to illuminate your consciousness and expand it more and more, into open spaces. Remove yourself from your body and physicality. The Spirit inhabits you and you already hear It, although with difficulty. Soon enough, the time will come when the Spirit will speak through you. There will be no need for you to have a personal life of your own. You will be at Its service – completely and permanently. You are due to receive this honour, but keep working so as to be worthy of it, until you become pure Spirit again. On earth, fatal events will pour in, but you are called to stay, to bring relief wherever I send you – overseas, in distant lands. I will always be by your side – never forget that.*

You will release an incredible force and nothing will oppose your will, which is why it will always have to be My Will, Mine only, and this is the only way for Me to continue being by your side.

My dearest, your days will be utilized to spread My voice and My word everywhere you go, never forget. You will transcend the mind. Only then will you reveal the divine game you have been called to play. I will not keep you waiting for a long time if you can row against the current of mundane life that would like to be your sovereign master again. I have not established that for you. You will be safe, you'll soon be rewarded for your trust in Me. Keep loving Me and honouring Me in every instant of the life I gave you. I want you to be a witness of My presence, of My essence.

Benevolent you will be with whoever may be at your side. Your eyes will no longer see the evil and this will be the salt of your future life. You will leave your present surrounding and return to being a wave in the ocean that I represent for every well-intentioned human being. On the path, you will meet only people full of godliness. Now is the time to change the pace of your currently sad and tough life. I proclaim you messenger of Joy and it will be clear to everyone that I love you.

My Love will have to expand from your heart, to fill with pure gold the becoming of your future. Everything you touch will turn into something precious. May you always be dressed in humility and may Love be your favourite food. Warm yourself up against My flame and you will be amma[160], adored by everyone. I will have no more secrets for you, as you are now becoming Me. You have passed the last test of the voice I had sent in order to tempt you Your pure heart did not give in to the admittedly tough impact. I hereby declare you sovereign over life and arcane death. You have the keys of the kingdom of the door that denies access to those who care not about the kingdom. Do come in, My dearest, take this opportunity, it is so rare nowadays. Just take care of Me and the rest will come naturally to you, without any pretext."

It is not my wish to elaborate at length the content of the message, but I also realize it is the only way for the reader of these lines to comprehend what the author experienced then and is still experiencing.

The first day of the year, perhaps to inaugurate the new millennium, I received another message from this 'soundless' voice that inserted itself in my thoughts (which were no longer mine in those instances, but belonged to the Spirit). That was how I received all my interior messages. The message said:

"Awake, a new life is about to be born in you and in a thousand other creatures. Together, you will illuminate the Earth with a new Light – My Light, the Light of cosmic Love. I will be guiding you all along. I will direct your footsteps towards other creatures, and they will be many!

The new world is here, help them discover it so that everybody can let their hearts know that I have always been there and will always be, that I will always have Love for you, human beings. You are part of Me, and I am the most beautiful part in you. Make it shine like a star. You are the firmament you see reflected in the convex space around you.

Your home is waiting for you, but it is rare to find someone who understands this. When you clear the mind of all the thoughts of the past, you will be the gardener helping those who refuse to see that the time has come to bloom in the sun illuminating a new life made of nothing but Love, Love and Love. You will water the seeds with the water of life so they can grow stronger, with ease. I will take care of the harvest and you will take care of the goodness you have found in every seed[161]. The Spirit will give you more and more support, with each new bud. The number of flowers in my garden will grow, until each seed becomes essence[162] and realizes that only Oneness exists."

The last words reminded me of another phrase I had heard before, which was repeated later on: "*I am the One who is, and everything dissolves in Me.*"

That was only the beginning. In the following months I received other messages, depicting a 'landscape' that I used to admire in astonishment and amazement, unable to orient myself in the sceneries described with accurate precision, especially in the passages referring to me. I couldn't tell which part of me, though. The way in which the Spirit spoke about me, an ordinary mortal, was overly grandiloquent and at the same time very exciting.

At any rate, I could only write down what I was told, nothing else. I did not feel like making questions or seeking clarifications regarding the content of the messages. Those sacred moments required absolute silence of the mind.

One day, walking down the street, I passed by a billboard, saying: "Caring for the Self: Harmony". That phrase struck me because it was divine in its perfect wholeness. Unfortunately, it was used to publicize alternative body wellness therapies. Those few words expressed a great truth, visible to the eyes of the heart. Only through Harmony can we attain the divine essence in us, the true Self.

The inner voice had announced that the Spirit would speak through me. I thought that the realization of the divine essence in me would mean, among other things, speaking from the heart, that is, spreading the word of God, i.e. the Truth. That was my own interpretation of what I had been told.

Many years before, I had written that I had only one expectation: "To feel at one with the Truth, with the Absolute". From that moment on, things have always been that way, even if my mind was quite unable to understand my prayer to God. I was also not quite clear about why I was so surprised by the fact that I had come so close to achieving this goal, because I'd worked very hard to get there. It might have been a game of the ego, to let me view the goal as something too ambitious or even unreachable, in order to demotivate me and drive me off the path I was on for so many years.

I knew with certainty that I hadn't had any mundane ambitions, since childhood. Was I perhaps trying to convince myself, like so many other people do, that God did not speak to ordinary mortals, but only to prophets and saints?

Leaving aside the prophets and the saints, why did Jesus say we must become children again to enter the Kingdom of Heaven, the abode of the Father? The condition I felt closest to was that of a child – not that of a prophet or saint. But there was nothing else for me to do except to simply accept the fact that I'd succeeded, by working hard over the years, searching for the real me, being a child again, or rather, finding in me the girl I had always been, the girl I never ceased to be. I believe the same thing happens to all of us, although not everyone comes to realize it.

The child in us sticks with us. Paradoxically so, I worked so hard to recover the dimension so simple and natural from which I addressed God at my earliest age. That is how I called Him then, without any additional epithets.

At that time, I was strongly convinced that He was my interlocutor – the Almighty – and I still preserve clear memories and written evidence of that.

Whoever reaches the true Self, the permanent centre of gravity in the heart, he stops desiring, having finally found what he has always been looking for –

completeness, wholeness, being no longer a 'fragment' but the 'Oneness' within. I have always nurtured such a yearning in my heart. So, why was I amazed that the Spirit manifested as a "living voice", albeit soundless, in my heart and in my thoughts?

I deeply realized the meaning of the saying: *"You are what you search for"*. No doubt, this other one is true, as well: *"You are what you think"*.

I came to realize that telling the truth implied speaking the language of God. Also, reporting what we hear from the voice within is prophecy – to put it briefly. I sometimes reasoned with myself, trying to play down what was happening. I would say to myself: Where is the problem? You're just a prophet of the third millennium. What is the big deal, compared to those – mere mortals like you – who fearlessly roam around sidereal spaces, waiting to land on Mars or who knows what other planet in the Solar System?

The first month of the year was not over yet, when a new message arrived:
"Focus on Me. I am the Light that shines forever. Love Me and I will love you every moment. Your breath will be an ode to joy and the air around you will observe the ritual of life every day, a life that will be divine, even in its most hidden corners from the sight of ordinary mortals.

Nothing will overshadow you any more, creature of Light – that is neither common nor mortal. You are life's relentless beat. Intoxicating is the scent emanating from your heart, filled by the desire to tell Me that you love Me.

It is Love that unites us, divine one, in arabesques of Light that will always be the morning light. The sun will set no more on you who found Me. Likewise, death, evil, sin or hatred will have no meaning for you any longer. You have crossed the gates of the clouds, built up to enormous proportions by the illusory vanity of worldly nature. The sky will always be clear for you, as an epiphany of new colours, more brilliant than those your eyes have ever enjoyed. You have offered Me seven petals, scarlet[163] flames, to propitiate this year blessed by Trinity. I married you in 2000. It was the year in which Oneness emerged from the two (mystic couple) and the soul and Spirit united. The three zeroes were achieved.

In this and the coming years, Unity, or Oneness, will be increasingly felt and Its powers will descend like gifts on you, so that you can bestow them on those who have no Light, Peace or Humility. You will give an example of Love to all Mankind, always hungry, albeit unknowingly, for more Divine Love that only Truth can yield, to satisfy the heart."

The last words alone were enough to explain the mystery of Love which was Sathya Sai Baba. He, the embodiment of Truth (Sathya), filled us up with the Love that emanated from His aura of Light, overwhelming us when His eyes rested on us, meeting our eyes. The three zeros mentioned by the voice were the three steps to annihilate the ego: overcoming material attachment, emotional ties and self-attachment (the ring materialized for me by Sai Baba had three diamonds).

By some strange coincidence, the same year Cartier came up with an ad of a ring (identical to mine) called Trilogy: for yesterday, for today, for tomorrow, for the next thousand years (of the golden Age, I'd say) to celebrate the third millennium. Two days later, I received another message (it was a continuous flow of nectar) which said:

"You must be certain about what you are going to do under My eternal guidance. You will come to Me and more Light will enter your life to bring clarity into every corner of your heart. You will see the weight you took upon yourself in distant times, in all its obviousness. This will help you get out of the narrowness of consciousness today, to acquire a galactic dimension of 'seeing'.

When you return, you'll find your star, Sirius, but you will not remain there for long, as other tasks await you. You will perform them like a faithful servant of your God, without rebelling. No one else will take your place of Light next to Me, if not your Self.

You are already aware that time has no consistency, and so nothing can upset you anymore.

I'll wait for you. You belong to My bosom and to My bosom you will come back. You are part of Me; you are Me - My eternal essence.

An ordeal of human experiences awaits you. It will serve to purify you of the last cravings.

After that, you will be free to move, at My command, to reach the farthest corners of the world. There will be nothing wrong in what you do, never forget that, as long as you remember to do the will of you-know-Who.

You must become detached to regain the freedom your soul aspires to all the time. What else can I say that you do not feel already? Yes, you have received gifts and you have recognized them. My flame of Love is burning in your heart. You can already see the Light shining and therefore it helps everyone to learn to love Me.

Build a huge fire of Love with My heat. Let it burn in every district, to illuminate everyone's path.

To you I will send people and you'll be their lens. You will be a microscope of Light, ready to discover the 'germs' of the Love you will find everywhere, even in unthinkable places; you will realize that you can't live without it.

Life changes incessantly. Always be the source of Light, disperse every shadow. Testify to everyone that shadow (hatred, evil, death) has no consistence and that the Light is here already, illuminating everyone. It is All-present and copious and what remains to be revealed now is the resonance of the heart."

This message announced the arrival of new trials, which were quick to come, so I did not have to 'wait' for a long time.

The gifts I was told to have recognized referred to what I had received with the Grace of charismas, that is, spiritual clairvoyance or intuitive vision, namely the ability to prophesize, or receive[164] messages from the Spirit, and the ability to heal – understood as the healing of the heart through listening and advice. The latter ability was mentioned in the messages several times, with regard to the task assigned to me to spiritualize matter and encourage inner understanding in others, the alchemical sublimation of lead into gold, or transformation of consciousness from individual to Cosmic, until the communion of the soul with the Spirit of Life takes place, followed by the liberation from *karma*, the rebirth into the Spirit, and finally the apostleship as the only possible practice of divine life.

A few days later, my heart was flooded by the wisdom of the Spirit and I received another message:

"What is there in front of you that you can't see you possess within? You are the clear mirror of a thousand rivers flowing from that One Source that has given life to all forms of creation. Soon, you will be asked to act and act you will have to, to affirm the sacred purpose that dwells in your heart. Soon[165], you will see the dawn of this new day. Rejoice, as you will carry the Light everywhere around. You will be recognized as the shiny[166] one.

Do not care about the ego. It will be replaced by Me so that you can do your best everywhere and sing My praises and My name, as long as you reside on this Earth full of sorrows, miseries and deceits.

You will illuminate everything with My effulgent splendour within the fullness of your heart. Yours or Mine, it will soon matter no more. Only Oneness counts, it gives life and warmth. You will no longer see the difference because all is essence and God is essential. Sublimate the energy that sustains you and you will be closer and closer to the Ray you belong to.

Assistants will come to your aid, rest assured, and you will soon find proof of this. You are about to inaugurate a new beginning - you who have been able to find lessons in the changes[167], with diligent patience, and tell good from evil. You have found out thus that nothing really exists, except for the Self of a pure and sincere heart. Like a diamond, that heart dwells in you, now that you have come to join Me. I vest you with the power to reconcile the irreconcilable and to restore the kingdom of true things, in the mission I gave you, and you will carry it on as long as you live. 'Black and white' (diversity) does not abide in the higher realms, where the union of opposites fears no diversity.

God loves you. If you love Him too, you become God!"

It was rather difficult for me to follow the concise and essential logic, by which I was vested with a mission I knew virtually nothing about.

I thought we could reconcile the irreconcilable only through Love and nothing else. And so, like always in similar circumstances, I laid down arms of reason at the feet of divine awareness and surrendered to God.

In those days there was another strange coincidence. I saw a billboard in the street, reading: "Do not think. Look at me".

I frequently received messages in rhyme. I subsequently discovered that Sai Baba, at His very young age, wrote letters in rhyme to His devotees.

In the same month I received two messages, very different from each other. The first said:

"Destiny is turning bright; the beloved may well come to honour Me. She will be given the fruits of patience, spent to overcome the uglier moments that are forever gone, together with the long disputes[168].

Harmony, from now on, will be your garment, woven with soft threads and colours, its warp yarn made of Love and Peace. In this way, the advice and the answers will be just right.

Point of Light in this vast world! Forever cheerful from now on will be your mood. In the upper realms of you we rejoice[169], although around you, one can't hear a voice.

Balance between firmness and clemency while you act as a fair and impartial judge of all those situations that cannot be settled by science. You will be exploring unknown worlds. Never reject help and be aware, with great humility, that everyone will be My messenger sent to you to enhance your divinity.

You'll have to be more and more unattached from everything, so that you can climb the mountain of your heart, higher and higher.

The peak is in you, My beloved one. You have always worked hard, courageously and relentlessly."

For decades I used to consult the *I Ching* (a Chinese oracle). Since I stopped talking to God, I consulted the ancient Chinese wisdom when I wished to be enlightened on important decisions. That habit remained even after I'd resumed the dialogue with Him, as I considered the *I Ching* to be an instrument of divine wisdom. The responses I received often informed me that I needed to accumulate power in righteousness, to be the source of life when I returned to the world with a task of great responsibility.

In my dreams I climbed and reached very high peaks several times. During an interview, Sai Baba told me that Tibet (referring to Kailash, the sacred mountain I wanted to visit) would come to me.

The inner voice told me that I would be a fair and impartial judge. My destiny number is eight, which in the Tarot corresponds to the arcane of Justice. Was there a connection? I didn't know the answer.

God's concept of justice does not correspond to that of humans. His free gift is the Law of Forgiveness and Grace. His justice is granted for free to those who live righteously, that is, with faith in God and according to His Will – as I had learned from experience.

Among the received messages, there was often a reference to non-attachment, a recurrent topic in the discourses of Jesus, such as when He said that one must die to be reborn, or to resurrect, and that we must disavow ourselves to be able to follow Him.

Non-attachment, along with renunciation, represents the so-called "initiatory death", which is a prelude to the rebirth in the Spirit. Through this journey we are offering life to God, making a gift of ourselves to humanity (which is God), through selfless service.

This choice is one of the possibilities to experience Christ Consciousness, through which all that is necessary for the evolution of the soul is revealed, because at that point there are no boundaries between us and the All. Supreme wisdom stems from devotion and hence we become pure consciousness (bodies of Light).

There are other possibilities (pathways) to reach this goal, such as meditation which, for those who practice it constantly and correctly, can be the simplest, although certainly not the most common way.

Another way accessible to everybody is the one suggested by Sai Baba, appropriate for the age we live in: the constant and continuous repetition of God's name (whatever it may be according to the various religions). In India it is called *namasmarana*.

Sai Baba says that the inner voice is the Christ Consciousness coming to bring Light, Love, Truth and Life. Those simple but great words hold the mystery of the initiatory transition from the 3rd, earthly dimension to the 5th, spiritual dimension (and even to the 6th and 7th dimension).

Jesus said that we had to become children again to enter the Kingdom of Heaven, that is, to get in touch with the Christ Consciousness within us. This confirmed that I had returned to being a child as I loosened the constraints life had imposed on me. When we realize the true Self within and attain imperturbability (by breaking free from the grip of the ego we become imperturbable), nothing can distract us from the divine centre, or the spiritual heart, and I was actually experiencing that.

Everything goes on the usual way in daily life; it's just that we don't get involved so much. Once we've settled the *karmic* debts of the past, we get ready for a new task: aiding those who are willing to take the same path to liberation. At this point, words like 'cross', 'sacrifice', 'blood' become synonymous with Love and spiritual growth and not with pain, just like light and water become synonymous with divine Knowledge and Christ Consciousness.

When the ego is no longer active, there is indeed no more pain, suffering, or fear of death.

The second message, received in January 2001, turned out to be prophetic months later:

"Don't be upset, there is nothing to explain. You have already been warned against what is going to happen. Sooner or later, profound disarray in the world will create concern and fear in the hearts.

With regard to the black clouds that will cover the sky this year, there is nothing to be afraid of. Everything will be fine eventually and Light will triumph. Dark days and bitter grievances will strike everybody, because every heart will have to melt down. Only those who have faith in God the Saviour will find peace and will be filled with Love. A cloudless sky will reflect the entire Universe, as the light reflects in the poor and the King, alike.

That Light is I, or what you call God, over and above the parties, sciences and arts. I see oneness in the opposites, without doing injustice to anyone. I bestow life and death and everyone gets his portion of fate, but I see neither difference, nor pain or suffering. Those who have understood the Truth stand in the middle. No religion will get you out of 'prison' – you must see oneness in everyone, without hurting anyone (Help ever, hurt never!)."

During the events of 11 September 2001, to which the message makes clear reference, I was in India, at Puttaparthi.

It was only upon my return to Italy the following month that I learned about what had happened in New York. I hadn't felt the awful 'shock wave' caused by the mass media in the wake of that devastating attack, a 'wave' that had not taken into account that the best protection against evil was Love, not fear and violence. Those are the sole makers of the war in Iraq unleashed subsequently, as the consequence of that event.

We should always bear in mind that both Sai Baba and Jesus invite to respond to evil with goodness.

Once again, the need to make a choice transpired from the messages I received because, although destiny does not depend on us, what does depend is whether we focus our mind within to find true peace, or on the outside world, littered with confusion, anxiety and restlessness.

It is hard to admit, but the fundamental decision concerns two possibilities: either to continue to follow this fake world and give up of the real life or do our utmost and seek the Truth, or the Spirit, and live by putting theory into practice. Living in God's Grace is the only 'real life'.

So many times I came across difficult, stagnant situations, or people who couldn't find solutions to their problems and therefore placed them for my attention. I noticed a clear tendency to hope that one day something would descend from above, by some kind of magic, and every problem will be resolved.

In most cases, this hope boils down to a disappointment because it is essentially an illusion.

The real determination to change things is based on the sound premise that we want to bring about changes by making specific, sometimes radical choices regarding something old, sterile or obsolete that has weighted upon our lives to the degree of immobilizing it in a chronic state of deadlock.

Starting from the mind (ego) – our thoughts – we must change the habits of a life sick with selfishness. This pathway can lead to incredible goals and, as Sai Baba says, you can become masters of your own destiny. This is the old story (but always instructive) of the glass, which must be emptied, or else it cannot be refilled. That year I went to India no less than three times. I had regenerating experiences and returned home filled with more and more Divine Grace and inner clarity each time.

I discovered that being obsessed with finding the true Self, was a manifestation of Divine Grace, as there is no real search without Grace.

I never ceased to be amazed with each new discovery, revelation or enlightenment. I was increasingly enthusiastic and attentive to any sign that I picked, as a gift from Heaven.

The world of the spirit is full of inexhaustible magic, whose wealth is like a gold-bearing vein. As it gradually comes to light, it manifests itself in all its splendour. The initiations I felt I had received through the eyes of the Divine Master were marked by Silence – His voice – which is the most eloquent of the divine teachings, since the Truth is beyond words and beyond any possible explanation of the mind.

All the effort to retell the story of my journey to the Truth eventually resulted in providing mere indications. It is not surprising that I often mentioned 'signs', speaking about my writing.

Hindu sacred scriptures report that, when the merits outweigh the demerits in a lifetime, the subtle body first goes to Heaven (higher astral realms and 5th dimension) and then returns to earth. When the merits and demerits are equal, we are reborn soon after, without an interval in other dimensions. But when the demerits outweigh the merits, we end up in hell (lower astral worlds) and then (in due time) we are reborn on earth (after we have served the sentence).

The *karma* related to the present life should be extinguished during the same life (ideally). The *karma* of the past lives (prior to the current incarnation) can be burned by a single spark of wisdom.

I was fascinated by this spiritual interpretation of life. It gave me inner peace because it finally helped me understand the origin of many "unresolved issues" that could not be explained solely with reference to my present life. Several years later, in India, by Divine Grace I experienced the aforementioned events, experienced firsthand, even though I considered them beyond the reach of human understanding. Because, it is indeed incomprehensible if assessed by reason, and yet it is perfectly credible to the intelligence of the heart.

I discovered something new every day. Life was more and more beautiful and God was increasingly generous with me.

I realized that the degree of freedom from unwanted thoughts and the degree of concentration on a single positive thought (e.g. the name of God) reflect our spiritual progress, in addition to the presence of joy which is an expression of God's presence in us.

The five virtues I wished to nurture to assure progress were Goodness, Justice, Truth, Wisdom and Love, comprising all of them.

Sai Baba talks about three steps to reach the desired ideal state of Self-realization. They are: "affirming that you are in the Light", "affirming that the Light is within you", and finally "affirming that you are the Light."

It is true, we can all climb to the last step and say that we are the Holy Spirit, the Trinity, that is, at the same time the Creator (the Father, the Power, the masculine within us), Creation (the Mother, Wisdom, the feminine within us), the Ethereal Light that characterizes them (the Son, the Love, the Holy Spirit in us), as the substance and fruit of the harmonious union of the first two. In this regard, I often described circumstances which gave me the uncommon and pleasant sensation of being guided by the hand by the Inner Master, or the Spirit of Life (or the Holy Spirit), or the Divine Master.

I discovered that the Self manifests to the awakening consciousness (more and more as we approach Christ Consciousness) through the "miracle" of synchronicity (what we commonly call coincidence).

Synchronicity is also described as a delicate relationship between prayer and fulfilment, as a consequence of surrendering to the Divine Will. Then Grace manifests through events that the mind finds bizarre. Here's an example: I must state beforehand that, to me, the robin represents the very presence of Sai Baba (that's how I experience it in the heart, without any plausible explanation). Every time I need to ask (Sai Baba) for an approval, a robin suddenly appears on the window sill or at the door or in the street. That modality of receiving His consent stirs up tremendous joy and gratitude in me.

A highly explanatory case occurred during a particularly bitter period of life. I was at the airport in Germany, waiting for my flight to India, when my heart sought help from Sai Baba. I wished for a positive make-over of my mood. I immediately turned my gaze towards a person sitting close to me, reading a book (by the way, he was Indian).

The title of his book was *The End of Sorrow*[170], *Bhagavad Gita*. The *Bhagavad Gita* is the Hindu Holy Scripture and it literally means "Song of the Lord". For me, it was a sudden intuition.

These incidents, inexplicable by common logic, for the language of the heart represent confirmations of the constant presence of the Divine within us and around us. They cheer up and enrich the monotony and the heaviness of the worldly life to those who long for the highest peaks of the Spirit.

Owing to those "divine" moments, I felt blessed by God, since everything aided me in the reawakening of consciousness and the meaning of life revealed itself more and more.

On this path, the study of the mysteries of ancient Wisdom, Mythologies of civilizations that left major marks on the ancient world and *Karmic* and Evolutionary Astrology induced me to view the human soul as closely connected to the Soul of the Universe. The messages I received confirmed this.

In Greek mythology, Harmony is born from the union of Aphrodite and Eros (Venus and Mars). In other words, the androgynous is born from the union of the feminine and the masculine. It is not by coincidence that philosopher Plato quoted Socrates (in a text) who said that *"just as the shortage of numbers, grace and harmony marks an undeveloped spirit and heart, the presence of the said qualities characterizes a developed heart and spirit."*

I received two messages in that period, speaking about the journey that awaited me. The first one said:

"Today, nature is wearing its Sunday best. Follow the path and forget about the rest. My Plan is perfect, just lull your little self again. Know that I am ready to hold you tight, just let go of yourself (of the ego). It's all right.

I want you to be naked and pure, and so a golden star should be your nature.

The path is already marked in the stars, just let destiny take you far. You'll go back to the stars, My dear love, and stay close to My heart like a dove. The only feeling your heart knows is the great, divine Love that flows. Hear the bells toll, the feast has begun, and so return to Me, there is nothing to be done. Love Me, honour Me, divine flower – I'll ways lighten your path, everywhere.

A life of Light for you I keep in store, don't think about the past any more. My dove, come to Me wearing white, shrouded only in bright light. Only essence counts, only essence is true, the rest around you is history, I'm telling you. With the eternal now you'll soon have to merge, and a complete picture will finally come forward."

The second message read:

"You have already finished rearranging your past, getting rid of big weights still hanging above your head. It's Love you have always longed for, now you know what it is. You know that His essence is harmony and you know how to find it within and pass it on (all around you).

I have poured My water on you three times. Three times you will be blessed if upon My Will you always act. In this perfect design, everything is done according to My divine plan.

A few specks have yet to be taken care of, residues of the big move, after everything is cleared away.

Your house will be neither here nor there, but the heart will find peace everywhere.

Nothing, as I said, will hamper you on the way, which is the wish of the Divine Game for you, My dear.

You will find new friends soon, but ahead of Me none of them you'll ever put. Arduous is the task I will entrust you with, but you can do it. Always clad in humility and patience, you'll overcome all the troubles, including those looming on the horizon, because the time is already due. You have already recognized the uselessness of your repeated attempts to convince those who have not discovered the key to Truth. Not the mind, but the heart, if open to the Truth, can allow the man to hear and understand. Otherwise, he is sentenced to a lifetime of ignorance. There is nothing you can do, or say or hope for. As in every game, in the game of life as well, someone wins and someone loses, even though those who apparently win, paradoxically so, are often those who lose, essentially, and vice versa.

It is in the destiny of saints and prophets to be distrusted and unrecognized and to move on to a new life, in silence. This is the life, the immortal life that awaits you, My dearest, divine star.

Many times you have returned down here, but soon enough the time will come when you will no longer have to come back, at least not to struggle and suffer. However, you will return to enlighten the path of those who linger in the dark, to show them all your empathy. I can already see your heart full of compassion, My lovely star. Fear not, for you will know how to break free from all the dark shadows, trust Me.

Do you remember when you had searched for Me in the silence, at thirteen? Now you have found Me in the silence, yet you've never been without My presence. It was silence you had to establish in your overactive mind, to finally realize that I Was, Am and Will Be abiding in your heart forever.

When you think, it is I who speak to you, or rather, I speak to Myself. In the silence, I am God at last. Therefore, spending more and more time in silence is the royal road to merge with Me and be the Self. My darling, nothing can then affect you, as your slavery to time and space will be undone.

Your pure essence will be free to vibrate with all of nature and raise into the upper spheres all the creatures that are true.

Your life alone will speak to those who are puzzled by My mystery, hence My message of Love and Truth will bounce from heart to heart, unstoppably."

The message mentioned a blessing with water.

Indeed, that month was the festival of Shivaratri in India. I was in Italy, so I went to a meditation retreat in Assisi.

On that occasion I received, no less than three times, a blessing with the water from the Ganges, brought for the occasion by some of the participants who had travelled to India during the great festival of Kumbamela, which takes place every twelve years. It was a double blessing, because I had always wished to take part in it, but the opportunity did not present itself and, although I couldn't go to Puttaparthi for the Shivaratri festival, I was still able to celebrate that sacred cosmic moment.

The message also alluded to the silence of mind, i.e. meditation, which I had been practicing regularly for years and which started to bear abundant fruits. The reference to compassion in the heart reminds me of what I have realized recently: compassion represents the highest vibration in the emotional realm, whereas depression, anger and fear are very low vibrations. The entire Universe is an ocean of vibrations, or pulsations of electromagnetic waves, more or less low and more or less high.

This approach to the surrounding physical realm allows a somewhat better understanding of what may happen very soon to planet Earth, according to various prophecies from different civilizations scattered throughout the world.

In the near future, planet Earth's vibration could (purportedly) change, which would entail a transition from the 3rd (earthly) to the 5th (spiritual) dimension, with the consequent disappearance of the lowest (or coarse) vibrations which cannot coexist with the high spiritual vibrations of the fifth dimension (pure consciousness, bodies of Light).

The above suggests that only those who are ready, or prepared through an appropriate spiritual discipline to support this quantum leap, i.e. those who have given full priority to Spirituality in their lives, will be able to survive and find themselves in the new Celestial Reality, to establish a society based on harmonic resonance and not on the acquisition of material goods and territorial defence, which has been the case on earth up till now.

Those that fail to overcome this transitional period will come back to an Earth-like planet, to resume the cycle of rebirths, to exhaust the remaining *karma* (see the advent of the *Avatar* Prema Sai, around 2030).

NOTES: CHAPTER XVII

157. According to Wirth, *"The child who collects the legacy of the Father as Wisdom and that of the Mother as Love, to inhale the Breath of the Universal Spirit and live the eternal life, is represented by the Solar Angel with a trumpet and the symbol of the Sun shining on his forehead."*

158. According to Wirth, *"It is the Vestal (female) of the fire that burns in every heart, the regenerating Spirit (Arcane no. 20) that manifests through her as Truth and removes the veil of appearance to express the secret of the essence of things"*. To be in the possession of this secret means to have the universal science and unlimited power that comes from it. It means to realize the ideal of the perfect aspirant ... Imbued with Divine Light, man is finally lifted from his fall. He becomes bright and concludes the cycle of his regeneration.

159. According to Wirth, it is *"the alienated, but also everything that is beyond the intelligible, the Infinite, the Absolute, that which exceeds our understanding."* This arcane expresses the consciousness of our nothingness, because without humility there can be no reinstatement in the primordial All.

160. *Amma* means 'mother' in India. By some strange coincidence, with whoever I was, in India or in Italy, with someone younger or older than me, I was asked if I was their mother. That question became a constant in my life.

161. Seed is implied as the human soul.

162. Essence is implied as the Spirit in terms of the divine spark within us (*Atma*). When the soul merges with the essence, that is, with the Spirit, it becomes at one with God, or Love.

163. I realized later that it was referred to the 7 red poinsettia petals I had placed on a seven-branched candelabrum, on the eve of 2000.

164. To prophesy means to be a receptive channel of the Word of God. It does not mean to predict the future or learn something new.

165. In the language of the Spirit, I discovered that 'soon' could imply several years.

166. My first name means 'shining'.

167. A few years later I received another message defining change as a source of spiritual evolution in my personal history.

168. It was very difficult to raise a child on my own, especially because my son had a very combative and assertive character.

169. Almost ten years before, the same words had been 'channelled' through the American therapist who'd come to the Sai Centre to speak to me, as mentioned earlier.

170. The end of suffering (physical, mental and spiritual) comes with liberation (from the ego) or with a holy life – a life lived to sing the praises of the Lord.

171. The bells were actually tolling. It was Sunday morning.

XVIII

There is one word that frees us of all the burdens and pains of life: the word is Love.

Sophocles.

With increasing awareness, all the teachings and the prompt support of the inner voice revealed the poetry of living. Having got rid of the hardness and heaviness of the ego, with its inevitable frustrations, deprivations and disappointments, I followed the heart and faced life with lightness, gently and joyfully.

Self-inquiry continued for years and I realized that my character – above all my personality – had been marked by the suffering I'd endured. The pain, the loneliness and the trials had hardened me.

Fortunately, I wisely came to the conclusion that sacrifice, which was the story of my life, served to obtain the benefit of freedom from slavery to the world[172]. I was still in the physical body, leading a normal life, but in my heart I knew that I was no longer subjugated to anything or anyone, except to my Creator, to whom I owed everything.

The understanding of the heart dissolved the shell I had retired into, perhaps for fear of being embroiled in the world I did not agree with, although I loved it. Every now and then, I would wonder if I was making a mistake by putting my inner experiences down on paper because I'd read that spiritual attainments should never be disclosed, perhaps because there is a risk of showing off. As for me, this likelihood was nonexistent.

When it comes to my commitment, I had no doubt whatsoever that my motivation came from the desire to serve God, the way He had asked me to do it.

I knew well how much I'd had to struggle, study, seek, renounce, meditate and pray to reach that stage – owing to the Divine Master who had stood by me all the time, in the heart, even when I hadn't been aware of it.

I could hardly believe that other people could follow such a path without a 'roadmap', i.e. a system of signposts, unless they had all the time I'd had at my disposal, in addition to the opportunities created by intuition (it has always been my gift) and the inclination towards self-inquiry.

I heeded Sai Baba's urge not to waste time but to make *the* comforting and reliable choice and believed that the best way to serve Him was by marking this 'treasure map'.

The most useful thing for me to do was to try and convey, the best way I could, the experience of the soul that knew and perceived the divine presence, in a constant communion, in the loving completeness of inner Harmony and Peace, waiting to attain the highest achievement – the union with the Spirit of Love and Truth.

I was blessed by Sai Baba's consent to undertake this task. This became the force that carried me through, all the way to the end, that helped me overcome the doubts and fears that the ego lodged in the mind once in a while. Despite all the progress, the disease of the ego wasn't eradicated altogether. But luckily, as Sophocles said, time unveils everything and brings it out into the light.

The ego's attempts to boycott me were regularly exposed and rendered harmless. Besides, the pleasure lies not in not falling, but in being able to recover after every fall and I, being a proper "Virgin", identified myself with the phoenix – the mythical bird that rises from its ashes.

The Truth is always rewarding, even when to 'prophesy' (i.e. to proclaim the Truth, the Word of God) is unpopular. The reason is that truth can be revolutionary, disturbing, uncomfortable, and therefore it is sometimes censored, depending on the dominant ideology in a modern society (just as in the past).

Having realized that I couldn't be relieved of narrating my "spiritual adventure", I wrote down the messages of the inner voice that arrived with increasing frequency. Enlightenment is awareness of the divine essence within, which brings fair-mindedness, peacefulness, tolerance, compassion and at oneness with the Cosmic Force.

As my consciousness awakened, I read the words of Jesus in a new light: *"Turn the other cheek, give even the cloak, pay no attention to praises or blames".* They were all expressions of equanimity. Only in this state of (enlarged) consciousness can we feel well everywhere, alone or in a company, knowing that we are part of the All.

He who has realized, on a deeper level, the Truth about his own nature, that of being a mere sparkle of the Divine Light, will also realize the spiritual power which is conferred by Wisdom and Love – Love being the only sacred instrument for encouraging those who aspire to reaching the Light. Being Light, loving others, nurturing (metaphorically) others and taking care of them has been the main concern in my life and the drive that has moved every choice of study, work and research. It has been my only true ideal, but also the true ideal that is really yours and no one can take it away from you.

From one life to another (I had seen this as I put together the puzzle of the past lives that I managed to reconstruct from various sources), the task entrusted to me was to take care of my fellow men, in one way or another.

I was now taking full responsibility for this 'extraordinary' way of making myself useful by being the solitary seeker of the Spirit within.

During the flight to India, I dreamt I was in a huge rose garden, full of orange roses in bloom. Many people approached me and I gave a rose to everyone. Eventually, when I realized that not a single one remained for me, I was glad for being consistent with the spiritual choice I'd made – to give without holding back. When I woke up, the following words were on my lips: "Dear God, may Harmony replace desire in the hearts of men."

I was at Puttaparthi again, to check my progress with regard to the previous journey.

Trust, Surrender, Acceptance, Peace, Harmony, Love and Unity are the steps of a single staircase we climb to reach the consciousness of the Supreme Truth. God and man are at one, the Absolute and the divine spark in every human being tuned to the eternal source (Love), are at one.

It was easier for me to experience this forgotten Truth while I was in that holy place, in the presence of the Divine Master.

I returned home on Easter Sunday morning and received the following message: *"You must feel Me and love Me with the heart; your life is now marked by the sun, ceaselessly illuminating and warming every moment of your existence. You have been given the go-ahead for Heaven, so you can walk the remaining stages of your path without breaking the rules of the divine game.*

On the earth, you are just a passenger passing through; your goal is inscribed in the Light. Do not suffer, My beloved child. You have always been Mine - you know that. Therefore, do not be afraid or distressed.

Your body is a leaf that falls with the change of season, your essence is what remains – eternal, immutable, just like eternal and immutable is My Love for you and for everyone and everything that emanated from Me, the Creator.

You are the indissoluble and immortal part of creation, have you heard Me? I have just called you to dry the salty tears.

Today is Easter or Resurrection Day: I will rise again in you every time you offer your heart, a thought or a deed to Me and I will rejoice. The divine joy I speak about is the flame that feeds the sacred fire of life, illuminating every moment of darkness with the Light of Love.

I shall keep every shadow away from you, so you can shine all the time and tap into the source[173] of Truth that will quench your thirst. You will never get tired of praising Me and testifying, with your presence, to divine Love as something a person cannot live without.

There is no void between Me and you. We are One, with a continuity that highlights the omnipresence of Divinity.

Rejoice, daughter, spouse, sister, friend, lover of your Creator, and turn your Love to Me. Animate it with sincere ardour, as an undeniable proof of a heart that is pure and true, and spread it among all mankind."

On Easter morning I was seized by a moment of despair, by a bitter nostalgia for the place that I had just left (Puttaparthi), when I heard the phone ring at eight-thirty. A friend was calling me directly from Puttaparthi to wish me a Happy Easter.

She was acting as a channel of Divine Love. I understood it at once and my tears of pain were transformed into tears of joy. I was deeply touched.

The same thing happened when, following a fall (I was hit by a car and the driver didn't even stop), I refused to go to the hospital, believing and trusting that the Divine Master would protect me.

Once home, sore and lame, the phone rang. It was a friend calling from Brindavan, Whitefield (the other *ashram* of Sai Baba). He said he didn't even know why he was calling. But I did. I was certain that Sai Baba wished to confirm that He was protecting me. These were His Divine Games to show His immense, constant Love.

A little more than a week passed, when, on Liberation Day, another message arrived:

"Today, when your country celebrates Liberation Day, I am going to reveal you the fruit you shall present Me with, the fruit of your deeds. It is a gift and a tribute to your perseverance that will have much resonance worldwide!

You shall finally make yourself useful to those who wish to hear about Me; at last you can give comfort to those who wish to fill their hearts with Me. My humble instrument you wanted to become, after you had been forgiven many shortcomings, as major signs of attachment to this vain world. My humble instrument you shall be as long as My Will resides in you, in this lifetime. So, there will never be anything to be afraid of.

You shall soon begin to work, to unravel the skein of each seemingly fatal event.

I'll let you do what you can do, what you were born to do and what you shall be sought to do. You will have to have ears for everyone's suffering, now that you know it is merely a question of lacking true Love. You shall be that Love, you will be the blessed food, the unique one, able to nourish every heart protected by Me and dear to Me.

I will be talking through you by means of words, sacred and true, that will be a prophecy to those who can see or start to see owing to these sincere words that will illuminate the path of every heart desiring to fill all the existential void with Love, as the Source of life and ancient wisdom. Harmony will prevail wherever you go under My guidance.

Balance will be your strength and your fate will be benevolent, even in those plans that involve many others. Their efforts will be great, resulting in the plea: 'Bestow grace on me'!

Eventually, the work performed with so many helping hands and so much effort will yield good results and you will see it was not done in vain.

You are not part of the herd any more. You guide and support every lost sheep – sad, alone and weakened by the ills of life, or overwhelmed by the troubles that betrayed it in the end.

You'll see again, very soon, what was once familiar to your lively Spirit. Very soon you will meet the One who will fill your void, without any pretext. According to the law of nature, or better still, the Divine Law, every void seeks to be filled. In the same way, every awakened Spirit seeks this Truth. Sweet is the awakening and the path leading to Me will be paved with fulfilment and harmony. Along the way you will encounter only Light and Love.

Be happy, My child, because I have already decreed a lasting peace for you and, from now on, your fate will always be benevolent. I will spread out before you blue, starry skies and evermore beautiful views of the subtlest dimension."

This message recalled familiar words, pronounced by the Divine Master Jesus: *"Blessed are the pure in heart, for they will contemplate God; blessed are the meek, for they will inherited the earth. He who has faith in Me will live forever. You cannot love two masters. He who wants to be great in My Kingdom must be a servant to his neighbour. The Wisdom of God will fill the earth, as water fills the oceans. The weeping voice will no longer be heard, there will be no more crime or injustice, the wolf and the lamb will walk together."*

How wonderful, I yearned for the advent of that day with all my heart.

The Indian poet Tagore wrote: *"Faith is a bird that feels the light and sings before sunrise"*, that is, it knows that the aurora will break, even though it is still in the darkness of the night.

Blessed is he who believes out of faith, out of trust in God. He who believes after he has seen, will have to make a much greater effort to reach the Light.

In effect, what we see lasts for an instant. What we don't see is eternal. What we see is ephemeral, and what we don't see is real.

I felt I could walk without the aid of mental crutches, but only with the Love of God, or the Spirit of Life that was permanently present in me.

I understood it from the inner peace that was increasingly becoming the natural state of being. How I wished to share it with all those who suffered, just as I did in the past, unable to make out the outlines of a way out of pain. As a former mental health professional, I became a healer of the soul, in accordance with what I had been announced by the inner voice which only confirmed what I felt in the heart.

I discovered firsthand that the only way to free ourselves from suffering was that of the Spirit. The way of the world cannot set us free, because to free mankind from the bondage of suffering, which leads them to perpetuate the same mistakes (binding them further to matter), would be counterproductive to the very existence of worldliness.

One could argue that the choice of the Spirit (understood as the spiritual life) is too demanding and difficult, and therefore impossible. This view conceals a danger which is insidious because it is occult. The absence of choice-making, remaining where you are, doing nothing, does not actually mean you are not taking any choice whatsoever. It means you are making a passive choice, maintaining the condition of slavery (to the world), with the resulting sentence to perpetuate the suffering. It would be like saying: it is easier to thrive on the energy of others than to change myself and live on my own. But this goes against the Divine (Cosmic) Law.

Therefore, it is useless to complain if you refuse to collect the courage to address the issues and resolve them, acting by the Will of God rather than by your own. Many a consciousness has been seduced by the chimeras of consumerism, or climbing to the top of the ladder of success in the mundane world. This, in turn, blocks the natural impulse to evolve, achieve the divine essence within and connect with the cosmic energy. In other words, this prevents humanity from thinking 'big' and discovering their 'immortality'.

Someone said that, if there is a way to know the best, then it must be by courageously acknowledging the worst. This is the effort each one of us should make to initiate their transformation.

According to the Divine (Cosmic)Law regulating life on planet Earth, according to the principle of duality, every coin has two sides. It is the law of antagonising opposites (the 3rd dimension).

Even this 'reality' should not be seen as an obstacle, but as an opportunity to redeem ourselves from the bondage of matter, from the constraints that have subjugated us to date. How? With positive thinking, being equidistant from the good and the evil, which makes us see the glass half full instead of half empty, which makes us catch a glimpse of benefit in every hindrance, which makes us experience every obstacle as an invitation to improve our personality and character, which makes us accept the disease as a way to grow and learn about our most hidden needs, by which we recognize in every loss a gift to raise our Self-awareness. At that point, what we previously considered negative becomes an opportunity we shouldn't miss. The differences gradually disappear and everything becomes positive, that is, spiritual, because in the realm of the Spirit (subtler dimensions, like the 5th dimension of the bodies of light) it is not duality but Unity that reigns, beyond good and evil.

The great qualitative leap that awaits us all is the shift from a nuclear family (which was once patriarchal and much wider) to the great family of mankind. All mankind is indeed one family. *Ekatma* (in Sanskrit) means "One single Spirit, in everything and in everyone" (Cosmic Love embracing and permeating all).

This ideal condition arises because there are no more differences between opposites, such as good and evil, good and bad, beautiful and ugly, that is, by overcoming the duality to achieve equanimity, perfect awareness, or enlightenment (*samadhi* in Hinduism, *nirvana* in Buddhism, *satori* in Zen, etc.). The inner voice referred to this goal when it announced that the essence of the future life would be seeing neither good nor bad.

Then, the Spirit fills us with Divine Power, sweetness, quintessence or shining ether, which constitutes the body of light of the one who is imbued with pure, unconditional Love and thus has access to the more subtle dimensions of the Universe, those that Jesus called 'the dwellings of the Father' and the inner voice calls 'the 5th dimension'.

This is how we cross the ocean of illusion (*samsara* or the cycle of rebirths), as lead turns into gold and we reach true ioy, Bliss (*Ananda*), or Eternal Life[174].

In this state, one has the power to reconcile the irreconcilable, as the inner voice had anticipated.

At that time I had a strange dream. I looked into the mirror and discovered I had a golden host, instead of a tongue. Many years before, I'd had a similar dream, in which I'd been given a golden host in church during communion, which I hadn't been able to swallow, of course.

That dream conveyed that the Word of Truth must be dictated by Christ Consciousness, i.e. the golden host, the Body of Christ, or the spiritual food, which is His Message, His Word, healthy food for the soul desirous to receive Him, that is, to receive pure, unconditional Love. This was the knowledge I had been invited to spread for the rest of my life. The greatest mystics, the 'prophetesses' of the Middle Ages, Catherine of Siena, Hildegard of Bingen, Bridget of Sweden, were masters of motherhood and universal brotherhood, the Cosmic vision of the world. Their conversation with God was continuous, steady, intoxicating, but also a trial. They were never spared of the cross of sacrifice, although they were full of Divine Power, understood as Love, Knowledge and Wisdom that manifested in them as self-offering, as the ultimate expression of charity. Their will remained firmly adherent to the Divine Will, throughout their lives. They yearned for God and nothing else, all the time.

Sai Baba says: *"Yearn only for Me, bear any torment for Me and I will deliver you from all sins and make you immortal."*

The trials of life, therefore, should not be seen as a penalty, but as a means to strengthen the will of goodness and consolidate virtues by experiencing their opposites.

For example, when I asked God for strength, I was confronted with my weaknesses. When I asked Him for Light, I was confronted with my shadows. The divine intention is totally benevolent, so everything happens always and only for the best.

I received another message of the inner voice that said:

"The time to indulge in useless thoughts is over. Act always for the goodness and in the best way you can because this is what I expect from you. Refine your feelings so that you can unify the most positive phenomena you encounter on your path. This will be My gift[175] for a springtime full of Light.

You will be joined by those who will work with you on this project I have conceived for the evolution of all humankind. You know that My thought is the invigorating and generative reality and the eternal, inextinguishable truth. This is why you will have to think big. Pay no attention to petty things; you have to go beyond that. When your will identifies with Mine, it will be transformed into power, joy and fullness, expressed through your actions and emotions.

Come out of that shell formed by the ego around your Self – it is already cracked. I want you to become a creature of Light, made to stay by My side always, without intermediaries and with clear thoughts of Love and Truth, as the only, eternal reality.

Do not humiliate your nature with unhealthy and ephemeral things. What is transitory has no value, as your heart already knows well. So, what are you waiting for? Fly away. Your wings are strong and they can challenge any height. Allow yourself to be carried by the wind of My Love and you will find Peace and Goodness everywhere you go."

The two wings that were supposed to help me fly were humility and patience (as well as confidence and courage), or in other words, Love for God and humanity – to keep reminding me that what I was told was not just about me. It was also about all those who would come to know it. My spiritual growth, as was explained to me, was an expression of the evolution of humanity, because we are all One[176].

To set out on a spiritual journey means to begin to Love in a new way. To think 'big' means to Love and act accordingly, in tune with Universal Love. This is what God expects of us today.

At the start of the third millennium, we have reached a pivotal point when the Divine Master does not ask for more devotion, but for a transformation. Our lives must express His message through sublimation (which means to lighten up, elevate) and not by suppressing the characteristics of the ego (desires, attachments, etc.).

The content of the messages, which may sometimes sound rhetorical, or epic, always express a clear invitation for a transformation.

I received another message a few days later, saying:

"My dear beloved, I am by your side in times of pain and confusion. In those moments you can not hear me because your heart is filled with useless torments and useless ideational speculations.

You are still unclear about the idea of God being pure Love. When this idea pervades you completely, it will absorb all of your denials, your resistance and your repression, and finally remove the confusing experiences that have disturbed and deviated you from the path of true reality, the reality of Unity. Oneness is in the All and All is in the Oneness. Be One with Me, and let the rest exhausted be.

Every single note by Me is played; every single thing or life by Me was made. Mine is the Universe and Mine is your every verse. It is I who write every breath in you, every heartbeat, every thought, so how could you possibly not feel Love, true Love?

My sweet child, take shelter in Me and abandon whatever is painful for you."

The above description of the soul possibly mirrors many people. Its calm, soothing and warm words provide them with the comfort and the confidence to. continue playing the game of life.

Came the day of Pentecost, blessed in the sky by a rainbow. It nailed me down to admire its majesty, as I was entranced by so much beauty and grandeur. It was double and immense and it embraced the whole horizon, from one end to another, isolating the ground and the landscape below from the sky, all black and grave with accumulated clouds.

Other people also stopped in the street to admire this unique and rare spectacle. It was a celestial sign, a gift of indescribable divine generosity to us, human beings, who admired in silence, small and stunned, the Majesty of God.

The rainbow also symbolizes the bridge that God sends from Heaven to earth, inviting us to recognize Unity in Diversity.

I accepted the concept of "sin" from the above mentioned Christian female mystics, implied as 'disorder', as a wound inflicted on the Divine Plan (which is pure Harmony) by the forces of the ego, in an attempt to break its harmony. Just as Sai Baba does today, they also warned of the danger we ran when we didn't make good use of the time and the forces we were given for temporary use.

As a result, according to the Divine Plan, we are forced to do what we failed to do out of Love, or rather, we have to learn through suffering what we could have learned through wisdom.

Never forget that evil cannot be defeated with more evil, but with goodness, because, eventually, the Light always prevails over darkness.

The 'pleasure of the senses' can easily make us lose the fear of God. Sai Baba says that modern man does not fear sin, but fears God because he can no longer discern good from evil, the real values from the false ones, being immersed in the illusory domain of matter.

In this regard, He continues, it is preferable to be either hot or cold, but not lukewarm (like people who hesitate all the time), because those who fail to choose the right path, following their ways of the world, are dead in the soul in the eyes of the Lord (the Spirit of Life leaves their body, and so the soul, being separated from the Spirit for a long time, withers).

At this point, the myth that passion is an expression of Love should be dispelled. Love is not passion, but understanding, forgiveness, faithfulness, respect, loyalty, humility, compassion and trust.

Where there is passion, there is no reason, says an ancient Chinese proverb, and there is no Love either. When Love is absent, the soul is gone – we should always bear this in mind if we wish to know the path of Light.

Quite predictably, recent studies made in the U.S. have shown that the so-called 'lovesickness' is triggered by the same biochemical (hormonal) mechanisms that cause a psychiatric disorder, known as 'obsessive compulsive personality disorder'.

In confirmation of this thesis, I remember a sad record: in Europe, the leading cause of death among women between the age of fourteen and forty, is not accidents, or tumours, but murders with a sexual background, by boyfriends, husbands or lovers. The incidence is greater in the North than in the South of Europe and it is perpetrated by males with a predominantly high level of education and social status and wealth.

In fact, all these events are characterized by an underlying fear of deprivation (in terms of abandonment, but also in terms of loss of possession or power) and, on a deeper level, fear of rejection (and the subsequent urge to control), but also anger, bitterness of betrayal, envy and jealousy (and the need for acknowledgment), as expressions of lacking self-esteem.

Those who are already able to discern can well understand that the true and only separation is what we feel when the soul is not in tune with the Will of God, or when we don't feel at peace with our consciousness.

On Corpus Christi Day, I received the following message:

"You don't know who you are, but you can understand it from what I have often said to you. Wanting to know more does not help you see. Moreover, it could prevent you from making true choices.

Free of the traces left by the past, you have to go forward without fearing fate. You have to let go of what you hold on to. It is superfluous and vain, and that does not surprise you.

Your road is paved with Light and each new stage will be enlightened by the sun, as you walk on. You still wonder who you are and your heart is discontent as long as it doesn't know about My sacred intent.

Wait, My beloved, until the road becomes clear and you will find out that you woke up in the right moment, without offending anyone.

You have a job to finish, even though you are oblivious to it. This is the way things should be; so don't hold back, as I will not burden your becoming with any additional karma. Be happy; be pleased and always intent on loving Me."

This message was quite enigmatic and I didn't understand what work I was supposed to finish. Was it related to my role as a mother or to the book that I (subsequently) revised? I didn't know.

In that same month, my son went in for the profession of graphic designer, with much enthusiasm and creative spirit (I was very proud of him.). He became independent in every sense, despite his young age.

The other reference to my past lifetimes pointed at what I had learned over the many years of search, namely that we should not persist in trying to go back to our past lives (to reconstruct them in the memory), because it may be harmful if the timing of the search is not right.

Someone might object: but how do you know when the timing is right? The answer is simple: when the disciple is ready, the Master arrives. When we are ready to understand, the opportunities to learn more about our *karmic* past will present themselves. We simply have to seize them – rest assured that "the crops you collect will be ripe".

Another message came from the inner voice (that year was memorable for the numerous messages I received). It said:

"Too many things are worn and withered in order to give birth to something new. Let go of the hackneyed words and come out of the eggshell.

Indulge your deep feelings; there is no other way to discover another world. Everything is Light that opens every door onto the main road. Do not stop; keep uniting the left and the right side of all things.

All is one in your dimension, and that Oneness is you. Feel safe and be serene. There will be no more pain for you. Your karma is melting in the sun of divine Love and soon there will be no trace left of your bitter destiny.

Joy, kindness, harmony, an enchanting life, this is what you will experience for having worked so hard.

Your reward will be a gift for all those who are ready to collect the fruits of your labour. Wait patiently, for the right time will come and everything will fall into its right place.

Divine Thought is perfect in its slightest expression - it is flawless. You will put in place all the little things. Your aim is not to cover yourself with mundane glory – you will be working for heaven, relentlessly.

Your star belongs to Orion and that's where your most beautiful dwelling awaits you."

Once again, a very important aspect emerged, which I had already heard in the previous messages.

Just as the Holy Spirit was a "gift" for me, I too would be a "gift" for others, as a useful instrument for those who wished to attain what one is born for – the awareness of the inner divine essence. Once we have reached the goal, we come to a new life – the life of the Spirit, eternal and immortal.

What was emerging was a 'treasure map', where 'treasure' was associated to a secure access to the inner spiritual life, which is not really hidden, but it is often invisible to those who are unable to look (with the eyes of the Spirit) into their heart.

In this regard I learned that the centre of the heart (the fourth chakra) governs our fate and it has the potential to reshape the future, depending on the level of spiritual evolution we are at.

When the heart is open to unconditional Love, indeed, it attracts the Grace of God to intercede for us and alleviate our *karmic* debts, possibly until they are extinguished.

Soon I received another message, saying:

"Vain is the glory that accompanies those who persist to walk a path that is not spiritual.

May your example be a compass in the world submerged in human illusions, to show the blue of a cloudless sky as an expression of the will of the Father who guides all those who are lost.

Be a careful and attentive guide, chosen by My Will. Bring words of Love wherever you go, and get your way. May Love be the greatest force to affirm the divine power that always strives to help the redeemed mankind to 'see'.

In these years of difficult transition, I have materialized a 'lingam' several times, in order to restore the original energy of the entire creation and dissolve the past karma of man and the Earth, to make fate more agreeable and acceptable to all.

Use this time to teach everyone to love. There is already a dwelling that awaits everyone if they stop hesitating and choose kindliness. We mustn't put it off, since the turning point is nearby.

Help everyone in every way and bring them to the realization that there is no time to waste – we have to learn to 'perceive'. It will be no use rebelling against what will happen and you will not be able to escape the events fate is in charge of plotting.

Forgive Me for the crudeness of My words – human bad habits have forced Me to say with certainty that, unless everyone tries to feed their hearts with tenderness, they will be eventually forced, against their will, to perish in bitterness.

Receive wisely everything you've heard and use it with kindness, with everyone who repents for having wasted the great gift that was misunderstood at the time. They can take this last chance to show their courage."

The message preceded the attack on the Twin Towers in New York, but, in my opinion, the scenarios it hinted at were even gloomier than what happened a few months later, in the USA.

It was the first time the inner voice apologized for the alarming tone used in describing what in truth is merely the product of our own actions, for the way we have misused the "great gift", which is human life (not animal but divine) with our free will, given to us by God the Creator.

The materialization of the *lingam* (as the primordial form of matter, the cosmic egg or *Hiranyagarba*), took place during the festival of Shivaratri (for twenty years it had taken place in private, in the presence of students and a few devotees). It has been celebrated publicly since 1999 and it takes place every year, on the same date.

In Hinduism, the lingam represents the power of authentic wisdom (*Jnana Shakti*), i.e. the power of enlightenment, as a mental body of Light (or causal body, or *lingasharira*), in which the forms and the differences disappear. It is the flow of vital energy that lights the divine spark (*Atma Shakti*), that is, the divine energy in us, as a living force that transforms an ordinary person into Divine Power.

At that time, I kept repeating this phrase (like a mantra), to myself: *"I recognize the power of wisdom in me and I light up the body of light to go beyond the duality of this world of illusions."*

Soon enough, I received another message:

"The music of the cosmos begins to resonate in your blood. Ever closer you are to the step that will set you free from that yoke that continues to imprison the languishing humankind.

You made a healthy choice when you decided to act upon My Supreme Will.

In Me continue to reside, as there is no hope outside this abode. Care about everyone who approaches you; may your advice be impartial and fair-minded. The labour of childbirth is clad in pain, but Joy and Love soon follow. When the inevitable occurs, time will lose its sense.

While witnessing the torments, struggles and upheavals on Earth, your heart will remain fixed in the Light.

Now that your human destiny has finally stopped opposing you, your body will soon be made of unworldly Light – and new. Your Light will be sovereign.

You have understood the value of life and its essence, one with the All your presence will become. This union is the seal you saw marked on your forehead a few years ago. You've chosen to become a child of the sun, although you were that already. You finally realize that your long journey is a pilgrimage, at times hard, at others easy, to return tò the Self. You have come close to that Self, I announce it firmly, you have been put on the list of those who are going to ascend, and I can assure you.

There will be a lot of work to be done but you will not get tired. You have taken a fairly good rest and now you can work hard for others.

I heard your vow, this is what you asked for, and so this is what I'm going to give you to save you from the fatal events. Only those who think about others will have another chance to live, to create a new world that will know peace. The others will have to scatter so as not to cause more damage, and there will be a life, which is a "non-life" for those who will be reborn.

There will be daylight only for the former – Light, plenty of Peace – but for the latter I foresee only a thousand obstacles. Your heart will guide you to many a path. You will always clearly distinguish the false from the true objectives. My gifts I have showered you with, so fate will always be well disposed to you. As I told you, I reiterate, it is no secret: those who love Me have never lacked anything.

Sweet darling, beloved one, in peace may you rest, may beauty and fullness rest upon you forever. I have filled you with kindness, you can testify to that. Have faith and you will share your ability to Love with the entire creation."

Jesus said: *"Rejoice, your names are written in Heaven"* (the inner voice told me that I was on "the list of those who will ascend"), but He also said: *"The Lord will arrive like a thief in the night. Don't wait for tomorrow – tomorrow may never come."*, i.e. do not put off until tomorrow what you can do today. The inner voice was making it clear to me that the time was due, urging me to make the right choice, the choice of Goodness, Altruism and unconditional Love.

My life seemed more and more like a magic gift – amazing and wonderful. Faith and loyalty to the Holy Spirit filled it with so much joy and fulfilment, renewing His alliance with me, day after day.

Although there were occasionally brief moments of discomfort (someone said we must pay the price of our dreams, for them to come true), it was clear that I was no longer on my own and that I would never be on my own again.

The greatest miracle is being able to have a first-hand experience of the presence of God and act upon His Will. That's why the healing of the heart is most spectacular. Indeed, I was going to act upon His Will. But, the task I was to be entrusted with not only seemed to be arduous and challenging. I didn't even know what it would consist in.

In all honesty, I did not have a clue about what I could do, except to continue doing what I had been incarnated to do, so many times, although from now on I was going to be a direct channel of the Spirit (according to what had been announced to me). Offering the 'Word' of Truth with discernment, clarity, equanimity, patience, audacity, courage, coupled with the humility and purity of heart, was not a minor task.

Meanwhile, life became an eternal 'now' for me. The past and the future lost the meaning they once had. I had to take note of events with a time reference, so that I could respond to questions in that regard (for example, if someone asked me when the last time was I went to India or how many times I went there over a period of time, etc.).

I guessed that the dream in which Sai Baba presented me with a watch with two fastenings and the other one, when the hands of the watch went backwards, were related to the fact that time united with anti-time equalled to eternal 'now'.

The inner voice announced that I had been pardoned of the burden of the *karmic* past, at least in good part. There was nothing else for me to do except to offer my life as evidence of the sacredness of the divine sense of cosmic events, in their regular rotation (proceeding), but in order to do this, I first had to acknowledge that I was a living temple of the Spirit, in a stable and continuous manner, and the living expression of the Divine Master's message.

Two more messages arrived, just days apart. The first said:

"Your heart feels the truth: although you'll remain on Earth further on, you don't belong to it any more. The sun will be your home and you're expected to shine in the Light, with your eternal companions. You will then return to illuminate the darkness that will continue to dim this planet plagued by duality. Envoy of Oneness, you will bring the bounty of the essence everywhere you go, the greatest and the rarest – Love – to imbue with its scent every soul you meet. May your path be a garden full of flowers, of wondrous beauty. You will grow every flower with lucid dexterity, so that My Light can reverberate in all its purity.

Your life, your example will be useful to reveal the true essence of the Divine. You will not need to explain what becomes clear only with your presence.

You will have to meet many people and they will want to know the lymph that flows in you, that will become a true nourishment for the most open-minded souls. There will be no dispute, for you will become an example of harmony. My Will shall accompany you wherever you go.

Only I will guide you, My darling, rest assured, and there is nothing that can make you feel separated from Me. We are at one, always at one. May this be your eternal song."

Do not be surprised that this message deals exactly with what I wrote earlier, as my personal reflection.

For years I used to write (and I stopped being surprised) notes on different dates in my diary, without understanding why I chose that page rather than the other. For example, on January the 1st I wrote down a thought, or a phrase on the page marked as the 25th April of that year, only to find the phrase written months earlier perfectly appropriate for the events that actually occurred on that particular day.

The second message read:

"You are paying your debts accrued life after life. Do not worry. In a few years from now, you will settle the debts made in the distant past.

I will make sure that everything is squared, so that harmony can return to reign in your eternal, no longer worldly life.

Too many things you ask Me but I cannot reply. The time will come for you to understand the purpose of creation better. You'll know then that your faith in Me was well placed. Your small mind cannot contain the magnitude of what is still an unfathomable mystery for it, but this mystery will soon become the source of joyful

beauty. You will no longer need to ask, because you will know everything. What-
ever is in Me will be yours too. We will be at one and you will shine like the sun.
The true source of eternal life and Love will reign in you. You will share its fruit,
authentic Knowledge, and Divine Will, pure Power, will triumph.

You decided to remain alone in this lifetime to investigate the ultimate nature of all
things. You promised not to commit yourself and to do away with duality. Having
reached the brink of the abyss that still separates you from your true home, you have
already laid the bridge and it is well fixed. So wait for your time to come, with faith."

I finally understood that, when we discover that happiness, the source of Love, is
within us, we start savouring freedom because the taste of eternal life becomes
familiar and the certainty of the immortality of being keeps away every worry or
fear of loss, or fear of death.

I had a dream set in India. I was at Puttaparthi (during a *darshan*), and Sai Baba was
coming forward with a light, slow gait. When He came near me, He placed two
strange gold objects at my feet. They were two small marbles shaped like domes, one
was full and the other empty. I took them, considering them as sacred gifts, but
without understanding the meaning. Upon awakening, I thought with trepidation
that another period of change was appearing on the horizon for me (truly, although
fortunate and useful, changes may initially raise some concern). In moments of
tension, I repeated this refrain: *"If you want to hear the voice of the heart, love and*
be endlessly patient", which calmed me down. I realized that 'goodness' was
whatever accelerated my spiritual growth, and "evil" was whatever hampered it. This
assessment served to weigh my actions, words and thoughts, before they reached the
ears of God, for nothing escapes His attention (everything that concerns us is written
in what He calls 'the book of life'). Goodness is driven from within, by the Divine
Will, whereas evil from without, by desires. However, we do not have to fight evil, it
is enough to weaken its enthralling drive.

I woke up one morning with the following words on my lips: *"The pathway of*
perfection is narrow and lonely" . It was the narrow pathway Jesus talked about. At
night, I often received advice, messages, or commands and I was convinced that the
masters of Light, the messengers of God, took care of my soul during sleep. This gave
me peace of mind, although certain commands were not easily assimilated. I
remember one in particular, which was a thorn in my side for quite some time. It
said: *"The goblet should be drained to the last drop."*

Years passed, until I realized that that phrase referred to the *karma* that was to be
settled in this lifetime, because it couldn't be delayed any longer (for reasons of
higher order I didn't know). I discovered that a soul could choose, depending on its
degree of development, a 'script' (i.e. a life) for a future incarnation, open to
unexpected challenges. According to the principle of *"grace being in proportion to*
the effort", the 'script' allows for a wide margin of possibilities to accelerate the

karma. It is also possible to choose the kind of family we are born into, but this option is available only to more evolved souls.

For the less developed souls, however, their future reincarnations are planned in a more schematic way, as if to protect them against the risks of involution (related to the misuse of free will).

This was a subject with regard to which I asked the Spirit to enlighten me and the inner voice made it clear that my little mind could not contain such great mysteries. In respect of this reply, I continued to work to increase the level of awareness, confident that this job was not for the earth but for Heaven and it would be useful not only for me but also to others (remember the hundredth monkey effect, which demonstrates that All is at one, like a hologram which includes the manifest reality including man, mankind and the entire Universe).

Once again the sensations I felt were reflected in a message that arrived shortly afterwards, before I left for India:

"You will experience an acceleration of events, thanks to the many interventions made by the Masters of Light in your favour. You are well taken care of. You can already perceive the constant presence of the essence, and your heart will soon manifest its (spiritual) power, when it surrenders to it, immaculately clean. With the right astral conjunctions in heaven, you will be fully conscious to dare and act, to address and solve the trials before you. The trials will not be marked by suffering but by the need to witness your maturity at any time, whenever the true or the false make the difference.

Isolation will end soon, My sweet, beloved one, and you will be asked to go among the people. You will discover the innate truth of balance and discernment. There is only one heart, one Love in the Universe. I want to see you as a witness to the Oneness, with My force (the Word) pushing you through all the difficulties (far from any point of controversy).

You will come out unscathed from every situation, however difficult, inaccessible or complicated, because your Light will find the solution immediately. Fear not therefore to face the world, no part of you can be injured or hurt, as you are immersed in Me like a dot in the middle of a full circle.

The symbol of the sun shines in you – your nature becomes the Body of Light since it understands only the language of my My Power and My Will".

Actually, in the same year I fell five times –it was pretty serious every time – three of which were bicycle accidents (one caused by a car which quickly drove away after it had run into me). All in all, I was not badly injured. I was no longer a tower of strength, given the consequences of the operation I'd had many years before. It was a miracle that I could still walk. Life itself became a miracle that repeated itself every day, owing to the constant presence of the Spirit within.

NOTES: CHAPTER XVIII

172. I later found out that the Grace of God would set me free from the cycle of rebirths – the true liberation according to Sai Baba.

173. Years later I dreamt of a sacred spring that gushed in the garden.

174. Lead, represented by planet Saturn, the Lord of fate (of *karma*), turning into gold, represented by the Sun, the enlightenment (the solar angel), represents the realization of the Divine within, transcending the *karma*, becoming beings of light, messengers, God's envoys, His apostles.

175. The Holy Spirit is the gift *par excellence*.

176. This phrase reminded me of the hundredth monkey effect, which in summary expresses the Unity of All! We are all made, essentially, of the same eternal substance: Divine Light. So, at some level, albeit very subtle, there is an exchange of energy that puts in communication the content of the experiences made by different individuals who use this interchange and amplify their individual knowledge.

177. This phrase reminded me that in Buddhism, as in Taoism, waiting is preferred to acting. This is so, because acting implies expectations and therefore disappointments and suffering.

178. In this regard Einstein said that: "As the speed of mass approaches the speed of light, time approaches zero.".

179. The Golden Age – a thousand years without wars and violence that will be inaugurated by the Avatar Prema Sai (in 2030), the next incarnation of Sai Baba.

180. That is, a life similar to a mundane life, neither eternal nor immortal.

181. The spouse of the Spirit is every soul that is at one with Him.

182. I recalled the dream in which I was on the brink of an abyss.

183. The inner voice subsequently confirmed this statement many times: "There is only one heart in the Universe, which contains all the hearts."

184. A circle with a dot in the centre is the Astrological symbol of the Sun.

XIX

"Wherever I look, God, I see Your immensity, I admire You in Your Work, I recognize You in me".

Metastasio.

For some time I was wondering if I was suffering from a messianic obsession, or perhaps from a saviour complex. At any rate, I still believed that there was but one way to serve everybody, according to Christ's message and that of Sai Baba: I had to become Love and Light and hence realize, together with the rest of humanity, the new myth of the Golden Age, i.e. bringing Heaven down to earth, or the Kingdom of Heaven within us (those who know the true Self and that they are part of the Divine have realized the Kingdom of Heaven within). No less than a 'real' fairy tale with a happy ending.

Jesus said: *"Seek you first the Kingdom of Heaven within you, then everything else you will be given in abundance,"* and again: *"He who tries to save his own life* (understood as earthly life, related to the ego) *will lose it* (lose the real life, that of the Spirit), *and he who loses his life* (ego) *for Me* (for the Spirit) *shall find it* (will find the Self, the divine essence, the life of the Spirit)".

That was just what I believed and what I pursued in the search of the true Self within, with perseverance and tenacity. Nonetheless, I wasn't prepared yet to face (or rather have an insight into) a reality so, I dare say, Cosmic.

I managed, with decreasing effort, to keep the forces of the heart and mind in balance, when a new message arrived, which I interpreted as another invitation to head off for India[185] at once:

"You have been warned of what is already happening slowly but inevitably, be-cause what was written was not written in vain. You can no longer belong to this deceitful world, even if you wanted because from this fate by your true friends you would surely be rescued.

Your path is marked and you know that; nothing can derail you. Soon, you'll come to Me and I will honour your presence.

Since your luggage will be light, I will reward you, have no doubt. Coming alone will not be a mistake because, you, I will never forsake.

The world, you know, is not your home, but a place of transition, which is why it is important to live here and now, and get ready for the journey to a new world, or the fifth dimension – as you call the life in its pure essence – always expanding towards that which you love most.

371

I am the gentle breeze, the Aura Placida, or the Holy Spirit, I am the scent of flowers, I am the blue of the sky and I am the fearless heart.

With the silence that fills you up I embrace you, My love, as you love Me without a reason.

Loving for the Love of Love is the verb that animates the heart – the one that beats in each entity and the other that is one with the Creator. That Creator is I. You have always called Me God, but I am also what you now call "I". My darling, nobody can ever keep us apart, you are part of Me. I have never repudiated you; with Me you will be, eternally.

Love all of creation; love even the smallest of worlds. There is no mistake in Love – it is ineffable life, truth and Light.

With Love regenerate all that you touch and see; candid like snow, always be part of Me."

Emotional devotion to the Divine Master (bearing in mind that the intimacy between the student and the Divine Master is the most profound and sacred of all) grew into non-attached Love, aimed to serve humanity.

The gates of transcendence were opened for me, although I still failed to understand certain parts of the message, like the warning about what was going to happen very soon (which I eventually understood, the following month, upon my return in Italy).

The reference to repudiation (I shall get back to it later) made me realize that the Spirit did not address "my" soul only, but used me as a channel to communicate with any human soul, because, as I said and believe, we are all essentially at one.

Hence, whoever was ready to wake up was the target of the messages. Or perhaps I felt like interpreting the messages in that way, in general, leaving aside the references that concerned me personally.

After a few days, with my ticket in hand and my visa renewed, without thinking twice, I was already on the flight to Puttaparthi. It happened more and more often to respond to His inner command and rush to Him, the Most High, and so my son and the few remaining friends were no longer surprised when I disappeared overnight.

As soon as I arrived, the Divine Master honoured His promise expressed through the inner voice, i.e. His voice, or the voice of the Spirit.

During the *darshan*, He stopped in front of me and materialized some *vibuthi*.

No one knew how immensely honoured I'd always felt when the Divine Master 'offered' the *vibuthi*, the sacred ashes, as the ultimate expression of earthly reality and, most importantly, the overcoming of all attachments to it.

One of the things that remained unclear in the message received just prior to my departure was the phrase "I have never repudiated you". If I was to interpret it personally, what was the Spirit trying to get across with this unusual term, considering this age and the Christian culture to which I belonged? As at every time

I couldn't grasp the meaning, there was nothing else for me to do except to surrender to the Will of God and continue my journey, with utter obedience to Him. During my stay in India I received several "divine commands". One said: *"Break the chains of subservience to matter"*, and another: *"There is only one marriage that lasts forever: the marriage of the mystical Soul to the Spirit"*, and again: *"Learn to read from the book of life, and to know each marginal note of My law"*, and finally: *"When you are 'at your place', I am with you, I am you – we are One."* My place was the sacred abode *par excellence*: the heart of God who is at one with the heart of each one of us.

I also received a message for a friend who had returned to India after many years, saying *"The prodigal son has come home."*

About the *vibuthi*, it is worth noting that the holy ashes remind us that the human body is dust, attachments are dust, According to Christian religious symbolism, *"Dust thou art, and unto dust shalt thou return"*. In the Hindu religion, it symbolizes infinity and the cosmic and immortal nature of all forms of God. To strew ashes upon our head means to prevail over all our desires[186], having purified the thoughts, words and actions, as if to say: you were divine once and you will be divine again. You will return to God. In summary, it is an invitation to become non-attached, to be free again, to be a pure *Atma* (divine spark, or essence). But, in order to become incorruptible, we must incinerate the ego.

"Break the chains of subservience to matter," said the inner voice after I'd received the gift of the holy ashes from Sai Baba. As if it meant: "you will be able to comprehend great things when you have given up on the small, or at least when you have given up on thinking small."

With regard to the frailty of the human body, something very touching happened to me on my birthday, during the same stay.

I visited the hospital at Puttaparthi to bid my last farewell to Mario Mazzoleni, a former priest and a devotee of Sai Baba, who had been excommunicated from the Church of Rome for failing to repudiate his faith in the divinity of Sathya Sai Baba.

He was in the intensive care unit, with a cancer in its terminal phase. He left his body the next day. His last wish was to be accompanied to Puttaparthi, to spend his last days on Earth there and leave his mortal remains in the vicinity of the Divine Master.

We had two things in common, besides our love for the Divine Master: we both understood that we had lived in vain until we met Sai Baba and were convinced that we lived more than one life in the same incarnation.

The time spent by his side, at the hospital, was for me an initiatory trial. I became aware that only the Knowledge of the Spirit, being the only true reality, and the awareness of His presence and the essence within can assist us in the moment of death and help us leave the body without feeling alone.

I returned to Italy, but shortly after I was back (for the third time that year) with the Beloved Goodness.

It was the tenth 'close' encounter with the Light manifested as the 'Living God', the *Avatar* Sathya Sai Baba.

He told me on that occasion: *"Be happy, be happy, be happy"*. In all kinds of circumstances - joyous or bitter – He often expresses His imperturbability and equidistance from everything and His Loving nature.

I inaugurated the new millennium under the best auspices for my spiritual growth. According to a book dealing with the body of Light, I learned that the Earth had approached the 4th dimension through a process called "harmonic convergence", in 1987. The next fourteen years were indicated as the period when our lives would be transformed and our bodies made lighter and purer (i.e. of finer vibrations), until they became bodies of Light (by sublimating energy). The year 2002 would mark an evolutionary leap, when the vibrations of the energies gravitating round the Earth would accelerate further.

In my case, the fact that the year (1987) when the New Age began coincided with the year when I chose to take the spiritual path was nothing short of remarkable. It was as if the soul felt the need to regenerate itself, in perfect harmony with the epochal, cosmic change, even though the mind was oblivious to it. When it comes to forms of life renewal on the planet, humanity in general was also unaware of what was known in certain narrow cultural circles of the so-called New Age current. Another extraordinary fact was that I was told, in the same message, about the shift into the 5th dimension. We were right at the end of 2001, at the beginning of 2002, which coincided with what was indicated in the book as the final year of the 'purification of the masses'.

Texts on the prophecies dealing with the first decades of the third millennium unanimously consider 2012 as the turning point and a transition into the 5th dimension, through a collective ascension of one part of humanity.

Since 2002, Sai Baba has repeatedly stated that the entire process of transformation on Earth has been anticipated and that unspecified changes are foreseen for the near future.

During the last trip, I realized that the path of the Spirit offers the opportunity to get on the same wavelength with the Universal Mind, or Cosmic Consciousness. It was this alignment that allowed the heart, purified by unconditional Love, to hear the inner voice.

The Divine Revelation felt in the heart was the True Knowledge I had aspired for all my life (the Intelligence of the heart).

Proust said that the real journey consisted not in seeking new lands but in seeing with new eyes (that is, becoming a new person – a divine one, if I may add).

This Knowledge, however, does not suffice to heal the wounds of the heart and to purify it. Curing the heart from self-centredness and transcending the traumas and conflicts of the past requires self-forgiveness.

Only then the heart can become the channel of the Spirit and read from the book of life, as the inner voice foretold. This means reading from the very existence – which is the book of life, written by everyone and no one at the same time. Nevertheless, God remembers even its 'commas'.

Jesus said: *"Be perfect, even as perfect is My Father in Heaven."*

This invitation to perfection by Jesus is what Sai Baba calls 'Constant Integrated Awareness'. It is the inner perfection that can be achieved by hosting Heaven within, by living again in the perfect balance featured by Love and Wisdom. To know God, we must be 'perfect'. Once the inner harmony of opposites is achieved and Androgyny realized, we are able to tune in with the divine energy. Those who have attained the wisdom of the heart (i.e. the harmonious balance between male and female) can see the magnificence of God with the single eye, i.e. by intuition (the third eye), wherever they look. With the heart they can hear the voice of God, i.e. the divine energy which becomes the 'Word of Truth' when it reaches human consciousness.

According to Gnostics, in the passage from the 3rd dimension (that of the ego, or worldly life) to the 4th, 5th, 6th and the 7th (the last possible dimension for those who are in a physical body), there are fewer laws regulating these realms and man becomes lighter and lighter, until he is completely weightless – he becomes a body of Light.

In this state of pure awareness (with a fully balanced intellect), God permeates the entire body with Quintessence, or Divine Light, or Divine Power.

The resulting magnetic force, at this level of evolution, manifests through unconditional service to mankind[187] and self-sacrifice for others, until the body becomes Light (being no longer human but divine).

Just a brief comment on the various dimensions: the 4th is that of the upper and lower astral planes, the 5th is that of the higher mental plane (characterized by pure awareness, by the bodies of Light; it is the Light that frees us from the physical form and the cycle of birth and death), the 6th one is that of the causal, or *Buddhic* plane (characterized by perfect equilibrium and solar angels) and the 7th is that of the Inner Master, the true Self or *Atma* (the divine spark in us). It is the dimension in which we can hear the voice of the Inner Master, where the union with the Spirit takes place and Christ or Cosmic Consciousness is attained.

As I did not think I'd reached that level of evolution, I thought I'd simply received the Grace to hear the inner voice because of the efforts made to reach the Light of Knowledge. I was bestowed the gift of hearing the voice of the heart, the voice of silence, by the generosity of the Divine Master.

I realized I should experience every day as if it were the last if I wanted to reach the dimension of *Atma*, of the Union with the Spirit, the realization of the divine essence in me. This approach indeed favoured non-attachment to the world and surrender to the Will of God.

During the previous stay in India, I'd promised I would always be a beacon of Light and Love for humanity. Nothing else could give more sense to life.

Time went by and then I had a strange dream: there was blood, bright red, gushing from my forehead. I was quite upset for a while, until, thank God, I came across an old book on alchemy. I read that "red indicates that the operator is born into a new, spiritual existence, representing the Holy Spirit" (it is also the colour of the mantle of Our Lady, as the Mother of God).

I thanked the Divine Master for having come to my rescue so quickly, through that book. For the first time I realized with lucid clarity that the Divine Master, or the Inner Master, and the disciple are so totally united. *"He who seeks is the Sought one."*

That is why ancient wisdoms claimed that "when the disciple is ready, the Master arrives", that is, manifests Himself to the awakened consciousness that was, is and will always be within us, as our true Self.

Having arrived thus far, it is very important to remain centred in the heart (Spirit), or in other words, not to be distracted (in our intentions) by emotional stress (our personality), which keeps trying to engage us, bypassing reason (the mind). A good exercise to practice what has just been said is trying to live as a witness. Life becomes a film and you are the star in role and the spectator – both at the same time.

It seems impossible at first, but with continuous and constant practice and a firm determination to succeed, it becomes almost like child's play.

Finally and with great relief, the soul can express its best qualities when it is no longer emotionally involved (although people generally don't think they can do without it) – which is a paradox. Consequently, creativity and freedom of thought (fruits of emotional independence) are unleashed.

The door of the heart opens to the Cosmic, or Christ Consciousness when the combination of heart and mind produces the gift of discernment.

But, beware! Do not confuse your emotions with the heart. It is the spiritual heart I speak about. Let me specify: the evil is in the mind[188], while goodness is in the heart. When the two are in harmony, evil becomes goodness and we become divine (new people, or angels).

Having crossed the threshold of the heart, we are back home, to the true Self (Spirit).

After the great renunciation of the world of matter (the crucifixion of the ego, as the most important Christly symbol) and the rebirth into the body of Light, the human and the Divine fuse together.

This is Resurrection and Ascension. They are expressions of the vibration of unconditional Love (i.e., the sacrifice of the ego for the love of humanity), leading to eternal inner Peace, the Harmony of Oneness, the 5th dimension, or the Kingdom of Heaven.

In this dimension, the law of resonance and permeability replaces the law of attraction and repulsion of the dual physical world.

The first year of the third millennium ended in a somewhat unusual manner: with a message followed by an enigmatic, synthetic communication.

The message read:

"You will ascend when the time comes and reunite with your companions, to fulfil the task for which you were chosen.

This Earth is waiting to go through some dark moments. You will be the ever-vivid Light guiding others through the dark storm, helping your brothers and sisters to stick to the path of salvation, against all odds.

You will be the calm harbour for the souls weary of coping with the raging waves of life. Peace must reign in you, sovereign, so that you can soothe and heal the ills of others.

Non-attached to the world, you will have to wander far and wide to bring words of strength and courage everywhere, to continue the never ending journey, until you finally realize that you are the goal. Then, Unity will bring forth the day of reckoning for all mankind."

The message that followed said:

"The heart has gone to the centre of its being. It will return renewed and fragrant like a flower".

It was astonishing, also because the same day I felt a powerful pang in my heart. I was concerned a bit, but then everything went back to normal.

The following summer I received an unexpected gift from a friend: a beautiful, rose-coloured lotus flower, with a delicate scent.

For me it was a sign that "the heart returned, like a fragrant flower", that is, that the moment described in the message had arrived. As for the meaning of the phrase, allow me a personal interpretation: I'd become centred in the heart. The Eternal Judge takes into account exclusively the efforts made on the path of liberation. I could have been rewarded because mine were so great.

The Hindu Holy Scripture, the *Bhagavad-Gita* says in this regard: *"But those who always worship Me with exclusive devotion, meditating on My transcendental form- -to them I carry what they lack, and I preserve what they have."* (Chapter 9, Sloka 22).

Sai Baba has always claimed that, when we surrender to God, He takes our burden and possibly erases, by His Grace, our heavy debts (as He did for me). I personally experienced this divine support - it was increasingly evident and decisive in achieving unity with God.

The Age of Pisces came to an end – two thousand years in which man fully delegated religious institutions to intercede for him with the Divine Power. We are now in the Age of Aquarius, the bearer of Spiritual Knowledge for the new man who wants to learn the Truth and think for himself instead of delegating an institution to be the intermediary with God.

The first message of the second year of the third millennium didn't take long to arrive. It said:

"The inner journey takes man to the conquest of celestial realms. I have bestowed the greatest grace upon you: I will lead you to the realms your soul has longed for so much.

May your word always be My Word and we will be at one as we awaken other souls to the divine inspiration of true life and heal every obstructing tendency. Be a messenger of Light and Peace, be pure Love, be Me, as I am you. We are at one now. I will soon bless the book – which is both yours and Mine – rest assured. Be happy.

I want you to be happy. Shiny like a rare diamond, your soul will look through your eyes and it will finally enlighten your single eye. My gift to you is the loving touch, to regenerate you. Enjoy the renewal of the soul, rejuvenate your awakened mind and ensure its vital space. This is the only way for you to stay on the path you have chosen and reach your destination – with confidence, serenity and satisfaction."

My perception of being centred in the heart was therefore appropriate – I was finally at one with the Spirit within.

The book the inner voice referred to is the one you are reading.

The Spirit's gift of the loving touch was the practice of Reiki on me by a friend of mine, which alleviated my temporary fatigue.

I had a dream full of Christian symbolism more or less at that time. I was in a Catholic church and after the communion the celebrant priest gave me a gold chalice, full of hosts. I laid it on the altar (thinking it was the altar of the sacrifice of the ego).

Was that a hint that I was ready to pass on to others what I had received? From what I'd learned from the study of symbology, the golden chalice represented the purified heart. The hosts, or the body of Christ, stood for His message we should bring to light as a message of a lifetime – to be practiced daily, and not just during the Sunday sermon.

After meditation, one day, I heard the voice say:

"I love you, you will be the bait for a miraculous fishing. Small and large fish will be caught, so they can discover how little they know."

I no longer learned through bitterness and suffering – I could finally do it through wisdom. At least, that's what I hoped for.

Sai Baba says: *"True happiness is Unity with God", and* I knew that was true. I also knew that heartfelt joy could be communicated to others and by joy I imply the fulfilment (happiness) of feeling at one with God.

The final tribute a person pays to the Absolute prior to liberation is the voluntary and irrevocable self-offering. This is because real life comes from the kind of self-giving that does not expect anything in return.

That was where I was at that point. Having devoted myself to the Most High, I felt I would soon have to make another leap in the dark (or in the abyss, as the inner voice said), but I also sensed His support (with the total faith I had in God).

One morning, after meditation, I had a marvellous vision. I saw a huge, white lotus. It disappeared immediately, leaving a white glow which also disappeared. I discovered that the white lotus symbolized pure (*Aditi*), Immaculate Divine Consciousness, the Divine Mother, the golden bridge connecting us to the Absolute. It depicts the seventh or crown chakra (the thousand-petalled lotus, where God resides) through which divine energy flows and awakens man to Christ Consciousness. The rose-coloured lotus, instead, symbolizes the incarnation of God on Earth – the *Avatar* (Sai Baba in our time).

The consciousness of being free can only come by Divine Grace. Whenever I couldn't figure out what I was going through, I would put myself into the hands of God, so that His Will could become mine.

After many years of complete solitude, I took in that my soul was not granted an "exterior" (someone to compare myself with) Master, but the Inner Master who followed me for years in silence, until I started hearing the inner voice (His manifestation).

Constantly supported by the Divine Grace, I've always had to discover everything by myself and on my own.

My aim was to achieve Self-realization – in silence, through dreams, meditation, the study of sacred and esoteric texts, reading the signs, the symbols, the *I Ching*, the Tarot, the stars and everything else which came to my attention – through self-inquiry, self-criticism and self-knowledge. I could not complain about the means, given the variety and richness of material that the Divine Master placed at my disposal over the years.

To monitor my progress (or regression), I also studied the miracle of synchronicity – which occurs daily when life flows with the *Dharma*, in the right direction, the direction of the Divine Light.

I finally understood that the 'Word' was the most powerful gift available to us as human beings, like the Word of Truth, or the Word of God (crystal clear, transparent).

In this regard I would like to underscore the importance of transparency in the words, thoughts and actions. Nothing brings equanimity, balance and harmony faster than transparency (or visibility) which is synonymous with truth.

The 'treasure map' I was completing had to meet the said requirements if I didn't want to disappoint the Divine Master (who is also the Inner Master). He was the invariable witness and friend in the adventure I had promised not only to speak about, but also to live up to – as any other 'Virgin' worthy of respect would do.

Sai Baba says that *"God is the only true Friend, the only One who has no ego and never lets you down."*

Jesus said: *"You will be given the possibility to know the mysteries of the Kingdom of God"*, and *"The Kingdom of God is within you. Seek the Kingdom of God and all the rest will be given to you in addition"*.

The Kingdom of God is the condition of the one who has realized that the Holy Spirit is within, being part of him, or her.

I've personally heard Sai Baba say: *"I am the Holy Ghost"* when I was in India. While in Italy, the inner voice, which is a manifestation of the Holy Spirit (or Divine Master, or Inner Master), kept repeating it.

This is the time of the return of the Holy Spirit, or the Christ Consciousness. It is taking place now.

The Holy Spirit has always been in us (and It always will be), as the inner voice reiterated (*"I have always been there, but you neither saw nor heard me"*) but we haven't been aware of it, at least until today.

The Holy Spirit is the source that quenches the thirst once and for all. It is the Master of the Masters, the Inner Master (*Sadguru* in Sanskrit) guiding us all the time. It is the Divine Mother, it is the Christ, or Cosmic Consciousness, it is the inner voice, it is the seeker and the sought, is the divine essence in us but also the divine essence of all the manifest reality, it is the very breath as the Divine Breath (*Prana* in Sanskrit, *Pneuma* in Greek), it is the Word, the word that heals, it is the pure soul of the initiate.

There is a poem by Hildegard of Bingen on the Holy Spirit, in which she explained what It represented to her (Translator's note: translation taken from Stephen Mitchell's anthology of poetry, *The Enlightened Heart*):

"Holy Spirit, giving life to all life, enlivening all creatures, root of all things that you wash clean, wiping out the mistakes, healing the wounds. You are our true life, luminous, wonderful, awakening the heart after a very long sleep."

When it comes to vibration frequencies, I compared my personal experience with the various books I'd studied and came to understand that frequencies were directly proportional to the degree to which we have mastered the ego, or the mind, so that we can live our destiny harmoniously (implying the harmony of thoughts, words and actions) and transparently (implying truth, honesty, loyalty and spontaneity).

The more evolved we are within – the more authentic, consistent, spontaneous, heart-centred we are – the higher the vibration frequencies. They protect us from low frequencies (anxiety, fear, depression, etc..), thereby shielding us from negative energies. That is how righteousness preserves itself and defends us from danger.

The highest frequencies (inner peace, joy, compassion, etc..) allow us to tune in with Divine Love, or the presence of God in each one of us.

In other words, the less evolved we are, the more susceptible we become to other people's energies. We consequently become dependent, frustrated, confused, indecisive, depressed, apathetic, abulic and so on, because if our inner vibration is low, we cannot avoid getting in tune with the worst of what life has to offer today, like spiritual slavery (until death) in the dungeon of the ego.

It thus becomes apparent that a 'realized' person is the one who understands his or her own divinity (*Atma*, essence, divine spark), who is the master of himself, or herself, and is no longer subservient to or conditioned by anything outwardly. This one is certainly a difficult figure in a society where 'collective' brainwashing fuels the ever stronger economic, political, religious and scientific power of the rulers of planet Earth. For this reason, spiritual quests are extremely unpopular in the consumer society we live in, as they absolve people from social restraints. To master the mind with the Spirit within means to take control over our emotions and ultimately our physical body.

Understandably, the capability to make decisions is directly proportional to the ability to discern between good and evil, true and false, that is, the ability to manage (instead of being managed by) emotions and thoughts. The capability to take decisions is also linked to the level of awareness. Once again, the outcome is quite unpopular: people thinking and acting for themselves, finding easier and easier solutions to life problems. Of course, their personal wellbeing and growth are not in the interest of the lobbies controlling the planet – they could jeopardize their power and have undesirable effects on it.

Jesus said: *"I have come to bring the sword."* The sword is the Truth, the Word of God, which is not always pleasant to hear, because our life is not always in line with His Will. So, His message of two thousand years ago and that of Sai Baba alike have been quite unpopular to this day. Advocating them can be a risky undertaking, falling short of attracting the praises of the silent majority.

Someone said Heaven is for adventurous spirits. I agree.

However, all this did not stop me in my intention to actualize the message of Love, in the direct experience of life. I was increasingly convinced that the more centred we are in our heart (i.e. in harmony with the divine message), the more pure Light we unleash – pure Love being the force, the irrepressible, unstoppable power, difficult to control or govern by the sophisticated and widespread systems of power control in today's society.

Coming back to the topic of Light, when we are centred in the heart, the Light emanated thereupon enables us to get in touch with God, as the Divine Spark,
llowing the individual consciousness to awaken (expand) and become Christ or Cosmic Consciousness.

I was going to return to India for the fourth time in the third millennium, feeling lighter under the increasing protection of God.

A friend of mine (a clairvoyant) saw palish colours in my aura, like that of a child. It was a pleasant revelation that supported a secret I held back: I was becoming a "child" again!

I don't think this new interior condition had anything to do with the recurrent dreams of children I'd had for years. I dreamt almost every night of taking care, in a variety of ways, and looking after small children, ranging from a few months to a couple of years of age. They were all in trouble and I rescued them from danger (fire, water, snow, etc..), pampered them, fed them and changed their nappies or clothes. Children were really a constant in my dreamworld.

I was already in India, at Whitefield, when I received the following message: *"You will soon find the aids who will support you in your difficult task of bringing peace on Earth. Do not be afraid, you will not be on your own. You'll finally witness the realization of your distant dream: assisting everyone in need and helping them disentangle from the maze of human passions. I want you to be free, I want you to know what is the right thing to do in every circumstance. The word of wisdom will be the tool for practicing the art of healing. This is the only way for you to serve Me, according to My Will."*

Inside the *ashram*, I found the thought of the day written on the board. It said: *"The only thing relevant to the Divine is the union of the devotee's heart with Him."* On the day of the departure, I woke up happy, after a fantastic dream: Sai Baba invited me to lunch. He ordered two large silver trays for me – one was full of soft, white bread[189], and the other was full of soft, white butter. In the dream I was puzzled and embarrassed at the sight of so much food and did not think I would be able to eat all that.

I woke up joyous and surprised by the fulfilment I felt in my heart. This feeling stuck with me ever since.

On the way back, I walked on thin air, I was so elated.

Sai Baba says: *"A true devotee is the one who cares about the happiness of God first, then about that of his fellow men, and finally about his own"* I hoped with all my heart that the Divine Master was pleased with the book I was writing. The words He told me during the last interview resounded in the heart: *"Be happy, be happy, be happy"* and that gave me the strength and support to continue my journey on the challenging path.

I dreamt about the end of the world once again. At three o'clock in the afternoon, the sky became very dark and the people in the street stopped to watch, lost in the all-embracing darkness. No one understood what was going on.

I tried to get in touch with my son by cell phone, but it didn't work. There was no electricity and people started to panic. Then I woke up, also agitated, incredulous of being at home, in my bed.

The age I experienced in the dream would see the rise of the Golden Age and the presence of the Great Comforter, the Holy Spirit. All the great mysteries that had remained hidden from the human eye for millennia would be revealed. We do not have to wait for Him. He is already here with us (as an incarnation of God), even though so many people have not recognized Him yet.

I was relieved, because I felt in tune with this age, so special, and shared what I had learned in the relentless pursuit of myself.

I considered the dream in which Sai Baba invited me to lunch as an initiation into the New Age. An I talked about the dream with an English friend of mine and she reminded me of the metaphor commonly used in the English language, denoting essential, basic elements. This interpretation was appropriate for that dream: indeed, my heart knew I had everything I needed.

Sai Baba says: "*The desire to serve God appears when you are on friendly terms with God. Therefore, friendship comes first and then we surrender to Him.*" Surrender is followed by Joy, Peace, Wisdom, Love and Bliss. Guaranteed. Try and see.

Shortly after my return to Italy, the inner voice came up with a new message:

"*Do not fret for what is happening, it will mould you for the work I am offering to you. You know that the time is ripe for long-term plans.*

Your have regained your strength, so nothing and no one can stand in your way. You must complete your task and find someone to relieve you from your burden when you are tired or confused, always patching up thought with action. I want you to be a master in coherence and wisdom because you've already leafed through the Book of Life. You know you have reached the tipping point and you don't need a cue to start a real dialogue with those you meet on your way, whom you want to assist.

My shining star, there is nothing else for you to do but to shine your Light; it will be dim or radiant, depending on the soul's life.

Oh sweet beloved, your soul can not live for you alone any longer – it would fade away, knowing that nothing but unconditional Love could soothe it and enrich with joy and virtue the remaining years of your stay here on Earth."

This message was also partly vague. However, I knew it was still useless to try and interpret it with reason, that being entirely useless in this context.

Only intuitive intelligence goes beyond the barriers of rationality, but it is activated only by the Grace of God – not by our own will.

I received another message a few days later:

"You are both a mother and a baby, My sweet darling. You are the All that is found everywhere, like a gold nugget, like the divine spark belonging to the golden star to which it will return when the time is due, stripped of appearance which has moved you away from the essence. What is has always been. What sometimes is and other times isn't, in reality is but a trivial illusion of the egoic Self."

I realized that the inner voice was speaking about the Holy Spirit, which is both form and substance, or rather the "essence" which becomes manifest form, but still remains essence (i.e. Light that becomes matter), albeit invisible.

I asked the Divine Master, in my heart, to keep me with Him all the time, for eternity, while I gave full availability to return to the earthly world as often as He deemed it necessary, not for my sake but for the sake of my brothers and sisters in Him.

That night, the inner voice told me, calling me by the name:

"... Wake up! Listen! I am He who is and I will always be with you!".

Words cannot describe that magical moment. My heart was flooded with gratitude for the gentle and watchful kindness of the Divine Master.

Jesus said: *"He who loves his mother, father, brothers and sisters more than Me is not worthy of My name."* What did the Divine Master of two thousand years ago mean by these words? That we must put God first so as to be worthy of the gift of the Christ Consciousness, that is, of the Constant Integrated Awareness, as defined by Sai Baba, who is the Christly Light of unconditional Love, the bulwark of 'His Name' (the attributes of God are: Beauty, Kindness, Splendour, Love), of the 'abode of the Father', of the subtle spiritual worlds that await us when we become purified and centred in the heart.

Another message (through the inner voice) arrived:

"Love, Love and more Love is the sweet music that invites each heart to sing – every heart awakened in the Light of the never-ending day, the eternal day which is the only reality. Sounds and colours, sweet and soft, welcome the awakening of those who have made, like you, the best choice[190] by heeding the messages of the Light and the heart and thereby pursue the goal on the direct path, the path of righteousness. When you gain full consciousness of your life, as Essence, you will understand that darkness has never existed, except for those who allow their source of all-enlightening light to be obscured by ignorance.

Do not worry, your son will, like you, choose the Truth. This is the reason why he came to this world that also consists of fatuity. It is no coincidence that with you he has had to mature, by making tough choices, albeit wise, and this will prevent him from sinking. You are hosts of the same nature and heavenly origin. You are here to fight, to save people, affirming righteousness, truth and beauty[191], by setting examples and speaking words that bear the seal of Love."

I had always hoped that my son would become a 'warrior of light'[192]. The inner voice confirmed it and that is the greatest reward a mother can receive. I thanked the Holy Spirit, the Divine Master, for this gift. I felt I was pardoned. Pardoned are those who no longer belong to the world they live in, those whose penalty (the weight of *karma*) has been "condoned".

In my case, I felt relieved of the *karma* of this lifetime. When it comes to the previous lives, I didn't know anything that far, except that the Divine Grace could annul that too.

The inner voice was back in a little while:

"In order not to disperse the lightness and transparency of your eternal, natural essence, I invite you to feed yourself with subtle joys, which hold the strings of the Universe.

The Scent of Love in the air you breathe, the touch of Love in the light that you attract, are continuous confirmations of life (which is Love), every day and every moment.

Let your Guru[193] be the centre of gravity around which your will rotates. His task will be to give you fulfilment, and then you will firmly honour this choice.

I have spoken about what is without foundation to the world, yet it represents, like your essence, the only reality."

A few days later, another message arrived:

"Sweet girl, you are loved beyond measure by the Self, the 'I am' that in you suc-cumbs every time you think you are on your own. The Life of the entire Universe is in you; the Light of the whole firmament is in you.

You are a star of supreme beauty; diamonds set in the crown of creation are the thousand facets of the multiple lives lived in the shade of your virtues.

Weary you are by now of treading the boundaries of the mundane world that holds no surprise for you.

More than ever, you long to taste the delicate nectar of eternal life – you, who have always aspired to immortality. Words can no longer express the gentle melodies played by the divine music to soothe the extension of your exile.

You will soon come to Me, to be refreshed. I will quench your heart so that it can face the commitment of the last steps to the goal.

No, you will not succumb under the weight of the long wait you have filled with various searches for the meaning of your life, the sense of which is now clear. You have completed the embroidery and you will soon present it to Me. It will have My approval, so you can continue your eternal life in other dimensions. Blessed flower, fragrant flower, your colour is of incomparable beauty because your substance, or essence, is Love. I bless you ever more. Remain in peace, My sweet love."

In a month's time, I was back in India. I began to think that the said "embroidery" was the book I was finishing. I really hoped it was so, because it would mean that I had the Divine Master's blessing, as He had disclosed to me years earlier.

185. I left a week before the attack on the Twin Towers in New York.

186. Hindu Holy Scriptures say that Shiva transformed *Kama* (desires) into ashes and strewed His body with it, to show that He had mastered them.

187. Mother Teresa of Calcutta was a living example of unconditional Love in the previous century.

188. When it is the mind that hears, and not the heart, it does not understand but it judges, removes, denies, distracts, circumvents. For instance, the mind would not be able to say something like this: "I recommend everyone who is 'attached' to someone, to have the courage to leave the wrong person and start a new life." Why? Simply because the mind calls attraction 'Love'.

189. Bread and butter are considered sacred food in India. In the Western esoteric tradition, bread is the 'body of Christ', the Word of God (the Truth), which Jesus incarnated. In the Hindu tradition, butter represents the pure heart, filled with Love for God.

190. An ad in the street caught my attention. It said: "You are free to choose, so choose the best."

191. These are the same inalienable principles emphasized in the philosophy of Socrates (in Classical Greece). My son had the following one-liner by Dante Alighieri posted on a wall in his studio: "Heat cannot be separated from fire, or beauty from The Eternal". What a coincidence!

192. In a letter to the Romans, Apostle Paul said: "We wear the weapons of light", referring, I believe, to Christ Consciousness.

193. *Guru* means Master. It is about the Inner Master who resides in the heart. *Gu* – darkness, *Ru* – light, that is, the one who dispels the darkness of ignorance.

194. I recalled the dreams I'd had, with so many peacocks symbolizing immortality.

XX

"Wherever there is Love, God is manifest."

Sai Baba.

I was about to leave for India, when I received this message:

"All of nature vibrates in the sublime beauty of the autumn air. From the sacred spring you have drunk clear and pure water in order to cleanse your natural essence – that wanted to incarnate in this season – from any residual waste. The day of your birth was the day of perfect balance[195], of complete harmony, to remind you of your task as a warrior of light.

The leaves blown by the wind play the game to interrupt the flow of light that the sunrays[196] direct straight into your heart. Do you see Me? I am the Light, I am the essence, a hymn of joy that assumes your appearance for the time of your earthly life. However, it will shine in Me eternally as essence, or Light, when you leave the Earth to join Me, luminous and serene. In silence you wonder how you deserved this honour, as you reread the messages I have often sent you over the last few years.

There is nothing you need to discover. You can recognize My voice by now, and you can feel the warmth of My rays. I am warming and lighting up your face out of Love, only out of Love. I have sent you those messages out of Love, to sweeten your bitter fate[197] as much as possible.

You have to be patient, only for a little while, and you will soon be able to start serving Me, according to your role. You will then understand what the present appears obscure and vague. Your life will be enlightened and you will be at one with your goal while immersed in the Divine Knowledge. You will know how to move around. You will become a wise aide to those who meet you because you will have crossed the shores of the white lake you visited in the past, which is now within you.

You are the Love and the Knowledge, My dear essence. Now that you know it, do not ever stop rejoicing at My Glory[198] – which is yours, it belongs to you – at My joy that contains your entire being.

As you identify with Me, you discover that there is no void that is not readily filled with the vital fullness of life, or essence, with My all-encompassing presence that represents everything because it is the All."

This message confirmed to me that the so-called "holy waters" verily contained special vibrations. I had been collecting them for years, from various sacred sites of Europe, but also from India (like the water from Patal, visited years earlier). That particular reference was to the water source of Arunachala, the mountain sacred to Shiva, in southern India, where the great saint Ramana Maharishi lived and died.

About the honours, it was true that the more I reread the messages I'd received (I never let anyone else read them), the more I wondered how come they were addressed to me. I was acknowledged the so-called sixth sense, or intuition, but also the seventh sense, or Divine Knowledge, which seemed like a huge honour – too great considering my little person.

I was fairly struck by the reference to the white lake that I had visited years before, in an astral journey. I would never expect the inner voice to mention *Shamballa*, the meeting venue of all the great sages who protect the Earth in this transitional age, located in a subtle dimension I know nothing else about (is it the 4th dimension?).

The reference to the sunlight clarified that the divine presence was also manifest as sunlight, which might seem obvious, but it is not, because if that were the case, we would all be aware of being kissed by God, every day and every moment, of being embraced by Him just as we are enveloped by the sunlight, unconditionally and lovingly. It gives us life and energy, moment by moment, without ever asking anything in return.

That afternoon (it was five o'clock when I received the message) I was sitting at the table, staring through the window at the sunrays playing hide and seek with me, peeking through the branches of the peach tree, the only tree in the garden. I was wondering if the inner voice belonged to the Guardian Angel, the Inner Master, the Self or the Holy Spirit, the unconscious mind, and then I realized that God was One, and included everything, so I could never be wrong if I believed that it was He – as I had always felt in the heart.

This is the problem when you are a grown up – you've lost the original innocence. As a child, I never raised such questions. I was simply convinced I was talking to God and this sufficed. This didn't make me proud, because I thought it was just a normal thing to do.

I tried to go to India for the Dasara Festival (which lasts ten days and I had never attended it) but the trip was rescheduled for the following month due to some unexpected events. In this regard, I received an illuminating message:

"The ten days of purification are now inaugurated. Take part in this festival in the heart, sacrificing every bond, to rediscover your innate purity.

You wished to attend the rites here with Me, but although you are not physically present, you can achieve the scope, provided you don't add any obstacles to your ascent that has already begun.

The clamour of worldly life cannot attract you any more, let the others perform the tasks of everyday life. Do not confuse what you feel with the feelings of others: different needs separate you from those who are next to you. You cannot refuse your divine mission, although you are still suffering and nobody can ease your pain.

Only purity can give you peace of mind. By invoking Me all the time, pain will be taken over by joy.

You will soon have[199] the confirmation of My love, you who never tire of feeling My presence, although you still struggle to leave behind the 'personal issues' that prevent you from living beyond good and evil (beyond the mind). This path is destined to you, now that you have fulfilled the tasks you had set yourself. You will soon be able to enter eternity and become part of My body. You will no longer remember the taste of pain, as you will be experiencing only Love."

For the first time, the ascension with the body of Light was being mentioned, which I was supposed to go through in a near future, according to the inner voice. Bonds affect our original purity. This sore of human life had been the subject of attention for decades in the many speeches of the Divine Master. Sai Baba often reiterates that man is born free (walking on two legs), then he gets married (the legs are now 'four'), then he has his own child (the legs become six), and so on, until he becomes like a cockroach (many legs – much slavery!).

I departed for the twenty-seventh trip to India (the fifth in the third millennium), where wonderful experiences awaited me and I concluded that year with a flourish, once again kissed by Divine Grace.

As soon as I arrived at the *ashram*, I rushed to the temple (*Mandir*), without even changing my clothes. I was right in time for Sai Baba's *darshan*.

I asked a *seva* (usher) if He had come out and suddenly I heard a reply, "He is waiting for you". At that precise moment Sai Baba came out of His home to enter the *Mandir*. Deeply moved, I couldn't suppress the tears of joy. I remembered one of His lines: *"The ocean of ever-lasting life is waiting for you"*. The Absolute had waited for this little person, for me.

In the year two thousand, the inner voice announced that *"I will once again become an ocean wave in the ocean He represents."* It was the crowning of the work of a lifetime, unfolding before the Divine Master who had descended to Earth in His physical form. What else could I wish for, now that I had everything – having found Him?

During that stay I dreamt of Our Lady. She was beautiful, with the Infant Jesus in Her arms, His head covered with golden curls in a radiant frame, set in a blue sky glittering with stars.

Then I dreamt that Sai Baba called me for an interview (in fact, He did call me a few days later). He anointed my head with oil while telling me about a task He would assign me to. I kissed His hands, as a sign of gratitude.

I woke up filled with energy and peace of mind, even though I couldn't remember a thing about the task assigned to me.

A day before my departure, I had another *interview*, unexpectedly, in His private room, and He told me: 'How are you, sir?'"

He had never addressed me in this way before, even though He does use this appellation, albeit rarely, with some women, for reasons unknown to me. He then added that I should work harder. At the time I thought He referred to the inner work, I realized later it was about the book I subsequently finished.

As I watched the Divine Master seated, beating the time of the *bhajans* with His hand on the armchair, I silently repeated some verses dedicated to Him, coming from the heart in the moment of inspiration.

The verses went like this: *"Your throne is my heart, Lord, on which You beat the time of life, which is Your song of Love".*

The heartbeat, as well as the breath, is the song that the Spirit of Life (God) sings within us, through us. But the true throne of God is humility, thus God can be seated only in a pure and humble heart. My heart wanted to be like that – humble and full of gratitude for the Love He lavished on me. The Bible says: *"With humility comes wisdom".*

The Grace bestowed by the Sacred Heart of the Lord is proportionate to the trust and gratitude we manifest. And so, this is the kind of effort He asks us to make: to be in tune with the Divine within.

These are the most powerful magnets attracting Grace upon us, which heals not only the heart, but also the body.

Since I chose the path of the Spirit, I have never been ill again in all these years. Diseases belong to history, prior to my forties, when I decided to detach myself, slowly but steadily, from the delusions of the world.

I understood that, when they strike, diseases signal that there is something wrong on our pathway, hence we should always welcome them, respectfully and without fear, take the message in (it being the message of the soul, coming from the Spirit, to help us know ourselves better), understand it fully and make the shift – or at least adjust the course.

We should always remember that joy and the love of life are not accompanied by diseases, for wherever joy is, there is God. God is pure joy, pure energy, pure life, pure harmony, whereas the disease is an expression of disharmony, just as sin is an expression of disarray and ignorance.

Here's how Sai Baba comes to our aid in this respect: *"Do not worry about the future, do not bear any grudges against the past. Just try to be correct today, in the present. Do not care about the fruits of your actions, this is your Dharma and everything will be given to you."* (here *Dharma* is understood as 'task in this incarnation').

I had just returned to Italy when I heard the news. The Pope was embittered and claimed that God did not reveal Himself any more since He was so disgusted by the behaviour of mankind and alluded to wars, world hunger, rampant corruption, and so on.

I was really outside the norm, as I was increasingly convinced that I was continuously receiving Divine Revelations and that they duly manifested in 'normal', everyday life.

Man must return to being his own priest if he wants to hear the voice of God being revealed to him. There is no other way, I've learned it from personal experience. The force of the mystic idealism I was driven by – if I may define so my profound aspiration to Pure Love, to the Absolute – made me live through a passionate search for Eternal Love, until I realized it was incompatible with human nature – so limited by the ego and its faults and miseries, that is, still a prey to spiritual ignorance.

An idea finally dawned in me: having searched for the real me and for Divine, unconditional Love my entire life, I finally deduced I had been reincarnated to realize the following irrefutable fact: that the Divine Love is at one with the real me being the divine essence.

The price I had agreed to pay for this revelation was the life of bitter loneliness and inexplicable suffering, until I found God. On the other hand, only by offering everything to Him, the true Friend within, can we access the Knowledge of the Self.

This accomplishment made me see that it was worth it. Suffering without understanding why we suffered (i.e. without knowing the Truth) was tremendous and it lasted most of my life. In the past ten years, however, I was fully repaid for the torments I had gone through.

I can well say I was reborn to a new life – not as a trivial remark, but literally. I could feel it in my heart.

The year ended with yet another message and a very meaningful vision. The message said:

"My beloved companion, to Me ever closer you are. You shall make this quantum leap into Oneness quite soon. And so I will be able to reveal you the mysteries hidden in the Universe. You shall know the laws of balance and harmony, and take scrupulous care that they be manifest in every creature.

You've realized that pain no longer echoes in your heart. Its strings vibrate other notes. You'll need to work harder to focus on the Self. Be unattached from everything and everyone so that you can soar to Me. Your journey will be light, sublime and radiant. Wherever you are, I'll always be there. You will always be close to Me.

I felt your furtive touch of Love and humility.

Your life will be far away from the clamour of the world, although you will be My messenger in the world, to announce the Gospel of your Sai.

Beloved girl, you will be close to Me soon, in the physicality, to expresses your Love through acts of obedience and kindness. Go ahead, spread the flame of Sai in every country, so that everyone can take the path to Me.

As I said, you shall be the sovereign master of this human life. You shall leave the body without fear, being at one with your Creator. Polarity will be but a mere re-

membrance. *Those who have not broken free of the memory and the flattering of the world will continue coming back as humans and consider themselves lucky.*

Another life awaits you at the place you are going to. Your essence shall unite in one Body of Light with those who have chosen to live in My presence, where you shall finally find Peace, Love and Light."

I remembered the words spoken in the previous interview (*"You have to work harder."*). In the message I was again asked to work harder and explained why. During the interview, I secretly and timidly touched the garment of the Divine Master, and I was reminded of that in the message. Once again, there was an allusion to my role as messenger of Him. That role had been recognized ten years earlier, by my son. What an extraordinary coincidence!

The beginning and the end of the message mentioned the transition to the 5th dimension, previously mentioned in several messages. My heart perceived those references to ascension, or resurrection, as the greatest manifestation of Divine Love in my regard through the delicate 'touch' of the inner voice.

The reference to 'spread the flame' was symbolically related to a photograph (of a flame) of a devotee (Italian) who had received a miracle from Sai Baba in Australia: the materialization of an unidentified substance (similar to wood) lit up by self-combustion, producing a beautiful flame that keeps burning. He called it 'the flame of Sai for Australia'.

On my return from India, I made several copies of that photo and I was going to give them to some people who were touched by it in a way.

The vision I had towards the end of the year in a sense completed the picture of the inner work done thus far and highlighted, albeit symbolically, the obtained results. I woke up during the night and saw a torch burning in front of a large book and two chains (like handcuffs) that broke apart. As they opened, they released what they had kept locked in. I could not clearly see what it was (probably two hands), because it was too dark.

I realized that, when the torch of Love and Wisdom lights up the "book of life" (the consciousness), the chains of illusion and attachment break apart and we are free from the ego. In other words, we progress from the small individual self (tied to the delusions of the world) to the realization of the true, universal Self (the macrocosm in the microcosm, the hologram of the Universe contained in a single human entity, as a spark or divine essence).

St. Paul wrote in a letter to the Ephesians: *"All of you are one body and Spirit."* He was telling the Truth, but how many of us experience this Truth in the body and Spirit?

Modern physicists have reached the same conclusion, nearly two thousand years later. (the Quantum Field, the Divine Matrix or the Divine Mind).

The inner voice announcing an upcoming trip to India seemed like a good omen for the new year. And it actually was a very important year because the knowledge of the inner world was deepened further. Astrologically, there were many aspects of sextile and trine in the solar revolution (astrological chart of that year). They formed a perfect hexagon within the circle. The corners of the hexagon were made by the conjunction of the points of a perfect "seal of Solomon, or Star of David" (a six pointed star). This symbol (as I have learned from sacred geometry) depicts the ascension of the body of Light (the *Merkaba*) to the 5th dimension. Therefore, the fact that I found it in the astrological chart of that year stirred enthusiasm and gratitude to the Divine Master for the new life He granted me with, full of Light and Divine Love.

To add a magic touch of Grace to the afore said, something special took place on the 1st January.

I was on my way to my friends' place in the countryside, when a huge rainbow appeared suddenly in the blue sky. Due to an optical (or divine) game, it reminded me of a triumphal arch and I had the feeling it was welcoming me as I was driving underneath it. I was not alone, so I could share that magnificent feeling of union with the Divine with my friends.

I learned, especially after I'd gone through the messages received over the years, that sometimes high-sounding words stand for simple albeit important truths, for example: reaching (the first) enlightenment[200] implies having attained balance of mind and heart and acknowledged the value and priority of Love and Wisdom over worldly things.

Once rid of the illusion[201] of the ego, we can access the dimension of the Eternal Present we already live in, without being aware of it. Where are the past and the future, as we live moment by moment, always and only in the present? In reality, instead of being masters of our time – which we erroneously believe we are – we are slaves of the categories of time and space we came up with (see the different calendars in different world cultures – the Chinese, the Jews and the Muslims observe different calendars, thus confirming the fact that everything connected to human nature is relative and impermanent).

Another great truth is that we should maintain a stable inner peace.

This is what Sai Baba says on this subject:

"Virtues allow God to settle in the temple that is our heart. To be a friend of all people (Maitri or cosmic friendship), *to take care of everyone (Karuna*, or compassion), *to be joyful (Mudita* or equanimity of mind) *and to have no attachments or desires (Upeksa* or non-involvement) *is the way to make the heart a dwelling place of eternal peace[202]"*.

Therefore, a lasting peace of mind is within reach. It is not impossible to attain. With Love, Wisdom, Peace and Bliss in the heart ... there is no room for suffering, pain or fear. This was announced to me as a reward for having reached non-attachment to worldly entanglements and the resulting awareness of the natural essence of God in me.

When the Light of unconditional Love overwhelms the heart, the body lights up as well. It becomes the body of Light. What does this actually mean?

I've read that the body of Light is a radiant vibratory infrastructure (radiant energy ranges from radio waves to cosmic radiation – a high frequency vibration). Its task is to transmit information through the pure energy of Light. The Universe is an ocean of radiant energy (the quantum hologram) in which the bodies of Light of the chosen souls, or the solar warriors, 'surf' beyond the stars and the planets, including Earth.

I've decided to tackle this subject to move away from the idea that these are sheer New Age fantasies. I was of the same opinion many years before, but by studying and experiencing the revelations of the Spirit firsthand, I recognized that what had been announced to me corresponded perfectly to the ancient wisdom reported in the ''Emerald Tables', whose author, Thoth (Hermes) the Atlantean[203], had influenced the Egyptian and the Greek culture with his writings. Moreover, it is also in line with the recent discoveries of Quantum Physics.

Returning to the body of Light, positive thoughts, feelings[204] and actions make us resonate with the more subtle vibrations, until we reach the frequency of Light, the so-called cosmic radiation.

I received the first message in that year, welcomed as a positive presage.

"You will be an arrow of pink Light in the vast blue horizon. Clad in the colours of the rainbow, you shall live in My presence as immaculate essence. The games of human darkness will be far away from your sight, vibrating only in the light.

Eternal and absolute Love you have sought since you were born in that human form that challenged your quest until you discovered the path to return to Me. I am and always will be Love. I will always give you Love because to Me you belong, indissolubly.

Your awakening will make you rise again, since resurrection is for every elected soul the last thing to experiment before returning to the Absolute, which you also make part of, by My Will. I am Love and so you shall be Love – eternal and absolute. You have My promise."

After mentioning the ascension of the body of Light, Resurrection is mentioned for the first time in a message. The topics were too elevated and holy for my little mind that continued to be frightened and confused about each new truth revealed to me.

A few days later I received another message:

"Remember what I have told. You shall be the lantern to light up the approaching dark time. Do not dwell on what befalls upon you merely to test the strength of your soul and its beauty. Yes, you feel confused, but this state of mind will not last long.

What now appears increasingly fatuous, this burdensome luggage will soon be taken away.

You will soon come to Me, light and sparkling, to be filled with Love and Light, like never before, since a long journey awaits you and you must take it as God intends. At one with Me in heart and mind, you will travel tirelessly from one continent to the other. My name will reign supreme in the words you spread everywhere, albeit on your own. In fact, I'll always be by your side to ensure that your heart is always ready to Love.

Love, Love, Love – that is what you and your life will be about. There will be no more space left in it, until the trial is over."

Even if the mind remained perplexed by the scenario depicted in the message, completely at odds with the life I was living (almost always alone and at home, reading or writing or meditating in my "hermitage"), when I was told that I would travel around the world, the more I reread the words of the message, the more I became convinced in my heart that liberation was a natural event, hidden behind the closed door of my heart. Once that door was open (owing to Spiritual Knowledge) nothing but Love and still more Love could come out.

As it was said in the most recent message, I left for India soon after.

On the eve of my departure, I dreamt of Sai Baba telling me: *"I have allowed this encounter to confirm My friendship to you."*

The message made me feel sparkling like a glass of champagne and sweet like chocolate, but most of all I felt weightless, as never before.

During this trip to India, twenty-eighth in a row, I started making a synthesis of my major inner experiences in the recent years, up till then.

I realized that, in 1998 Sai Baba asked me to give Him a pure heart and a stable mind and in 1999 He asked for a life suffused with Love. These requests were made in public, during the speeches made on the Gurupurnima (Guru Festival).

In 2000 He "married" me, in the mystical marriage of the soul and the Spirit (the alchemical wedding), in the presence of the devotees, during the interview. Since then, over the next two years, the messages of the inner voice intensified, instructing me on the Divine Knowledge revealed to me from time to time. As the Androgynous figure in me was gradually completed (as I achieved Peace and Harmony), Love and Wisdom interpenetrated the Divine Power and Will. As Thoth the Atlantean (Hermes Trismegistus) said,: *"Every step you make elevates the mountain; overall progress increases the goal."*

2003 seemed like the year of the awakening of Christ Consciousness, Resurrection and Ascension into the 5th dimension.

Indeed, the more I progressed, the more I started from scratch, even though the inner peace was stable. The third zero was reached – denying the individual self, that is, renouncing self-attachment (ego), having overcome material attachments and emotional ties and offering myself to God to serve humanity, which is what God had asked me to do.

One can understand better the meaning of the last part by recalling, to simplify things, the "hundredth monkey" effect (or rather the holographic nature of manifest reality). The resonance of an individual's choice is amplified (being the expression of an inherent part of the Whole), extending the individual effect on the entire community, in the sense that all mankind is to benefit from the right choice of an individual.

By setting an example, Jesus Christ as the Divine Master taught us the value of the principle known in Gnosticism as "Sacrifice for humanity", which is sacred work for the benefit of the human race.

But I would like to go back to sacred geometry and the Star of David in the chart of the Solar revolution of that year, characterized by the conjunction of two astral cycles – the Lunar cycle of twenty-eight years (28 + 28 = 56) and the cycle of seven years for Saturn and Uranus – confirming the revolutionary, radical change in life. The Star of David is the hexagram of the perfect man, the Androgyne, who has succeeded in harmonizing the masculine qualities (Knowledge, Wisdom) with the feminine ones (Love, Compassion), the body-mind principle (the soul) with the Spirit and the heart (the divine essence).

I was in India during the festival of Shivaratri. Sai Baba materialized two gold *lingams*, which I had the grace to see.

During a *darshan,* one morning, I had a mysterious vision of an Indian noble-looking woman approaching me, offering me a heart-shaped amber[205] amulet with the word "TURIYA" inscribed[206] on it. She then disappeared into thin air, just as she had appeared.

My imagination was caught by that vision, but as I always did in similar circumstances, whenever intuition did not support the interpretation of events, to stop fuelling my imagination any further, I put everything in God's hands.

I later learned the spiritual meaning of that sacred word.

During that stay at Puttaparthi, I had a prophetic dream (which became reality after a few months). I saw a white goose (symbol of the purified soul, like the swan, *Hamsa* in Sanskrit) that flew out of my home window and alighted gently on a golden pond surrounded by lush vegetation. In the dream, I knew that the vegetation was tropical and that hardly reconciled with the garden back home, in Italy. I stated: 'the goose finally broke free from captivity and returned to its natural habitat'.

The next day I had another dream in which I saw a spring of miraculous water gushing out in my home garden. There was immediately a procession of people coming to collect some. I was confused because they kept coming in greater and greater numbers and I didn't know how to manage such an enormous flow of people.

Upon awakening, I could not explain what I'd seen.

When I returned to Italy, I realized that many questions had been somehow clarified within. I understood that the "awakened" one is he who recognizes the futility of the world of dualities and puts into practice true human values, that the "resurrected" one is he who, once rid of the illusion of the ego and *karma* (related to it), rises again in the light of divine awareness, and, having stepped out of the cycle of rebirths, returns to earth merely to fulfil a task of service entrusted by God for the sake of humanity.

According to the *Bhagavad-Gita*, there are two ways to exit the world: the path of light leading to liberation, and the path of darkness leading to rebirth. Therefore, there are two modalities of returning down here – the first one is without a *karma*, that is, according to the Divine Will as His assistants (or as Masters), and the other to pay off the *karma* of the past, as common mortals.

Sai Baba says, *"By taking refuge in Me, all beings can attain the ultimate realization"* and again: *"If you look at Me, your image will be in My eyes and My image will be in your eyes."* I was still keeping His look in my heart, in His room a few months before, when He bid farewell at the end of the interview. He made me feel "absorbed in Him," or rather "At one with Him."

I finally understood the words of Jesus when He said: "W*hoever has, to him shall more be given; and whoever does not have, even what he thinks he has shall be taken away from him."* I hadn't been able to comprehend those words for many years. Now everything was clear: those who had pure intentions, saw the doors of knowledge wide open, while those who lacked virtue saw every opportunity to make use of their own ingeniousness cut short, inexorably. What a waste!

I had another dream, whose symbolism was incredibly eloquent. I climbed, against common sense, a high cliff falling sheer to the sea, all the way to the top, around me only a storm that raged, rain and wind lashing against my body, hovering between life and death, afraid of falling at any moment. Suddenly, a giant human-like face emerged on the surface of the sea, rippled by huge and menacing waves. There was something monstrous about the face I was staring at in horror, a huge mouth that opened and closed swallowing the waves above.

I was still dizzy when I woke up. After a few days I was in a bookstore, with the intent to look for some books. My attention was drawn to the section of "Astrology" which I hadn't visited for years and, in particular, my eyes focused on a monograph on planet Neptune.

I immediately decided to buy it and left the bookstore. At home I began to leaf through it, as if with a presentiment that I would discover something. Indeed, I was to be revealed something that would enlighten the esoteric meaning of the dream of the night before. Towards the end of the book, I read that planet Neptune granted true inspiration only to a few, whereas it was associated with self-deception with the majority of people, or the spiritually less evolved.

According to this text, the interpretation of this planet's esoteric meaning, compared with the overall astrological birth chart, preludes a path leading to the integration of the emotional (individual) plane into universal life. So, this was my evolutionary task of this lifetime. Once this task was accomplished, I could transcend the physical plane and set out for the path of transpersonal growth.

The big face from the dream was that of Poseidon (in the ancient Greek culture), Neptune (in ancient Roman culture), Kether (in the Jewish Kabbalah), and the Freudian unconscious mind (in the psychoanalytic culture).

Neptune represents the realized Unity with the Divine, the crown of consecration. I was deeply moved. I had no words to express what I felt in the presence of such great generosity demonstrated by the Creator of the Universe, the Almighty, the Oneness, with regard to a small ray of light like me.

After this revelation, I remembered that, the previous year, I had heard the inner voice utter a word I didn't know the meaning of: "CHOCHMA" (another *sephira* from the cabalistic tree). I realized it implied the gaining of wisdom, the Divine Knowledge, the water of life of the Aquarius (Ascendant in my astrological birth chart).

I sometimes missed the inner voice, but I never dared to invoke it. I always put myself in the hands of God and let things manifest according to the Will from High above.

As I spent much time alone, in silence, at times I felt a need for a conversation partner. And so I would consult the *I Ching*, the Tarot (the Major Arcana), the Runes[207], or the Cards of the Universe[208]. One day I received the following response:

"You are now ready for the work of transformation the Creator has entrusted you with. Be happy and brave, you are a divine being. Think like God, act like God, Love like God and God is now powerfully realizing the desires He had put into you, for His Will to manifest. The pathway of your life is free and bright."

It was just a confirmation of what I had been told by the inner voice, and so all I could do was to go on and persevere.

J. Williams said: *"Life becomes a wonderful journey when your travelling companion is God."* I couldn't agree more.

The great enlightened genius Leonardo da Vinci said he was happy when he was on his own, because in those moments he belonged only to himself and that self was the true Self.

In those days, my friend the robin would come to see me almost every day, to confirm that everything around me spoke of rebirth and immortality, although apparently nothing changed in the daily routine. The alchemy of awakening had been triggered in the inner world, bringing renewal in every cell of the body, in every thought that arose in me.

It became obvious that I had undertaken a new 'journey' to freedom from ignorance (the mother of all evils), to remove the veil of illusion obscuring the light of true knowledge. One of the stairheads of the stairway to the stars was the ability to master our senses and our emotions.

When the seven chakras (energy wheels) are functional and in harmony with each other, they become the keys to the awakening of consciousness (through an exchange of cosmic energy) from individual to collective, and finally universal – the enlightenment of the true Self, as the divine essence in us.

The will is crucial on this evolutionary path (to liberation), being indispensable to subdue the mind[209], the emotions and the defects of the ego (such as attraction-repulsion, pride, prejudice, fear, etc.).

One day, eager to speak to the Divine Intelligence, I took a rune to delve into a particular moment I was going through. I chose the one representing the Cosmic Mother, perseverance, safety, protection, wisdom, deep knowledge, but also change as a tool for improvement: the crux of a lifetime.

Indeed, the prospects of life had changed radically. Up until a few years before, I was convinced that I would soon leave the physical world, and so I stopped worrying. It was God's work to decide on my earthly time and beyond – not my business any more.

One revelation after another, my understanding of the significance of what I'd been told deepened. I realized that the rosary, as a wreath of blood and peace, represented renunciation (blood) and wisdom (inner peace). The greater the renunciation, the greater the understanding, that is, we have more access to true knowledge and thus we evolve spiritually.

I understood the words of Jesus with the heart and it became clear that the parable: *"What is bound on earth is bound in Heaven and what is released on earth is released in Heaven"* implied that emotional dependencies, or attachments, are passed on from one lifetime to another, until we succeed in overcoming them. The emotional freedom we achieve will be supported by the eternal becoming.

Among other things, I found out that the farther we progressed on the spiritual path, the sooner we were "billed" for the mistakes. It is like: do not put off until tomorrow ... the settling of your bills.

At the end of the day, this was an advantage granted by the Divine Intelligence, to help the seeker of Truth get rid of the *karmic* burden, as quickly as possible.

On certain occasions, I had the distinct feeling of being watched and followed and it had nothing to do with any kind of "persecution mania". It was about making an impartial evaluation, based on constant and scathing self-scrutiny, of every thought, every action, every word that seemed at odds with the well pondered choice to do the Will of God (the food Jesus Christ was fed by – the Will of the Father) instead of mine (namely that of the ego).

Jokingly, I charged my guardian angel or guiding spirit (some people prefer the Freudian term 'unconscious mind' when alluding to the supervisor watching our conduct from the depth of our being) with censoring. A thought out of place sufficed and, in a flash, something would happen to call me to order – a fall in the street, or I would drop something (a serious trial for my patience, if, for example, it was a jar of sugar or rice). The inner voice was prophetic in 2000, when it foretold that my *karma* would be paid off within two years (to foretell means to be the receptive channel of the Word of God) and that I would transcend[210] the mind.

The transcendent mind becomes enlightened and then universal, since transcending the ego means being at one with God, or with the Supreme Truth. In other words, when you know yourself, you know everything.

The awakened consciousness is destined to become Cosmic Consciousness or Christ Consciousness. It returns to the source of life and fuses with the Oneness, the Almighty, the Absolute. This was going to be the goal for the next leg of the journey (to the Absolute), although my hologram[211] had already completed the journey into the timeless Universe containing realms that are subtler than ours, and so the return into the Light had already been registered. Meanwhile, I was still intent on discerning the true from the false in the mundane and illusory reality down here on earth.

Deep down, I felt that the period of withdrawal that lasted nearly ten years had come to an end. I was asked to go back into the world, although I no longer belonged to it.

When we overcome the fear of loss and death, we can resonate with the music of the heart, with unconditional Love. With this quality, we become the bridge between Heaven and earth and thereby discover that Paradise, the Kingdom of the Father, is not a place in Heaven, but a state of being: *"To be perfect like our Father in Heaven"*, said Jesus. This is why we returned to earth, to discover perfection in ourselves and pass it on in the form of Light and Love to our brothers and sisters.

The sacrifice of ego (ism) on the altar of our freedom allows us to regain perfection, be free at last from the major cause of our 'crucifixion' on matter and return to being our own priests.

Do not confuse the cross with spirituality. As a matter of fact, we are not crucified by the world of the Spirit or by choosing It – as one might erroneously think, drawing a superficial conclusion about the limitations this choice might entail – but by the choice to live in the world and for the world, because our cross actually consists of fear, doubt, guilt, pain, loneliness, confusion, ignorance, etc.. Who can contradict this?

The time finally arrived when I clearly saw, through an enlightening read, that going public about the experiences I'd had over the years was not a mistake (I had moments of serious perplexity, but continued to write nevertheless).

A man of wisdom of the past century, Master Aivanhov, claimed: *"We should jealously cherish the knowledge within, until we have enlivened it. Then, no one can take it away from us and it will help us triumph over the trials we have to face."*

This was another confirmation that the time was ripe to go back into the world (as I had already been foretold by the inner voice).

Jesus said: *"If you abide in Me and My words remain in you, ask what you wish and it will be given to you."*

A few days later, with the right circumstances, my wish to return to the Divine Master turned into reality. Beyond all expectations, my dream (the white goose that would find its natural habitat) came to life.

Two messages arrived with a two day interval, but, for clarity's sake, let me tell you the background story first.

I dreamt of being called to Kodaikanal (India), where Sai Baba hadn't been for more than five years (when I went there and met Him was the last time He had visited it). In the dream, I was told that I'd passed all the tests, including the physical fitness test, and had been selected for a job there (to work with His spiritual association).

Puzzled and surprised by the news, I replied that the altitude (two thousand meters of altitude) wasn't good for my health condition. I asked if I could work in another Sai centre (there are *ashrams* in other Indian cities, besides Puttaparthi and Whitefield).

The next morning (after the dream) I went to the airport to greet some devotees who were back from Whitefield (near Bangalore). I learned from them that Sai Baba had returned to Kodaikanal, after five years of absence.

My first thought was that those were only rumours. However, a friend of mine was leaving for India in a few days and I asked her to let me know where He was.

And so, in this context, the first message arrived:

"Why don't you join Me here, where I'm waiting for you, as you well know? You will be granted creative inspiration when you purify the mind, following the path of the Guru, and when you become unattached from the transitory things perceived by the mind and the senses."

I understood with increasing clarity that transcending egotism meant to become One with the Universe, with the Truth, but I still lingered over my departure.

The next morning I received a call from India. My friend informed me that Sai Baba was leaving for Kodaikanal. It was all true, then. I had to decide whether to leave or not.

Then I received the second message (a warning):

"Why did you doubt the message I gave you? Doubt does not do honour to those who have Me, here and now. From your father you inherited a very hard fate, from which I will deliver you and honour your name. Very soon you will come to Me, to discover your gifts. At last, you will love only Me, with all the Love you possess.

I called to reassure you. I never stopped loving you. I went to the mountain, you know that, but I obliged no one to follow Me. It is Love that prompts Me to call you. You can turn to Me now that you are so close to the turning point that will see your life turned upside down. It is Love that moves everything and resolves all the problems, sometimes causing pain due to 'ignorance' or for the fear of something 'new'.

Do you remember what I said in 1997? My words did not suit you at the time but now, you see, they fit you well because your heart no longer hurts, nor the world troubles you any more, now that you live quietly in the Dharma. You have been acknowledged as the messenger of Truth and this makes you feel light. Peace now dwells in you who are reaching the higher Self.

And so you are apt for the place[212] for which everything is already prepared. You are neither crazy nor a visionary, you're just breathing the air of true life. It is a subtle joy that comes from the heart, as you are aware of being Love.

SAI is you. My dear beloved, always stay close to Me. May you hold My name in your bosom, may your garment be a piece of Heaven.

The Divine Mother embodies as a woman[213] and you too will be a Madonna. To you – the beloved amma to many – I wish good night, dear mother."

That day was in fact Mother's Day – the Divine Master expressed so much tender love and I was still hesitant to go there.

The message confirmed that I would be pardoned the past *karma*, to which Sai Baba had referred already in a dream (telling me that I was paying for 100 years, for my father in Samaria).

With regard to change, the reference to '97, when I was upset by a command of His voice (or inner voice - it is always the same Oneness speaking in the heart), was just perfect – I was no longer afraid of losing.

Among other things, The Divine Master confirmed that I was neither crazy nor a visionary, but simply living in the *Dharma*, i.e. for the task assigned by the Divine Will. That is why I started savouring inner peace.

I left at once (I already had the visa and immediately bought the ticket) for the journey of surrender and obedience to His Will. It was the twenty-ninth journey, the seventh one in the third millennium.

NOTES: CHAPTER XX

195. I was born on the day of the autumnal equinox.

196. In Esotericism, the Sun symbolizes the Messiah, or the Cosmic Christ.

197. This phrase reminded me of the command received a while earlier: "The goblet should be drained.", and it really was terribly bitter.

198. I thought it right to use a pseudonym for the book, "Yor Glory". Yor appears like the phonetic spelling of the word *your*; the 'misspelling' was deliberate. Whatever they do, the American Indians always leave an imperfection. It is done on purpose, as a reminder that only God is perfect. The point is that I left this imperfection, totally unaware that God had a surprise for me in store: Yor Glory *was* my spiritual name, according to what the Divine Master revealed to me in India shortly before the book was published.

199. During the next journey, I had an interview with the Divine Master.

200. In esoteric terms, the second, the third and other enlightenments are also contemplated.

201. Sai Baba says that the entire manifest world is an illusion and the individual self (ego) of every human being is only a small facet of this great illusion.

202. The name of the *ashram* at Puttaparthi is *Prashanthi Nilayam*, which means "Abode of Eternal Peace."

203. I was repeatedly told that I had lived in Atlantis.

204. Compassion is the highest vibratory frequency.

205. Symbolically, amber represents the mental thread that connects individual and cosmic energy. It represents solar, spiritual or divine attraction.

206. After waking, dreaming and deep sleep, there is a fourth state, that of celestial consciousness, or pure awareness, which is reached after the first three states have been transcended. In Sanskrit it is called "Turiya".

207. Celtic Oracle.

208. New Age Cards.

209. Only when there are no more desires, the mind can get rid of the thoughts and focus on the true Self.

210. Destiny is transcended by surrendering to God, or through constant self-inquiry and concentration on the Divine.

211. The hologram is created when a light source is irradiated through a mirror (spiritual reality) into a photographic field (physical reality), thus creating a three-dimensional image. The entire manifest reality (including us, human beings) is probably a hologram. This is in accord with the ancient Vedic wisdom and with Sai Baba's words today, claiming that the manifest world is an illusion and that the Spirit is the only true reality (invisible).

212. Was it the job from the aforementioned dream?

213. I was increasingly convinced that, to Sai Baba, every woman should embody the Divine Mother, considering the great spiritual task assigned to her by the Creator – the task to hold the keys of Love and Wisdom for all mankind.

XXI

"Beyond the senses, there are objects and beyond the objects, there is the mind. Beyond the mind, there is pure reason and beyond pure reason, there is the Human Spirit".

Katha Upanishad

The journey to the Absolute still held in store fantastic surprises: I was soon going to discover something truly unforgettable.

I was in Kodaikanal for the fourth time in 10 years. The first day was dawning and I was queuing, on the lake shore, to enter the abode of Sai Baba, where I would have His *darshan*, the first one in the course of that journey.

Absorbed in my thoughts, I was staring at the lake in front of me, when I suddenly remembered the image from the dream a few months earlier and everything became patently clear.

The golden pond on which the white goose had alighted was the lake of Kodaikanal. It was the same lush vegetation, with forests of centennial eucalyptus trees like a wreath all around it. In that moment the lake was reflecting the golden rays of the sun rising in front of me.

The white goose was hence the soul that was going to regain the freedom. What a striking association.

The next morning, the inner voice confirmed the interpretation from the previous day. In my heart, I heard it say: "I have returned you the dignity of a free Spirit", but I hardly had time to get excited about this sacred event, when something else happened, both incredible and unexpected.

After the morning *darshan*, Sai Baba invited all the participants to lunch and did His best, assisted by His "angels", the students, to serve everyone with abundant food, savoury and sweet, according to the Indian custom.

I was sitting next to the friend of mine who had also been invited to lunch by Sai Baba in the dream I had eight years before.

We looked at each other and I realized that she was deeply moved by the coincidence, as she recalled the dream I'd told her about.

Life is really a daydream when you live in the *Dharma*, doing the Will of God, aware of being divine.

Seized with wonder for the Cosmic Game I was part of, during that stay I asked the Divine Master to be united with Him and to attain equanimity – the ability to see everyone as His equal and to love everyone indistinctively.

In His speech, Sai Baba spoke about Unity as Love and Truth, and said: *"Those who pray God to be United with Him, shall attain it."*

He also says: *"Near to Me, dear to Me, One With Me".*

What a magical journey it was! The said prayer was also immediately confirmed by a message of the inner voice:

"You have answered the call. I confer you the gift to bless, in the name of the Holy Spirit, everyone on your path. This gift shall be enacted with My blessing. This is the honour you have deserved." (to Bless = to invoke Divine Protection and Divine Favour).

This message arrived while I was in the Temple (*Mandir*) of Brindavan (Whitefield), to which I had moved in the meantime, since Sai Baba had returned to His summer residence.

There, after a few days, I received His blessing and heard the following words in the heart, already overflowing with joy and happiness: *"Be a heart of butter and you will give your blessings in the first person because you'll be divine. Do you remember when I told you: 'Be nothing but Love and you will realize, in one lifetime, what you did not realize in the many past lives'? The time has come, and it is NOW."*

That journey lasted for two months, ending with a *Gurupurnima*, the festival of the Guru, the Divine Master. It widely opened the door of the heart to Divine Love: every cell in the body was filled with His Light. Someone said: *"When God speaks within us, we are God."*

All I knew was that I was no longer my old self. I was regenerated by the Grace of Divine Love, embodied in the *Avatar* Sathya Sai Baba.

I was back in Italy for a week when, on the night of the Feast of the Redeemer (a holiday of the City of Venice), the inner voice solemnly announced: *"I am the Holy Ghost".*

When you become nothing, in that very moment you become everything and vice versa – this means achieving the Self, that is, knowing that we are a speck in the infinite All and, at the same time, sparks of the Absolute. I wrote these autobiographic lines, inspired by the Love for the Divine Love, dedicated to Him:

"The afflicted soul wandered aimlessly,
until it saw the first lights of the everlasting day.
The awakening shook its depths,
and made it the elect witness of this dawn.
Its essence finally broke free
from the lifelong imprisonment.
It could finally begin to love, again,
those who were true and real.
The infinite might of the Creator

returned to speak, at Its height.

Bold and bright in its splendour,

that ray of light returned into the Universe".

The revelation of the inner voice concerning the heart of butter pointed at the sacred meaning of the dream I'd made the previous year (in Whitefield), when Sai Baba offered me some bread and butter. Butter symbolizes Absolute Realization, the Christ (or Krishna) Consciousness which is sweet and tender, like butter (in Sanskrit *Sakshatkara*, meaning 'full of bliss, completely absorbed in God'), allowing you to see God in everyone.

The Divine Master fulfilled the wish I'd made shortly before. Indeed, unknowingly, that was precisely what I had asked Sai Baba during the last trip – to meet Him and enjoy the vision of Him all the time and everywhere.

Step by step, I was constantly guided by Him in the completion of the Divine Plan designed for me, even when it comes to the requests I'd considered 'personal'. I came to understand that the inner voice was the voice of the awareness of the Self in us (of the *buddhi*).

I talked to the Divine Master, telling Him more and more often: "My Love, My Lord, My Life, My Light, Your Will, Your Glory"…may they be done all the time. It eventually became my favourite mantra[214].

Confucius said: "To bless means to help". The *I Ching* says: "Heaven helps the devotees, men help the truthful."

The easiest thing in the world seemed to be extremely difficult, until I realized that, to bless others or the entire world, I didn't have to speak aloud – which would have been embarrassing anyway. Doing it in the heart was enough. In this way, the limitations of time or space are bypassed and so, to bless becomes as easy as breathing. It is a way to channel to others the joy and gratitude that increasingly flooded my heart. This river of Love generated by the gratitude I felt for the Creator could regenerate everything around me.

Despite this state of inner well-being, once in a while I dreamt of catastrophic events hitting the earth, like tidal waves wiping out entire cities, including my house, or giant tornadoes of uncontrollable rage, erasing every sign of life on earth, wherever they passed[215].

I received a new message:

"Dear daughter, beloved one, divine mother, do not fear the violence of strange events, now that you have put your fate in My hands. In the face of any danger you will run for Me, the divine blessing will always be bestowed upon you, always intent to protect you and to refine your feelings.

Continue to count on Me. I reside within you. Together, we are an invincible force.

That the Spirit governs matter is no longer a futuristic statement, but a reality. It is now accepted by those who begin to understand that there is little time left for ma-

terialism to finish burning out the glories of an epic on the exit. Now that your desires have calmed down at last, it will be possible to check your potential as 'transmission channel' of the highest entities, which will use you as an instrument that has overcome many ordeals, to spread the knowledge and the life-giving Love everywhere. May Glory be eternal for you and your descendants."

The inner voice brought to light the concerns generated by those dreams and it promptly came to comfort me.

Clearly, the purpose of incarnation, as human beings, is not just individual but also collective, or better, universal.

Therefore, the yearning for the awakening of consciousness from individual to cosmic is the natural consequence of this "memory in us", which is in turn responsible (in my opinion) for that atavistic longing to return to the roots we are all stricken by at least once in a lifetime, regardless of gender, race, faith or culture.

I believe that one's attachment to one's mother, family or homeland reflects the attachment to something more subtle in us, something that brings us back to our true origin, which is not to be found in the family tree, but in Heaven, understood as a spiritual dimension, where memories of angelic lives from the distant past are stored (albeit deleted from our individual consciousness). In fact, we can revert to being angels and it is easier than human imagination can imagine. Truth is, sometimes reality exceeds imagination.

When we stir receptivity (which is esoterically feminine – the Cosmic Virgin) and creativity (which esoterically represents the male principle, the Cosmic Father), i.e. our dormant highest potential, and restore the perfect balance of polarities, we can even defeat disease and death (life = order, disease = disorder).

The Balance and Harmony of the awakened (or Christ) consciousness connect us with the entire Universe: this is the pathway that leads us back to the origins: the abode of the Father, the Kingdom of Heaven (*Kaivalya* in Sanskrit), the pure heart.

Love, blessing, forgiveness, compassion and tolerance are the keys to salvation, or 'the new eyes' (I think) Proust spoke about.

Since my return to Italy, I felt that the approaching change would be so great that it would upset the daily routine at home, where I was living with my son for twenty years, also because I felt an increasingly pressing need to experience the 'dimension of silence', being at peace with God, without interfering with his life.

So I formulated a precise request in the heart, which was unusual for me because God already had given me everything I needed. In general, I would just say "Thy will be done!" in the daily prayers, which were actually a dialogue with Him who was an integral part of me.

The same day I found just what I wanted – which was almost unbelievable. I found the "nest" (a home) I had asked for – small, isolated, well-lighted, on the upper floor and in my favourite neighbourhood.

Everything was perfect, except for one problem: the price was too high. I decided to give it up. After several days, the inner voice spoke up:

"Relieved at last you feel of all the weight created solely by the mind. This September day is rainy, to quench all Nature's thirst. You too have drunk My 'water' and you will never be thirsty again, lucky woman. Real luck is finding God in the heart and therefore being able to live in Love forever. So, the 'water of life' is the Love that represents the fervour of the fire of the Spirit. Oh, beloved daughter, you will soon have a nest[216], where you will rest by merging with Me, completely. You are blessed, My dear beloved. Under your touch, every bitter thing will turn sweet.

Continue to bless everyone you meet, so that everyone can find evidence of My Glory."

I immediately realized that the 'nest' I had found was a gift from Him, so I decided to sign the contract the same day, certain that He would help me resolve all the practicalities.

Generally, when we get old enough to become independent, we venture into a new life and start living on our own. In my case, the opposite happened. It was I (the mother) who became mature enough to decide to leave home for a new life, in union with God. Besides, He said I would never have to worry about anything. I would never be thirsty again after I'd drunk from the fountain of life.

The water of life that quenches thirst once and for all is unconditional Love. Jesus offered it to Mary Magdalene at Jacob's well (my favourite parable from the Gospel).

I've read that the elevation of the mind is a way to transcend it. It occurs when the sharpness of intelligence, enlightened by God, transcends human capacity. What the mind perceives transcends it, but at the same time the mind is not completely alienated from ordinary life because that is the only way for us to express our gratitude to God: by bringing His Word among men every day.

I was increasingly aware that it was not God who made us suffer – it was our ingratitude and ignorance about the gifts He keeps bestowing on us.

We should correct the course of life and tune in with the 'waves' of gratitude, unconditional Love, for us to see the end of suffering in our lives. By knowing and practicing the Word of God, we become our own priests, celebrating life every day, as the most sacred gift from the Divine.

I was getting ready to return to India (it was the third trip of the year) for Sai Baba's birthday when, before departure, I received this message:

"You never seem to be tired of receiving confirmations about your choice. Soon enough, you will be certain that Ruah[217], no one but Ruah, is always by your side. The fact that the world gives only disappointments is an unquestionable constant and your soul knows it well. Soon, it will long only to be united with the essence and it will get rid of the worldly things, as quickly as possible. Only you now feel what I

410

announced earlier. Six years have elapsed from that Christmas, yet you are lighter and firmer every day, since you have realized that you are Ruah".

During this stay at Puttaparthi I had two particularly meaningful dreams. In the first dream, Sai Baba offered me some vibuthi and in the second He placed a gold necklace[218] on my neck, telling me: *"Be happy, be happy, be happy, I am forever with you."*.

Those were His very words of farewell at the end of the last interview, the year before. They mean, in reality: "Be Love, or *Atma*, the divine essence."

One night, the inner voice told me:

"You are given the ability to probe the subtlest dimensions of the Universe." As on other, similar occasions, I could not comprehend the message. However, I was aware that the Self knew everything, so the secret meaning was in me.

Upon returning to Italy, I had to move from one house to another, from one life to another, because my life was going to change with the change of home. After twenty-seven years (living with my son), I was on my own again (this time with God), starting another chapter of my adventurous life, in search of the true Self, the divine essence in me. The search was in its final phase.

I was happy about the choice I'd made and this gave me a lot of energy to address all the difficulties on the way. I could envisage them 'melting like snow in the Sun' that is, resolved by the Divine Grace.

Jesus said: *"If any man will come after Me, let him deny himself and take up his cross, and follow Me"* To deny oneself means to act upon the Will of God – not one's own will. To take the cross means to render the ego harmless (i.e. not to give in to its allurements) and to follow Jesus means to offer oneself to Him, i.e. work for humanity (which is an expression of God).

And then, your heart will be filled with the Holy Spirit, with unconditional Love, and it will no longer experience sorrow and suffering. There will be eternal joy and peace, nothing else. To substantiate this, the inner voice announced that my heart would always be joyful.

Jesus said: *"The man became a living being."* By choosing Light and Divine Love, man attains real life instead of sheer survival.

That was when I met a friend who had been the channel of the Divine in the past, who passed me messages of eternal wisdom. He told me: *"You are ready to ask Him to show you His face."*

I was stunned by this unexpected statement.

A few days later, prompted by the Spirit, I was pondering on those words when I realized that the 'Face' of God was manifest in the Christ Light of the Revealed Knowledge (which leads to enlightenment) and in unconditional Love (which brings the gifts of the Holy Spirit[219]). By revealing It to me in everyone's face and by letting me see His favourite expression (God is joy) in everyone's smile, Sai Baba confirmed me the gifts I'd received (*"You are Love and Knowledge, my dear essence"* His message said).

As the Truth revealed itself in the heart, my eyes saw old things in a new way. I finally understood the meaning of the anointing of my head by Sai Baba, during an 'initiatory' dream.

In the Psalms (the Bible), Grace is called 'the oil of Joyfulness'. The 'anointing' of the head signifies baptism by the Grace of the Holy Spirit, teaching us, through inner inspiration, everything pertaining to the salvation of the soul and preparing us to share it with our brothers. The anointed (Christ) of the Lord is the just (the Angel), he who strives with all his heart (albeit still living an earthly life, in a physical body) to model the soul according to the purity of Heaven.

Reading a book on Hinduism, I discovered that the anointing of the disciple by the Master is also an expression of the elimination of his or her *karma.* That was what the inner voice revealed. Everything coincided perfectly.

With discipline and discernment, all the people of good will can attain this goal and return to being 'angels'. The time is ripe, or rather, salvation time is here and now. The chances to save ourselves are multiplied by a hundred.

Initiates, masters, angels, all the heavenly armies are no longer hidden in the temples or in Heaven (other dimensions). They are among us, so let's try to recognize and accept their assistance, without hesitation. Jesus used to say: *"At the end of time, the Son of man shall come in the Glory of His Father, with 'His Angels'".*

Sai Baba is the Holy Spirit (Grace), the Spouse of the soul that, when "taken as His bride, is clothed with the power from Above, so that it does not yield to temptation, so that it perseveres to the end, so that it can rise again, after each fall."

This extract from the Psalms recalls the revelation made by the inner voice: power (the new clothing of the soul) stems from the discovery of the divine nature in us (made of freedom, inner peace and bliss) or, in a word, being 'Love'.

Sai Baba claims that intention qualifies the deeds, or better: *"Intention is more important than action".*

There was one intention in the heart (like a treasure I watched over): to be the living model of what I had experienced, read, searched for, discovered and written on the true Self, or rather, on the presence of the Holy Spirit in us. These lines were conceived as a road map which would speed up the discovery of the Truth within us, about us, as an additional tool for the seekers of Truth, the real sisters and brothers[220] in God.

I often remembered the key words of the Bhagavad-Gita: *"Leave all the duties behind and take refuge only in Me. I shall free you from all sins."*

In this regard, I had a propitiatory dream. I was offered a huge and beautiful branch of mistletoe[221] (symbolically representing all that heals, thus considered sacred by the Celtic priests). The year was ending in flourish and harmony, with a clarity in the heart about the meaning of certain words, such as 'Essence', 'Awareness' and 'Bliss', incorporated in the Vedic phrase 'Sat Chit Ananda'.

Anyone conscious of being divine (*Atma* = divine spark), having found the true Self, becomes One with the All and can only live in bliss.

During the last night of the year, I dreamt of numerous Tulsi plants (sacred plant to Krishna, the *Avatar* with the heart of butter, or Pure Love). Being able to read the Words of God in the dreams, signs and symbols was another great gift bestowed on me.

On the first day of the New Year, I received the most anticipated present – a message from Him (by that time I was sure that the inner voice was His voice in me):

"I am within you, I am your breath, I am the Love emanating from your heart. Merge with Me. May your form be Love so that we are at one always and every-where.

You will soon make that quantum shift, undoing every bond that still keeps you tied to the world.

You will soon come to Me and so a phase of life will end. You will return renewed to undertake a new, long journey in all directions, as My messenger of Love.

Gender will no longer distinguish you (androgyne) from those around you, because your soul will see the brightness of those who have the honour of meeting you and serving the cause for which you will stay on Earth a bit longer, before you take off for that dimension you are already part of, where you will remain, as long as your evolution benefits from it.

May your heart rejoice in the peace and serenity coming from My heart. Lavish them on all humanity because one heart unites us all, in the embrace of God."
The last phrase was repeated in my heart by the Divine Master throughout the following journey, to substantiate the fact that we all belong to one single heart - the heart of the Universe.

The message reminded me again that I had achieved Androgyny, the Harmony of opposites within, which made me fit to pass into the 5th Dimension, in a near future. I hence managed to overcome the trials of the previous year, aided by my faithful companion, the Spirit. I was well aware that God's clock was never slow and that everything happened perfectly on time and for our own good, not for the benefit of our desires (which often go against our well-being). Everything is Divine Grace (as Aurobindo claimed, too), in thick and thin (so to say) as long as we are in the earthly world of dualities.

It is the destiny of every soul to become free from the bondage of dualities, sooner or later, and I'll never tire of repeating it. We return to earth to overcome the ties imposed by the ego(ism). The ultimate desire of every human being, though often well obscured by the flattery and the illusions of the mind, is to attain perfection and eternal happiness that can be granted only by the Absolute, as the Spirit of Life in us.

In the new year – the year of the harvest, the elimination of the past *karma*, the union with God, the fusion into Oneness and the discovery of new realms (as Sai Baba had announced to me nine years before) – a friend presented me with a silver rose. That gift touched the strings of a distant memory in the heart, linked to the symbolism of this flower: uprightness and invincible courage in the service of the ideal of Pure Love, which has been the ideal of a lifetime.

During that trip to India, I prayed the Divine Master, from the bottom of my heart, to give me the possibility to serve and honour Him for good, to be forever illuminated by His Light, like a pure diamond, and to testify of His greatness and of the beauty of the soul.

I had been at Puttaparthi for a week, and I was repeatedly the first to enter the Temple of all the people in the group, every day, until one morning I heard Him address me in the heart:

"You are in My heart, the heart of the Universe, just like everyone else. The difference is that you know that, while many others don't.

Your conscious presence in Me will grant you the perfect knowledge of all things. The number one is just a small example[223]", and then again, *"Be in the essence and you shall be free. You will be able to accomplish great things, beyond time and space, without limits."*

The message arrived after the request I'd made to the Divine Master, deep in my heart, to clarify something that went on for a week (and continued thereafter): I could sense what was about to take place and that promptly came true.

That continued for a few weeks, perhaps for me to grasp the inner potential and to be able to testify of it. Then everything returned to normal, with a great relief.

In the *ashram* garden, Sai Baba's Thought of the Day is posted on the board daily. That day (when I received the message), the quotation read:

"The sweetness of wisdom comes from good company, solitude and meditation. But in any case, it is found only within us, when we get rid of hatred, envy and jealousy."

A few days later, it was the Day of Rama (the *Avatar* of Righteousness, or *Dharma*) and I remembered the same day exactly ten years earlier. I had been with Sai Baba, in Kodaikanal. What a magical moment! This time it was going to be even more so. Unexpectedly, He spoke to me in the heart, telling me something I never thought I could hear: *"Your past I have wiped off because you have won My favour with your Love."*

In all honesty, I did not feel I had done that much for Him. Out of His infinite kindness and generosity, He rewarded not the efforts I'd made but the manifestations of Love.

During the last *darshan* before leaving, when Sai Baba got up to say goodbye to the devotees, He raised both hands in a gesture of blessing. At the same time, I made the same gesture, which was untypical of me, and our hands joined in the blessing of

414

Oneness. The fusion with Him took place on the physical as well as on the subtle plane, in the heart.

On the way back, on the plane, I read on the front page of an on-board magazine: "Adios tristeza" (Farewell, sadness), as a confirmation that the wish to eliminate suffering from my life was fulfilled. The power of the Spirit is limitless.

Although still 'scientifically' unproven, an incredible but true fact goes in favour of this truth: the concept of man originating from the divine spark, understood as the immortal, mother cell of the body of Light - and not the other way round.

The most important effort that gives access to this Grace is the work on transforming yourself into a better[224] person, changing the quality of your thoughts, no longer thinking small, in terms of your self, but starting to think big, in terms of mankind – the great human family.

This process directs cosmic energy to us, our consciousnesses is awakened to awareness and the unstoppable flow of Divine Love fills us with Beauty, Power and inner Peace.

Those who live immersed in God (as Truth and Love, Peace and Righteousness) are unassailable, protected from every peril, because, as we know, Righteousness protects those who abide by it.

In this regard, Sai Baba says: *"God is incarnated from one age to another – not to protect individuals, but to protect the Dharma (righteous behaviour), the Divine Law."*

So the popular adage is true: *"God helps those who help themselves"*, that is, behave well, according to the Divine Will, and It will come to your aid in the moment of need.

Someone said: *"We are all flowers in the garden of God, it is up to us to choose whether to fall at His feet or simply on the ground."*

I remember another one-liner full of wisdom, coming from a mountain priest: *"In a desert, even leaves turn into thorns"*, i.e. in the absence of True Love, in the absence of Truth, life retreats, too, the soul dies out and the soil remains dry and barren. This is what the life of the one who loses contact with the Spirit can be like.

I had another uncommon dream. I was surrounded by ten beautiful peacocks and in front of me there was a huge number '21'.

The card of the Major Arcana, 'The World' came to my mind. The reference to completeness was real, as I had been living in the new apartment for a few months. I had 'settled down' in the new home and life. Purity of heart was my major yearning and the peacocks that surrounded me in my dream made sense.

I felt Heavenly[225] because the natural inclination to inner Peace and Harmony were fully realized in this new environment. Essentially, number 21, in synthesis, divinely confirmed this experience.

I was ready to seize what didn't take long to appear: short but significant phrases, to announce the transition to a new level of inner peace which would allow me to live, with lightness, the life that had weighed upon me like a burden for many years.

I was deeply convinced that the greeting and blessing exchanged with Sai Baba was yet another infusion of Divine Love. I could finally flow with the river of Love, always ready to be amazed by the events. I never changed in this respect. Since childhood, I have been a hopeless dreamer who marvelled, time and again, like the very first time, at every dream that came true, especially if it had seemed to be impossible.

My dreams became "speaking symbols", or revealing images. I dreamt of being in the shade of a giant cypress tree. Struck by its magnificence, I quietly admired its silence (the silence of God). I subsequently discovered that the cypress symbolizes immortality, resurrection, incorruptibility and spiritual virtues: that is why it is often found in cemeteries.

I also dreamt of being on a train, travelling to an unknown destination in Europe. It was called 'Le Monde 21'. It confirmed the dream in which the same number had appeared. (21 – completion of the Divine Work).

I bought an item for the house and saw the following slogan on the receipt "Follow your dreams". My greatest desire was to realize the most beautiful dream, or the highest ideal: Pure, Absolute Love. When you follow your heart, your desires come true, someone said. So how come we are so surprised when dreams come true?

I wanted to maintain a pure heart, to be useful in the art of healing – as I was often told by the inner voice. The art of healing (with cosmic, divine energies) is based essentially on the healer's purity of heart.

I consulted the *I Ching* (the Chinese oracle) about it and received a clear response, through the hexagram called 'The Well', reading that He, who is the source, will quench everyone's thirst. Drinking from our own source means putting words into practice and arriving at the end of suffering. After purification, we are ready to unite[226] with God (as in the greeting, or blessing gesture, shared with Sai Baba), and complete the Divine Work.

Jesus said: *"The greatest among you shall become the smallest."*

It is yet another call to humility and kindness, the major forces we can express in the world, besides Love, because force understood as violence and power implied as wealth are nothing compared to the power of awareness of being divine, emanating from a pure, humble, kind, compassionate, virtuous heart.

God as the source of life offers Love and Kindness to those who have managed to walk through the storms of life without losing their soul in the depths of selfishness. There are no limits to what can be obtained with faith. So much so that one can move a mountain, as Jesus said. He also stated: *"Ask and you shall be given"*, *"Search and you will find"*, *"Knock and it shall be open"*. In other words: rediscover the

Divine in you and you will be everything and nothing – powerful and humble, enlightened and simple, wise and sinless, in His image and likeness.

Cosmic (Divine) Intelligence speaks through the hearts, if we manage to silence the mind (i.e. make it pure) through meditation (or contemplation) and if we have the good will to live righteously every single day.

One night I had a beautiful vision: an angel, illuminated with a white glow, stood majestically (it reached the ceiling) on my head, leaning against the headboard of the bed.

I got up, but He vanished. I was sure He had come to bless my new home.

It is written in the Upanishads (Hindu Holy Scripture): *"Know That (the true Self), and this Knowledge will make you know all the rest."*

The circle was closing, as I came across the same wording I'd been impressed by many years ago (in my youth), that left an indelible mark in my soul.

Those words were written on the temple of Delphi, in Greece, *"Know thyself"*, and I add today: …and you will know the rest because All is One.

I received another message 'of Love' from the inner voice:

"You have been chosen to carry the torch of Love everywhere. You have learned by now to come out of the trouble created by the world. I want you to be completely unattached and free to follow My command.

There is no tide strong enough to break this cane. Its strength comes from its flexibility and its unrelenting readiness to straighten up and turn its head to Me, as soon as the weight it had to endure is gone.

Confident and attentive to every sign expressing My Will, you will follow, with passion, the pathway I have outlined for you. As you have already seen, there are no more obstacles[227] on your way up. You will soon reach the top on your own, only to contemplate the enchanting scenery created by yourself, as you shaped your life on a model made of pious acquiescence to My Will[228].

You are divine, beloved daughter and mother of the one and only God, the God of all things visible and invisible, the God of everything and nothingness, the God made of Love and Truth, as the only everlasting and immortal reality that makes your current world and the other wonderful and invisible worlds 'real'.

Wonderful creature, do not fret, you will not have to wait much longer. A semester separates you from the meeting that will clarify everything about the task you are to perform. You will finally reach completion so that you can visit new worlds and create new realities, together with those who ride the same wave as you do in the 'endless sea' that surrounds and supports the galaxies in their perpetual motion, renewing the energy of life, the source and substance of creation, every moment.

Your enchanted eyes will hardly believe that all the boundaries have been removed. No one will trespass onto your nest, rest assured, it is My Will. You are going to leave it empty more and more often and for longer periods, because your presence will be required elsewhere and you will have to comply. You will be a messenger of Light and Goodness, enlightening with your example all those who wish to be nurtured with it."

For four long, wonderful years, as He had promised, I heard Him speak in the heart. Everything was in His hands, including this new promise of a meeting that would clarify the task that awaited me.

He had already anticipated in the previous messages that I would work beyond all limits (would I leave the body or move definitely into the astral dimension - who knows?! I was not allowed to know it yet, so I put everything in His hands). This message inaugurated a period of major revelations in the heart.

One morning I sensed almost physically inside me the fountain of living water, gushing from the heart, the same water that Jesus revealed to Mary Magdalene, proclaiming: *"Whoever drinks the water I give, will never be thirsty again and will become himself the fountain of eternal life"*, that is, Pure Love will flow out of Him.

The period of thirst was over. I discovered that the water that quenches the thirst once and for all dwells in us. It is life itself, or Divine Love.

Shortly after that, I became aware of the gift offered by the Spirit of Life: 'to Bless' means to help everyone and everything and distribute a load of Divine Love that consequently multiplies geometrically and spreads everywhere, on earth and in Heaven.

Power, Wisdom and Divine Love poured into my heart, for me to set an 'example' and show that only by sharing the fullness and the joy we could continue to enjoy those bounties.

I was about to finish the venturesome story about a soul in search of God, when I realized it was the time of the year when daylight was at its peak, the summer solstice, the Festival of Light. What a magic coincidence!

In that moment I realized the remarkable similarity between the words I had heard in the heart (during the most recent stay in India): *"Your past I have erased because you have won My favour with your Love"* and the words of the Divine Master Jesus who said, two thousand years ago to Mary Magdalene: *"Therefore, I tell you, her many sins have been forgiven – for she loved much"*. Did those words hold the key, or better, the pass[229] for a new dimension?

Was the dimension most frequently mentioned by the inner voice the same as the one shown to me by the Indian woman with a heart-shaped amulet (with the inscription 'Turiya', i.e. the dimension of pure essence), in the vision I had at the ashram of Sai Baba? It seemed unbelievable, and so I put my queries in God's hands.

I believe the Kingdom of Oneness is the last we can reach, while still occupying the physical body. In reality, he who has found the Light in the heart, cannot help seeing it in everything and everyone's heart – this is the Kingdom of Oneness. This is the pass to enter the freedom from desires, attachments and conditionings of the world of duality. I had a dream that filled me with wonder and inner peace because it expressed the mood of the moment.

I was in an enchanted garden[230], full of flowers and lush vegetation. Children were playing carefree and happy on the trees, with many animals, white swans, brightly coloured peacocks (one of which was white), elephants (one of them was also white) and numerous colourful parrots. Upon waking, I couldn't tell if I had visited a heavenly dimension. I probably had.

The next day, in a bookstore, I spotted a book (on mystical ecstasy) with a picture of a peacock on the cover. On the back, I read: *"The peacock is the bird of immortality, the symbol of Paradise"*.

The answer to my query arrived, along with the explanation of the dream made so many years before, of the feast of the peacock in the *ashram* of Sai Baba.

The story came to a conclusion, but new memories emerged, such as the words of the inner voice saying *"You have chosen to remain on your own in order to overcome duality and return to Oneness"*.

I reached the mountain peak in the heart, as I had done so many times in the dreams, sometimes with difficulty, other times not, as the years went by. That peak finally had a name: "I am" (the Spirit).

Sai Baba says: *"The mind is like a thousand petalled lotus, each petal is oriented toward an object or a goal. In the centre of the lotus is a flame representing the Anthakarana* (the set of intelligence, memory, and individual self). *When the flame is tilted towards one of the petals, we are influenced by duality* (success-failure, joy-pain, etc..), *when it is straight and stable, it is not limited by the body and its senses. We then reach impassiveness and become impartial witnesses, uncontaminated, unattached to our life or that of others and we identify with the 'I am, the Spirit'"*.

Jesus said, *"God is the Spirit of Truth and those who worship Him must worship Him in Spirit and Truth"*, and also: *"You shall do greater things than Me."*

What is greater than finding 'Unity in Diversity', after we have forgiven ourselves for our limitations, transformed the individual self and been reborn into the life of the Spirit, the true Self? This is an invitation to celebrate the New Age of the Third Millennium. Everything that happens serves to awaken the consciousness to the inner divinity residing in us all the time.

Sai Baba says: *"Ages[231] change only with the changing of the Dharma and not with the passing of time. The Dharma establishes the age of every one of us. He who possesses the four virtues* (Truth, Compassion, Forgiveness, Charity) *is in the age of Krita, or the age of perfection* (gold). *It is man's behaviour that creates or harasses history and transforms the Golden Age into the Iron Age* (Kali Yuga)*"*.

Today, like yesterday, life offers two possibilities: awakening or continuing to sleep, that is, surrendering to the Father's Will or continuing to go against Him by the will of the individual self or ego.

419

In the former case we choose to live with God, in the latter we choose to live on our own. In the first case we achieve inner Peace and Bliss, in the second we are bound to suffer and fret.

As a matter of fact, God has given us everything we need, 'we lack nothing'. If only we could become aware of that and focus on the real values, the true goodness, we would discover that we can be the winners in the obstacle race, which is the game of life.

Will these lines (this 'road map') help you find the treasure hidden in every seeker of Truth? I wish you that, with all my heart. It worked with me and I'm like you, being one of the six billion divine seeds[232] scattered around the earth by the Love of God, a seed that has discovered a new world within the heart, enlightened by the Light of the Creator. The new world is called 'Love', which means that God resides in the heart.

We come from Love, we are Love and we return to Love.

Allow me to give you one recommendation: start looking for it today, tomorrow may be too late. May this true story inspire you to transform every challenge that life brings your way into a victory.

Peace be with you, always.

P.S. The last words of the inner voice were: "*The Seekers of Truth are not friends, they are brothers and sisters.*"

Jesus said: "*I have no mother and I have no brothers, but those who act upon the Will of My Father are my mother, my brothers and my sisters*".

He spoke about a great family, humankind united by a single sacred bond and the observance of the Will of God as Love and Truth to realize the Highest Goodness – True, Eternal Life.

Sai Baba says: "*Truth is the mother, Wisdom is the father, Righteousness is the brother, Compassion is the friend, Peace is the wife, Indulgence is the son. These are man's true relatives.*"

OM SAI RAM

NOTES: CHAPTER XXI

214. A *mantra* (repetition of the name of God, whatever it may be, according to a given religion or belief) has the power to change the vibration frequency of every cell in the body and bring harmony. That is why the *namasmarana* (a constant repetition of the Name of God) is important. It is actually more effective when recited mentally.

215. I might have been alarmed by the news on the health of planet Earth I occasionally heard. For example, the radiant energy of the sun has grown by 0.05% per decade, since the 70s; terrestrial magnetism (the force that allows the earth to maintain the axis of the poles in the present position) is dangerously close to zero; the moon is moving closer to earth; at least 400 asteroids risk colliding with earth, day after day, and so on.

216. I used the same word to express my plea to Him.

217. *Ruah* is the Holy Spirit.

218. In India it is called *mangalasutram,* and it augurs well for the marriage, like the wedding ring in the West.

219. The gifts of the Holy Spirit (the Spirit of Truth, the Paraclete) are seven: Knowledge, Intellect, Counsel, Fortitude, Science, Piety, Fear of God
220. This was later confirmed by the inner voice.

221. Being generally considered propitiatory, mistletoe branches are given for Christmas to bring good luck for the coming year.

222. I was called 'My messenger' for the first time and explanations followed shortly after.

223. Numbers were extracted to determine the order of entering the temple. To my embarrassment, I kept drawing out number one in those days. Deep inside, I knew beforehand that I was going to extract it, without resorting to any tricks whatsoever.

224. Allow me to point out the following, as an invitation to a makeover and to imprint it in the reader's mind: it is easier to thrive on other people's energies than to change ourselves and rely on our own energies. But I have to specify: this applies to the eyes of the world. In the eyes of the Spirit, this 'facilitation' weighs seriously on our destiny, as it costs us dearly in terms of perpetuated slavery and dependence.

225. This feeling was confirmed to me in a dream and in an episode I will mention later.

226. It can only be experienced firsthand. It cannot be described or known through an intermediary, merely to sense the ecstatic thrill of to reach the highest peak. If we are to fully enjoy our achievement, we must climb it with our own force – no one else can do it in our stead.

227. I dreamt of climbing a mountain with velvet sides, which facilitated my climb to the top.

228. According to esoteric books, we shape our 'future' in the subtle realms, depending on the luggage we carry with us in the moment of death.
229. Years before, I dreamt I was given a (passport) visa till 2007.

230. Etymologically, Paradise means 'garden'.

231. There are four successive ages (*Yugas*) over the millennia, according to Hinduism:

Krita Yuga or the Golden Age (when the *Dharma* walks on four legs or four virtues);
Treta Yuga or the Silver Age (the *Dharma* walks on three legs or three virtues);
Dwapara Yuga or the Bronze Age (when the *Dharma* walks on two legs or two virtues);
Kali Yuga or the Iron Age (when the *Dharma* walks on one leg or one virtue).

232. Meister Eckart writes: "The seed of God is within us ... pear seeds grow into pear trees, hazel seeds grow into hazel trees and the seed of God grows into God."

"No matter where you go,
always fulfil your duty the way you feel.
Know that I will be there within you,
to watch over you, every step of the way.
In the years to come, you will be able to experience Me
in my numerous manifestations.
You belong to Me.
You are more precious to me than any treasure.
I will protect you
as the eyelid protects the eye.
I already have you.
You possess Me.
I will never leave you
and you can never leave Me.
From now on, you will not have to worry about anything.
Do the task entrusted to you
with unconditional Love.
See God in all things.
Be patient.
In due time, you will be given everything.
Be happy! There is no reason to worry.
Whatever happened, whatever you experienced,
know that it is the Avatar who wants it.
There is no force on Earth that can slow down,
not even for a moment,
the mission for which this Avatar has come.
You are all sacred souls.
You must play your parts in the show
that is about to begin,
that of the dawning New, Golden Age."

Sathya Sai Baba .

Omnia Sunt Operae Ad Te Domine
(All the works come from You, Lord)

Invocation to the Holy Spirit

May these lines reach every place,
unmindful of me, remembering Your splendour.
In the years to come, may those who read,
having shed the sad yoke of the ego,
offer their cured minds and hearts,
recover from their toils, and merge with You.

INDEX

G·16